Presiden

"It is now established as an irreversible precedent, that the President of the United States has but to declare that War exists, with any Nation upon Earth, by act of that Nation's Government, and the War is essentially declared."

—John Quincy Adams on the start of the Mexican War

The Constitution is clear: the president is commander in chief of the armed forces, but Congress alone has the power to declare war. Yet, while war has been declared war only five times since the nation's birth, American forces have taken part in more than two hundred armed conflicts, large and small, overt and covert, on orders from the commander in chief.

In *Presidents at War,* military historian Gerald Astor examines the history and evolution of the president's most crucial role. Focusing on the period following World War II, he traces the history of America's post-war conflicts and asks probing questions about the meaning and import of each event. Did the president overstep his authority? Could Congress have prevented the commander in chief's actions? Is the Constitution, despite its apparent clarity, deliberately ambiguous on these matters? Does the United States' role as a superpower nullify constitutional restraints and laws enacted by Congress on a president's executive authority?

Drawing on new interviews with current and former members of Congress, unpublished oral histories by senior military officers, official papers, and other literature, Astor analyzes presidential justification for the United States' military adventures. His investigation deals with major actions, such as Truman's "police action" in Korea and George W. Bush's invasion of Iraq, as well as limited and covert measures, including Kennedy's Bay of Pigs invasion and Ronald Reagan's support for the Contras in El Salvador. While each of these presidents offered specific reasons for each action, an overriding theme emerges: as commander in chief, the president has assumed he has the authority to direct American military and paramilitary actions as he sees fit.

At the center of Astor's discussion are the Vietnam War, which involved four successive presidents, and an escalating series of actions taken under the commander-in-chief authority by George W. Bush in the current war in Iraq. Even more troubling, many of the commander in chief's specific justifications for and descriptions of these actions are now known to have been exaggerated or even false.

Are there no limits on a commander in chief's power to take military action without congressional consultation? Would any such limitation endanger the nation in times of crisis? Astor makes numerous suggestions that would allow Congress to exercise its constitutional obligations without hamstringing the president during an emergency.

Few issues have a greater impact on the United States and the world than the president's prerogative to take military action. *Presidents at War* is the only book that tackles this complex and singularly important subject head on.

A former magazine writer and editor, **GERALD ASTOR** has published twenty-four books, twelve on World War II, including *The Jungle War: Mavericks, Marauders, and Madmen in the China-Burma-India Theater of World War II,* also available from Wiley. He lives in Scarsdale, New York.

Jacket Design: Michael Rutkowski
Jacket Photographs: Battleship USS Iowa;
U.S. Presidential Seal/©CorbisU.S. Presidential Seal/©Corbis

wiley.com

PRESIDENTS AT WAR

From Truman to Bush,
the Gathering of Military Power
to Our Commanders in Chief

Gerald Astor

Foreword by Congressman John P. Murtha

WILEY

John Wiley & Sons, Inc.

For general information about our other products and services, please contact our Cus-
tomer Care Department within the United States at (800) 762-2974, outside the United
States at (317) 572-3993 or fax (317) 572-4002.

Wiley also publishes its books in a variety of electronic formats. Some content that appears
in print may not be available in electronic books. For more information about Wiley products, visit our web site at www.wiley.com.

Library of Congress Cataloging-in-Publication Data:

Astor, Gerald, date.
    Presidents at war : from Truman to Bush, the gathering of military power
  to our Commanders in Chief / Gerald Astor.
       p.   cm.
    Includes bibliographical references and index.
    ISBN-13 978-0-471-69655-1 (cloth)
    ISBN-10 0-471-69655-2 (cloth)
    1. Presidents—United States—History—20th century. 2. Presidents—
  United States—History—21st century. 3. United States—Foreign relations—
  20th century. 4. United States—Foreign relations—2001– 5. United
  States—Military policy. 6. United States—History, Military. I. Title.
    E176.1.A825 2006
    355'.03357309045—dc22

                                                              2005030780

Printed in the United States of America
10 9 8 7 6 5 4 3 2 1

To my indomitable wife, Sonia; our sons, Ted and Larry;
Ted's wife, Karen, and their daughter, Lindsay;
and our daughter-in-law Stacy, who gave our beloved Andy
so much pleasure and support the last ten years of his life

CONTENTS

Foreword by Congressman John P. Murtha   vii

Acknowledgments   xv

Introduction: Commander in Chief   1

1   The Evolution of War Powers and Precedents   11

2   World War I, World War II   21

3   The Truman Years   31

4   The Reign of Ike   47

5   Camelot's Commander in Chief   64

6   The Missile Crisis   78

7   Resolution and Reverberations   94

8   LBJ, Part of the Way   108

9   Down the Slope   122

10   Toward Peace with Honor   136

11   Pieces of Peace   153

12   The Bitter End   167

13   Iran, Afghanistan, and Lebanon   182

14   Beirut, Central America, and Iran   196

15   Iran-Contra   209

16   Bush One   221

17   Nation-Building and Genocide   233

18   Prevention and Retaliation   246

19   Between Iraq and Hard Places   257

20   Winning the War, Fighting On   271

21   Power and Abdication   286

Notes   295

Bibliography   303

Index   307

FOREWORD

by Congressman John P. Murtha

I've served seven presidents and in my experience, a president's strength lies not in his simply being commander in chief, but in his public support and the perception of his power. President Richard Nixon, for instance, was reelected in 1972 in a 520-to-17 electoral vote landslide. By 1974, though, when I was first elected to the House, he was powerless. As Watergate unfolded that year, Nixon was virtually confined to the White House. Even as the North Vietnamese were violating the Paris Peace Accords that Nixon had himself secretly authorized and supervised, he could not react because he had lost the support of the public. His approval rating in February was 27 percent. The weaker he became, the more the North Vietnamese ignored the peace agreement. The House Judiciary Committee voted to impeach President Nixon at the end of July 1974. He resigned on August 9, 1974. Eight months later Saigon fell to the North Vietnamese.

Democratic and Republican members of Congress all thought highly of Nixon's successor, Gerald Ford. He was knowledgeable in domestic and foreign policy issues and was as well prepared as a president could be. And despite being unelected to both the vice presidency and the presidency, his approval rating was 75 percent. After he pardoned Nixon a month later, though, this rating dropped precipitously to 54 percent. Their party, undermined by Ford's and Nixon's unpopularity, would suffer a worse fate. In the congressional elections that November, forty incumbents, thirty-six of them Republican, were defeated. In addition, thirteen retiring Republicans were replaced by Democrats. The House Democratic majority thus expanded from 56 percent to 67 percent. Of thirty-four Senate seats up for grabs that year, the Democrats netted four additional seats and lost no incumbents.

In 1976 the country was looking for competent leadership and, after Watergate and the Vietnam War, someone to tackle two major emerging issues: inflation and energy problems. Jimmy Carter, a Naval Academy graduate, nuclear submarine expert, former Georgia state senator and governor, was elected president. Former Speaker Thomas "Tip" O'Neill said Carter was the smartest president he'd served with and certainly the hardest working. Jimmy Carter was a master of detail. He could stand before fifty members of Congress and answer in-depth questions with ease, without ever turning to his staff for help.

A meeting at the White House in 1977 illustrates the importance of public support. The Democratic leadership was invited to discuss the president's proposal to raise the gasoline tax ten cents in reaction to the oil embargo. The goal of the tax was to curtail demand. The president believed consumers would get the money back in the form of lower payroll taxes. The leadership pledged to support the president on the tax but I knew the public would not buy it. I spoke up, and, as a junior member, all eyes were on me. I said, "Mr. President, you won't get fifty votes." By the time the vote got to the floor, the gas tax proposal had gone from the original ten cents down to four cents. Nevertheless, the vote failed miserably. The president received only fifty-two votes.

The Iran hostage crisis, which began in November 1979, a year before the next election, further eroded the public's confidence in President Carter. Fifty-two U.S. diplomats were held hostage for 444 days. The president ordered a rescue attempt, but it failed because he overestimated the capability of our military. General Peter J. Schoomaker, the current army chief of staff, participated in that raid as a young soldier. He reflected on that time in history during a recent hearing of the House Appropriations Subcommittee and said he learned a valuable lesson from the failed attempt: "We should never confuse enthusiasm for capability."

Six months after the 1980 election I asked President Carter why he had lost to Ronald Reagan. He said he had paid too much attention to detail. After all, he was an engineer. In my view, however, it was because he was unable to recover from the Iran hostage fiasco. The public perceived him as weak and incapable of dealing with our enemies. Thus this highly intelligent president would be remembered primarily as a peanut farmer who was in over his head.

Ronald Reagan was an affable, charismatic actor and governor of California who exuded paternalistic patriotism. As soon as he took office, he began a crusade to upgrade the military, which had been suffering from low morale, low pay, and outdated equipment. The defense budget increased 43 percent during Reagan's presidency. He raised military entrance standards and discharged thousands of unqualified service members. As a result, the American public enthusiastically supported Reagan, whom they viewed as strong and decisive.

In 1982 President Reagan sent sixteen hundred marines into Beirut to help restore order. But that was not nearly enough, particularly when compared to the Lebanon crisis of 1958, when President Eisenhower sent fourteen thousand soldiers and marines into Beirut. I was sent to Lebanon to assess the situation and I recommended that we get out. The rules of engagement were unclear and there were not enough troops to patrol the high ground. On October 23, 1983, we lost 241 marines in Beirut. The public was outraged. They asked, "Why should our young men be dying in Lebanon?" President Reagan argued that peace in the Middle East was of vital concern to the security of our nation and that the terrorists were trying to weaken American will and force the withdrawal of U.S. troops. But in the end, President Reagan was forced to withdraw. The American public had spoken.

I admire President Reagan's willingness to compromise at the right time and his ability to read the public's mood. I supported him through his Central American forays—El Salvador, Nicaragua, and Panama, though a majority of Democrats were against his policies. I chaired election oversight committees to El Salvador and Panama and was gratified by the democratic results. But even as democracies emerged, the president's foreign policy goals in Central America became untenable due to waning public support.

George Herbert Walker Bush took office during the peak of America's military power. He had been a naval aviator and was shot down in the Pacific Ocean during World War II, and he had been a member of Congress, director of the CIA, ambassador to China and to the United Nations, and vice president. Because he'd "been there," he was very cautious about putting our men and women in harm's way. He knew well the consequences of going to war.

On August 2, 1990, Saddam Hussein ordered a military blitz of Kuwait. More than a hundred thousand Iraqi soldiers backed up by seven hundred tanks invaded Kuwait, overwhelming the small Kuwaiti military in less than twenty-four hours. Soon Iraqi troops were plundering and pillaging the tiny country.

Because of its strategic location in the midst of the world's largest oil supply, the unfolding crisis was obviously of enormous consequence to the United States and the world. Within days, President Bush sent his secretary of defense, Dick Cheney, to Saudi Arabia to meet with King Fahd. The king agreed to allow the deployment of U.S. fighter aircraft and troops to Saudi Arabia to deter Iraqi forces from making a run on that country. The army's 82nd Airborne and the air force's F-15 fighters were immediately deployed.

The shape of the post–cold war world was still evolving. The Berlin Wall had come down just eleven months earlier. The Warsaw Pact in the Soviet Union had not yet imploded. As U.S. military buildup of our troops in Saudi Arabia steadily increased, the question arose as to what, if any, congressional authorization was needed for conducting military operations. President Bush was in constant communication with the leaders of the international coalition and members of Congress to keep them apprised of the unfolding events and to ask for their support.

On September 21, 1990, about a month after his initial order to deploy U.S. troops, the president invited a small group of members of Congress to the White House to discuss the crisis. We met in the president's private dining room. The president's secretary of state, James Baker, and Brent Scowcroft, director of national security, were the only representatives from the executive branch in addition to the president himself. The meeting was interrupted twice when the president answered phone calls from heads of state involved in the deployment.

President Bush began the meeting by explaining why he had felt it was necessary to order the deployment of U.S. troops. He hoped each of us would support him. While most present were supportive of the actions taken thus far, there were many words of caution expressed. President Bush astutely asked how long we thought our troops could remain in Saudi Arabia with the support of the American people. Some members thought our troops could remain for a prolonged period of time. I was not among this group and said that only about six months could pass before we would lose the morale of our deployed troops and the support of the American people. I provided the following rationale: Our troops would be in one of the most hostile physical environments on earth. The longer they sat idle without combat action, the more impatient they would become. Although the polls indicated strong support for the president's policy, the percentage of those who opposed it was rising. President Bush knew the public would not tolerate an extended deployment and realized the benefit of quick and decisive military action.

I don't think that any president could have handled a foreign policy crisis or war better than President George H. W. Bush. When the war ended, he received a lot of criticism from Washington insiders, particularly conservatives, who believed that he should have gone after Saddam Hussein. But the president followed the UN resolution that clearly called only for the eradication of Iraq from Kuwait. He later said, in his book *A World Transformed* written with Brent Scowcroft, "Trying to eliminate Saddam, extending the ground war into an occupation of Iraq, would have violated our guideline about not changing objectives in midstream, engaged in 'mission creep,' and would have incurred incalculable human and political costs. Apprehending him was probably impossible. We had not yet been able to find Noriega in Panama, which we knew intimately. We would have been forced to occupy Baghdad and, in effect, rule Iraq. The coalition would instantly have collapsed, the Arabs deserting it in anger and other allies pulling out as well."

President George H. W. Bush does not receive enough credit. He came from a generation that realized results are what counts, and that results speak for themselves. He consulted, listened, and then acted. He is the quintessential model of how the commander in chief should operate.

President Bill Clinton won the presidency with less than a majority of the popular vote, 43 percent. Initially, he misunderstood his mandate and how that mandate translated into results. He took on the chairman of the Joint Chiefs of Staff, who had just won an overwhelming military victory in Kuwait, on the divisive issue of gays in the military. Clinton lost. Then he took on a massive, powerful, and diverse health care insurance industry with a twenty-million-dollar advertising budget to influence public opinion—and he lost. But he learned quickly.

President Clinton was a gifted orator and he knew public support was imperative to a president's effectiveness. In my view, the State of the Union Address is purely show and I usually watch it on television. But after President Clinton's indiscretions, I felt compelled to go in person to see how he would perform. He was masterful. The American public responded favorably and his poll numbers immediately went up.

As commander in chief, President Clinton also garnered support on military matters by consulting with both Democrats and Republicans in Congress. Two prominent Republican senators recently told me they were consulted more under President Clinton than under his successor, George W. Bush.

When the United States intervened in the conflict in Kosovo with aerial attacks, the president's advisers predicted it would take four days to get the conflict under control. I thought it would take thirty days or more. The president called me after forty-four days and said the bombing was not going well, but we could not afford to fail. Although I originally opposed the use of ground forces, I thought we needed to use them. The president adamantly replied, "No way!" I said, "Mr. President, I intend to send you a letter recommending it." But before my letter was formalized, his national security adviser leaked to the press that all options were on the table; in other words, ground forces were being considered. Milosevic folded. The perception of power.

In Somalia, it was a different situation. The president let his advisers change the mission from a humanitarian one to a nation-building one that culminated catastrophically in the failed kidnapping of Somali warlord Mohamed Farrah Aidid by U.S. Army Special Forces soldiers. We paid a heavy price for the debacle. This was mission creep. Clinton's secretary of defense, Les Aspin, was forced to resign over the affair as Clinton attempted to regain public and military support.

Democrats and Republicans had high hopes for President George W. Bush. He campaigned strongly against nation-building and the use of our military to police the world. He pledged to work in a bipartisan fashion in the pursuit of humble foreign policy objectives. In fact, he even attended the first Democratic caucus to be held during his presidency.

After September 11, 2001, President Bush's public polling figures were off the charts. He had the support of 80 to 90 percent of the public. When we went into Afghanistan, the world was with us. But then he diverted us from Afghanistan to Iraq, and the reasons for going into Iraq turned out to be false. Mistakes and miscalculations were made but nobody was held accountable, although this country is paying a heavy price for those mistakes. We have lost more than twenty-three hundred Americans, and more than sixteen thousand have been wounded, half of whom have not returned to duty. The president's military mission in Iraq has grown and morphed so often that the public has lost confidence in him. As of this writing, his approval polls are in the midthirties and still sinking.

Nonetheless, in no time in history have I seen the power in our government so unbalanced as it has been under the Bush 2 administration. President G. W. Bush has insisted on absolute deference to the executive branch from Congress and the judiciary. I am not proud of how the president has rolled over Congress, but in a one-party monopoly, such as the Republicans enjoy today, it is nearly impossible to fight the party in control. That is, unless the public reacts vehemently and public outcry forces the president to change direction. We saw this scenario play out perfectly in George W.'s push for Social Security reform. No matter how he packaged it, the public was against reforming Social Security and they would not allow it.

The legislative branch reads and reacts to public mood far faster than any other branch of government. The House of Representatives, whose members must be elected every other year, is in particular the voice of America. Members of Congress, even under a one-party system, will stand by the president for only so long before the pendulum swings and Congress reasserts its constitutional powers.

A classic case of this change in tides came as the American public learned of a Dubai-owned company's acquisition of operations at six major U.S. ports. The public's outcry was loud and clear—they thought the acquisition was a slap in the face to our homeland security efforts. As support for the president and the vice president was at an all-time low, Congress reacted. In a 62-to-2 vote of an amendment to the Emergency Supplemental Spending Bill of 2006, the committee voted essentially to confront the president and to kill the Dubai port deal.

The public spoke. Congress reacted. The balance of power began to shift. The perception has changed.

ACKNOWLEDGMENTS

I am indebted to Caspar Weinberger, George McGovern, Brent Scowcroft, Al Haig, Dick Holbrooke, Nita Lowey, Gary Hart, and Anthony Lake for their responses to my interviews. I'd also like to cite Woody Goldberg, General Haig's associate, and Doris Blank and Julie Edwards with Nita Lowey's office. As in the past, the U.S. Naval Institute in Annapolis, Maryland, gave me access to its library of oral histories. I received similar help from the U.S. Military History Library at Washington, D.C., and the U.S. Air Force Library at Maxwell Field, Alabama.

My friend Alan Shapiro and my brother Burt both offered valuable suggestions and sources. I would be remiss if I did not express my thanks to Stephen Power, my editor, for his work that helped shape the finished book.

INTRODUCTION

COMMANDER IN CHIEF

The United States is at war and has been for most of the twentieth century as well as the twenty-first. Officially there are just the two world wars, the conflicts in Korea and Vietnam, the invasions of Grenada and Panama, Operation Desert Storm to liberate Kuwait, and the current struggles in Afghanistan and Iraq. But although some actions may not even merit a footnote in the ledgers of history, U.S. military and paramilitary units have been almost constantly under fire in small wars in Latin America, Europe, the Middle East, and Asia. The frequent deployment of armed forces, which goes beyond those in uniform to include covert agents and surrogates, is a natural phenomenon for a world power. It fits neatly into the thesis of Carl von Clausewitz: "war is the extension of politics by other means."

How has the country gone about the business of war? The U.S. Constitution, drafted at the end of the eighteenth century, employed disarmingly simple language. Article II, Section 2: "The president shall be commander in chief of the army and navy of the United States, and of the militia of the several states, when called into the actual service of the United States." However, under the theory of separation of powers, Article I, Section 8 states, "The Congress shall have power . . . To declare war; . . . To raise and support armies; . . . To provide and maintain a navy; . . . To provide for calling forth the militia; . . . To provide for organizing, arming, and disciplining the militia."

But, as with many provisions of the Constitution, the interpretation of who has the right to do what and how has always been a contentious matter. It's fine to codify a theory for representative government, but, in a Clausewitzian context, action confronts evolving actual conditions. It falls to the executive branch, the president, to deal with them. White House residents bring to the situations their beliefs, ambitions, and prejudices, and, most formidably in recent years, the intelligence gathered. At the same time, the presidents are subject to the influences of precedents, political ramifications, congressional attitudes, public opinion, and the media.

As the foremost world power, the United States now faces challenges that the founding fathers never could have imagined. The once fine line between the power to declare war and the authority to conduct that war has been smudged, if not erased. To understand what has happened, it is useful to examine the role of the chief executive, who, when the trumpets sound, replaces his civilian character with a military one. The authors of the Constitution, anxious to avoid the trappings of royal courts, in 1787 named the head of the executive branch "president." There's a prosaic quality to "president," but when the assembled statesmen decided on the powers of the office, in Article II, Section 2, they may have opened the door to mischief by using a commander in chief never imagined by the authors. "The president shall be commander in chief."

"Commander in chief": can there be any title more grand, more all-encompassing? It far surpasses the simple "king," "emperor," or any of the fanciful titles some maximum leaders and tinpot dictators have bestowed upon themselves. The honorarium dubs its holder supreme over the most potent arm of any government, and might infect almost anyone with tumescent hubris. When the commander in chief alights from an airplane or arrives at a military base, the senior officer salutes him. Bands blare his personal anthem, "Hail to the Chief," vesting the president with majesty.

According to the historian Arthur Schlesinger Jr., Secretary of State Cordell Hull said that during World War II, Franklin Delano Roosevelt preferred the title of commander in chief to that of president.[1] How else would one explain the incident when President Lyndon Johnson visited Vietnam and as he headed for a helicopter, a young officer said, "Sir, that's not yours." "They're all mine," grandly announced LBJ. Or how in 1986, upon first hearing of the scheme to free Americans seized as hostages in Lebanon by dealing weapons to Iran, Admiral William J. Crowe Jr., chairman of the Joint Chiefs of Staff, braced Secretary of Defense Caspar Weinberger, asking why he and his fellow military leaders had been kept ignorant. Weinberger rebuffed Crowe with the retort that President Ronald Reagan, as commander in chief, "can do anything he wants to do."[2] In an interview with the author in 2004, Weinberger insisted that this should be understood in the context of the time.

When Richard M. Nixon in 1970 broadened the American front in Vietnam by invading Cambodia, he announced, "I shall meet my responsibility as Commander-in-Chief of our Armed Forces, to take the action necessary to defend the security of our American men." He declared his decision as worthy of his office. "The legal justification . . . is the right of the President of the United States under the Constitution to protect the lives of American men. As Commander-in-Chief, I had no choice but to act to defend these men. And as Commander-in-Chief, if I am faced with that decision again, I shall exercise that power to defend those men."[3]

Nor was the ascension of the president into the highest rank decried by the legislative counterweights. Senator J. William Fulbright, the Arkansas Democrat regarded as one of the most thoughtful legislators, wrote that when confronted by the prospect of nuclear war, expediency demanded sole authority. "As Commander-in-Chief of the armed forces, the President has full responsibility, which cannot be shared, for military decisions in a world in which differences between safety and cataclysm can be a matter of hours or even minutes."[4]

In 2004, President George W. Bush, in claiming the right to detain captives from Afghanistan and Iraq without their access to standard legal procedures, invoked his power as commander in chief. Bush, particularly as his campaign for reelection gathered steam, frequently referred to himself as commander in chief, and his rival, Senator John Kerry, starting with his anointment at the Democratic Party convention in July 2004, countered with oratory about what he would do as commander in chief. *Time* magazine even billed its September 20, 2004, campaign accounts as "The Commander-in-Chief Election."

A look through American history finds that the only individuals who in their presidency seem to have been less assertive of that omnipotent title were those professional soldiers who once actually led the military — Washington, Grant, and Eisenhower. Acording to General Maxwell Taylor, who commanded the 101st Airborne Division in World War II and during Eisenhower's terms held the job of army deputy chief of staff, said that Ike, while president, was "very loathe to make decisions in the military field." Taylor reported that Eisenhower refused to even offer advice to Charles Wilson, his secretary of defense, about problems in the Pentagon.[5]

Historian Schlesinger, in his 1973 book *The Imperial Presidency*, said, "The repeated use of the term Commander-in-Chief as if it were an incantation would have confounded the Founding Fathers . . . the office through most of American history had a strictly technical connotation; it meant no more than the topmost officer in the armed forces." Schlesinger believed World War II conferred "new glamor" upon the title, and its implied power led to its use even when dealing with purposes outside of war. As the United States began to accept and develop its role as a world military power after World War II, it followed that the title assumed greater gravitas.

So seductive is the title that it may encourage entry to armed conflict. In 1990, during the run-up to Desert Storm, the coalition that drove Saddam Hussein from Kuwait, Admiral Crowe, chatting with General Colin Powell, his successor as chairman of the Joint Chiefs, said, "First, to be a great president, you have to have a war. All the great presidents have had their wars." When Powell laughed in agreement, Crowe continued, "Two, you have to be attacked."[6]

In fact, the last dozen chief executives, with the possible exceptions of Gerald Ford and Jimmy Carter but including George W. Bush, have all been full-scale war presidents. Franklin D. Roosevelt commanded during most of World War II, and when he died, Harry S. Truman held office for the final months and then later presided over the Korean War. Dwight D. Eisenhower took office with the war in Korea still ablaze. His successor, John F. Kennedy, waded through the Bay of Pigs, negotiated the Cuban Missile Crisis, and then inserted the first sixteen thousand soldiers in Vietnam. Lyndon B. Johnson expanded the conflict there, and Richard Nixon, who implied he had a plan to end the war, carried on until 1973. The only use of U.S. military force during the time of Gerald Ford was an abortive effort to rescue the crew of the U.S. merchant ship *Mayaguez* in 1975. Jimmy Carter's regime saw the seizure of the hostages in Iran, and his single exercise of armed force was a disastrous expedition to rescue them. Ronald Reagan put marines in harm's way in Lebanon, with deadly effects, and U.S. airmen combated Syrian pilots and antiaircraft. The invasion of Grenada also occurred on Reagan's watch. Under the first George Bush, Americans, as part of a vast coalition, drove Iraq out of Kuwait and invaded Panama. Bill Clinton used American Rangers to pursue a Somali warlord, with unhappy results, and through NATO dispatched U.S. forces to suppress ethnic cleansing in the Balkans. He hurled missiles at suspected sites of WMDs and nests of terrorists in Iraq, the Sudan, and Libya. George W. Bush launched an attack on al-Qaeda and the Taliban in Afghanistan before starting a war against Iraq.

While one can argue whether Crowe's principle is accurate—does anyone regard Zachary Taylor or William McKinley, both of whom had wars, as great?—the second requirement, that the country must be attacked, and the war a defense of national security, has generated the most controversy. As this book will detail, history reports but a few instances where the United States was actually attacked, although certainly on some occasions American interests were perceived as threatened. Under strict interpretation of the powers of the Constitution, although the charter for the original United States anointed the president with a grandiose status, that document's authors had no intention of giving the president carte blanche to exercise his role as commander in chief and the choice of when to wage war. The founding fathers knew that any pretense of democracy would collapse if an American president, like the British king, possessed the sole authority to originate and then wage war. Hence the language of Article I, Section 8, quoted at the beginning of this introduction, which would seem to severely circumscribe the actions of a commander in chief. The founding fathers believed that by insisting upon deliberations by the legislative branch, they kept the head of state from ever hurrying the nation into war.

Even here, the language had undergone revision. Originally, it read, "To make war." While many delegates feared any extension of war powers to the chief executive, they also realized that the commander in chief should, in the event of a surprise attack, be able to instantly retaliate without waiting for Congress to assemble and act. James Madison and Elbridge Gerry suggested that "declare" replace "make," understanding that the change provided the necessary latitude for a quick defensive response.[7] In the eighteenth century that might have seemed a foolproof solution. Alexander Hamilton knew better and warned in number 23 of the *Federalist Papers*, "The authorities essential to the care of the common defense are these: to raise armies; to build and equip fleets; to prescribe rules for the government of both; to direct their operations; to provide for their support. These powers ought to exist without limitation, *Because it is impossible to foresee or define the extent and variety of national exigencies, or the correspondent extent and variety of the means which may be necessary to satisfy them* [Hamilton's italics]."

In fact, not only did the problem lie in the inability to divine the future, but also in the inexactitude of definition, inherent when words stand for things. This created fertile soil for differing interpretations. The disconnect has become more obvious in the events of the twentieth and twenty-first centuries, where the "common defense" has come to include terms such as "preventive" and "preemptive." It is thus not surprising that over some 220 years, the policies, ambitions, and agendas of presidents wearing their commander in chief's hats have tested, bent, and even broken the constraints prescribed in the language of the Constitution, if not also the intent of its authors.

A further complication lies in the definition of war. Former national security adviser Lieutenant General Brent Scowcroft has said, "An act of war is not necessarily a war."[8] Perhaps so, but for those reeling from the sting of bombs or missiles, this may split an irrelevant hair.

The relationship in matters of war has been complicated by the natural expansion of government. In the eighteenth-century infant nation, the commander in chief relied on secretaries of the army and navy, a mere two or three generals and admirals, while the legislative branch operated with a minimum of committees. Today, the apex of the presidential pyramid descends through a secretary of defense backed up by a number of undersecretaries in the military along with a chief of staff for each of the armed forces, themselves under a chairman of the Joint Chiefs. In this infrastructure, those in uniform, while expected to carry out the policies of the commander in chief, can exercise a certain amount of independence, not only arguing with their bosses but also covertly or overtly (at the peril of their careers) with members of Congress. That body also now fields multiple committees and subcommittees to poke into the doings of the armed forces and foreign policies.

To stress an already delicate balance, the process and the deliberations today usually hinge on that vast netherworld known as intelligence. Many eras ago, information flowed from embassy contacts, commercial travelers, and even casual tourists. Not until World War II, with the creation of the Office of Strategic Services, the precursor of the Central Intelligence Agency, did the United States systematically enter into the gathering of data about the military strength, political forces, and prime movers in other lands. Along with the CIA, the armed services themselves, the State Department, and other agencies began building up their own intelligence forces. Furthermore, the CIA has since the 1950s been more than just a collector of information; it has been "proactive," funding and arming foes of unfriendly governments, destabilizing and even assisting in the overthrow of them, what could be construed as acts of war, if not actually war itself.

Intelligence has become the whipping boy for wartime failures, and not without justification. Errors of judgment committed because of missing or wrong information have left the landscape strewn with corpses. That holds for the debacle at Pearl Harbor, through Korea, Vietnam, and with the most recent struggles against terrorists and the twenty-first-century Iraq war.

In the eighteenth century we understood war as being conducted by organized armed forces. Since the twentieth century, however, another kind of war, that of guerrillas, combatants without uniforms, frequently sponsored by nations with their own agendas and movements lacking clearly defined home states, have shed blood around the world. To protect U.S. interests, but unwilling to openly contest those considered hostile, commanders in chief have increasingly resorted to covert actions. While handfuls of Americans, as members of intelligence services, have participated in some of these hidden wars, often the strategy has been to fund and arm friendly indigenous people. Under these circumstances, a president seemingly is not directing American armed forces. However, the law in the United States recognizes that hiring a person to injure or even kill another human being makes one an accomplice, as guilty as the individual who actually commits the deed. Therefore, the use of surrogates, whether Afghan warlords, Contras in Nicaragua, or loyalists in El Salvador, puts a president at war.

When he left office, George Washington warned against "foreign entanglements." He believed it unnecessary to enter into alliances that could bring war because the huge oceans separating the United States from the existing powers limited American interests abroad. In the interdependent world of the twenty-first century, isolationism has lost credence. We belong to the United Nations, the North Atlantic Treaty Organization, the Southeast Asia Treaty Organization, and the Organization of American States, to name but a few groups that influence decisions to make war and have encroached upon the original authority solely owned by Congress.

Still, when issues about war and peace arise, the specter of the Constitution hangs over the debate. Did those who drafted the Constitution and fought for its adoption know what they were about? In a landmark decision of 1952, *Youngstown Co. v. Sawyer*, Supreme Court justice Robert Jackson delved into the title of commander in chief. He wrote that the Constitution implies "something more than an empty title." Just what that more amounts to, however, is vague. Jackson commented that the designation might be invoked in "support for any presidential action, internal or external, involving use of force, the idea being that it vests power to do anything, anywhere, that can be done with an army or navy." *Youngstown* pivoted on the question of whether commander in chief Truman had the right to seize struck steel mills during a war (Korea). Jackson warned of "more sinister and alarming" possibilities through extrapolation of meaning to the commander-in-chief clause. He foresaw situations in which "a President whose conduct of foreign affairs is so largely uncontrolled, and often even is unknown, can vastly enlarge his mastery over the internal affairs of the country by his own commitment of the nation's armed forces to some foreign venture." Indeed, in the reign of George W. Bush, his administration legitimized the imprisonment of some suspected terrorists without the usual protections of habeas corpus or due process by dint of his status as commander in chief. It was also argued that it was within his power to order wiretaps that involved citizens inside the United States without warrants.

General Scowcroft remarked, "The founding fathers had it about right, but there is a lot of ambiguity." The president has the right to veto legislation, requiring a two-thirds majority to override, but as Scowcroft pointed out, "Congress, with the power of the purse and the ability to cut off funding if they feel strongly enough, has the last word."[9] In theory that may stand, but as Americans have come to realize, once the men and women of the armed forces are under fire, stopping appropriations for war is an exceedingly hard political sell to those in the national legislature, as senators and representatives learned during the Vietnam War of the 1960s and '70s and the invasion of Iraq in 2003.

Just as Justice Jackson suggested in 1952, commanders in chief have been able to thrust their armies, navies, and air forces in harm's way with little restraint and often with the country and its elected representatives in the dark. In fact, although the United States through its armed forces has fired shots heard in various parts of the world dozens of times, committed deeds that could be construed as acts of war, and openly engaged in large-scale hostile engagements, Congress has declared war only five times—the War of 1812, the Mexican War in 1846, the Spanish-American War in 1898, World War I in 1917, and World War II in 1941. Yet the armed forces have been in harm's way close to two hundred times. Historically, for the most part these have been deployed in small wars—the word "guerrilla" literally translates as "small war"—because of affronts to citizens, to aid U.S. commercial interests, and to gain territory as part of Manifest Destiny.

The erosion of Congress's responsibilities markedly increased during the twentieth and twenty-first centuries with full-scale wars in Korea, Vietnam, Panama, Afghanistan, and Iraq (twice). On a lesser scale, we have invaded Grenada, bombed Yugoslavia, and launched missiles and air attacks at targets in Lebanon, Libya, and Sudan. In addition, administrations have directed secret operations to overthrow unfriendly governments in Iran, Chile, Nicaragua, and elsewhere, infringed upon the borders of sovereign nations with espionage ranging from old-fashioned human agents to spy-plane overflights, submarine listening posts, satellite eyes in space, and the sophisticated technology of electronics roaming the World Wide Web of communications.

In the post–World War II era, Truman chose not to ask for a resolution that approved his intervention in Korea. Congress tacitly accepted the president's action by authorizing funds for military operations and extending the draft. That papered over a usurpation, occasioned by Truman's deployment of the armed forces under the rubric of a "police action," a wildly untenable label. Then there are instances such as that of President John F. Kennedy during the 1963 Cuban Missile Crisis, where he ordered a blockade and faced a potential shooting war. JFK had the Monroe Doctrine and a Congress that endorsed a policy designed to prevent by any means importation of weaponry into the Western Hemisphere by those hostile to the United States. Succeeding presidents have relied on congressional resolutions, and findings that authorize them to take action but not to declare war—Lyndon Johnson in Vietnam, George H. W. Bush in Desert Storm, Bill Clinton in Bosnia and Kosovo, and George W. Bush in Iraq. Under Ronald Reagan, American forces overthrew the government of Grenada, a Caribbean island, without input from the legislative branch.

The contentious relationship between the commander in chief and Congress over the use of the military owes, as General Scowcroft remarked, much to the ambiguity of the Constitution. But that was not because those who drafted the document were careless or unknowing. As the history of the debates in the eighteenth century shows, they recognized the potential risks to a democracy if they did not get it right. How they decided on the language, how it has been interpreted, and how the world has evolved is crucial to the conduct of presidents at war and their partners in Congress.

1

THE EVOLUTION OF
WAR POWERS AND
PRECEDENTS

When the founding fathers met in Philadelphia in 1787 to draft a charter for the newly independent country, they were acutely aware of two antecedents: the rule of a near-absolute monarchy in England, and the Articles of Confederation that had loosely held the colonies together during the Revolution. When it came to matters of war, they recognized the perils illustrated by King George III with his control over the military and what the legal authority Blackstone said was "the sole prerogative of making war and peace." The Articles of Confederation, in contrast, had created no central power over war and the armed forces. That had weakened the effort against England and obviously would not serve for future foreign affairs.

The conundrum that faced the delegates was how to maintain civilian authority over the armed forces, prevent war at the whim of an individual, and yet manage war when the cannons began to boom. They struggled for a solution that would separate governmental powers. Ideally, entry into war would devolve upon the people's elected representatives, but once engaged, the country would be led by a civilian commander in chief, the president. But these were only the basics. What was undefined was how the two branches of government would interact when war clouds gathered, the resources that would be available, and how the influence of experience and precedent would effect a functioning system.

The commander in chief was to control both the army and navy of the United States, but in the debate following the drafting of the Constitution in Philadelphia, whether or not there would even be standing armed forces became an issue. One critic, "Brutus," a foe of the proposed federalism, spoke for several opponents as he disputed the need for a standing army. In January 1788 issues of the *New York Journal*, Brutus posted diatribes asserting that the history of almost every nation demonstrated that such armies are dangerous to the liberties of a people, and "a cloud of the most illustrious patriots of every age and country, where freedom has been enjoyed, might be adduced as witnesses in support of the sentiment." (Considering that in the eighteenth century it would have been difficult to find lands where even the barest freedom was enjoyed, Brutus had little empirical evidence for his claim.)

Brutus thrust damning words into the mouths of the federalists: "It is a language common among them, 'That no people can be kept in order, unless the government have an army to awe them into obedience; it is necessary to support the dignity of government, to have a military establishment.'" However, he allowed some plausible reasons for raising a permanent armed force, based upon danger from "Indians on our frontiers," or "European provinces in our neighborhood." He proposed that, "as standing armies in time of peace are dangerous to liberty, and have often been the means of overturning the best constitutions of government, no standing army, or troops of any description whatsoever, shall be raised or kept up by the legislature, except so many as shall be necessary for guards to the arsenals of the United States, or for garrisons to such posts on the frontiers, as it shall be deemed absolutely necessary to hold, to secure the inhabitants, and facilitate the trade with the Indians; unless when the United States are threatened with an attack or invasion from foreign power in which case the legislature shall be authorised to raise an army to be prepared to repel the attack."

A bare two days after this polemic by Brutus was published, James Madison, using the pen name of "Publius" for number 41 of the *Federalist Papers*, printed in the New York *Independent Journal*, insisted that the very independence of the nation required it to have a ready military. He noted that those who disputed the extensive powers of government under the Constitution ignored the necessity of such authority as a means to obtain a desired end. "They have chosen rather to dwell on the inconveniences which must be unavoidably blended with all political advantages; and on the possible abuses which must be incident to every power or trust of which a beneficial use can be made." Between Brutus and Madison reverberated the classic argument of whether government, with its potential for oppression, can be rendered benign or is so intrinsically susceptible to evil as to be uncontrollable.

Madison asserted that security against foreign dangers was one of the prime desires of a civil society and was essential to the preservation of the

"American Union. . . . Is the power of raising armies, and equipping fleets necessary? . . . It is involved in the power of self-defense." The final version of the Constitution accepted the need for a trained, full-time army and navy.

One of the foremost contributors to the language of the Constitution, Madison emphasized Article I, Section 9, "No money shall be drawn from the Treasury but in consequence of appropriations made by law." He stressed that "the legislative department alone has access to the pockets of the people," and confirmed the intent to ensure that Congress not only possessed the sole authority to go to war, but, with its grip on the national wallet, reigned over the size and regulation of the armed forces. By these means, even in time of war, the commander in chief did not have a free hand. (Notably, the power of the purse shut down the war in Vietnam.)

Mindful that such an army should be small and with recognition of the states' needs for their own security, there was acceptance of militias controlled by the governors. Outlining "the real characters of the proposed chief executive," Alexander Hamilton in number 69 of the *Federalist Papers* argued that the president's authority "will resemble equally that of the king of Great Britain and the governor of New York. . . . The President will have only occasional command of such part of the militia of the nation, as by legislative provision may be called into the actual service of the Union [federalization of the National Guard]." While the original language of the Constitution flatly gave to the legislature the authority "for calling forth the militia to execute the laws of the Union, suppress insurrections, and repel invasions," numerous presidents have federalized National Guard units for these duties. Lyndon Johnson did so during the urban disorders of the mid-1960s, without benefit of a congressional imprimatur.

Hamilton observed that while as commander in chief of the army and navy the president's authority might seem the same as that of King George, it was actually "in substance much inferior. . . . It would amount to nothing more than the supreme command and direction of the military and naval forces, as first general and admiral of the confederacy, while that of the British king extends to the *declaring* and to the *raising* and *regulating* [all italics Hamilton's] of fleets and armies; . . . which by the Constitution . . . would appertain to the Legislature."

Hamilton, a former officer and aide to George Washington in the Continental Army, recognized the importance of a supreme military leader. He observed in number 74 of the *Federalist Papers* that conduct of war "most peculiarly demands those qualities which distinguish the exercise of power by a single head." As the constitutional scholar Louis Fisher wrote,

Hamilton "understood that 'command and direction' [words defining the commander in chief] are more than clerical tasks. They can be powerful forces in determining the scope and duration of a war. Furthermore, the designation awarded a president meant that a civilian would govern the military. The Declaration of Independence contained the grievance that King George III had sought to make the military separate and superior to the civil officials."[1]

Refining the constitutional imperatives, Congress in 1792 enabled the chief executive to call out the state militias in the event of invasion or an imminent threat from any foreign country or Indian tribe. The statute also provided for similar action to suppress domestic insurrections.

In 1794, farmers in western Pennsylvania refused to pay a federal excise tax on their distilled spirits and violently rebuffed the revenue collectors. As the so-called Whiskey Rebellion started to infect a wider area of the country, Washington, with the imprimatur of a Supreme Court judge, summoned the militias from four states, which quashed the revolt.

During the period from 1798 to 1800, disputes with former friend France brought the nation to the brink of hostilities. Although 166 years later the State Department attempted to cite the "undeclared war" with France as a precedent for the Johnson administration's offensive operations in Vietnam, Louis Fisher reported that President John Adams did not decide to go to war with France on his own authority. Instead, he asked Congress to prepare the nation for war, similar to Franklin D. Roosevelt's persuading the legislators during 1940–1941 to pass a number of measures to beef up the armed forces.[2]

One day after Thomas Jefferson succeeded to the presidency in 1801, Congress appropriated the funds for a "naval peace establishment" to go along with the standing army. The bill stated that the half dozen frigates would be "manned as the President of the United States may direct." Of particular concern was the $10 million in tributes exacted from the country by four North African states in return for guarantees not to interfere with American ships. Jefferson had decided the ransoms extorted by the "Barbary pirates" were intolerable. He dispatched warships to the Mediterranean with instructions that should the North African governments then declare war on the United States the infant navy should "protect our commerce & chastise their insolence—by sinking, burning or destroying their ships & Vessels wherever you shall find them."[3]

Having strode to the potential brink of war, Jefferson tossed the issue to Congress, commenting that he was "unauthorized by the Constitution, without the sanction of Congress, to go beyond the line of defense."

Hamilton, as usual, argued that Jefferson was defining presidential war power too narrowly. A declaration of war against the country eliminated the need for congressional approval of a response because, how is it that "one nation can be in full war with another, and the other not in the same state"? It did not matter, said Hamilton, if one was the attacker and the other defender; "the rights of both, as to measures of hostility, are equal."

Revisionist historians have claimed that Jefferson initiated military actions without benefit of congressional sanction. Actually, the Congress of the day enthusiastically voted for a number of bills that authorized Jefferson to deploy armed force against the Barbary States. Likewise, it was enough for Panama to declare war on the United States in 1989 to permit President George H. W. Bush to invade the isthmus without need for a congressional declaration of war.

Congress first availed itself of its right to declare war in 1812, following messages from President James Madison condemning the British, in their conflict with the French, for having engaged in gross affronts to American shipping on the high seas. They had seized U.S. seamen and impressed them into their own navy, confiscated what they called contraband supplies bound for France, and instituted a blockade of American ports. Certainly these amounted to acts of war, and Congress had little choice but to declare war against Great Britain.

The conflict stretched over two and a half years, with severe economic losses caused by a British blockade of Atlantic ports, the burning of Washington, D.C., and significant casualties along the border of Canada. The War of 1812, which became known as "Mr. Madison's War," ended in a stalemate—the biggest American victory, the battle of New Orleans, occurred three weeks after a peace treaty was signed. Contrary to the assertions of some jingoists, the United States did not have an unbroken string of victories at war until Korea.

To prosecute the campaigns against the enemy, Madison had called up the state militias, as spelled out in the Constitution, once Congress issued its declaration. But the governors of New England refused to hand over their militias to the secretary of war. The defiance outraged James Madison. He observed that if the states could ignore a legitimate exercise of constitutional principles, the United States could not be considered "one nation for the purpose most of all requiring it." Furthermore, he declared that without the authorized use of such militias, the country would need to create "large and permanent military establishments which are forbidden by the principles of our free government."[4]

Fifteen years later, the challenge by the New England governors to Congress and the Militia Act reached the Supreme Court in the form of *Martin v. Mott.* The decision rejected the stand taken by the governors. In the 1827 opinion, the Court not only upheld the right of the commander in chief to call up the militia in these circumstances, it also gave him added muscle. It ruled he had the "authority to decide whether the exigency has arisen belongs exclusively to the President . . . his decision is conclusive upon all other persons."

While the Court said this applied only to sudden dangers, the question of who defined an imminent threat, as opposed to an open attack, went unanswered. Arthur Schlesinger Jr. remarked, "There started to accumulate within the Presidency the means to force the issue of war on the branch supposedly empowered by the Constitution to make the decision. For the President had the ability to contrive circumstances that left Congress little choice but to ratify his policy."[5]

Chief executives Lyndon Johnson and Richard Nixon both "contrived circumstances" to legitimize attacks on North Vietnam and Cambodia. Thirty years later, President George W. Bush would appear to have swallowed the 1827 decision whole, as his administration took the country to war in a presumed preemptive strike against Iraq that was endorsed by a Congress that accepted the premises handed it. (That the Bush government sincerely believed what was later proven faulty intelligence does not contravene the issue of contrived circumstances.)

From 1787 until the close of World War II, the United States had dutifully followed Washington's precept to avoid foreign entanglements—with one exception. That was the 1825 Monroe Doctrine, which said the country would resist any foreign encroachments into the Western Hemisphere. While a unilateral declaration, it did potentially encumber the nation with responsibilities for other countries, and presidents entered into small overt wars in Latin America.

When residents of Texas, aided by an influx of expansionist and opportunistic American adventurers, announced the independence of Texas in 1836, President Andrew Jackson hesitated to recognize the new nation, aware that to the Mexican government the Republic of Texas was merely a province in revolt. Mexico might perceive legitimization of the breakaway state as a "declaration of war." Jackson deferred to Congress, which did not hesitate to acknowledge the independence of Texas.

After Mexico rejected Texas independence President John Tyler in 1844 mobilized the armed forces in the Gulf of Mexico and along the southwestern border of Texas. His secretary of state, John C. Calhoun, said

Tyler would protect Texas against an invasion. Calhoun claimed that such an action fell within the scope of a defensive war that could be waged until Congress approved or forbade it. That hardly squared with the demands of the Constitution. After nearly ten years the United States annexed Texas, which the Mexican government regarded as a just cause of war. Still, the foreign minister indicated a willingness to negotiate on this and other points of dispute.

When Mexico broke diplomatic relations with the United States, President James Polk instructed General Zachary Taylor to move troops across the Nueces River in Texas and into an area that extended to the Rio Grande, then a patch of territory unclaimed by Texas and assumed by Mexico as its turf. Units of its army attacked. Polk ignored doubts about whether the Americans had infringed upon a sovereign nation's turf and advised Congress, "The cup of forbearance has been exhausted. . . . Mexico has passed the boundary of the United States, has invaded our territory and shed American blood upon the American soil. By act of the Republic of Mexico, a state of war exists between the Government and the United States." That galvanized the majority of Congress to consider a declaration of war. Rather than a formal declaration, on May 13, by a vote of 174 to 14 in the House and 40 to 2 in the Senate, they chose to recognize that "a state of war exists."

Senator Henry Clay of Kentucky denounced Polk's policy. "This is no war of defense, but one of unnecessary and of offensive aggression. It is Mexico that is defending her firesides, her castles and her altars, not we." Elder statesman John Quincy Adams prophesied unforeseen consequences as a result of a serious wound to the spirit if not the letter of the Constitution. He observed that the recognition of a state of war evaded the provision for a declaration of war. To a comrade he wrote, "It is now established as an irreversible precedent, that the President of the United Sates has but to declare that War exists, with any Nation upon Earth, by act of that Nation's Government, and the War is essentially declared."[6]

In 1846, as he campaigned for Congress in Illinois, Abraham Lincoln, although he held private doubts, along with others urged a quick and united response toward the enemy. It was an acute example of the syndrome of how when the guns begin to boom, politicians tend to support the armed forces no matter what their misgivings, fearful of appearing disloyal to their constituents.

With the passage of time a groundswell of opinion increasingly questioned the events that had led to the war. Early in 1848, freshman Illinois representative Abraham Lincoln now joined fellow dissidents in adding, to a resolution that praised General Taylor, the statement that the attack on Mexico had been "unnecessarily and unconstitutionally begun by the President of the United States." The Senate eliminated the comment from the bill. Lincoln had challenged Polk to identify the exact "spot" upon American soil where American blood was shed.[7]

Lincoln followed up with a reply to a letter from W. H. Herndon, his law partner back home and an enthusiastic supporter of the war. "I understand to be your position . . . that if it shall be become *necessary, to repel invasion,* the President may, without violation of the Constitution, cross the line and *invade* the territory of another country; and that, whether such *necessity* exists in any given case, the President is to be the *sole* judge [Lincoln's italics]." Polk actually had gone to Congress to obtain the requisite declaration, but under circumstances that seemed to have left the legislators little wiggle room.

Lincoln cautioned, "Allow the President to invade a neighboring nation, whenever *he* shall deem it necessary to repel an invasion . . . and you allow him to make war at pleasure."[8] Notably, for all his reservations about the Mexican venture, Lincoln never availed himself of the means by which Congress could control use of the armed forces. He unfailingly voted funds to support the troops. In the 2004 election, John Kerry was forced to square his vote that permitted the president to invade Iraq with a vote against the appropriations bill. Actually, he had voted for a similar measure with an amendment attached that required a rollback of tax cuts on upper-income earners. That proposal lost in Congress, particularly after President George W. Bush said he would veto it, meaning Bush would have blocked money for the military under fire.

The Mexican War was the most egregious case where Article II, Section 2 bumped up against Article I, Section 8, but during the nineteenth century presidents deployed the armed forces without benefit of congressional authority in a number of less celebrated instances. On several occasions, seagoing bandits captured and looted merchant ships. U.S. Navy ships retaliated, notably in Sumatra and Puerto Rico, by attacking towns rather than seizing the criminals.

President Millard Fillmore in 1852 dispatched Commodore Matthew C. Perry to open up Japan. Ostensibly Perry sailed to the Far East on a peaceful mission to rescue shipwrecked American seamen who had been stranded in Japan and abused while incarcerated. The instructions to him reportedly cautioned, "He will bear in mind that as the President has no power to declare war his mission is necessarily of a pacific character, and will not resort to force unless in self-defense."[9] The reigning mikado bowed to the westerners but left unresolved the question as to how, if the Japanese had resisted, Perry could truly meet the requirements for a permissible "defensive" war.

Two years later, the first American gunboats began to prowl China's Yangtze River, beginning more than seventy-five years of foreign warships plying the inland waters of that sovereign nation, to battle pirates, warlords, and rebels in defense of private American interests and citizens, all without benefit of approval by Congress, other than through appropriations to the navy.

Upon the secessionists' firing on Fort Sumter on April 12, 1861, President Abraham Lincoln, who little more than a decade earlier had castigated Polk for taking upon himself war powers that belonged to Congress, without convening the legislators added to the army and navy without regard to the limits set by Congress, mobilized the militia, called for volunteers, spent public money not appropriated upon the armed forces, suspended the basic right of habeas corpus, allowed the arrest of citizens denounced as disloyal, and authorized a blockade of the newly formed Confederacy. It was an encyclopedia of violations of the Constitution. Not until some twelve weeks later did the Great Emancipator face a sitting Congress.

While seeking the benediction of the legislators, Lincoln claimed that because a state of emergency existed, threatening the extinction of free government, he had a constitutional right to act. Actually, Article I, Section 8 reserved those powers for Congress.

In his argument, one that resonates still, that emergencies required immediate steps, Lincoln asked, "Must a Government, of necessity, be too *strong* for the liberties of its own people, or too *weak* to maintain its own existence?"[10] No language in the Constitution defined an emergency, and the use of it as a rationale reverberated in President Harry Truman's June 1950 deployment of the U.S. military in Korea as well as President George W. Bush's invasion of Iraq predicated on the imminent danger of a mushroom cloud over the country courtesy of Saddam Hussein.

In only one instance was Commander in Chief Lincoln challenged. Chief Justice Roger B. Taney ruled that the president had no right to suspend habeas corpus for a prisoner accused of leading a secessionist engaged in sabotage. However, officials refused to free the incarcerated man when presented with the writ from Taney. The justice suspended further action with the note that it would be referred to Lincoln with "his constitutional obligation to 'take care that the laws be faithfully executed.'"

In 2004, Lincoln's handling of a prisoner would be cited when questions of jurisdiction arose over foreigners and even American citizens in

alleged instances of terrorism or support for foes in both Afghanistan and
Iraq. Again, a Supreme Court decision that prisoners were entitled to the
standard rights of an accused did not bring relief.

"All theories leak," theorized the educator Alan Shapiro, paraphrasing
an analyst of grammar rules. Theories are dependent upon words whose
definitions are subjective, and the Constitution, while a model of precise
language, has always been open to interpretation. Even the fullest of pre-
scriptions cannot cover every contingency. Invariably it is the president,
whose role as chief executive means he must react to a situation, who has
led. It is the president who dispatches the troops, who calls upon Congress
to declare war. Under these circumstances, whether it has been whiskey
tax resisters, border disputes, or secessionists, the commanders in chief
during the eighteenth and nineteenth centuries felt compelled to make a
stand. While the measures taken settled the issue of the day, they also
established precedents that would further the use of military force and
confound the roles of commander in chief and Congress.

2

WORLD WAR I,
WORLD WAR II

It would not be far-fetched to suggest that invention mothered the necessity of presidents to expand and intensify their roles as commanders in chief. The steam-powered ships that replaced those dependent upon wind carried American interests to the farthest reaches of the world, and the telegraph and cable beneath the seas meant swift if not instant messaging. Whiffs of imperialism wafted through government and public policy. Expansionism in commerce and influence abroad inevitably increased the potential for conflict with competing governments. With this came new challenges to the traditional ways of dealing with issues surrounding war.

The first scratch at the imperialist itch occurred at the end of the nineteenth century. During the 1890s, Cubans seeking independence from Spain drew substantial support from émigrés in the United States. Commercial interests, disturbed by the destruction of their tobacco and sugar plantations in Cuba during the battles between rebels and the government, wanted resolution of the conflict. Congress offered the "friendly offices" of the United States in brokering independence from Spain, a proposition Spain rejected. Undaunted, a delegation from Congress informed President Grover Cleveland, "We have decided to declare war against Spain over the Cuban question." The president coldly rebuffed them: "There will be no war with Spain while I am President."[1] When the legislators argued they had the right to declare war, Cleveland parried that the Constitution named him commander in chief and in that capacity he would refuse to mobilize the army.

However, in 1898, with William McKinley in the White House, the battleship *Maine* blew up while anchored in Havana harbor. The headline of the *New York World* asked, "Maine Explosions Caused By a Bomb or a Torpedo?" Five days later, newspaper magnate Joseph Pulitzer advised readers, "*World's* discoveries prove the mine theory," and then falsely claimed, "Government accepts mine theory of the *World*." No less bellicose, William Randolph Hearst's *Journal* trumpeted, "The Warship *Maine* Was Split in Two By an Enemy's Secret Infernal Machine." "The Whole Country Thrills with War Fever." And it sounded a mantra, "Remember the *Maine*! To Hell with Spain!" In contrast, two newspapers, the *New York Sun* and the *New York Evening Post*, decried the rush to judgment and war. The Spanish authorities in Havana conducted an elaborate funeral service for nineteen dead sailors (some 260 navy men were killed). Every dignitary in the city turned out in a demonstration of mourning.

Inquiries by the Spanish and the Americans proceeded separately. The former concluded the *Maine* a victim of an accident, but the U.S. naval officers diagnosed a mine, planted by an unknown party, but with no connection to Spain. Arguing that the ship while in Havana harbor had merited better protection from the local authorities, McKinley asked for a significant sum of money as compensation. He and his mentor, Senator Mark Hanna of Ohio, hoped to avoid war.

Ultimately, while the Spanish agreed to an unconditional armistice in Cuba, they would not yield on the matter of independence for Cuba, a sticking point. However, the American minister to Spain cabled that he believed the issue might be resolved later. It was too late for the war-hungry. Wrangling over various resolutions ended with a declaration of war against Spain.

Although Secretary of State John Hay would describe it as a "splendid little war," it was hardly that for those who fought it. Resistance in Cuba was strong; terrain, climate, putrid beef rations, and typhoid epidemics exacted serious tolls. When it was over, Cuba stood as an independent nation while the United States possessed a modest empire, most prominently Puerto Rico in the Caribbean and the Philippine Islands and Guam in the Pacific. The niceties of the Constitution appear to have been observed, but this was a case when there was no threat to the United States but a tide of public opinion, something new to the body politic, pushed a president into asking for Congress to create a war.

Following the Spanish-American War, executive actions that evaded the monopoly on treaty ratifications held by the Senate potentially expanded the power of the president, bending if not breaking the line defining the authority to wage war. The mechanism for the shift lay in acceptance of the president's right to enter agreements that involved a single act, as opposed to obligations that required repeated actions. A president could recognize foreign governments, settle foreign claims, arrange cease-fires or armistices, and carry out provisions of policy such as the Monroe Doctrine without approval by the legislators. Recognition of a foreign government put the president in a position to legally aid those who had formerly been rebels. This would impact questions about whether the United States was engaging in acts of war by supporting insurgencies or merely responding to a legitimate request for aid from a sovereign government.

With victory over Spain, McKinley expanded the American reach. He claimed that his right to protect American citizens and their property allowed him to dispatch five thousand troops to China. The expeditionary force joined an international army that would eventually suppress the Boxer Rebellion and prop open the doors of China. Under executive orders from Theodore Roosevelt, "the great white fleet" steamed around the world in a display of American military might. TR intervened to arrange a peace between Russia and Japan, acquired the Panama Canal Zone, and, wielding his "big stick," inserted American troops into Central America, trespassing upon sovereign governments. Isolationism was mortally wounded, although a substantial portion of the country tried to breathe life into the moribund political idea for nearly fifty years, until World War II.

When his authority was questioned, Roosevelt answered, "I managed without consultation with anyone; for when a matter is of capital importance, it is well to have it handled by one man only."[2] It was hardly a ringing endorsement of the constitutional philosophy of checks and balances.

In 1912, during the term of President William Howard Taft, Senator Augustus O. Bacon tried to rein in executive power with a proposal to block money for military forces sent without congressional approval beyond the United States, except for emergencies when Congress was out of session. After the Bacon amendment was defeated, Senator Elihu Root argued that nothing prohibited the president from sending troops "into any country where he considers it to be his duty as Commander-in-Chief of the Army . . . unless it be for the purpose of making war, which of course, he cannot do."[3]

Four years later, Taft acknowledged that the right to station the military wherever a president pleased could bring consequences that fractured the limits imposed by the Constitution. If soldiers beyond the American borders became embroiled in a shooting war, it would "leave Congress no option but to declare it or to recognize its existence," thereby usurping the legislators' authority.[4]

During the administration of President Woodrow Wilson, starting in
1914, conflict with Mexico, which was racked by revolutionary movements, rose anew. Foreign investments were destroyed by the opposing
forces and some civilians, including some seventy Americans, were killed.
In 1914, Mexican forces arrested the crew of an American naval barge at
Tampico. Although the sailors were quickly released, when Admiral Henry
Thomas Mayo, commander of the Caribbean fleet, demanded a formal
apology and a twenty-one-gun salute to the Stars and Stripes, the Mexican president declined unless the Americans boomed their own guns in
honor of Mexico. On his request, Congress granted Wilson the authority
to bring the armed might of the United States to bear. The navy put
ashore armed bluejackets and marines at the port of Vera Cruz. In less
than a day the Americans seized the objective, although nineteen men
were killed and another seventy-one wounded. Mexican casualties were
considerably greater.

A full-scale war was avoided only when Argentina, Brazil, and Chile
offered to mediate. The border continued to rumble, however, and Francisco "Pancho" Villa, a former lieutenant of the insurgent leader Venustiano
Carranza who combined a career of banditry and revolution, massacred
eighteen American mining engineers. Villa then crossed the border to rav-
age Columbus, New Mexico, killing another seventeen Americans. Amid
loud cries of revenge, and with no need for endorsement by Congress—the
territorial United States had been attacked—Wilson again asked for an
approval by the legislators to commit the armed forces. With grudging
permission from Mexico's president, General John J. Pershing's twelve-
thousand-man-strong punitive expedition pursued Villa across the border.
The venture may have salved American pride, but the target vanished
into the wilds of Mexico. Wilson eventually withdrew the troops.

Elected for another four years in 1916, Wilson continued his policy of
neutrality in World War I, although the sympathies of Americans lay with
Great Britain, France, and Italy. But it became difficult, if not impossible,
to avoid coming under fire and protecting American lives and property
as the war bridged the oceans. The president honored the Constitution,
going before Congress for such matters as arming American merchant
ships. Elected to his second term with the slogan "He kept us out of war,"
Wilson teetered between war preparations that would clearly signal to the
Germans entry on the side of the Allies, and failure to mobilize for the
inevitable.

The Germans, seeing the United States as a silent partner for the
Allies and probably a future adversary, began to ignore professions of neu-

trality. Unable to penetrate the blockade of their ports, they attempted to stop shipments to the Allies by torpedoing American merchantmen with their U-boats. The sinking of ships under the U.S. flag inflamed hostility toward Germany, and when British espionage artfully uncovered a plot by the Germans that promised Mexico restoration of its lost territory, Wilson had the essential casus belli to call for a declaration.

He reported to Congress on April 2, 1917, "Neutrality is no longer feasible or desirable when the peace of the world is involved with the freedom of its peoples, and the menace to that peace and freedom lies in the existence of autocratic governments. . . . The world must be made safe for democracy." Between the two houses of Congress, the vote to declare war passed by 455 to 56. By Armistice Day, November 11, 1918, the American Expeditionary Force in France numbered more than one million.

The Bolshevik Revolution overthrew the Russian czarist government in 1917. As the guns fell silent on the Western Front, Wilson, without approval by Congress, shipped five thousand American soldiers to Siberia to join an ill-conceived international force against the Reds. A few legislators complained, but the swirling currents that enveloped peace treaty squabbles obscured the intervention in Siberia. Wilson had preached his Fourteen Points, much of which was designed to lessen armed conflict, ten months before the armistice. Point 14 called for a League of Nations through which international cooperation and international peace and security could be promoted. Unlike future multinational combines like the UN or NATO, it contained no provisions for operations by polyglot armies. An isolationist Senate defeated Wilson's campaign for membership in the League.

While the United States rejected internationalism, the armed interventions in Central and South America continued. The nominally strict isolationist Calvin Coolidge in 1927 dispatched five thousand men to Nicaragua to help suppress an insurgency led by a man named Sandino. Some in Congress argued that the power to declare war was in danger of being usurped and tried to control the Nicaraguan adventure by snapping shut the purse, but a majority endorsed the action.

By the time Franklin D. Roosevelt entered the White House in 1933, Congress would seem to have held a tight rein on military force despite exceptions such as Nicaragua. FDR sought to enlarge his authority with a request for the Senate to allow him, at his discretion, to embargo arm shipments to countries he identified as aggressors. The legislators only agreed on an embargo placed on all nations in a war, rather than simply punishing those who fomented it. Neutrality legislation enabled Congress to curb the ability of the president to take sides and perhaps drag the nation into a war.

In 1940, after the fall of France and with Great Britain barely hanging on against the Axis juggernaut, Roosevelt traded fifty over-age destroyers to Great Britain in return for leases on bases. The deal provoked charges that the executive agreement, without the advice and consent of the Senate, violated the Constitution. Clearly, Germany could have regarded the transfer of the destroyers as an act that enabled Adolf Hitler to declare war against the United States. Public opinion, by a nearly two-to-one margin, supported the exchange, and the administration argued that if the matter had gone before Congress, that body would have unleashed the Capitol's Aeolian bag, stretching out debate until Britain had succumbed.

While many viewed Roosevelt as a high-handed autocrat, in the perilous days leading up to U.S. entry into the war he tended to enlist Congress in the buildup of American war power. The legislators, as specified in the Constitution, mobilized the armed forces with passage of the first peacetime draft in the autumn of 1940. Roosevelt must have held his breath when the Selective Service Act was renewed by a single vote. Lend-Lease, which helped sustain the opponents of the Axis, also required the approval of Congress.

In May 1941, FDR by presidential proclamation declared a state of "unlimited national emergency." Having already stationed American soldiers in Greenland, through an agreement with Denmark, he created an American defense zone extending the country's reach to Iceland, which is not in the Western Hemisphere. That drew the ire of Senator Robert A. Taft of Ohio, who still clung to the vestiges of isolationism, but only a single senator supported Taft's cry that the president had nullified the constitutional authority reserved for Congress.

The American defense zone included waters regarded by the Germans as hunting grounds for U-boats. As the summer of 1941 faded away, the U.S. destroyer Greer, carrying mail to Iceland, came in contact with a British patrol plane, which signaled that a submerged submarine lay ten miles dead ahead. The Greer sounded general quarters and accelerated toward the sub. Having located it by sonar, the destroyer began to relay data to the RAF aircraft. It dropped four depth charges, to no effect. The Greer continued to track the U-boat but made no offensive moves. Suddenly the submarine pitched several torpedoes at the warship. The Greer dodged the missiles and retaliated with a series of depth charges before breaking away.

The commander in chief seized upon the incident and in a fireside chat announced, "She [the *Greer*] was flying the American flag. Her identity as an American ship was unmistakable. She was then . . . attacked by a submarine. Germany admits it was a German submarine. . . . I tell you the blunt fact that the German submarine fired first upon this American destroyer without warning and with deliberate design to sink her. Our destroyer at the time was in waters which the Government of the United States had declared to be waters of self-defense—surrounding outposts of American protection in the Atlantic [Iceland]."

After labeling the attack as "piracy" and recalling earlier incidents of hostile fire from the Germans, FDR announced a policy: "If German or Italian vessels of war enter the waters, the protection of which is necessary for American defense, they do so at their own peril." His words were interpreted as an authority to "shoot on sight."

The commander in chief had omitted the fact that the *Greer* had clearly cooperated with the British airmen seeking to sink the U-boat. The attack on the American ship was hardly unprovoked. More than two decades later, in the Gulf of Tonkin, a similar escapade would be used to justify expanding the war in Vietnam.

On the other side of the world, in September 1940, executive action by the president imposed an embargo on scrap iron and steel to Japan, retaliation for that nation's ongoing aggression in China and its extortion of bases in northern Indochina from the puppet government of Vichy France. Less than a year later, with the Japanese gaining bases in southern Indochina, the Roosevelt administration froze Nipponese assets in the United States and in partnership with Great Britain banned all war matériel exports to Japan, shutting off access to oil. To the Japanese that translated into a declaration of economic war.

According to Arthur Schlesinger, Roosevelt, in some eighty-three press conferences that led up to December 7, 1941, never invoked his role as commander in chief to justify special powers in foreign affairs. When he did cite the title, it was confined to his authority over the armed forces.[5]

Diplomatic exchanges in 1941 could not resolve the conflict between the American determination to halt Japanese expansion and the militant desires emanating from Tokyo. Right-wing revisionists still accuse FDR of a devious plot to bring on war, but short of capitulation to the imperialist drives of Japan the steps taken by Roosevelt before Pearl Harbor cannot be faulted. It is even more absurd to believe that Roosevelt knew in advance of the coming attack on Pearl Harbor, as if he was prepared to go to war knowing that much of his fleet would be destroyed. And it was several days after December 7, 1941, that Germany and Italy declared war on the United States, requiring Congress then to declare against those two Axis powers.

In 1942, little more than two months after the Japanese attack on Pearl Harbor, under an executive order from President Franklin D. Roosevelt, all persons of Japanese ancestry, including those of American birth, were designated "enemy aliens." Congress ratified Roosevelt's action, which denied Fifth Amendment rights such as due process to those who were summarily relocated in internment camps without charges against them or trials. A handful of individuals who resisted received no redress from the courts. The Supreme Court approved of the measures as part of the government's power to wage war. It took more than forty years for U.S. authorities to recognize a terrible injustice and compensate the incarcerated. Nevertheless, in the twenty-first century, the administration of George W. Bush used the precedent of 1942 to seize and imprison alleged enemies of the state.

A second event of World War II that surfaced in the twenty-first century involved eight German saboteurs captured in late spring 1942 on Long Island, New York. They were tried and convicted by a military court through an edict of FDR, who proclaimed his right to deal with them in this manner as commander in chief. Again, the Supreme Court supported the administration. Confronted with prisoners seized in Afghanistan and Iraq as well as some allegedly involved in terrorism against the United States, the legal team for George W. Bush cited the decisions on the Japanese Americans and the German saboteurs as conferring upon the commander in chief the power to detain anyone, anywhere in the world, for any length of time if he believed them enemy fighters.

Roosevelt exercised his commander-in-chief authority in several major strategic areas. Having established a policy to war in Europe first, he overruled General George Marshall's proposals for an early invasion of France and agreed with British prime minister Winston Churchill that the first offensive strike would hit North Africa. The president accepted the British plan to drive through Sicily and into Italy, going against the advice of his trusted army chief of staff. In the Far East, Roosevelt showed far more tolerance for the importuning of China's Chiang Kai-shek, to the fury of the top American general on the scene, Joseph Stilwell. Notably, the commander in chief bought into Operation Matterhorn, which invested huge resources in men, matériel, and money for B-29s to stage through India and China on their way to bomb Japan. The B-29 program only began to pay off when the aircraft were shifted to Pacific island bases.

During the Casablanca Conference in January 1943, Churchill and Roosevelt held a press conference. In the president's opening remarks, he enunciated a policy of "unconditional surrender" that had critical implications for future strategy and the postwar era. Aside from its appeal to an emotionally charged public, unconditional surrender was aimed at pacifying the Soviet Union, which feared a separately negotiated peace by its allies. Churchill had discussed the idea with FDR, and the State Department advisory group favored the policy. A few in Congress reviled unconditional surrender as "brutal" and "asinine," but legislators did not dispute the right of the commander in chief to establish the requirements for a cease-fire. Against a foe bent on global or regional domination, the policy for ending a war would not ordinarily generate dissent from legislators. After World War II, the terms for ending the wars in Korea, Vietnam, and Iraq in 1991, as well as the twenty-first-century "war on terror" and that of Iraq beginning in 2003 would be problematic.

As the victors of World War II discussed the creation of an effective worldwide organization to maintain peace, the sticking point for the United States lay in an outside authority's power to commit the armed forces of its members. If the organization were to be effective it had to possess the strength to use force or intimidate by threat of military action. Secretary of State Cordell Hull counseled the president that he must be able to contribute American troops for use by the UN (although at this point the organization did not even have a name) in order to preserve collective security. A key Republican, Senator Arthur Vandenberg of Michigan, initially fought against a free hand for a president who wanted to respond to a UN request for troops. He allowed that in lesser crises, as in Latin America, where presidents had committed the military without sanction of Congress, it might be permissible. But for conflicts of greater magnitude, Vandenberg insisted, "I would never consent that our delegate . . . should have the power to vote us into a *major* military operation [tantamount to declaring war] without a vote of Congress, as required by the Constitution."[6]

Vandenberg's position meant a legislative veto for any significant role in collective security by the United States outside the area covered by the Monroe Doctrine. He claimed that any clear-cut case of aggression would result in congressional approval for American participation. Florida Democratic senator Claude Pepper opposed granting any of the decision-making about use of U.S. forces to an international body, but observed that it would be acceptable for the American military, without congressional authorization, to become involved in a "police force" to combat aggression in a small war.

Privately, Roosevelt believed it necessary that the president should hold the right without recourse to Congress to send in troops on request from the UN, or else the mechanism for collective security would jam. During his campaign for a fourth term, he simplified the issue as he explained, "A policeman would not be a very effective policeman if, when he saw a felon break into a house, he had to go to the Town Hall and call a town meeting to issue a warrant before the felon could be arrested."

The United States entered the twentieth century pursuing a policy of going it alone. World War I saw the first "foreign entanglement" as the American armed forces became part of the Allied armies. Although the effort by Woodrow Wilson failed to commit the country to participation in an international body, isolationism was moribund. The Axis powers nailed shut its coffin. The United States now perceived national security as a global matter. That would profoundly affect the role of the commander in chief, the deliberations of Congress, and the use of America's armed forces.

3

THE TRUMAN YEARS

Franklin Delano Roosevelt died on April 12, 1945, and Vice President Harry S. Truman succeeded him. FDR had expanded the war powers of the presidency, but it would be his successor who would apply them to a new world in which the major players had changed and the functioning of the U.S. government would evolve. Truman and the Congresses wrestled with how to meet the latest challenges to national security while maintaining the integrity of the Constitution.

Before Truman attended the Potsdam Conference with other Allied leaders in the final days of the war with Japan, on April 25 the countries eligible for the United Nations began a nine-week conference in San Francisco on the structure of the organization. John Foster Dulles, a Republican adviser to the U.S. delegation, seemed to steadfastly argue upon total control at least by the Senate when it came to using the troops. "It is clearly my view, and it was the view of the entire United States delegation, that the agreement which will provide for the United States military contingent will have to be negotiated and then submitted to the Senate for ratification in the same way as a treaty."[1]

Another Republican, Senator Eugene Millikin of Colorado, offered a compromise, allowing executive action for "policing powers" under exclusive authority of the president, and "real war problems" that should be reserved for Congress. Dulles relented slightly: "If we are talking about a little bit of force necessary to be used as a police demonstration, that is the sort of thing that the President of the United States has done without concurrence by Congress since this Nation was founded."[2] Indeed, but the "little bit of force" in a "police demonstration" could easily prove the first tentative step upon a very slippery slope, as evidenced by what happened in Korea in 1950.

The final version of the United Nations Charter said that military forces contributed by its members should, under Article 43, be based upon special agreements negotiated by the Security Council (where the United States along with the other permanent members held a veto) and ratified by the various nations "in accordance with their respective constitutional processes." In the UN Participation Act passed by Congress, the issue became fudged with language that said the president should not be deemed "to require authorization of the Congress" to supply troops under the agreement as spelled out in Article 43. However, during the sixty years following the adoption of the UN Charter and the UN Participation Act, special agreements were never initiated.

The UN Participation Act, which would green-light American membership in the world body, restated the congressional monopoly on matters of war and peace. When an amendment that would have enabled the president to negotiate a special agreement with the Security Council upon a two-thirds vote in the Senate, as with international treaties, was offered, Senator Vandenberg denounced it. "If we go to war, a majority of the House and Senate puts us into war. . . . The House has equal responsibility with the Senate in respect of raising armies and supporting and sustaining them."[3] An overwhelming nay vote vanquished the amendment that would have given the Senate special power.

In 1945, Vandenberg, now a convert to the principle that a president should be able to deploy the U.S. military, wrote, "To implement a disarmament treaty . . . is the exercise of the same constitutional prerogative in behalf of the 'national defense,' which he has used (I believe seventy-one times) without challenge for 150 years."[4] Vandenberg undoubtedly felt relieved when he consulted retired chief justice Charles Evans Hughes, who answered, "Our Presidents have used our armed forces repeatedly without authorization by Congress when they thought the interests of the country required it."[5]

Amendments slightly modified the president's right to use the military. The chief executive could provide armed forces, without prior approval from the legislators, for a UN "cooperative action." However, the numbers were restricted to one thousand and they were only to serve as observers and guards—no combat duty.

Harry S. Truman thus became president with the issue of the commitment of American military force through the United Nations undefined. The new commander in chief seemed to firmly resolve any questions with a statement cabled from the Potsdam Conference late in July 1945. He asserted that all agreements involving U.S. troop commitments to the United Nations would first have to be approved by both houses of Congress.

Truman's most momentous early decision as commander in chief approved the use of nuclear bombs against Japan. While the necessity to use a weapon of mass destruction at that moment in World War II can be debated, there is no question that as president Truman was well within his constitutional rights. From the standpoint of logic, the atomic bomb in a single blow replicated the casualties and destruction wreaked by a multitude of incendiary raids that had killed tens of thousands of people. The total deaths in Tokyo from repeated firebombing raids, including a hundred thousand in a single night, topped those of Hiroshima.

During the Truman administration, Congress in 1947 passed the National Security Act, which created a National Security Council, originally composed of an advisory board that included the president, vice president, the secretaries of state and defense, plus several other civilian officials dealing with foreign and military affairs. The net result was to put in tandem diplomacy and armed force as instruments of policy. The NSC would play an ever larger role in government, with the commander in chief soon appointing a personal national security adviser who steadily ascended the ladder to power. The CIA, established that same year as a successor to the Office of Strategic Services during World War II, soon developed its own charter by means of national security directives and cut its congressional umbilicus to become a semi-independent organization, sometimes beyond either the control or oversight of Congress. It would become a powerful tool for a commander in chief loath to seek legislative approval for ventures that sometimes had all the characteristics of a small war.

An underlying assumption in the United States was the belief that communism meant an unquenchable thirst for expansion and that the heart and brain of all communist ventures lay in Moscow. That there might be communist movements that forsook the Marxist-Leninist dogma of internationalism to pursue narrower goals based on national, ethnic, or religious aspirations did not figure in the calculations of the democracies. And in the late 1940s, with the Soviet Union a most active sponsor of communists beyond its borders, the diagnosis was reasonable. The United States faced off against the only other world superpower in a foreign policy, as enunciated by the State Department's George F. Kennan, labeled "containment."

Acting in accord with the notion of containment, Truman announced to a joint session of Congress on March 12, 1947, what was tagged as the Truman Doctrine. He said, "One of the prime objectives of the foreign policy of the United States is the creation of conditions in which we and other nations will be able to work out a way of life free from coercion. . . .

We shall not realize our objectives, however, unless we are willing to help free peoples to maintain their free institutions and their national integrity against aggressive movements that seek to impose upon them totalitarian regimes. This is no more than a rank recognition that totalitarian regimes imposed on free peoples, by direct or indirect aggression, undermine the foundations of international peace and hence the security of the United States . . . it must be the policy of the United States to support free peoples who are resisting attempted subjugation by armed authorities or outside pressures."

To implement the Truman Doctrine for the benefit of Greece and Turkey, both possibly susceptible to Soviet dominance, the president requested an appropriation of $400 million in economic and military aid to these two countries. It was a shot across the Soviet bow, signaling the start of the cold war. A few die-hard isolationists and some left-wingers who thought they detected an odor of American imperialism objected. Others expressed concern that the effort bypassed a responsibility of the UN and opened the faucets for what could become an enormous drain on American resources. Nevertheless, Congress bought the Truman Doctrine. It was truly precedent-setting as the country entered the sphere of power diplomacy beyond the Western Hemisphere. At the same time, the appeal to the legislators to shell out the money confirmed the role of Congress. The Truman Doctrine differed significantly from the much larger Marshall Plan in that it was articulated as an American response to insurgencies believed to be actively supported by communists inside and outside the two countries, and the aid included a substantial contribution of hardware to enable governments to suppress insurrection and resist outside aggression. The Marshall Plan focused much more on economic rebuilding.

The cold war nearly ignited into a shooting one on June 24, 1948, when the Soviet Union pinched one of the many pressure points, access to Berlin by the West. The Kremlin believed that by choking off all supplies to garrisons and civilians in the western sector of the city, the three former allies, Great Britain, France, and the United States, would be forced to abandon their toehold. Instead, the commander in chief mobilized the newly minted U.S. Air Force and along with the British RAF began "Operation Vittles." It ferried by air some 4,500 tons of supplies a day to West Berlin, from coal to food, clothing, and the gear to maintain the garrisons as well as the civilians. While Soviet fighter aircraft occasionally menaced the transports, no shots were fired.

Having scored an upset victory with his reelection in 1948, Truman expanded U.S. responsibilities with membership in the North Atlantic

Treaty Organization. Britain, France, Belgium, the Netherlands, and Luxembourg had joined in a fifty-year defensive pact that required mutual aid if any came under attack. The Senate issued an approval for American participation through a resolution sponsored by Senator Vandenberg. Seven more countries, including the United States, signed the treaty on April 4, 1949. (Canada, Norway, Denmark, Iceland, Italy, and Portugal were the other additions.) The final version of the treaty said that in the event of an attack upon a member, the others could undertake "such action as it deems necessary," including but not requiring "armed force." By this language, the United States retained its constitutional provisions when the question of war arose.

The cold war featured a long series of confrontations with the communist powers and a frenzy of anticommunism at home. The legal scholar Nicholas Katzenbach wrote, "Presidents became prisoner of the cold war view of politics. . . . The general public and congressional perception of the cold war—and incidentally, of an exaggerated American power to influence and control events—made it virtually impossible for any President to be candid about the costs and risk of our foreign policy. The 'China Syndrome'—the aftermath of Joe McCarthy [the rabid anticommunist senator]—meant politically that it was easier to accept the premise of 'no loss of territory' in the hope that his Presidency would not be called to account than to attempt to gain public and congressional acceptance that the premise might involve unacceptable risks and costs."[6]

The commander in chief grappled with a feverish anticommunism that viewed the ship of state as on the verge of sinking from the wormholes bored by subversives. The aforementioned McCarthy from Wisconsin flourished a fake list of Reds in government; others accused the administration of losing China to communism, and a drumfire of criticism labeled Secretary of State Dean Acheson and his boss as appeasers.

In 1949 Chiang Kai-shek transported his Nationalist Party to Formosa (soon renamed Taiwan), an island traditionally accepted as Chinese territory, which the State Department under Secretary George C. Marshall, with the acquiescence of other U.S. agencies, had decided in October 1948 that the United States would not defend.[7] Undeterred, the generalissimo maintained a belligerent stance and talked of a return to the mainland to conquer the Red Chinese. A so-called China lobby in Congress constantly pressed the case of the Nationalists and protested the administration's attitude.

The Korean peninsula, held by the Japanese from 1910 to 1945, had been divided at the end of World War II. The Soviet Union had declared war on Japan very late in the game, which was sufficient grounds for it to occupy a chunk of the northern part of the country, while Americans entered the south. Governments acceptable to the occupiers ruled in an uneasy peace over the two sections, while both the Soviet Union and the United States removed their own troops. The American pullback had the blessing of the Joint Chiefs of Staff, Truman, General Douglas MacArthur, and the State Department. Budgetary constraints figured into the decision, along with the idea that any real conflict with the Soviet Union would involve atomic weapons. The emphasis was upon the favored notion of money-conscious politicos, "lean and mean," a "bigger bang for the buck," with added funds for a long-range, strategic air force that carried nuclear weapons.

U.S. diplomacy, with the potential for the ultimate resort to military action, stretched across the entire globe. It was with some awareness of how far and wide the country seemed ready to deploy its armed forces that Secretary of State Dean Acheson on January 12, 1950, seeking to clarify the containment policy, described the American defense perimeter in the Far East. He drew a line that stretched from the Aleutians through Japan, Okinawa, and the Philippines. He told the Senate Foreign Relations Committee, "We should not [use] military forces of the United States to take, secure or defend Formosa."[8] The line drawn by the secretary of state also did not include South Korea, but while he placed responsibility for its defense on the indigenous people, he remarked that the United States had "a direct responsibility" for South Korea. After the Korean War began, opponents of the Truman administration charged that Acheson, by his omission of Korea, had signaled permission for North Korea and its Soviet ally to overrun the south. However, Acheson coolly responded by noting that MacArthur, the U.S. suzerain ensconced in Tokyo, had drawn the same perimeter. Furthermore, Congress had refused to provide the military aid the State Department had requested to bolster South Korea.

On June 24, 1950, North Korean soldiers with tanks and artillery poured across the 38th parallel into South Korea, sweeping aside the ill-equipped, ill-trained troops of President Syngman Rhee and the handful of Americans still garrisoned there. President Truman, a day later, called upon the Security Council of the UN to act. The Soviet Union, in a snit over the refusal to seat a representative of Communist China on the council, boycotted the meetings, eliminating its ability to cast a veto. The United States then led the council into a unanimous resolution that branded North Korea the aggressor, urged an immediate cease-fire, and asked all UN members to "render every assistance" for restoration of peace.

"Acheson's man in Tokyo," remembered Alexander Haig, then a MacArthur aide, "sent a message directly to Truman saying it was essential for the U.S. to intervene."[9] The envoy had bypassed MacArthur, but when the general talked to Truman they agreed the United States had to get involved.

On June 26, Truman announced that the North Korean forces had not obeyed the order from the UN and had continued their attack. Citing the danger to Formosa, he said, "I have ordered the Seventh Fleet to prevent any attack on Formosa. As a corollary of this action, I am calling upon the Chinese government of Formosa to cease all air and sea operations against the mainland. . . . I have also directed acceleration in the furnishing of military assistance to the forces of France and the associated states in Indochina and the dispatch of a military mission to provide close working relations with these forces." This last would have far-reaching consequences.

In his memoirs Truman said, "In my generation, this was not the first occasion when the strong had attacked the weak. I recalled some earlier instances; Manchuria, Ethiopia, Austria. I remembered each time that the democracies failed to act it had just encouraged the aggressors to keep going ahead. Communism was acting in Korea just as Hitler, Mussolini and the Japanese had acted ten, fifteen, twenty years earlier. I felt certain that if South Korea was allowed to fall Communist leaders would be emboldened to override nations closer to our shores."[10]

The president, hewing to the theory that all things communist emanated from the Kremlin, in his memoirs wrote that the invasion was designed by "the Russians . . . to get Korea by default, gambling that we would be afraid of starting a third world war and would offer no resistance." Truman did not include Communist China as seeking control over Korea.

In the Senate, some questioned Truman's power to commit the armed forces. But Republican senator William Knowland applauded the executive action. "I believe that in this very important step which the President of the United States has taken in order to uphold the hands of the United Nations and the free people of the world, he would have the overwhelming support of all Americans."[11]

The League of Nations, according to many historians, had foundered after its members failed to act when the Japanese in 1931 attacked Manchuria. Korea served as the first test of whether the UN could provide security. With no indications of a pullback by North Korea, the American commander in chief ordered American naval and air forces to attack the aggressors a few hours before the Security Council formally asked for its members to supply military aid to South Korea. On June 30, with the rout by the North Koreans in full swing, the president committed ground forces, drawn from the occupation soldiers in Japan. General Douglas MacArthur assumed command of the international forces fighting what was to become the Korean War.

The president had sounded the call for war without waiting for congressional action. He only met with leaders of the Senate and House on June 27, after he had decided to act and issued orders to implement the policy. On June 29, at a press conference, someone questioned whether the nation was at war. Truman barked, "We are not at war," but when asked whether this might be "a police action," he agreed.

That term had frequently been invoked during the debates about authority of a president to deploy U.S. armed forces in a UN venture, but never, even by its most ardent advocates, with the investment of men and materials that the Korean War consumed. During 1951 Senate hearings, Acheson went so far as to admit, "In the usual sense of the word there is a war."[12]

Democratic senator Paul Douglas of Illinois threw his weight behind the presidential contention, using the UN resolutions as signs that the use of the military wasn't a war but "the exercise of police power under international sanction." To justify the unilateral decision by the president, Douglas noted the necessity for swift reaction in the emergencies typical of the post–World War II era. "With tanks, airplanes and the atom bomb, war can become instantaneous and disaster can occur while Congress is assembling and debating." Douglas pointed out that even if the two-thirds majority invoked cloture to shut off palaver from as few as one or two senators, the procedure required a minimum of two days. He added, "the retail [small quantity, as opposed to wholesale] use of force" ought to be allowed under historical precedents. He claimed that presidents had deployed the armed forces more than a hundred times "without any declaration of war." His examples, drawn from a 1933 State Department paper, included Jefferson's expedition against the Barbary pirates, the Seminole War of 1817, Polk in Mexico, the Boxer Rebellion in China, and interventions in Santo Domingo, Nicaragua, and Russia.

Douglas admitted, "Up to the invasion of Korea, the use of armed force has been almost invariably ordered by our presidents as a protection against immediate and direct attacks or threats to American lives and property. . . . Our present intervention to check the provocatory [sic] invasion of South Korea by the north Korean Communists under almost certain Russian direction is of a somewhat different kind."

The senator conjured an image of unchecked Soviet-sponsored aggression that could conquer "Burma, Indochina, Persia, Jugoslavia, Greece, Berlin and West Germany." An expansion of Soviet dominance around the world would force other nations to accommodate the communists. Douglas invoked the results of appeasement by Western democracies of Adolf Hitler and said, "The ultimate security of the United States depends upon convincing the Communist aggressors that we will resist aggression and will check it in its earliest states." Thus a liberal senator defined a policy that would guide American military actions for most of the remainder of the twentieth century and justify the ways that commanders in chief and legislators met challenges.

Douglas indicated that one could count on the cautious discretion that pervaded the office of the president and that an overreacher could always be impeached. Given the consequences that might befall the nation if an inhabitant of the Oval Office embarked on a disastrous course, his consolations are hardly convincing. On the other hand, no one can deny that without an immediate armed response, South Korea would have been overrun and beyond help even if Congress could have reached a conclusion within a week.[13]

Senator Robert Taft straddled the line. He supported the use of force in Korea but saw "no legal authority" for it. He would, however, vote for a joint resolution that approved it. Although a Gallup poll reported that 81 percent of the citizens approved of the intervention shortly after it began,[14] during the early weeks, as the poorly trained and poorly outfitted GIs also absorbed horrific punishment from the North Korean armies, the debate about whether the president had overstepped his bounds boiled over in Congress. The legislators found themselves in that uncomfortable bind: to criticize the president could be construed as disloyalty to the troops, undermining the commander in chief. (Most recently, that syndrome has dominated much of the debate about the wisdom of the second war in Iraq.)

The president wavered on the question of whether he should seek that formal backing. He consulted with Secretary of State Acheson, a lawyer who had once served as a clerk for Justice Louis Brandeis, a constitutional scholar. The president decided not to go to Congress but instead commissioned Acheson to draw up a bill of particulars that justified the executive action.

The State Department reiterated the Douglas list of cases where presidents had deployed troops in combat situations on their own initiative. The white paper argued that the "Commander in Chief of the Armed

Forces . . . has full control over the use thereof," that there existed "a traditional power of the President to use the armed forces of the United States without consulting Congress," and that this had often occurred in "the broad interests of American foreign policy."

All the citations of instances where the president, on his own, had sounded the trumpet for battle ignored the fact that previous actions were always aimed at pirates or protection of American citizens and their property. Never had there been a case that involved a sustained and major war against a sovereign state. Also, no matter how many or how strong the UN resolutions, they could not override the language and spirit of the Constitution.

The initial campaign to halt the onslaught of the North Koreans produced dismal results, as the enemy reduced the toehold of the battered American and South Korean forces to a small portion of land at the southern tip of the peninsula. General Curtis LeMay, who had innovated the tactics of the Eighth Air Force in Europe and then the use of B-29s against Japan and now commanded the Strategic Air Command (SAC), urged an attack upon North Korea "with incendiaries and delete four or five of their largest towns."[15] The White House refused to approve LeMay's proposal.

Bringing in reinforcements from a number of garrisons and bolstered by a British division, MacArthur, against the advice of the Joint Chiefs of Staff, the navy, and even members of his own staff, on September 15, 1950, outflanked the foe with an amphibious operation at Inchon, near the capital, Seoul, cutting off the communist troops south of the 38th parallel. Within a few weeks, the North Koreans had either been wiped out or driven back across the border.

On October 7, the UN General Assembly approved an offensive across the 38th parallel that would unite Korea. A warning from Beijing that it would not stand by if North Korea were invaded went ignored. As the United Nations forces, the X Corps, and the Eighth Army, in a strategic error, split to meet along the Yalu River that formed the border with China, MacArthur confidently advised that the Chinese would not intervene. To his chagrin, two hundred thousand well-armed and -equipped Chinese soldiers crossed the frozen Yalu. They routed the Americans and their allies and penetrated South Korea.

Alexander Haig commented, "There was a big mistake made by the Truman administration when it drew the line of defense to include Formosa and the Pescadores Islands. It wasn't necessary to pledge support for Formosa. I was as anticommunist as anyone but what the hell did Formosa have to do with Korea! The Chinese were already nervous about the role of the Soviet Union and its expansion. North Korea was considered under the influence of the Soviet Union. It was evident that Moscow was advising the North Koreans. When we crossed the 38th parallel, it suggested to the Chinese an envelopment of their country and they felt bound to enter. We were the victims of a lack of intelligence; the CIA was newly formed and not equipped yet to collect intelligence. The military were not to conduct strategic intelligence that would have revealed the attitudes of the Chinese."[16] The debacle was an early demonstration of intelligence failure.

Haig was correct about the influence of the Soviets. North Korea's dictator, Kim Il Sung, had gained the halfhearted approval of Joseph Stalin for a military offensive to unite the two Koreas. Mao Tse-tung of China was even less enthusiastic but did not object strongly. But perhaps he was confused by mixed messages. Secretary of State Acheson had specifically ruled out defending Formosa in testimony to Congress, but the president announced that the United States would not accept an invasion by the Red Chinese.

What undoubtedly added to Beijing's concern, however, flowed from the behavior of MacArthur. The general, without advance notice to Washington, visited Formosa toward the end of July 1950 and conferred with Chiang Kai-shek. Although MacArthur declined an offer to send Nationalist troops to South Korea, the generalissimo felt encouraged enough to declare that "victory" over Mao's mainland forces was now "assured." The American commander, praising Chiang for his leadership, ordered three squadrons of fighter planes to the island. The saber-rattling and the intrusion of MacArthur into the area of diplomatic strategy discomfited Washington.

In January 1951, the attitude of Americans had dramatically shifted. In place of the 81 percent favorable to the original police action, two-thirds of the country told Gallup they wanted to pull out altogether.[17] The unpopularity of what his opponents now called "Truman's War" incited some of the people's representatives. Truman had announced that he intended to send four more infantry divisions to Europe, and Frederick Coudert Jr., a New York Republican, offered a resolution that "no additional military forces" could be sent abroad "without prior authorization of the Congress in each instance." Furthermore, the proposal denied the president the right to use any funds to send troops overseas except for the purpose of removing those in Korea.

The compromise that emerged settled little. A "sense of the Senate" resolution approved the shipment of the divisions to Europe with the stipulation that no additional ground forces could be deployed there, a provision carried against the wishes of the administration by forty-nine votes to forty-three. Among those who voted for this restriction of presidential authority was a young senator from California, Richard M. Nixon. Haig has contended that the Eurocentric focus in Washington that continued to ship troops and supplies to Europe denied MacArthur the military force that might have ended the Korean War earlier.[18]

After Eighth Army commander General Walton Walker was killed in December 1950, General Matthew Ridgway, who had led airborne GIs during World War II, replaced him. Ridgway revitalized the shattered UN troops, building up a force of 365,000 buttressed by naval forces that hammered the Chinese from offshore. Under brutal winter conditions the Eighth Army regained the territory of South Korea and then set up a defensive perimeter.

The standoff in Korea produced a showdown between Truman and MacArthur. The Joint Chiefs, under instructions from the president, had advised MacArthur that while he should be prepared to defend all of Korea, this was a limited war and no attack upon China would be countenanced nor would Chiang's armies on Taiwan become engaged. MacArthur, after having wrongly predicted little or no response from the Chinese across the Yalu, renewed his proposals to carry the war to China—bombing bases in Manchuria, instituting a full-scale blockade of China, and even strewing nuclear waste across the supply lines of the enemy.

As a naval officer in the Pentagon, David Richardson was familiar with the relationship of Washington to MacArthur. "None of the Joint Chiefs had faith in him; they didn't trust him. . . . We knew that the Joint Chiefs weren't inclined to cross him up . . . but weren't at all inclined to support him. . . . He wanted to destroy the bridges before the Yalu froze over. He wanted to use a nuclear weapon to do that . . . we always have to remember that [nuclear weapons] then [were] very dirty."[19]

MacArthur entreated Washington to permit the use of Chiang Kai-shek's soldiers on Formosa. To his staff, which included twenty-seven-year-old Alexander Haig, he preached a gospel, "There is no substitute for victory." Many years later, Haig scorned the idea of "limited war" as dictated by those who objected to an offensive. "It was in fact a policy of war without victory. MacArthur said, 'War's very object is victory.'"[20] Some of the more ardent hawks even considered the use of the atomic bomb against Beijing. In fact, American conflicts had frequently been limited wars—the War of 1812, the Mexican War, the Spanish-American War.

While victory seemingly meant nothing less than the overthrow of the Red Chinese, MacArthur did issue a communiqué in which he said, "I stand ready at any time to confer in the field with the Commander-in-Chief of the enemy forces in the earnest effort to find any military means whereby realization of the political objectives of the United Nations in Korea, to which no nation may justly take exception, might be accomplished without further bloodshed."[21] That sounds like at least an endorsement of limited objectives, if not a limited war.

The administration, shell-shocked by the sudden reversal of fortune in Korea, and its UN allies, alarmed by the ferocity of the Chinese intervention, refused to accept MacArthur's strategy. Strikes across the border into China risked widening the war, possibly bringing in the Soviet Union, whose Siberia actually touched the northeast corner of Korea. In Moscow in 1950, dictator Joseph Stalin had signed a mutual assistance pact that obligated the Soviets to aid the Chinese if they were attacked by either Japan or the Western Allies. The Soviets had recently exploded their first nuclear bomb. The worst-case scenario saw mushroom clouds over British cities. Furthermore, the Western powers, clinging to remnants of empire in French Indochina and British Malaya, could ill afford to see the Korean War expand.

General Dwight D. Eisenhower, departing for Europe to serve as supreme commander of NATO, opposed MacArthur's plans, as did General Omar Bradley, chairman of the Joint Chiefs of Staff. Bradley would advise Congress that MacArthur proposed "the wrong war, at the wrong place and at the wrong time, and with the wrong enemy."[22]

In challenging civilian control over the military, enshrined in the Constitution's nomination of the president as commander in chief, MacArthur crossed the Rubicon. The general released to the press an appraisal of the military situation and declared that the Chinese lacked the industrial capability to wage a full-scale war. He argued that a move across the Yalu would persuade the Chinese that unless they negotiated the regime would collapse. Having already flouted the order to keep his silence, MacArthur appeared to go over the president's head. He wrote a letter to the Republican leader of the House, Representative Joseph Martin, in which he said, "Here we fight Europe's war with arms while diplomats there still fight it with words." He concluded with his mantra, "There is no substitute for victory." In his book *Reminiscences*, he said he had only responded to a request for his views from Martin and had never agreed that his letter should be made public.

The lobbying of the general outraged Truman. He hurriedly consulted with the sages of his administration—Bradley, Marshall, Dean Acheson, and W. Averell Harriman, director of the Mutual Security Agency—all of whom agreed that MacArthur must be dismissed. Because of fears of a leak, the announcement that MacArthur had been cashiered was abrupt. It acted like pheromones to those who lusted for Truman's downfall. Joseph McCarthy called the president "an s.o.b. who decided to remove Mac-Arthur when drunk." Richard Nixon demanded immediate reinstatement of the general, and Senator William Jenner fulminated about impeachment. Gallup reported that 69 percent of the public favored MacArthur, versus only 29 percent supporting Truman.[23]

According to the historian Samuel Eliot Morison, MacArthur several years later said, "A theater commander should be allowed to act independently, with no orders from President, United Nations or anyone."[24] The remark clearly indicates an attitude wholly incompatible with the spirit and language of the Constitution and representative government. Nevertheless, in *Reminiscences*, MacArthur clearly accepted the supremacy of the commander in chief. "The legal authority of a President to relieve a field commander, irrespective of the wisdom or stupidity of the action has never been questioned by anyone. The supremacy of the civil over the military is fundamental to the American system of government, and is wholeheartedly accepted by every officer and soldier in the military establishment. It was not an issue in this case."[25]

In 1954, after Truman had been out of office for two years, he posed the question of what would have happened had he gone along with MacArthur. "The Generals say that a few bombs on airfields in Manchuria would have caused a Korean victory to the Yalu. To have been effective, Peking [Beijing], Shanghai, Mukden, Dairen, Vladivostok and Central Siberia at Ulan-Ude on Lake Baikal would have had to be destroyed. It would have been a unilateral action." He predicted that as a result, "The Russians would have marched to the North Sea and the Channel. We had six divisions of our own and about that many of our allies to oppose them. They had over 4,000,000 men in their ground forces. They could not have been stopped." In his scenario it would have been "World War III and no allies." He foresaw the unacceptable destruction of Chinese cities, killing some twenty-five million innocent women and children and noncombatants. "In 1945 I had ordered the A Bomb dropped on Japan at two places devoted almost exclusively to war production [actually a secondary industrial complex, Hiroshima was targeted as home to the Japanese Second Army]. We were trying to end it [the war] in order to save the lives of our soldiers and sailors. . . . In my opinion it had to be used to end the unnecessary slaughter on both sides. It was an entirely different situation from Korea. We stopped the war and saved thousands of casualties on both sides."[26]

MacArthur returned to the States from Korea triumphant even in his defeat. A ticker-tape parade was organized in New York City and he addressed Congress. At the conclusion, he quoted words from an army ballad: "Old soldiers never die, they just fade away." While he retained his popularity, his attempt to usurp the powers of his commander in chief had failed.

Truman had little time to savor this victory. In 1952, with the Korean stalemate still a sore point, the steelworkers struck their industry. Under the Taft-Hartley Act, passed by a Republican Congress, the president could have directed an eighty-day "cooling off" period during which the parties might reach a settlement. Truman had opposed the law, and because stoppage of the mills might curtail production of war materials, he chose instead to take over the companies on the basis of the emergency war powers vested in a commander in chief. Although Truman asked Congress to publicly endorse his action, he did not request special legislation. He explained that it was within his right to have taken over the steel industry. "We are in one of the greatest emergencies the country has ever been in. . . . I feel sure that the Constitution does not require me to endanger our national safety by letting all the steel mills shut down." He allowed that if the legislators disagreed they could reject the confiscation. Congress declined to either veto his decision or to enact legislation of its own.[27]

Youngstown Sheet & Tube Company sued, naming the secretary of commerce, Charles E. Sawyer, as the defendant. Lawyers for the company did not deny that in times of emergency the government could seize their property, but contended that the executive branch was the wrong one to do it. In essence their suit was on behalf of Congress. The Supreme Court ruled six to three against the president, although including the dissents there were seven different opinions.

Justice Hugo Black wrote the most commonly quoted opinion, which refuted the claim that the seizure order followed as "an exercise of the President's military power as Commander in Chief of the Armed Forces. The Government attempts to do so by citing a number of cases upholding broad powers in military commanders engaged in day-to-day fighting in a theater of war. . . . Even though 'theater of war' can be an expanding concept, we cannot with faithfulness to our constitutional system hold that the Commander in Chief of the Armed Forces has the ultimate power as such to take possession of private property in order to keep labor disputes from stopping production. This is a job for the Nation's lawmakers, not for its military authorities." The Supreme Court ruling had reminded the executive branch of the limitations upon it when it attempted to ride the back of a nag named emergency.

Justice Robert H. Jackson commented, "The purpose of lodging dual titles [president and commander in chief] in one man was to insure that the civilian would control the military, not to enable the military to subordinate the presidential office. No penance would ever expiate the sin against free government of holding that a President can escape control of executive powers by law through assuming his military role. . . . I think it is not a military prerogative, without support of law, to seize persons or property because they are important or even essential for the military and naval establishment." In his opinion, Jackson specifically condemned suspension of habeas corpus, Lincoln's sin. In 2004, the title of commander in chief would be invoked in the legal brawls over the habeas corpus rights of those captured in Afghanistan and Iraq.

Harry Truman broke fresh ground with his interpretation of the powers of a president and commander in chief. In Korea, for the first time, the president had engaged the nation in a major war without benefit of a prior declaration by Congress or even post-combat benediction from that body. Furthermore, the legislators did not reprimand him for having usurped their authority. In retrospect, his failure to request their blessing was a mistake. It was a momentous precedent, and one that would haunt the White House and Capitol Hill. At the same time, Truman's decision to meet North Korean aggression with armed resistance enlarged the definition of national security and was ratified by the infant United Nations. While overstepping the mandates of the Constitution, the president had dramatically strengthened the world body, providing an object lesson in what it could do.

4

THE REIGN OF IKE

T he use of American forces to halt aggression by communist North Korea signaled a policy that fully met the Clausewitz theory. The effort to confront communism would not be restricted to diplomacy but would extend into open warfare if deemed appropriate. For the next forty years and through seven presidencies, national security was being redefined and not only covered Southeast Asia but also the Middle East with its vital oil. For the first time, covert war would become an accepted tool.

But it was a bloody conventional war that gripped the nation in the final years of the Truman White House. The president had intervened in Korea but he could not gain victory. In July 1951, protracted truce talks began at a neutral site in Korea. Eventually, the parties agreed to a cease-fire along the front. The diplomats bickered over terms for a permanent cessation of hostilities and the negotiations dragged on into 1952 as the United States geared up for the presidential elections. Admiral David C. Richardson, a member of the American team working with NATO, was in Washington during the negotiations at Panmunjon. "We were insisting that the North Koreans not be allowed to rebuild their airfields and re-create their aircraft strength. They weren't willing to agree to that.

"The Joint Chiefs . . . had sent Truman a message and recommended that we acquiesce on that point. He [the president] said, 'I do not understand why we should grant them this. We have defeated them at a cost of much blood and money, and I don't see any reason why we should allow them to reconstitute.' I thought, 'My God, he thinks we've won this war. We haven't won this war.'"[1]

For the 1952 presidential elections the Republicans nominated Eisenhower, rejecting by a narrow margin Robert Taft, the representative of the isolationist wing of the party. The World War II commander of the Allied armies in Europe exhibited a smiley congeniality, although the private

Eisenhower could be a more prickly personality. As the "We like Ike" sentiment inundated the country, Eisenhower cemented his appeal with a promise to go to Korea and personally bring the state of war to an end. He buried Democratic candidate Adlai E. Stevenson in an electoral avalanche.

President elect Eisenhower fulfilled his vow by visiting Korea in December 1952, an unprecedented step for a commander in chief-to-be. It was more show than substance, however—the administration and the UN appeared determined not to trigger an excuse for a full expression of war. Although the Chinese and Koreans attempted several offensives that cost them dearly against the now well-entrenched UN forces, the latter basically stayed put, to the chagrin of some military leaders. Lieutenant General Maxwell Taylor, commander of the 101st Airborne during World War II and head of the Eighth Army in Korea in 1953–1954, champed at the bit. "We couldn't move more than two battalions in an offensive without permission from Tokyo [headquarters for the UN command]. And Tokyo would probably have to get it from Washington, so the latitude to display initiative was zero point zero."[2] Foreign policy and political considerations dictated military strategy and tactics, much more so than during World War II.

After seemingly endless palaver, a harbinger of what would come with the Vietnam War, a cease-fire and restoration of the 38th parallel boundary marked the conclusion of combat. Less than a true peace but an end to the shooting, the settlement in the eyes of some scholars nevertheless demonstrated that the UN could effect international security, using armed force if necessary. Although the Truman administration had tried to paste a UN label upon the Korean War, it was still largely an American war. The nation invested one million soldiers over time, spent $15 billion, and suffered 150,000 casualties, including 33,000 dead. And the understanding of the war powers shared by the two branches of government had absorbed some serious shaking. Alexander Haig contended that the war ended when Eisenhower threatened to use nuclear weapons.[3]

As the commander in chief, Eisenhower became the first senior military commander since Ulysses S. Grant to occupy 1600 Pennsylvania Avenue. He eschewed both the military trappings and references to his career in uniform. At the same time, he presided over a substantial reduction in funds for the armed forces. The mostly civilian analysts believed the days of conventional wars were over. Since the Soviet Union had revealed its nuclear capability, the new theory of war rested upon the concept of mutual assured destruction, or MAD, which in light of the damage potential from a wholesale exchange of atomic bombs seems appropriate.

Actually, a whole new line of quasi-military action entered the U.S. arsenal, covert operations designed to unseat hostile governments or to support friendly ones battling insurgencies. The first case involved Iran, where radical—in the eyes of British and American oil interests certainly—prime minister Mohammad Mossadegh inveighed against the foreign interests that controlled his country's natural resources. BP, the British oil company, had refused to grant Iran a fifty-fifty profit-sharing deal on Iranian oil as proposed by Mossadegh, although they had such an agreement with Saudi Arabia. When Mossadegh subsequently nationalized the British oil refineries in 1951, he said, "It is better to be independent and produce only one ton of oil a year, than to produce 32 million tons and be a slave to Britain."[4]

The British had quickly instituted a series of financial actions, all but turning off the spigots for that country's oil. Initially, the United States offered support to Tehran. The Truman administration attempted to involve U.S. oil companies as a means to prevent an economic collapse that would enable local communists supported by Moscow to gain power.

Shortly after Eisenhower entered the White House, the policy changed. The dearth of income from oil exports crippled the Iranian economy. Mossadegh could not make good on promises of reforms. As the country teetered on the brink of civil war, he attempted to take command of the armed forces and institute emergency powers, giving him the appearance of a dictator. Propaganda from the British and Iranian opposition to Mossadegh painted him as under the influence of the Tudeh, the local communist party. Actually, as a member of the parliament, the Majlis, he had rejected an oil concession to the Soviets. Furthermore, dating back to 1907 and through World War II, the czars and then the communists from the USSR had enjoyed a sphere of influence in the country that had culminated with the presence of Soviet soldiers during World War II. The occupying force had been a sore point with many Iranians.

In the United States there was little understanding of Iranian attitudes and Mossadegh. He was ridiculed by the American press: *Time* labeled him "The New Menace" and called him "by Western standards an appalling caricature of a statesman." A cover story that pronounced him "Man of the Year" carried the line, "He oiled the wheels of chaos."[5] In his memoirs, Eisenhower described the Iranian leader as "a semi-invalid, with tears and fainting fits and street mobs of followers."[6]

Members of Congress, the media, churches, and oil interests whipped up a groundswell of anticommunism that became an irresistible tidal wave. The White House rejected a plea for economic assistance. Iranian mobs rampaged in the streets. Shah Reza Pahlavi fled his country. The CIA, working through the Tehran embassy, distributed thousands of dollars to support the shah and conservative forces. Loy Henderson, the new ambassador, estimated the amount at "millions of dollars."[7]

The shah returned to his Peacock Throne with a promise of $85 million in economic aid to ensure his future. A court sentenced Mossadegh to three years of solitary confinement. For the State Department and its helpmates in the CIA, this was a grand triumph. Covert operations had wrought regime change of a sovereign government. It was as much an act of war as an invasion of armed forces. The shah would rule for twenty-five years, tied to the West, sometimes a benevolent despot and sometimes a tyrant through the offices of his secret police.

Closer to home, Washington became increasingly alarmed at the spread of communist movements in Latin American countries, which drew philosophic sustenance from Moscow if not arms, money, and agents. Guatemala under democratically elected president Jacobo Arbenz took on a distinctly pink hue through the looking glass of the United States as its government expropriated the holdings of the banana king, United Fruit Company, offering a pittance of the worth of the property. Indiana representative Ray J. Madden warned, "We know now that the Kremlin has succeeded in making Guatemala a Communist beachhead in America."[8]

When the tenth Inter-American Conference met at Caracas, Venezuela, in March 1954, the prevailing attitude toward Uncle Sam was palpably hostile. The United States, however, twisted enough wrists to obtain a resolution that branded communist infiltration into the hemisphere as a threat to all. For Guatemala, push came to shove after a shipment of arms from Poland arrived and the United States countered with airlifts of weaponry to Guatemala's nearest neighbors. The CIA created an operation code-named PBSUCCESS, directed by Richard Bissell, which combined black propaganda inside Guatemala with an insurgency mounted from Honduras. An "army" of two hundred, allegedly composed of that country's exiles, led by Colonel Castillo Armas, marched into Guatemala, with air support from three ancient World War II bombers.

According to Eisenhower, his CIA director Allen Dulles reported that two of the three airplanes had been lost. In his book *Mandate for Change*, Eisenhower said he asked Dulles, "What do you think Castillo's chances would be without the aircraft? His answer was unequivocal. 'About zero.' 'Suppose we supply the aircraft. What would the chances be then?' . . . 'About 20 percent.'" Dulles told the president that "the country which had originally supplied this equipment to Castillo was willing now to supply him two P-51 fighter bombers if the United States would agree to replace them." Henry F. Holland, the assistant secretary of state, warned that the new planes would signal U.S. intervention and remind other Latin Americans of the history of American meddling. However, Eisenhower believed the Caracas resolution against communist infiltration justified the shipment of the P-51s.[9]

CIA official Richard Drain later told the agency's historian Jack Pfeiffer, "PBSUCCESS was a success, through dumb luck more than anything else." The invasion withered as the rebels refused to engage in active combat. However, the CIA's psychological barrage intimidated the Guatemalan army, which refused to fight for Arbenz and forced his resignation. "We won more because of incompetence on the other side than anything else," said another key CIA operative, Jake Esterline.[10] Again, covert aid by the CIA had paved the route for the change.

Singularly, the commander in chief, who more or less scrupulously engaged Congress when it came to overt use of the military, kept covert operations in Iran and Guatemala within the White House. The administration excluded the legislators from a decisive role.

From the beginning of the Eisenhower regime, the State Department grew increasingly disturbed by events in Indochina, where since 1946 a war for independence and for control had pitted the former French colonial masters and their Vietnam loyalists against the communist Viet Minh rebels backed by China. Unlike the British, who quickly granted independence to India, the French stubbornly resisted yielding anything more than a loose confederation of protectorates with titular control by indigenous princes.

In 1945, recalled *New York Times* Far East correspondent Seymour Topping, Truman had abandoned Roosevelt's proposal that Indochina become a UN trusteeship and yielded to Charles de Gaulle's demand that the colony be returned to French control. Truman, said Topping, ignored eight appeals from Ho Chi Minh for U.S. backing for a Philippine style of independence. That caused Ho to turn to the USSR and China for aid against French forces.[11]

In 1952, a unanimous NATO resolution stated that the French resistance to the rebels was consonant with the aims of the organization. It agreed that "the campaign waged by the French Union forces in Indochina deserves continued support from the NATO governments."[12] In its final days, the Truman administration furnished $30.5 million for military use there and an equal sum for economic aid and resettlement of refugees. Furthermore, the U.S. government nominated Vietnam, Cambodia, and Laos, the three pieces of Indochina granted "independence within the French Union" in 1949, for membership in the UN.

Secretary of State John Foster Dulles, who was fiercely hostile toward any expression of communism, voiced a common sentiment: "The propagandists of Red China and Russia make it apparent that their purpose is to dominate all of Southeast Asia." In the years to come the clichéd metaphor of falling dominoes, originally uttered by Eisenhower, would punctuate the speeches of similarly alarmed officials.[13]

As the news from the Far East worsened, the administration approved the dispatch of air force mechanics to maintain bombers and other aircraft used by the French forces. Senator John Stennis, a Democrat from Mississippi, commented that the request for this aid was "reasonable" but added, "It proves my contention that step by step, we are moving into this war in Indochina. I am afraid we will move to a point from which there will be no return."[14]

On February 11, 1954, the president held a press conference. He said the members of the armed forces sent to Vietnam were from training and administrative units, part of the Military Assistance Advisory Group (MAAG) to service aircraft. They were not combat troops. He assured Americans that no one could be more bitterly opposed to ever getting the United States involved in a hot war in that region than he was.[15]

As the situation for the French rapidly deteriorated, Washington's military and civilian leaders considered the alternatives. In a disastrous strategy, the French command placed ten thousand of its crack troops at Dien Bien Phu in the northwest area of Vietnam, close to the Laotian border. Eisenhower had always doubted the wisdom of the Dien Bien Phu venture. "When a French diplomat had told me of their plans at the time, I said, 'You *cannot* do this!'"[16]

Within weeks the garrison at Dien Bien Phu, as Ike indicated, became trapped. They could only be supplied by air. A state of siege began. The stronghold became a symbol for the French presence in Indochina, and if it fell, the defeat would shatter any hope for Western domination. Starting early in April 1954, the Eisenhower administration seriously contemplated deploying elements of the U.S. military to sustain the French.

Eisenhower had already approved shipments of material aid, and was not totally opposed to using the American armed forces in Indochina, but he insisted on several preconditions. He said, "Any intervention on the part of the United States would scarcely be possible save on urgent request of the French government, which request would have to reflect, without question, the desire of the local governments."[17] The reference to the local governments meant that the United States was insisting upon full independence for the three parts of Indochina. Even some of those stalwartly opposed to the spread of communism argued against helping the French if that meant enabling them to maintain an empire.

In addition, Eisenhower wanted international support, either through the United Nations, through a coalition of some Southeast Asian countries, or at least with Australia and New Zealand. Furthermore, he wanted the British to participate in any venture. And while he contemplated the use of air and perhaps naval units, he notified Winston Churchill, "I do not envisage the need of any appreciable ground forces on your or our part." U.S. intervention, said Eisenhower, also required "favorable action by Congress."[18]

The reporter Chalmers M. Roberts, working for the *Washington Post and Times-Herald*, ferreted out a sequence of events. He wrote, "The United States twice during April proposed using American Navy carrier planes and Air Force planes based in the Philippines to intervene in the Indochina war provided Congress and our allies agreed. But the British would not agree." According to Roberts—and his account was never disputed—"Secretary of State John Foster Dulles and Admiral Arthur Radford, Chairman of the Joint Chiefs of Staff, broached the idea at a secret April 3d meeting of the bipartisan leaders of Congress." No ground troops were contemplated for the action. Dulles advised that the situation was "grave but not hopeless."[19]

Dulles dismissed the notion of a UN operation, saying that it would take too long to go into effect and the French required more immediate help. When questioned, Radford admitted that army chief of staff Matthew Ridgway, after the experience of commanding the forces in the Korean War, foresaw a grim, bloody struggle at least as difficult as Korea. He and the other Joint Chiefs did not support the proposal to use the navy aircraft and army B-29s. At the very least, it was suggested, B-29 raids might ease the pressure on the Dien Bien Phu garrison.

Dulles, reported Roberts, then flew to London to consult with British prime minister Winston Churchill and his foreign minister, Anthony Eden. The American could not persuade them to commit to armed intervention. In Paris Dulles heard that the French commander in Indochina had claimed a five-hundred-plane raid "would be sufficient to save Dien Bien Phu." But the British air chiefs had said it was not possible to save the site through air attacks.[20]

On April 16, Vice President Richard Nixon set off alarm bells in a speech to the American Society of Newspaper Editors. His remarks, supposedly off the record but soon widely distributed, included, "Loss of Dien Bien Phu [would be] almost catastrophic." Nixon said that as a leader of the free world the nation could not afford further retreat in Asia. "If to avoid further Communist expansion in Asia and Indochina we must take the risk now by putting our boys in, I think the Executive has to take the politically unpopular decision and do it."[21]

The newspaper reports stirred senatorial wind. Senator William Jenner of Indiana, one of the more vociferous anticommunists, offered a bellicose version of a popular American thesis—Asians should fight Asians. "There is only one way to stop the Red Chinese help to the rebels [in Indochina]. That is to release the armed forces of the free nations of Asia. Once the free Chinese [from Formosa] land on the mainland with sufficient equipment, millions of Chinese will rise up to join them."[22] Having personally seen what it required to mobilize for the June 6, 1944, invasion of France, Eisenhower knew a preposterous proposal when he heard one and ignored it.

Others in Congress angrily denounced Nixon's remarks. Senator Edwin Johnson of Colorado declared, "As a guest at a private party in the company of Democratic Senators a few weeks ago, I heard Vice-President Nixon 'whooping it up for war' in Indochina. I thought he was expressing a private opinion. Now that the editors of the *Nation* [along with other publications] have exposed his off the record war-in-the-jungles speech, I feel free to speak. I am against sending American GIs into the mud and muck of Indochina on a blood-letting spree to perpetuate colonialism and white man's exploitation in Asia."[23]

Ralph Flanders of Vermont voiced concerns that the breakdown of French resistance in Indochina might open further advances in Southeast Asia by the communists. In a prescient statement he remarked, "It is impossible to win in a war in such territory if the people are opposed or even if they hold themselves neutral."[24]

American military leaders were equally dubious about involvement. George Anderson, chief of naval operations, said, "There was grave concern of the JCS of the U.S. being overextended in Indochina, grave concern that the French would not do the things that were necessary to prevent the loss of Indochina to the communists, grave concern that the French would not do the things that would enable what U.S. assistance was being provided . . . grave concern that the French operation out there . . . was purely to regain the status quo ante of the French. The question of the United States coming to the assistance of the French at Dienbien Phu . . . came to a head in 1954. Admiral Radford [Arthur, chairman of the Joint Chiefs of Staff] doubted and I think the army at that time doubted the ability of the French to hold Dienbien Phu."[25]

Concerned about the investment of American men, legislators tacked an amendment to an appropriations bill, seeking to restrict Eisenhower's authority to dispatch troops anywhere in the world without the consent of Congress. Ike said the limitations would reduce his flexibility and if it passed he would veto the bill. The rider lost.

"There is going to be no involvement of America in war," Eisenhower told a press conference, "unless it is a result of the constitutional process that is placed upon Congress to declare it."[26] Having observed the torrent of criticism heaped on Truman when he went to war in Korea without prior support from the legislators, Eisenhower would not expose himself to a hostile Congress. His chief of staff, Sherman Adams, remarked that his boss was determined "not to resort to any kind of military action without the approval of Congress."[27]

According to Chalmers Roberts, an attack in Indochina by American airpower was a much closer thing than Eisenhower's memoirs indicate. Eisenhower was prepared to go to Congress on April 26, 1954, to ask passage of a joint resolution to permit American intervention. If granted, the strike would launch on April 28. The timetable left no room for Congress to investigate or debate, but the argument would claim that without immediate action the cause would be lost. It is difficult to believe that Vice President Nixon could have taken upon himself so serious a policy question as an armed intervention in Indochina. If Eisenhower did not know what his vice president was going to say, he should have and should have given consent.

Any chance for use of the U.S. military in Indochina had foundered as the British pushed a negotiated peace rather than pledging armed aid. The insurgents overran Dien Bien Phu. An international conference in Geneva hammered out peace terms for Indochina, creating four separate and independent entities. Vietnam was split in two, like Korea, with the north under a communist government tied to China and the Soviet Union, the south connected to the West. Laos and Cambodia became independent nations. Some in Congress grumbled that the West had caved in with a "Far Eastern Munich." The Eisenhower administration tried to keep its skirts clean by refusing to sign any of the agreements while tacitly accepting them.

Secretary of State John Foster Dulles engaged a number of those who had attended the Geneva meetings to form a replica of NATO in the Southeast Asia Treaty Organization (SEATO). It obliged its members to

support one another in the event of aggression, but, like NATO, the signatories maintained the right to determine whether to commit their
armed forces. While U.S. membership did not supersede the role of Congress in declaring war, nevertheless, SEATO tended to further dilute the
role of the legislators.

The fractious state of affairs between the communist Chinese government in Beijing and Generalissimo Chiang on Taiwan nearly ignited into
a war over two offshore islands, Quemoy and Matsu, which were occupied
by forces loyal to Chiang but lay only about a half dozen miles from the
mainland. The Strait of Formosa, 120 miles wide, separated Chiang's
Nationalist stronghold from his opponents. On the morning of September
3, 1954, the president received word that the Red Chinese had started a
heavy artillery bombardment of Quemoy. The casualties included two
American soldiers.

The shelling did not surprise Washington. The two Chinas had been
sparring ever since 1949 when Chiang fled to Formosa as the Red armies
swept the field. On New Year's Day 1954, the Nationalist leader had
vowed an invasion of the mainland "in the not distant future," and he had
renewed his promise with an Easter message calling for a "holy war." Ships
and planes from both sides had intermittently swapped gunfire. In fact,
ten days earlier, a band of some forty Chinese raiders had probed the
defenses of Quemoy, killing ten Nationalist soldiers.

In August 1954, Syngman Rhee, the South Korean president, addressed
a joint session of Congress and made the startling proposal that the United
States join his country and Nationalist China in a war against Beijing,
with American air and naval power in support of an invasion by troops
from Korea and Formosa. Premier Chou En-lai promptly picked up the
gauntlet, with a call for the "liberation of Formosa." He warned that his
government would not tolerate any interference from Washington.

The positioning of American naval forces after the onset of the barrage adhered to a White House policy. Eisenhower less than three weeks
earlier had told a press conference, "In January or February of 1953,
instruction went out to the Seventh Fleet. Those instructions regarding
the defense of Formosa merely reaffirmed orders that had been in force in
that fleet since 1950. . . . I would assume what would happen is this: any
invasion of Formosa would have to run over the Seventh Fleet."[28]

The two offshore islands, Quemoy and Matsu, figured into the Formosa
equation. Eisenhower's Joint Chiefs could not agree on whether to defend
these islands, though the majority concluded that while they were not
strategically necessary to protect Formosa itself, they were worth fighting

for because of their psychological value. On two points everyone concurred: that the islands were not militarily necessary for the security of Formosa, and that the Chinese Nationalists on their own could not stave off an aggression against them.

Admiral Radford, Admiral William Carney, chief of naval operations, and General Nathan Twining, the air force commander, urged support for the Nationalists by a bombing campaign against the mainland. Eisenhower rejected their view. "We're not talking about a limited, brush-fire war. We're talking about going to the threshold of World War III. If we attack China, we're not going to impose limits on our military actions, as in Korea. . . . If we get into a general war, the logical enemy will be Russia, not China, and we'll have to strike there."[29]

The issue was complicated by the emotional reaction to the treatment of American flyers who were shot down on the day Ike took office in 1953. The Chinese announced sentences of from four years to life imprisonment for the crime of espionage. Within his own Republican Party, the president met forceful opposition to his measured responses, and to enlist congressional support he met with leading legislators. At a breakfast session, he tried to calm one of the more belligerent congressmen, Senator William Knowland of California, whose ardent advocacy for Chiang earned him the sneering epithet of the "senator from Formosa." Despite Eisenhower's pleading for patience, Knowland took the Senate floor to demand the navy blockade the Chinese coast and thereby force the release of the airmen. Eisenhower rejected Knowland's strategy and in this he had drawn some support even across the aisle from Democratic senators.

The crisis over the offshore islands continued. To clear up any misconceptions, Dulles and Dr. George K. C. Yeh, the Chinese Nationalists' foreign minister, drafted a treaty in which the signatories pledged to "maintain and develop their individual and collective capacity to resist armed attack." The document specified Taiwan and the Pescadores, a group of islands within the Formosa Strait and much nearer Chiang's domain. However, the language also said the agreement could be extended to other areas by mutual consent. A key component, covered by a letter between Dulles and his counterpart, added, "It is agreed that such use of force will be a matter of joint agreement, subject to action of an emergency character which is clearly an exercise of inherent right of self defense." The import was that the Chinese Nationalists would not attack the mainland unilaterally.[30]

Tensions increased as Chiang forecast war "at any time," while across the water, the Chinese Communists constructed jet airfields that could bring supremacy in the skies over the two islands. Beijing invaded the island of Ichiang, a mere seven miles north of the Tachens, another group of islands occupied by the Nationalists. Backed by intense bombardment from the air, an amphibious force landed four thousand soldiers, who quickly subdued the thousand Nationalist irregulars guarding Ichiang.

The president hewed to his course, explaining that neither Ichiang nor the Tachens figured in the defense of Formosa and the Pescadores. However, he now wanted to modify the policy regarding Quemoy and Matsu. Accordingly, Eisenhower sent a special message to Congress on January 11, 1955, in which he requested presidential authority to use American armed forces to protect Formosa and the Pescadores and "related positions," which would cover the two offshore outposts. Eisenhower later explained that he was aware of the possible confusion that had encouraged the North Koreans to invade and therefore he had resolved to leave no uncertainty in the minds of the Chinese Communists.

The January 24, 1955, Formosa Resolution read: "That the President of the United States be and he hereby is authorized to employ the Armed Forces of the United States as he deems necessary for the specific purpose of securing and protecting Formosa and the Pescadores against armed attack, this authority to include the securing and protection of such related positions and territories of that area now in friendly hands." The measure won 410 yea votes in the House and 85 in the Senate.

At the same time, the White House seemed to include Congress if the possibility of military engagement arose. In 1955, Ike requested from legislators a joint resolution covering armed forces operations to protect Formosa. He noted, "Authority for some of the actions which might be required would be inherent in the authority of the Commander-in-Chief," while allowing that approval by Congress would publicly affirm this authority.

Congress dutifully voted to give him the right to deploy the military "as he deems necessary," a rather extraordinary power in the absence of a specific action other than the oft-voiced threats of the Mainland Chinese. Arthur Schlesinger pointed out that similar congressional sanction had been voted against Tripoli and Algeria in the early nineteenth century, but the Formosa Resolution did not order any action or name an enemy. The president's personal popularity and the decline of the "dinosaur wing"—taken by age, death, and replacement by younger individuals—provided the capital to support this blank check. Previously, Congress had refused to grant this type of contingency authorization, but now the legislators ceded a fundamental privilege to the executive branch.[31]

On the surface, Eisenhower had respected the provisions of the Constitution by asking for authority rather than assuming he held it. However, he had also procured the credit card of Congress and little limit on how he would use it in a particular situation. This advance approval by means of resolution would become an increasingly popular instrument. Its net effect was to provide a commander in chief with the freedom to act quickly in foreign affairs, but only five days of debate preceded the vote. Missing was any intense scrutiny of the political and military situation, an appraisal of what might be the consequences if the commander in chief did call on the armed forces and what end result would satisfy the parties involved.

Whatever the potential downside, tensions in the Far East abated. The Americans taken prisoner were released. While the United States adamantly stuck to an embargo on trade with China, by 1957 Great Britain and other countries had resumed commerce.

Meanwhile on the other side of Asia, though Iran had settled down, the Middle East, with the infant state of Israel and a bubbling cauldron of revolutionary and anti-Western attitudes, threatened to boil over into a series of shooting wars. President Gamal Nasser of Egypt, buoyed by a rising tide of nationalism, offended the West by bargaining for loans and arms from communist countries. Washington and London withdrew an offer to finance a high dam at Aswan on the upper Nile.

The Egyptian president retaliated by seizing the Suez Canal, owned mainly by British and French stockholders. Under international law, Nasser could have nationalized the waterway upon compensation to the investors. On October 29, 1956, Israeli armed forces attacked Egypt because of a series of raids that had started on Egyptian soil. Two days later, France and Great Britain joined in an attack to capture the area surrounding the canal, ostensibly to protect it from destruction in the Israeli-Egyptian war but in reality as a means to take control over the passage. The timing suggested collusion with the Israelis, something all parties denied.

With two NATO partners engaged, Eisenhower navigated some treacherous waters. Bucking the French and British could test the NATO ties. Eisenhower chose to give full support to a UN effort for an immediate cease-fire and a parley to settle the issues. International pressure forced the occupiers of the Suez territory to yield. A UN police force there established order.

The administration feared that the decline of French and British influence in the Middle East opened up fertile ground for communist movements. The president, pushed by his State Department, sought to replicate the arrangements that covered Formosa. He asked for a congressional resolution to provide him with the authority to furnish, upon request, economic aid and armed support to any Middle Eastern country that felt threatened by the communists.

Unlike the situation in the Far East, however, the legislators had second thoughts about giving carte blanche. Hearings and debates dragged on for weeks before passage. Notably, whereas with Formosa the resolution expired whenever the chief executive decided "the peace and security of the area is reasonably assured," in the Middle East Resolution Congress reserved the right to make that determination.

George McGovern was a freshman Democratic representative from South Dakota in the House. "I joined with 60 other House members," he recalled, "to oppose a request by the Eisenhower Administration for a 'blank check' to intervene in the Middle East. The resolution also called for $200 million in economic and military aid to the Arab states to strengthen them against Soviet inroads. Although it seemed to me a clear abdication of congressional authority over war-making, the measure passed the House by an overwhelming margin, 355–61. Hubert Humphrey called Congressman Eugene McCarthy and me to urge us not to oppose such a fundamental bipartisan foreign-policy proposal. The Congress should support the President on such questions, he said. It was a preview of the issue that . . . was to create differences between Hubert and me and eventually make us opponents inside the Democratic Party."[32]

The Middle East still wobbled. Gamal Nasser drew Syria into the bosom of Egypt to create a new state, the United Arab Republic. After a coup eliminated King Faisal II of Iraq in 1958 and both Jordan and Lebanon appeared shaky from internal disorder abetted by communist elements, the West reacted. The British landed paratroopers in Jordan, the Sixth Fleet maneuvered along the Mediterranean coastline, and an amphibious force deposited U.S. Marines on the beaches of Lebanon. To the astonishment of the marines who hit the beaches, they were greeted by sunbathers and music; whatever crisis had inspired the deployment had evaporated.

It was only partially on the basis of the Middle East Resolution that the White House, beset by word of a communist takeover in Lebanon, ordered the operations. The president did tell Congress that the troops were deployed under the rubric of the resolution's language about "preservation of the independence and integrity of the nations of the Middle East." He announced, "In response to the appeal from the government of Lebanon, the United States has dispatched a contingent of U.S. forces to

Lebanon to protect American lives [about two thousand American citizens were in the country] and by their presence to encourage the Lebanese government in defense of Lebanese sovereignty and integrity. These forces have not been sent there as an act of war. They will demonstrate the concern of the U.S. for the independence . . . of Lebanon which we deem vital to the national interest and world peace."[33]

Democratic senator Mike Mansfield of Montana complained that the White House seemed surprised and ill prepared for the chaos of the Middle East. "It seems clear that there has been a failure somewhere. . . . There are three possibilities: The intelligence services are not providing our government with the necessary information. . . . The information is not being properly evaluated in Washington. . . . The evaluation is not being properly acted upon by the policy makers." While he did not single out the CIA as the culprit, Mansfield was pointing out a serious weakness for the commander in chief—flawed intelligence.[34]

Intended to stabilize the Middle East on terms friendly to American interests, the "Eisenhower Doctrine" drew little support in the region. The United Arab Republic denounced it, and while aggressors from outside may have been deterred, the area remained racked by internal conflict. However, when the Arab governments after UN mediation agreed not to meddle in one another's internal affairs, the marines left Lebanon.

The situation in Latin America also seemed to be deteriorating as rebellious factions, some of which undoubtedly included communists aided by money if not weapons from the Soviet Union, twisted Uncle Sam's arm. A visit to countries south of the border by Vice President Richard M. Nixon in 1958 met barrages of stones and epithets in Lima and Caracas. Even in friendlier countries, the hosts confronted their guest with denunciations of U.S. support of despots. The disturbances so alarmed Washington that the president directed his generals to prepare paratroopers for a possible rescue mission of Nixon. The vice president reached home safely, but aware of the strife in the nation's backyard, Washington started a twin campaign. In one, Congress appropriated billions in foreign aid to Latin America, while in the second, the CIA opened up more ambitious covert operations to thwart those considered hostile to American interests.

Ambivalence governed relations between the administration and Cuba. Strongman Fulgencio Batista's excesses were difficult to ignore. His partnership with American gangsters in an economy fueled by corruption and vice hardly fitted the prim attitudes of Secretaries Dulles and Christian A. Herter, and the White House. The leading revolutionary, a bearded young lawyer named Fidel Castro, however, also bothered U. S. investors in Cuba, who worried that a change of regime might cost them. Castro started to receive weapons from well-wishers opposed to Batista, and the administration chose to embargo further arms to the dictator.

After Castro overthrew Batista early in 1959, his new government received quick recognition. At the same time, wary of his intentions, Washington held back on economic aid. Arthur Schlesinger wrote that the new Cuban government astonished Washington by not requesting any assistance.[35] As the revolutionaries systematically executed followers of Batista, Castro lost popularity with the United States and when the new Cuban government confiscated property owned by American companies, opposition toward the regime increased radically. Relations hit absolute zero as the Cuban dictator tried to export revolution to other countries.

The principals began to set the stage for a series of dramatic confrontations. Washington attempted to chop-block Castro, cutting off all sugar imports from the island while imposing an embargo on everything from the States except for medicine and food. The Soviet Union quickly stepped up, agreeing to buy the Cuban sugar and promising to compensate for the American trade bans with oil, machinery, arms, and technicians. Nikita Khrushchev, successor to Joseph Stalin, scorned the principles of the Monroe Doctrine, pronouncing it a corpse: "Bury it, just as you bury anything dead, so it will not poison the air." He went so far as to say that the United States could expect a rain of rockets should it strike at Cuba. Castro demanded the return of the American naval base at Guantanamo, granted in 1903 and more or less permanently ceded by a 1934 treaty. Rebuffed, the Cuban leader ordered a severe reduction in the Havana embassy staff, while describing the American president as a "gangster" and "senile White House golfer."

Teeth gnashed in Washington, but membership in the Organization of American States obliged the signatories not to act alone against an opponent. A number of other nations in Latin America, while not Marxist-Leninist states, still sympathized with the social and economic reforms undertaken by Cuba, and they traditionally resented the "big stick" periodically wielded by the mighty northern giant. No amount of cajoling nor economic promises could win acquiescence for intervention. Cuban refugees began to fly small bombing raids from Florida airfields. While these did not involve members of the U.S. military, the use of American soil to attack a sovereign nation violated UN and OAS rules for their members. Beyond these pinpricks, the CIA prepared a covert scenario that would enlist exiles in a military operation to depose Castro.

On March 17, 1960, the plan, entitled "A Program of Covert Action Against the Castro Regime," won Eisenhower's approval. Specifically, it called for the creation of an opposition movement against Castro located outside of Cuba; the development of a communications program to propagandize against Castro; the recruitment of agents within Cuba to feed intelligence to the exiled foes and take direction from them; and perhaps foremost, the organization of an armed force outside of Cuba capable of waging guerrilla warfare. The CIA document noted that all of this was to be done "in such a manner as to avoid the appearance of U.S. intervention."[36] For these purposes, the president granted an initial budget of $4.4 million. CIA deputy director Richard Bissell, the architect for the overthrow of Guatemala's Jacobo Arbenz, began to draw up the plans and directed the program.

By the end of the Eisenhower administration, a mere fifteen years after World War II, the American military and new, sub rosa, nonuniformed agencies were engaged in acts of undeclared war. Congress, with exceptions by a few members, had aided and abetted in its loss of authority through the weakening tactic of the resolution. The route for larger military adventures instigated by an administration, with enormous potential for abuses of power, opened wider.

5

CAMELOT'S COMMANDER
IN CHIEF

During the terms of Truman and Eisenhower, most of the focus had been outside the Western Hemisphere. Ike's successor, John F. Kennedy, with minimal input from Congress, continued to flourish the flag in far-off places in the fashion of his predecessors. But when a threat surfaced closer to home, he accepted the traditional responsibility of the president to defend the nation. His authority would go unquestioned, but it was significant that even where all signs pointed to a more than supportive Congress, the administration would largely ignore the people's representatives and go the distance without their advice, to say nothing of their prior consent.

Ike's second term in office would end in 1960, and Vice President Nixon, who had bared his hawk claws during the 1954 Indochina crisis, as the Republican candidate in the 1960 campaign hung the deadly label of appeasement upon his Democratic rival John Fitzgerald Kennedy after the latter indicated he would not defend Quemoy and Matsu but protect only Formosa itself. In a seeming contradiction, Nixon charged Kennedy as "dangerously irresponsible" in promoting talk of Cuban refugees returning to the island to overthrow Castro by force. But in fact, Nixon was an early and enthusiastic advocate of the CIA's proposed plans to carry out such an attack. Kennedy buckled under the charge of being soft on communism and changed his position regarding the two Asian islands and the Cuban revolution. According to Arthur Schlesinger, Kennedy had at first spoken of the need for consultation with other republics in the hemisphere before taking any measures against Cuba. But then he suddenly shifted in tone, with words about support of anti-Castro exiles and hopes of overthrowing the Cuban leader. The handsome, articulate, telegenic Kennedy eked out a win. He announced that the torch had been passed, but along with it came baggage for the new commander in chief.

JFK brought to the White House glamour in himself and his wife, Jacqueline. A Massachusetts Democrat, he could hardly be described as a "liberal," considering his flirtations with notorious Red-baiter Senator Joseph McCarthy and his nondescript record in Congress. A rich boy, he came from Irish Catholic stock fully aware of the contempt showered on his kind by the local Brahmins. His reign would be known as "Camelot," but in truth the flowering of the arts and cultural values during his administration came mainly through the influence of Jacqueline. The media of the day hid his sexual peccadilloes, allowing him to carry on without the murk of scandal to distract him from his purposes—unlike the forty-second president, William Jefferson Clinton. Never an ideologue imprisoned by ideology, he encouraged associates to speak their minds.

Like his predecessor he upheld a policy of opposition to Soviet and Chinese communism under the heading of "containment," a posture of confrontation whenever they appeared to be attempting to expand their hegemony. At his inauguration, JFK announced, "Let every nation know whether they wish us good or evil that we will fight any fight, pay any price, make any sacrifice in order to ensure that liberty is not removed from the earth." The statement implied a more assertive policy, even use of military force, to halt the perceived enemies of freedom.

Dwight D. Eisenhower bequeathed to his successor the muddled scenario for an invasion of Cuba by exiles who expected strong support at sea and in the air from the United States. The author and producer of the final shooting script was the CIA, which, building upon its successes in the removal of Mossadegh and then the less well concealed overthrow of the Arbenz regime in Guatemala, fattened its secret budget to roughly $1 billion a year. The agency, under a 1960 plan, formed an army of about fifteen hundred Cuban refugees, trained with American weapons and equipment.

According to Richard Bissell, the CIA deputy director of plans during the Eisenhower presidency, at a meeting on January 3, 1961, with the incoming chief executive's inauguration less than three weeks away, Eisenhower "seemed eager to take forceful action against Castro, and breaking off diplomatic relations appeared to be his best card. He noted that he was prepared to 'move against Castro' before Kennedy's inauguration, if a 'really good excuse' was provided by Castro. Failing that, the commander in chief speculated, 'Perhaps we could think of manufacturing something that would be generally acceptable.'"[1] Neither a provocation from Castro nor a suitable fake incident occurred. Eisenhower could only sever diplomatic relations.

The newly inaugurated president faced a choice of whether to allow the operation to proceed. During his campaign for the presidency, Kennedy had criticized the Eisenhower administration for not doing enough to oust Fidel Castro. He thus took office with the implicit imperative to take action against Cuba. Furthermore, as a Harvard graduate, one with a large stock of so-called liberals in his administration, JFK offered a target for anti-intellectual and partisan forces slinging the epithet "soft-headed." Arthur Schlesinger wrote that after a discussion of the matter at the White House, "I could not help feeling that the desire to prove to the CIA and the Joint Chiefs that they were not soft-headed idealists but were really tough guys, too, influenced State's representatives at the cabinet table."[2] Playing what they called "hardball" was a highly valued characteristic for those trying out for the Kennedy team.

Senator J. William Fulbright, who chaired the Senate Foreign Relations Committee, after the president confided that the rumors of an invasion were factual, decried the move in a memorandum. "The Castro regime is a thorn in the flesh; it is not a dagger in the heart," he wrote. Given a seat at the table for a conference at the State Department, Fulbright reiterated his opposition, calling fears about Cuba "wildly out of proportion to the threat."[3]

Most of those in the State Department had lined up early alongside the CIA in favor of the attack. According to Schlesinger, Secretary of State Dean Rusk teetered on the fence but eventually agreed with the plans. Secretary of Defense Robert McNamara and the heads of the armed forces studied the military aspects and eventually pronounced them feasible. However, the Joint Chiefs warned that without a massive anti-Castro reaction beyond the beaches the fifteen hundred invaders could not hope to conquer the two-hundred-thousand-strong Cuban army and militia.

On April 12, 1961, Kennedy announced that in no circumstances would U.S. armed forces become directly involved in any attack on the island. Five days later, the ragtag invasion force began landing on the southern coast of Cuba at Bahia de Cochinos, the Bay of Pigs. The original blueprints for the invasion had plotted daylight landings at Trinidad, a city on the southern coast, near the Escambray Mountains. Commander in chief Kennedy had involved himself in the tactical details, albeit for diplomatic reasons. According to Bissell, the president argued for an after-dark operation at the Bay of Pigs because that would lessen exposure of the U.S. involvement. The beach might also provide an airstrip for bombing raids. Trinidad's field could not accommodate bombers. Schlesinger noted that JFK said the daylight invasion might be "too spectacular" and he preferred something "quiet." The alterations tailored by the president required vigorous revisions in logistics by the CIA in the confined space of four days. The new location also lessened the insurgents' ability to recruit the disaffected. Nevertheless, the agency went along, confident that Castro's air force would be destroyed prior to the landing. Attempts to reinforce loyal troops would be blasted by the bombers and a mass uprising against the government would sweep the island. A CIA briefer assured the anti-Castro soldiers of "an umbrella" that would shield them from enemy planes. Allen Dulles, in a book published two years later, claimed the CIA did not believe a spontaneous, widespread revolt would follow, but instead that the beachhead would begin a war of attrition that would ultimately cause the Castro government to collapse.[4]

If all went as hoped, the provisional Cuban government organized by the CIA would land and declare itself. Immediate recognition by the United States would follow, and when this regime requested military assistance, the United States could supply it, in what was surely a brazen maneuver to outflank congressional involvement in the use of armed forces abroad.

B-26 bombers, taking off from Puerto Cabezas, Nicaragua, struck at four Cuban airfields on April 15. Having expected the invasion, the Cuban air force had dispersed its planes. The Castro government had also cast a wide dragnet to sweep up anyone whom they suspected might aid the enemy, jailing as many as two hundred thousand. When Cuban minister of foreign affairs Raúl Roa complained to the United Nations about the raids, U.S. ambassador Adlai E. Stevenson, given a photograph of a B-26 with a Cuban defector standing by it, rebutted that this was the act of rebels in the Cuban air force. A few hours later, the truth surfaced as experts examined the picture and noted that the B-26 model was not the same as that used by Cuba. A chagrined Stevenson chafed even further upon hearing the president refer to him as "my official liar."

Frogmen from the U.S. Navy actually were the first to set foot on the beaches to set up guide markers for the invaders and to remove any barriers. However, the entire operation unraveled as the landing ships encountered unforeseen reefs. Cuban planes, using bombs and rockets, sank the vital supply ship *Houston* and the freighter *Rio Escondido*, then disabled a large landing craft. The indigenous militia, instead of joining the invaders, put up stout resistance until regular troops could arrive and steadily whittle down the CIA's recruits. A last-ditch airstrike by a few U.S.-piloted planes could not save the isolated anti-Castro force. Kennedy had agreed that six unmarked fighters from navy carriers could fly cover for these raiders. But the escorts missed their rendezvous and Cuban fighters knocked off two of the bombers. The White House tossed in the towel, leaving the invaders on their own. Pushed back to the water's edge, the rebels surrendered; two hundred had died and almost twelve hundred became prisoners. Four American pilots were killed.

In the final hours of the Bay of Pigs fiasco, Kennedy insisted that this had been "a struggle of Cuban patriots against a Cuban dictator. While we could not be expected to hide our sympathies, we made it repeatedly clear that the armed forces of this country would not intervene in any way." He ignored the use of U.S. Navy frogmen and escorts for ships, the training of pilots by the U.S. military, the activities on American soil, and the failed attempt by carrier planes to protect the bombers. However, he stuck to the hard line. "If the nations of this hemisphere should fail to meet their commitments against outside communist penetration—then I want it clearly understood that this government will not hesitate in meeting its primary obligations which are to the security of our nation." Both the president and his brother Robert F. Kennedy denied that air cover was ever promised to the rebels. The willingness to have unmarked navy fighters provide assistance makes their claim less meaningful.

Since the attack on Cuba had its inception during the Republican Eisenhower administration, Kennedy escaped partisan criticism. Indeed, as part of his "strategy of protection" the president had telephoned influential Americans, including Eisenhower, Truman, Nelson Rockefeller, Barry Goldwater, and Richard Nixon, whose advice had been to "find a proper legal cover . . . and go in."[5]

A report by Lyman Kirkpatrick, the inspector general of the CIA, blamed the agency for bad intelligence, wretched planning, and misinforming the White House. Kirkpatrick's investigation excused the Joint Chiefs of any culpability after they argued that the final plan was presented to them "only orally, which prevented normal staffing. They regarded the operation as solely the CIA's responsibility except for some minor support from the armed forces, that they assumed full air support would be furnished and control of the skies secured, and there would be huge influx of Cubans joining the insurgent ranks."[6] However, both Schlesinger and Kennedy aide Ted Sorenson attribute much more input to the Joint Chiefs who signed off on the plans even in the absence of a massive uprising by the island's residents. Kennedy had taken the precaution of obtaining written endorsements by General Lyman Lemnitzer, chairman of the Joint Chiefs, and by Admiral Arleigh Burke, chief of naval operations for the navy. And while Kirkpatrick may have given a pass to the military, the president scorched their contribution. "Those sons-of-bitches with all the fruit salad [medals and ribbons] just sat there nodding, saying it would work."[7] General Lemnitzer drew the bulk of JFK's fury.

Members of the military recalled the interplay with the Joint Chiefs quite differently. Former vice admiral Lloyd M. Mustin said:

> I had no inkling of that it [the Bay of Pigs invasion] was even going on, until as a member of Arleigh Burke's personal staff, I barged in on him in the morning of the disaster . . . the landings had begun. They were going very badly by the time I walked in. There was Arleigh Burke . . . tearing his hair out and telephoning the White House and everything else, trying to make head or tails out of things . . . and he wasn't getting very far.
>
> . . . he explained to me—later, when things had calmed way down—. . . that the CIA plan, for this invasion at the Bay of Pigs, had been kept secret from the Joint Chiefs of Staff, completely. They were not permitted to know even that a plan was being developed, let alone any details of what the plan was, until very late in the game the plan was shown to General Lemnitzer. . . . General Lemnitzer was told he could not even show it to his colleagues, but his opinion was requested as to whether or not it could be successful.
>
> He showed it to at least some of his colleagues, including Arleigh Burke, to whom this was absolutely the first notice that such a thing was impending . . . within a matter of days or hours—the time not firmly set. With their advice and agreement, he informed President Kennedy that it could succeed, provided the U.S. furnished air support. That was the essential proviso. If it was stated in the words that Arleigh used to me, it was stated with unmistakable clarity.
>
> Somehow or other, the U.S. carrier *Essex* was in the Caribbean area . . . with her air group on board. Arleigh unilaterally, on his own, moved her over from Guantanamo to the Bay of Pigs area—not far, several hundred miles . . . with her he moved a couple of destroyers. They were there the morning of that invasion. What Arleigh was literally frantic about was that . . . the *Essex* air group was in the air, ready, and he couldn't get permission to use them.
>
> The destroyers were in there so close that their whaleboats picked up survivors from the landing force. . . . The pilots, out of the *Essex* air group were down 50 feet over the beaches . . . the invasion force got in there successfully. The Cubans took to their heels. These people were advancing practically without opposition. [That does not square with the on-scene accounts that credit the locals with resisting sufficiently to delay the rebels.]
>
> So here we had something planned entirely outside the armed forces, . . . and not with any of their recommendations as to place, time or anything else. . . . The country was treated to the spectacle of the Arthur

Schlesinger, Juniors—and people of that stripe—explaining why it was that Kennedy lost his faith in the military and seemed unable to get decisions out of them.[8]

Mustin's comments emphasize the ongoing conflict between those in uniform and the civilians who, in a democracy, are elected to run the country. Schlesinger would later comment that the varied explanations for failure reminded him of historian Douglas Southall Freeman's lengthy apologia for Robert E. Lee's defeat, which never mentioned the element of the Union army. Indeed, the Bay of Pigs fiasco demonstrated the firm hold of Fidel Castro over his nation and the willingness and ability of his armed forces to fight, phenomena missed by the CIA.

The president offered a public mea culpa for the affair while firing Allen Dulles as head of the CIA and its planning director, Richard Bissell. There was much talk of reform within the intelligence community. From discussion with Eisenhower and some aides and his own introspection, Kennedy realized that his major mistake was in not thoroughly questioning the operation and the assumptions that came with it. He resolved to deliberate more intensively if confronted by a crisis of similar magnitude. Forty years later, President George W. Bush launched a war against Iraq freighted with even worse intelligence vetted by the CIA.

The experience of the Bay of Pigs did not dampen the ardor to remove Castro, and in fact the embarrassment may have heightened the zeal of the White House to rid Cuba of his troublesome presence. Bissell, understandably unhappy when the administration canned him for the misadventure, wrote, "To understand the Kennedy administration's obsession with Cuba, it is important to understand the Kennedys, especially Robert [John's brother and the attorney general]. From their perspective, Castro won the first round at the Bay of Pigs. He had defeated the Kennedy team; they were bitter and they could not tolerate his getting away with it. The president and his brother were ready to avenge their personal embarrassment by overthrowing their enemy at any cost. I don't believe there was any significant policy debate in the executive branch on the desirability of getting rid of Castro."[9]

Personal animosity by a commander in chief as an addendum to concern for national security should alert the watchdogs to a skewed policy. George W. Bush's attitude toward Saddam Hussein—"he tried to kill my dad"—surely reflected his familial grievance. The dark side of Camelot created Operation Mongoose, a catch-all for anti-Castro steps that included everything from fake photos calculated to embarrass him, to poisonous cigars and abortive attempts to build another army of refugees. The heroic portraits of JFK painted by Schlesinger and Sorenson do not mention Mongoose or the assassination schemes.

Two months later, in June 1961, Soviet premier Nikita Khrushchev, having met the new American president in Vienna for discussions about Germany, disarmament and a ban on nuclear testing, and Southeast Asia, renewed the threat to end the Western presence in Berlin. JFK responded with a request to Congress for strengthening the military and the call-up of a quarter of a million reservists. The legislators overwhelmingly approved, presenting the Soviets with a united and stiffening front. Instead of pursuing the objective to unify Berlin under East German control, the Soviets and the East Germans attempted to shut down the steady flow of people to the West. They bisected the city with a wall of concrete and barbed wire, overlooked by armed sentries.

After retiring from his post as chief of staff of the army, Maxwell Taylor wrote a book, *The Uncertain Trumpet*, in which he criticized the reliance of the Eisenhower administration upon nuclear weapons. Kennedy, finding that Taylor's theories on limited warfare suited his own ideas, brought him into his administration as a special adviser on military affairs, and in the aftermath of the Bay of Pigs later appointed him the successor to Lemnitzer as chairman of the Joint Chiefs.

Secretary of Defense Robert McNamara, whose well-thought-out, systematized management of the Ford Motor Company had dazzled the business and academic communities, with the Joint Chiefs began to organize the military for more limited conflicts dependent upon conventional arms. The administration opted for a more balanced military, with buildups of the navy, marines, and army ground forces. The air force added tactical wings, fighter-bombers that could support the ground troops. The growing guerrilla-type wars that menaced existing governments convinced the U.S. experts on military affairs to add counterinsurgency training.

As president, Kennedy also insisted that the leaders of the armed forces expand their horizons beyond the battlefield. Admiral Thomas Moorer, a hard-bitten conservative, southern segregationist, and an advocate of maximum force when the guns began to shoot, noted that he was present one day when Kennedy came to the Pentagon. "He was very strong in making the point that the senior military people must not confine their thinking and their studies to military problems per se. They must know how to integrate the economic and the political and international relations with the military and he expected us to do that."[10]

In Southeast Asia, fifty thousand U.S. troops guarded South Korea, but new U.S. clients in 1961 were Laos, Thailand, and South Vietnam. Laos, lying between Thailand and Vietnam along the Mekong River, and Thailand stood with the West, while Vietnam had been split, like Korea, into north and south, the former ruled by communists, the latter under the erratic reign of a quasi-democratic leader. Kennedy had actually visited the area in 1951. On his return to the States he warned, "We have allied ourselves to the desperate effort of a French regime to hang onto the remnants of empire. . . . To check the southern drive of communism makes sense but not only through reliance on the force of arms. The task is rather to build strong native non-Communist sentiment within these areas and rely on that as a spearhead of defense." He concluded that this could only be achieved by satisfying innate nationalism—implying independence.

During the final years of the Eisenhower presidency, the newly created state of Laos had benefited from an outpouring of $300 million in American largesse. Actually, 85 percent went to the Royal Laotian Army, whose Transportation Corps received jeeps and trucks although the country had no all-weather roads to accommodate vehicles in monsoon season. Furthermore, the training from American experts dealt with conventional warfare, rather than counterguerrilla tactics. The government, infested with corruption, frittered away such aid, and an insurgent movement by communist guerrillas gained control of increasing amounts of real estate.

On March 23, 1961, JFK issued a statement proclaiming that to preserve Laos from falling to the communists he would pursue a policy designed to ensure its independence and neutrality. Some thirty days later, however, the administration decided not to take its stand in Laos but instead to invest more heavily in South Vietnam. Republicans chided the White House for talking tough while waving a white flag. When the rebels in Laos gained even more ground, the Pentagon shipped five thousand soldiers to neighboring Thailand, which was also somewhat shaky. The Thais greeted the troops warmly and their presence somehow steadied the government.

A fourteen-nation meeting in Geneva drafted an agreement that guaranteed the neutralization of an independent Laos with a tripartite government composed of the communists, neutralists, and pro-westerners. Again, a drumfire of partisan sneers charged appeasement. In South Vietnam, Premier Ngo Dinh Diem, a Roman Catholic in a predominantly non-Christian nation, dealt harshly with noncommunist dissent, while the Viet Cong, South Vietnamese communist guerrillas, threatened his domain.

Seeking to maintain a bulwark against further encroachment by the communist elements, the administration sent its first military "advisers" to train and direct operations by soldiers loyal to Diem. Helicopters, piloted by Americans, began to assist missions. Recognizing the exposure to injury, JFK issued an executive order that servicemen wounded in Vietnam were entitled to Purple Hearts, the medal for those hurt while deployed by the American military.

The New York Times reported that the United States had written off the right-wing Laotian army. The rebel Pathet Lao had driven much of its opposition to seek refuge in Thailand. Secretary of Defense McNamara announced that the amount of aid to Saigon was ample and would level off, as he was confident of eventual victory because of great progress in the last eight to ten months. However, he expected the war might drag on for years. The chairman of the Joint Chiefs, General Lyman Lemnitzer, said he detected a greater feeling of self-confidence in the Civil Guard and Self-Defense units. There were now six thousand American servicemen in South Vietnam.[11]

General Paul Harkins told the U.S. troops, "We are here at the request of the government of South Vietnam and to support the people of South Vietnam in their fight against a vicious Communist enemy." He defined "support" as the training and matériel consistent with the endeavors in intelligence, communications, logistics, and application of modern tactics to counterguerrilla and counterinsurgency warfare.[12]

The administration policy drew applause in Congress. Senator Thomas Dodd, a conservative Democrat, said, "President Kennedy will . . . have the support of all of us in his decision to dispatch American troops to defensive positions on the Laotian frontier and for any further measures he may find it necessary to take to prevent the subjugation of Southeast Asia for international communism." The senator praised the administration for its "prompt and solitary decision to send American forces into Thailand." Whether the president had the authority to commit the military to this dangerous area did not seem to bother Dodd.[13]

The type of warfare evident in Southeast Asia impressed Kennedy enough for him to sponsor changes in strategy and tactics. A memorandum on Vietnam by Brigadier General Edwin Lansdale inspired the president to think in terms of counterguerrilla activities. Those in charge of the ground forces tended to plan in terms of battles in the mode of World War II and Korea, but the insurgents in Southeast Asia avoided conventional confrontations and achieved their successes by infiltration, hit-and-run tactics, and living off the land rather than relying on heavy equipment and the traditional means of supply, command, and control.

A program to expand the U.S. Special Forces, then only eighteen hundred men, began at Fort Bragg, North Carolina. Taylor, as JFK's special adviser on military affairs, played a key role in the army's development of the necessary skills and ordnance. The air force improved its techniques to supply or deploy men, while the navy intensified its training of SEALs, amphibious tactics, and small boat operations, and the marines stepped up their own instruction in counterinsurgency. By the beginning of 1963, ten thousand Americans from the armed forces were stationed in South Vietnam, and by the summer more than seventy had been killed. Without any involvement of Congress, the Kennedy White House had entered into a shooting war.

The growing investment of human U.S. military assets in Southeast Asia escaped notice partly because the administration kept it quiet, but mostly because of events in October 1962 known as the Cuban Missile Crisis. Triumphant after the Bay of Pigs, Fidel Castro came out of the closet on December 2, 1961, to declare, "I am a Marxist-Leninist and I shall be a Marxist-Leninist until the last day of my life." He welcomed shipments of arms and other aid from the Soviet Union, which was anxious to preserve a communist toehold less than a hundred miles from the United States. When Washington protested the influx of weaponry to Cuba, Moscow assured the White House that these were for defensive purposes only. Having sponsored the refugee attack, and continuing to assist anyone taking potshots at Cuba, the United States was in a weak position to argue. Cuba possessed the second largest army in the Western Hemisphere. On the plus side, from the White House standpoint, the Organization of American States, pushed by the United States, excluded Cuba from membership. More than a dozen Latin American countries severed diplomatic relations with the Castro government. Operation Mongoose percolated along, dabbling in schemes to assassinate the bearded Cuban leader and looking to foment an uprising in Cuba that would justify a massive U.S. intervention.

The genesis of what would become the Cuban Missile Crisis lay in an April 1962 chat between Soviet premier Nikita Khrushchev and his defense minister, Rodion Malinovsky, while the former vacationed in the Crimea. Malinosky pointed toward the Black Sea and spoke of U.S. missiles, armed with nuclear warheads, aimed at southern Soviet targets from Turkey across the water. "Why do the Americans have such a possibility?" Malinovsky asked. "They have surrounded us with bases on all sides and we have no possibility or right to do the same!"[14]

Khrushchev sought to redress the imbalance. Early in the summer of 1962, the Soviet and Cuban governments entered into an agreement that would dramatically boost the stakes. In autumn, they planned to install nuclear-armed missiles in Cuba, making the United States vulnerable to massive attacks from its tiny neighbor. Any attempt to dislodge Castro would expose American cities to devastation. The Soviets would feel freer to pursue their ends, knowing that just as U.S. missiles placed in Europe and Turkey could raise mushroom clouds over their population, the ability to strike from Cuba might weaken resistance to communist expansion. For Khrushchev the plan promised to double the number of nuclear missiles capable of destroying U.S. cities at a minimum investment of rubles in bombers or long-range missiles.

While the downing of a U-2 spy plane over the Soviet Union in 1959 had embarrassed the Eisenhower administration and curtailed the planes' usage there, no inhibitions existed for Cuba, which lacked the means to knock off the high-flying surveillance planes. On August 29, a U-2 brought back film that captured the building of surface-to-air (SAM) launching pads. The State Department warned Khrushchev that the administration would not tolerate the introduction of any offensive weapons. On September 11, the Kremlin assured, "The armaments and military equipment sent to Cuba are designed exclusively for defensive purposes." The message boasted, "There is no need for the Soviet Union to shift its weapons for the repulsion of aggression, for a retaliatory blow, to any other country, for instance Cuba. Our nuclear weapons are so powerful in their explosive force and the Soviet Union has . . . rockets to carry these nuclear warheads that there is no need to search for sites for them beyond the boundaries of the Soviet Union."

The statement accused the United States of "preparing for aggression against Cuba and other peace-loving states." Kennedy, recalled Schlesinger, told a September 13 press conference that he did not regard the latest arms from the Soviet Union as a serious threat, but if Cuba at any time seemed likely to become a military base for offensive actions by the Soviet Union, he would not hesitate to do whatever was necessary to preserve the security of the country.[15]

Schlesinger's account distorts what the president actually said. The text of his statements includes his belief that the "offensive missile sites" being readied could only be "to provide a nuclear strike capability against the Western Hemisphere." He remarked that as commander in chief, "I have full authority now to take such action" [military force against Cuba]. Questioned on whether he thought it necessary for the legislators to give him this authority, he answered no. He said he welcomed the viewpoints of the members of Congress, and "I'd be very glad to have those resolutions [supportive of the position taken on Cuba] passed if that should be the desire of the Congress." He warned that any nuclear missile launched from Cuba against any nation in the Western Hemisphere would be regarded "as an attack by the Soviet Union on the United States, requiring a full retaliatory response upon the Soviet Union."[16]

Actually, Congress was already raising a mighty hue and cry about the situation in Cuba. On September 5, Republican senator Kenneth Keating of New York told his colleagues that he had written to the State Department on August 14 for information about the buildup in Cuba. Sixteen days later, State replied that it had "no information that any Soviet troops have landed in Cuba . . . no evidence of supplies or technicians have arrived in such numbers as to provide for external aggression from Cuba." In his speech Keating made no mention of missiles but insisted that the importation of the armament violated the Monroe Doctrine.[17]

Washington representative Craig Hosmer claimed, accurately as it turned out, that three to five thousand Soviet personnel had arrived in Cuba toward the end of July along with eleven cargo ships packed with military equipment. He called for a ban on importation of all communist war materials. To carry out the program, Hosmer proposed a congressional resolution that in effect would give the president the right to use armed force to bar or blockade communist-bloc ships and to search them for contraband under the Monroe Doctrine. He cited Theodore Roosevelt's actions in Latin America, Franklin D. Roosevelt before World War II, Harry S. Truman in Korea, and Dwight D. Eisenhower with Berlin. Only TR's use of the military fell under the Monroe Doctrine, but Hosmer argued that all of the presidents were engaged in protecting U.S. interests.[18]

Congress duly passed a resolution that said the United States was "determined to prevent by whatever means may be necessary, including the use of arms, the Marxist-Leninist regime in Cuba from extending, by force or the threat of force, its aggressive or subversive activities in any part of this hemisphere." Additionally, the resolution declared the U.S. policy to prevent establishment in Cuba of any external military force that endangered American security.

The theory behind the license granted Kennedy was astonishingly cavalier. Senator George Smathers, a Florida Democrat and friend of JFK, said, "We all recognize that the final decision is left to the President of the United States by the Constitution."[19] Smathers did not cite the date on which the Constitution had been amended to hand such a power to the commander in chief. The anticommunist, anti-Castro fever was so virulent that even Republicans agreed. Senator Bourke Hickenlooper of Iowa, a conservative Republican, remarked, "Basically the Executive has the responsibility for and is in charge of foreign policy operations." He explained that the resolution "eliminated the question of whether or not the President shall declare war."[20]

The frequency of U-2 overflights doubled and the CIA intensified its efforts to determine the meaning of the buildup in Cuba. According to Schlesinger, almost no one in the administration believed that Khrushchev intended to install more than defensive capability within Cuba. John McCone, the CIA director, however, thought the Kremlin might well desire to create an offensive potential.

The "humint" (human intelligence) gathered by the CIA included references to nuclear bombs, but having been badly misled by their agents of the actual antipathy to Castro at the time of the Bay of Pigs, the analysts worried this might be more dubious information. While the administration awaited more definite data from the U-2s, Keating continued to orate about the creation of offensive bases in Cuba. On October 10 he said, "Construction has begun on at least a half-dozen launching sites for intermediate-range tactical missiles."[21]

Before the White House could respond, on October 14, after three days of bad weather, the skies over Cuba cleared and a U-2 took off for a more definitive look at an area in western Cuba. The aircraft returned and photo-interpretation specialists pored over frame-by-frame blowups. By Monday afternoon, October 15, they had identified a launching pad, buildings designed to house missiles, and even one medium-range missile lying on the ground at San Cristobal. That evening, the CIA notified McGeorge Bundy, coordinator for security affairs within the White House, of the findings. Bundy decided to collect all of the evidence and prepare an agenda for a meeting of the National Security Council's Executive Committee (ExCom). The preliminary data indicated weapons that could be used for offensive operations against the continental United States, notwithstanding assurances from Khrushchev and the ambassador to the United States, Anatoly Dobrynin, that the USSR had no intention of using Cuba as an offensive base.

Fear of international communism, particularly when the dreaded Reds ruled only ninety miles from Miami, strengthened John F. Kennedy's hand. If anything, the political voices in Washington favored a more aggressive stand than the administration had put forward.

6

THE MISSILE CRISIS

The White House responded to the challenge of Soviet missiles and aircraft in Cuba with a process for dealing with an imminent threat and the issues of preemptive and preventive war. Starting with the precedent of Truman's handling of the situation in Korea, Kennedy embroidered the pattern. There was a full debate within the administration, one dominated by civilians who held differing views. The views of military leaders were heard, but their input was really limited to questions of how a war should be conducted rather than foreign policy. Individual congressmen received briefings and could voice their opinions, but the decision-making stayed within the executive offices.

On the morning of October 16, 1962, ExCom assembled to deal with the reality of nuclear-armed missiles ninety miles from the continental United States. The cast included the president, Vice President Lyndon B. Johnson, Secretary of Defense Robert McNamara, Secretary of State Dean Rusk, Attorney General Robert Kennedy, acting director of the CIA General Marshall Carter (in place of the honeymooning John McCone), Treasury Secretary Douglas Dillon, UN ambassador Adlai Stevenson, Special Counsel McGeorge Bundy, Ted Sorenson, Deputy Secretary of Defense Roswell Gilpatrick, Undersecretary for Economic Affairs George Ball, Ambassador to the Soviet Union Llewellyn Thompson, Deputy Undersecretary of State for Political Affairs U. Alexis Johnson, Assistant Secretary of State for Inter-American Affairs Edwin Martin, and Chairman of the Joint Chiefs General Maxwell Taylor, two weeks on the job. Arthur Lundahl from the National Photographic Interpretation Center and CIA specialist Sidney Graybeal were on hand to interpret the images captured by the latest U-2 flights.

Presidents as far back as Franklin D. Roosevelt had experimented with means to record White House discussions, and JFK had arranged for a system to tape conversations. The transcripts cover the period of Tuesday,

October 16, through Monday, October 29. (Some historians have attempted to reproduce the pronunciation of words. I have rendered most of them according to the dictionary. Unless otherwise noted, the quotes from ExCom sessions that follow are from the transcriptions in the book *The Kennedy Tapes*, by Ernest May and Philip Zelikow.)

ExCom debated how soon the missiles would be operational. Taylor offered the gloomy assessment, "Very quickly, isn't that true?" Sidney Graybeal, while admitting that final preparation to fire would require "in the order of two to three hours," added that of the eight missiles detected, only one appeared near a launch position beside an erector.

While some believed action against the launch sites should not be delayed, McNamara insisted that any plans rest on the readiness to fire. "It seems extremely unlikely that they are now ready to fire, or may be ready to fire within a matter of hours, or even a day or two." His view prevailed; airstrikes did not need to be ordered, for the moment. According to Arthur Schlesinger, the final assessment concluded that a window of ten days remained before the missiles might be operational. On that basis he said the administration felt timely resolution of the issue would be stalled by Soviet representatives if brought to the UN.[1]

The president commented that even if the air attacks wiped out the known missiles, replacements could be brought to Cuba by submarine. He worried about whether it was politically and militarily feasible to mount sustained raids. Taylor pointed out that it might be necessary to go after the surface-to-air missile sites, the SAMs that protected the targets. The Pentagon estimated at a minimum that five hundred sorties would be required to achieve anything close to the desired results. Furthermore, unless the airstrikes eliminated every single missile before it was armed, the United States could be exposed to a devastating retaliation. McNamara noted that even if all missiles were destroyed, a fighter bearing a nuclear bomb could still penetrate U.S. airspace.

Secretary of State Dean Rusk reminded the group, "Mr. McCone suggested some weeks ago that one thing Mr. Khrushchev may have in mind is that he knows that we have a substantial nuclear superiority to the extent that he has to live under fear of ours. Also we have nuclear weapons nearby in Turkey and places like that." There were fifteen Jupiter missiles lodged inside the Turkish border. While these medium-range missiles were aimed at the Soviet Union, their value was declining since they were considered obsolete and other means to deliver nuclear payload into the heart of the Soviet Union already existed. The secretary of state also pointed toward Berlin as "very much involved."

The participants discussed bringing in other nations and organizations. Treasury Secretary Dillon cautioned, "Getting public opinion, and OAS action, and telling people in NATO . . . would appear to me to have the danger of getting us wide out in the open and forcing the Russians, Soviets, to take a position that if anything was done they would have to retaliate."

The president asked veep Lyndon Johnson for his sentiments. Johnson backed action to preserve national security but allowed that "the country's blood pressure is up, and they are fearful, and they're insecure, and we're getting divided." He cautioned that in all likelihood neither the OAS, NATO, nor even Congress might give strong support. The former Senate majority leader declared, "I'm not much for circularizing it over the Hill or our allies, even though it's a breach of faith, not to confer with them. We're not going to get much help from them."

After the president ticked off four steps, two dealing with airstrikes, one with a blockade, and then the degree of consultation with allies, Attorney General Robert Kennedy said, "We have the fifth one . . . which is the invasion." Despite Schlesinger's remarks about the president's brother as a "dove from the start,"[2] ExCom tapes reveal ambiguity. "I think we should also consider what Cuba's going to be a year from now, or two years from now. Assume that we go in and knock these sites out. I don't know what's going to stop them from saying: 'We're going to build the sites six months from now, bring them in [again].'"

When McNamara mentioned the blockade, Kennedy persisted. "Then we're going to have to sink Russian ships. Then we're going to have to sink Russian submarines."

JFK asked McNamara and Taylor about a timetable for a possible invasion. They thought ninety thousand men could be put in Cuba within five to eleven days, depending upon how much advance notice the armed forces received. The president inquired whether it might not take too long, a month or more, to mount a successful invasion. McNamara repeated an earlier claim that an invasion could follow within a week after the airstrikes. JFK uttered some doubts about whether sufficient troops could land within seven days. Taylor detailed plans for sea and airborne landings of as many as ninety thousand within five to eleven days. The president, burned by the military's estimates during the Bay of Pigs, remained dubious.

Robert Kennedy scoffed at the hesitancy of the military. "Is it absolutely essential that you wait seven days after you have an air strike?" General Taylor explained to the civilian that deployment of ships and amphibious forces too soon would tip the enemy off to the coming attacks. The attorney general countered that it might be harmful to wait even five days before an invasion. "The United States is going to be under such pressure by every-body not to do anything. And there's going to be also pressure . . . pressure on the Russians to do something against us. If you could get it in, get it started, so that there wasn't any turning back."

McNamara supported Taylor. "We haven't been able to figure out a way to shorten that five- to seven-day period while maintaining surprise in the air attack."

That first session of ExCom broke up shortly after the president's announcement that "I don't think we've got much time on these missiles. . . . We may just have to take them out. . . . We're certainly going to do number one [the limited airstrike]. We're going to take out these missiles." He told the appropriate parties to move forward with the planning for sec-ond airstrikes and prepare for a general invasion. An amphibious task force with forty thousand marines had begun a regularly scheduled exer-cise in the Caribbean and one hundred thousand army troops moved to Florida. Fighter-bombers replaced the long-range bombers on the airfields within easy reach of Cuba.

Any military operation seemed fraught with risks. A limited air attack on the missile bases inevitably would kill or maim Soviet technicians, per-haps triggering a strong military response. Massive raids and an invasion most likely would result in thousands of Cuban casualties, generating anger against the United States in the Western Hemisphere and around the world. Moscow might seize the American distraction with Cuba as an opportunity for a grab at Berlin. And looming over the entire situation lay the prospect of a World War III nuclear holocaust.

After the first ExCom discussion ended, a lunch for the crown prince of Libya afforded the president an opportunity to invite Adlai Stevenson, his UN ambassador, to the family quarters. JFK displayed the U-2 photo-graphs. When Kennedy remarked, "I suppose the alternatives are to go in by air and wipe them out, or to take other steps to render the weapons inoperable," Stevenson counseled, "Let's not go into an air strike until we have explored the possibilities of a peaceful solution."[3]

At the second ExCom session that evening, a review of the latest intelligence indicated that when completed, the missile sites would serve from sixteen to twenty-four birds with a range of about a thousand miles. However, no storage facilities for nuclear warheads had been found. Act-ing CIA director Marshall Carter dismissed the plaintive hope that the weapons in question were not a threat. "There's no question in our minds, sir," he said to the president. "And they are genuine. They are not a cam-ouflage or a covert attempt to fool us."

Robert Kennedy asked, if the United States chose the invasion option, "How long would it take to take over the island?" General Taylor answered that it was difficult to estimate but he thought perhaps five or six days before major resistance ended, though mopping up might drag on for months. He advised eradication of not only the missile sites and possible nuclear warhead storage sites but also the fighters and bombers. He admitted that a first strike might not complete the job. "We'll never get it all, Mr. President. But we then have to come back, day after day, for several days."

Elmo R. "Bud" Zumwalt Jr., on a career path to become chief of naval operations, in 1962 a captain, served as the navy's voice, providing talking points to Assistant Secretary of Defense Paul Nitze, who sat in on the meetings of the National Security Council. "As Paul described these meetings . . . it was clear to me that McNamara and the Joint Chiefs of Staff were like swinging back and forth on their positions. Initially, McNamara wanted to go in and bomb the missiles out, and the Chiefs were reluctant. Later on in the week, the Chiefs were getting far more war-like and McNamara was getting more reluctant."[4]

McNamara rejected a diplomatic approach—attempts to reach an agreement through talks with Khrushchev, Castro, NATO, and the OAS—as having no chance of satisfying U.S. needs. He suggested instead a strategy that fell between military and political efforts, a public announcement of surveillance of Cuban airspace and an indefinite naval blockade against offensive weapons shipped to Cuba. If Castro initiated any military action against the United States, the country would attack. "Attack who?" Bundy ungrammatically inquired. "The Soviet Union," replied McNamara dispassionately.

McNamara and Taylor related the ideas of the heads of the armed forces. They strongly recommended against a strike confined to air attacks on the missiles, storage facilities, and MIG planes, believing that would still leave too much capability undestroyed. They preferred a full-scale invasion. The plans called for a pre-landing five-day aerial bombardment, seven hundred to one thousand sorties per day. "To move beyond that, into an invasion, following the air attack," said McNamara, "means the assembly of . . . between 90 and 150,000 men. . . . " He added, "It seems to me almost certain that any one of these forms of direct military action will lead to a Soviet military response of some type, some place in the world. It may well be worth the price. Perhaps we should pay that. But I think we should recognize that possibility."

The president informed the group that he expected to see Andrei Gromyko, the Soviet foreign minister, two days hence. He wondered whether he should confront Gromyko. Most agreed that it would be useful to trap the minister in a lie asserting the USSR would not install missiles with an offensive capability in Cuba. The official Soviet news service, TASS, had already denied any such intention when the ordnance had already arrived or was on the way. Before either an ultimatum or even a preemptive attack, the administration sought to gain the upper hand in world opinion. No one in ExCom brought up the need or desirability to seek congressional approval or authority to go to war.

McNamara offered an analysis that covered "a domestic political problem." He noted that the president had said that if such weapons were introduced, "we'd act. Well how will we act? We want to act to prevent their use." He proposed an ultimatum tied to twenty-four-hour-a-day surveillance and a blockade that would stop every ship for search and removal of any offensive weapons. McGeorge Bundy remarked, "You have to make the guy stop to search him. And if he won't stop, you have to shoot, right?" Members of ExCom foresaw that overt military action could ignite tinder in a number of hot spots—Berlin, Turkey, Iran, and Korea. "All our forces should be put on alert," said McNamara.

When Kennedy again gathered with his ExCom on October 18, the principals began to coalesce around a diplomatic approach coupled with the blockade plan. CIA director McCone, who had visited Eisenhower at Gettysburg, related the former commander in chief's views. Ike felt the thrust by the Soviets was intolerable and believed limited action would not be satisfactory. "If I were to pin him down he would recommend . . . an all-out military action. He talked of [going] right to the jugular first not landing on the beach and working slowly across the island. But concentrate the attack right on Havana first and taking the heart of the government out."

They pondered what Khrushchev might do if confronted and whether the initiation of negotiations might prevent any U.S. action while the missiles moved closer to operational status. The president mused, "The only offer we would make, it seems to me . . . the point being to give him some out, would be giving him some of our Turkey missiles." Bundy agreed.

The president asked, "Now, to declare a blockade on Cuba, do we have to declare war on Cuba?" The tapes record a flurry of unattributable opinions. "Yes, yes, we do." "It is commonplace to make a declaration of war." "It makes it easier and better." "It makes it legal." JFK answered his own question. "I think we shouldn't assume we have to declare war." In rather fuzzy reasoning, he added, "If you're going to do that, you really . . . have to invade. . . . We do the message to Khrushchev and tell him that if work continues et cetera et cetera. At the same time, launch the blockade. If the work continues, then we go in and take them out." When someone insisted that without a declaration of war a blockade was illegal, JFK snapped, "There will be hardly anybody who gets excited because their ships are stopped under these conditions."

The president settled upon what he called "a prospective course of action. Tomorrow afternoon [October 19] I'll announce about the missiles and say we're calling Congress back. . . . It isn't Pearl Harbor . . . we've told everybody. Then we go ahead [October 20] and we take them [the missiles and bases] out, and announce they've been taken out. And if any more are put in, we're going to take those out." Maxwell Taylor advised that the air attacks could not be launched until October 21. The commander in chief, replying to a question about the summoning of Congress, said, "The advantage of calling Congress back . . . is that it gets the information that they are there before we attack. Whatever solidarity that may induce." Notably, he still expressed no need for their official imprimatur.

The moment came when the White House decided to issue an ultimatum. "I wrote the document," said Zumwalt, "dashed back in to Paul Nitze with it. He had said two days so [it read] 'We must have your answer within two days.' The rest of it was a mailed fist in a velvet glove. Paul made the one change, which was absolutely necessary. He changed, 'within two days' to 'within a couple of days' which to the Russians would come across as less definitively a deadline and that was the one that finally broke the back."[5]

The president invited Dean Acheson to the White House to gain his advice and support. Acheson, who had been flayed by critics as an appeaser and soft on communism while secretary of state for Truman, advanced a hard line. Ridiculing any analogy of an attack on the missile sites without prior warning as similar to Pearl Harbor, he favored immediate airstrikes. A letter from UN rep Stevenson urged "negotiations before we start anything."[6]

At their meeting, the president neatly trapped Soviet foreign minister Gromyko, who continued to insist that the only weapons supplied by his country to Cuba were defensive. Some time after Gromyko left the White House, JFK talked with Robert Lovett, Truman's secretary of defense. Lovett later reported, "He [the president] asked me if I had gotten the briefing and all the facts available, and I said that I had. He grinned and said, 'I ought to finish the story by telling you about Gromyko, who, in this very room not over 10 minutes ago, told more barefaced lies than I have ever heard in so short a time. All during his denial that the Russians had any missiles or weapons, or anything else, in Cuba, I had the low-level pictures in the center drawer of my desk, and it was an enormous temptation to show them to him.'" Lovett said he urged the "quarantine" route or blockade, and he recalled that when Robert Kennedy joined them and asked about the application of any blockade, "He felt as I did about the necessity for taking a less violent step at the outset, because as he said, we could always blow the place up."[7] Subsequently, a State Department lawyer suggested that the term "defensive quarantine" might be preferable to "blockade."

The commander in chief held only one formal meeting with his Joint Chiefs during the missile crisis, on the morning of October 19. Taylor had informed them of the decision to begin with a blockade. The Chiefs agreed to recommend a massive airstrike against the Cuban military targets without advance warning. They could not agree on whether an invasion should follow.

Historians Ernest R. May and Philip Zelikow describe JFK's view of his Joint Chiefs as "respectful but skeptical. . . . His most recent experience with the military in a crisis had angered him." The admission of a black student, James Meredith, to the University of Mississippi had generated campus violence. Kennedy had called on troops to provide security, but he had felt the military had been unresponsive. He groused to an aide, "They always give you that bullshit about their instant reaction and their split-second timing, but it never works out. No wonder it's so hard to win a war." He had already been unhappy with their performance during the Bay of Pigs invasion. Their input seems to have convinced him that the armed forces leaders boxed themselves in the narrow confines of military strategy, oblivious to matters that went beyond waging war.[8]

Relations between the civilians and the military in the Kennedy administration had deteriorated from the start. As secretary of defense, McNamara brought his tight-lipped managerial style into a culture that believed only those in uniform were qualified to judge weaponry and strategy. McNamara brushed aside Pentagon experts as he trimmed waste and bureaucracy and tried to reform the military, tromping on highly burnished shoes in the process.

In the session with the president, air force general Curtis LeMay scoffed at starting with a blockade. "The first thing that's going to happen is our missiles are going to disappear into the woods. . . . we can't find them . . . we're going to take some damage if we try to do anything later on." He refused to accept the theory that "if we knock off Cuba, they're going to knock off Berlin." LeMay continued, "This blockade and political action,

I see leading into war. . . . It will lead right into war. This is almost as bad as the appeasement at Munich."

Admiral George Anderson, chief of naval operations, then spoke. "I agree with General LeMay that this will escalate and then we will be required to take other military action at greater disadvantage to the United States. . . . I do not see that, as long as the Soviet Union is supporting Cuba, that there is any solution to the Cuban problem except a military solution."

General Earle Wheeler, the army chief of staff, said, "Mr. President, in my judgment, from a military point of view, the lowest-risk course of action it would take in protecting the people of the United States against a possible strike on us is to go ahead with a surprise air strike, the blockade, and an invasion."

Maxwell Taylor leaned toward the stance taken by the top officers without fully expressing himself. He did warn, "We can never talk about invading again, after they get these missiles, because they got the gun pointed at our head." All the armed forces heads agreed that Berlin and other potential flashpoints mattered little because if the Soviets wanted to move on them, they would do so without needing the excuse of a confrontation over Cuba.

The president mildly demurred from the overall tone. "I appreciate your views. These are unsatisfactory alternatives. The obvious argument for the blockade was [that] what we want to do is to avoid, if we can, nuclear war by escalation or imbalance." Kennedy inquired about the timetable for the first air attack and LeMay said the earliest would be October 21 but an optimal strategy would launch two days later. He asserted the airstrike as "guaranteed hitting." LeMay, who on several occasions showed little hesitation about resorting to the nuclear weapon, thought in terms of an inevitable military confrontation with the Soviet Union. He considered Cuba a "sideshow" and when asked how he would handle it, responded, "Fry it."[9]

The commander in chief was aghast at the presentations by the top command, which seemed to accept the high probability of nuclear war. "Those brass hats have one great advantage in their favor," he told his aide Dave Powers. "If we listen to them and do what they want us to do, none of us will be alive later to tell them that they were wrong."[10]

With the country and Congress still unaware of the crisis, the president flew off on a previously scheduled campaign trip to help elect Democratic candidates. Before his departure, he directed his brother and Ted Sorenson to persuade wavering members of ExCom of the desirability of the blockade option. He added that if no agreement should be reached,

"I'll make my own decision anyway."[11] It was reminiscent of an Abraham Lincoln cabinet meeting in which after a unanimous nay vote on a measure the president then said, "Aye, the ayes have it."

During an ExCom meeting on October 19 at the State Department, Bundy shed his dovish approach. He announced that following private conversations with JFK he now believed in a surprise air attack. Acheson, McCone, Dillon, and Maxwell Taylor all seconded him. McNamara, however, stubbornly clung to a phased approach that started with a blockade but sanctioned planning for airstrikes if the other side did not yield. He admitted that the United States might be forced to give up missile bases in Italy and Turkey. Robert Kennedy, "speaking with quiet intensity,"[12] reported that he too had spoken with the president and understood from him that a surprise attack à la Pearl Harbor was "not in our traditions." The attorney general spoke of the thousands of Cubans and hundreds of "Russians" who would be killed without warning. A sneak attack would besmirch American ideals and traditions. A blockade would demonstrate the seriousness of the U.S. position. It would also afford the Soviets an opportunity to retreat gracefully.

At the second session that evening the tide shifted. According to Schlesinger, the younger Kennedy's remarks had swayed his audience, particularly since a blockade did not prevent an airstrike if it were felt necessary. On Saturday afternoon, when the commander in chief returned to Washington, McNamara summed up the pluses and minuses of a blockade. The disadvantages, he said, were the long time required to eliminate strategic missiles from Cuba, the political trouble in the United States (from refugees and the more virulent anti-Castro people who wanted the dictator removed), and the potential weakening of the U.S. world position.

On the plus side of the ledger, a blockade would cause less trouble with allies and avoid the nation's committing a Pearl Harbor–style surprise. The quarantine "is the only military course of action compatible with our position as a leader of the free world." Finally, and certainly most important, it would sidestep the kind of military action that might trigger a violent response from the Soviets, escalating into a huge war.

Taylor said that he did not share McNamara's fear that if nuclear weapons were used against Cuba, nuclear weapons would hit the United States. He added that unless the missile sites were hit immediately, they would then be concealed or camouflaged sufficiently to make it impossible to destroy them later.

Robert Kennedy made the case for a combination of the blockade and airstrikes. He noted that there could be a short wait after the setting of the blockade to give the Soviets time to react, halting further development of missile capability. If they did not stop, then it would be legitimate to launch the airstrikes. His stance undoubtedly reflected that of his brother.

There were variations on the theme. McCone and Dillon proposed ultimatums: that unless the "Russians" did not dismantle the offending ordnance within seventy-two hours, the bombs would fall. Both men feared that protracted negotiations would mean an exorbitant price for peace and degrade the nation's prestige in Latin America. Adlai Stevenson and Robert McNamara, while partial to the blockade route, thought diplomatic negotiations at the highest level should begin immediately afterwards.

Schlesinger wrote that a straw vote found eleven favored a quarantine while seven opted for the airstrike.[13] The president rejected initiation of bargaining with the Soviets until the Kremlin complied with the American demands. He announced that he was prepared to proceed with the blockade and order the steps necessary to strike the missiles and the launching sites from the air within two or three days. When the meeting ended, the commander in chief spoke to Taylor, who recalled his words: "I know that you and your colleagues are unhappy with the decision, but I trust that you will support me in this decision." Taylor assured him they would.[14]

Perhaps even more so than in the time of the Bay of Pigs, word of a major event involving Cuba circulated. The mobilization and movement of ground forces, naval vessels, and aircraft could not escape notice. The frequency of high-level meetings in Washington, with the president canceling campaign stops, papered over with a phony explanation of a head cold, caught the attention of reporters. James Reston, the *New York Times* Washington bureau chief, and syndicated columnist Walter Lippmann both sensed an imminent denouement. The administration managed to convince the media to stop the presses and mute the broadcasters.

On October 22, the president prepared to go before television cameras that evening and inform the public about the crisis. A final tally from surveillance photographs indicated approximately forty launchers for missiles capable of hitting the United States. In the morning, General Walter C. Sweeney, the tactical air command chief responsible for formulating the air attacks on Cuba, presented the commander in chief with the plans to take out the missiles. The general recommended that the MIGs and IL-28 bombers also be targeted simultaneously. Kennedy agreed that that would probably be desirable.

Sweeney and Maxwell Taylor argued for a surprise attack, but both McCone and Robert Kennedy thought that unwise, not only for its effect on world opinion but also because it could start a general nuclear war. Everyone accepted that once the bombs began to fall, an invasion must follow. Vice President Johnson reluctantly endorsed the choice but complained, "We are telegraphing our punch" and "locking the barn after the horse was gone."[15]

During the final forty-eight hours before a public case was made, a blizzard of communications informed ninety-five American embassies around the world, and individual messages from the president went to the heads of friendly nations. At the same time, the State Department dispatched a text of Kennedy's speech and a letter from him to Khrushchev both to the embassy in Moscow and by hand to the Soviet ambassador in Washington.

White House aide Lawrence O'Brien had been tasked with rounding up congressional leaders for bipartisan approval of the policies. The legislators had not been in session. Brought in through military transport, twenty of them filed into the cabinet room at the White House. The Republican senators included Everett M. Dirksen of Illinois, minority leader; Bourke Hickenlooper of Iowa, chairman of the party's policy committee; and Leveret Saltonstall, the top minority man on the Armed Services Committee. Their Democratic colleagues were J. William Fulbright, who chaired the Foreign Relations Committee; Hubert Humphrey of Minnesota, the majority whip; Mike Mansfield of Montana, majority leader; Richard Russell, the Georgian who headed the Armed Services Committee; and Floridian George Smathers, a Kennedy pal who was on record as giving the president carte blanche to use the armed forces.

From the House, Minority Leader Charles Halleck of Indiana and John Tabor of New York of the Appropriations Committee took seats. Democrat Hale Boggs, the Louisiana whip, who had been fishing in the Gulf of Mexico and learned of the summons from a note dropped by an air force plane in a plastic bottle, had boarded a chopper to New Orleans and a jet to Washington. Carl Vinson of Georgia, chairman of the Armed Services Committee, and John McCormack, the Massachusetts Speaker of the House, were present. McCone, with support from Lundahl, detailed the intelligence. After a few questions from the congressmen, the president explained his reasoning for a blockade rather than immediately initiating an airstrike.

Richard Russell urged immediate application of armed force. "The Secretary of State says, 'give them time to pause and think.' They'll use that time to pause and think, to get better prepared. . . . Why, we have a complete justification for carrying out the announced foreign policy of the

United States. . . . I don't know whether Khrushchev will launch a nuclear war over Cuba or not. I don't believe he will." Russell stuck to his position even after rebuttals by both Rusk and McNamara.

The president said approval from the Organization of American States would be sought. "If they don't give us the 14 votes, the two-thirds vote, then we're going to do it anyway. But in that case we are going to have what's legally an illegal blockade or a declaration of war." Later, when asked about "illegal," the president answered, "We can always make it legal . . . by declaration of war."

Fulbright, who had forcefully argued against the Bay of Pigs invasion, took a hard line. "I think a blockade is the worst of the alternatives, because if you're confronted with a Russian ship, you are actually confronting Russia . . . if you have the invasion . . . this is not actually an affront to Russia. . . . I'm in favor . . . of this invasion, and an all-out one as quickly as possible."

When the commander in chief pointed out that at least seven days would elapse before an invasion could be mounted, the Arkansas senator answered, "I would do nothing until you're ready. A blockade leads into quibbling and delays . . . it will give them [the Soviets] a better excuse for retaliation." He stubbornly maintained, "They're Cuban sites. They're not Russia's sites . . . firing against Cuba is not the same as firing against Russia."

The president noted that with an invasion, "We do have the 7 or 8,000 Russians there. We are going to have to shoot them up . . . it would be foolish to expect that the Russians would not regard that as a far more direct thrust than they're going to regard on the ships."[16]

It was now late in the afternoon and the president excused himself to make his speech to the nation. He opened by saying, "This government, as promised, has maintained the closest surveillance of the Soviet military buildup on the island of Cuba. Within the last week, unmistakable evidence has established the fact that a series of offensive missile sites is now in preparation on that imprisoned island. The purpose of these bases can be none other than to provide a nuclear strike capability against the Western Hemisphere." He labeled the development as "an explicit threat to the peace and security of all the Americas." The president noted that previously the USSR and the United States had deployed strategic weapons in a manner that would not create an imbalance. He reported that American strategic missiles had never been placed within foreign soil "under a cloak of secrecy and deception," and continued with the charge that the situation in Cuba violated previous assurances from the Kremlin and was deliberately provocative.

The commander in chief cited the lesson of the 1930s, that aggressive conduct (by Nazi Germany), "if allowed to go unchecked and unchallenged, ultimately leads to war." He then laid out the steps taken by the United States, starting with the "initial" one of strict quarantine on all offensive military equipment shipped to Cuba. Second came continued and intensive scrutiny of the Cuban arms buildup. "Should these offensive military preparations continue, thus increasing the threat to the hemisphere, further action will be justified. I have directed the armed forces to prepare for any eventualities."

Third, he announced a policy to regard any nuclear missile launched from Cuba as an attack by the Soviet Union on the United States, "requiring a full retaliatory response upon the Soviet Union." He announced that he had asked for support from both the OAS and the UN, with resolutions calling for prompt dismantling of the offending weapons under UN supervision.

While Kennedy did not speak in terms of any specific areas of negotiation, he did say, "We are prepared to discuss new proposals for the removal of tensions on both sides." He added several paragraphs aimed at "the captive people of Cuba," suggesting that their leaders were "puppets and agents of an international conspiracy," and he looked forward to a free Cuba.

Just as JFK addressed his countrymen, Rusk handed Dobrynin an advance copy of the speech and a covering letter from the president. U.S. ambassador Foy Kohler in Moscow received a copy of the letter with instructions to deliver it to the Kremlin. In his letter, Kennedy recalled his meeting with Khrushchev in Vienna and said, "I made it clear that in view of the objectives of the ideology to which you adhere, the United States could not tolerate any action on your part which in a major way disturbed the existing overall balance of power in the world. I stated that an attempt to force abandonment of our responsibilities and commitments in Berlin would constitute such an action and that the United States would resist with all the power at its command. . . . I publicly stated that if certain developments in Cuba took place, the United States would do whatever must be done to protect its own security and that of its allies."

After pointing out that a congressional resolution supported this policy, the president continued, "Despite this, the rapid development of long-range missile bases and other offensive weapons systems in Cuba has proceeded. I must tell you that the United States is determined that this threat to the security of this hemisphere be removed. At the same time, I wish to point out that the action we are taking [the quarantine of shipping] is the minimum necessary to remove the threat to the security of the nations of this hemisphere. The fact of the minimum response should not be taken as a basis, however, for any misjudgment on your part." He had made clear that without a satisfactory response, more severe measures would follow.

Setting up the quarantine stuck Elmo Zumwalt in the middle of turbulent waters. He was summoned to McNamara's office and arrived without paper and pencil. The secretary of defense barked at him, "'Here's what I want you to do. Send an order to CinCLantFlt [Commander in Chief Atlantic Fleet]' and he went through point one, two, three, four. He got up to about point five, and he saw that I didn't have a paper and pencil. I will cheerfully admit that I should . . . have asked for [them] but I was busy memorizing these points. He picked up a tablet of paper and pencil, and instead of saying, 'Here!' he threw them at me. This infuriated me so much that I left them there—a really dumb thing to do—and he went on and finished his summary.

"I dashed back to my office and wrote down first words and then sentences and took about 30 minutes writing the message out. Then I went back into Paul Nitze and he spent about 15 minutes studying it. He said, 'Bud, it's all there; take it up to McNamara.'"

Transmitting McNamara's orders brought new woe to Zumwalt:

I had carried the directive down to [Admiral] Ike Kidd in CNO's office who sent it immediately down to Admiral Ulysses S. Grant Sharp, who was then [deputy chief of naval operations]. . . . Sharp sent for me and said, "Look, Bud, this isn't the way to do this. I want you to go back and tell McNamara that we're closer to a Russian ship, and that we want to go ahead and intercept a Russian ship first."

I said to him, "Admiral, I can tell you that this has been very carefully thought out and it's come from the highest levels," and I gave him the theory of what they were about.

Admiral Sharp said, "What's your rank?"

I said, "Captain, sir."

He said, "Do you understand a direct order when you get it?"

"Yes, sir."

"I order you to go back and tell McNamara what I want to do—what Admiral Anderson wants to do."

I . . . said to Paul Nitze, "This is the order I have been just given. Will you go with me to McNamara?" He said, "I most certainly will not. You get back to Admiral Sharp and tell him that I have personally directed that he is to carry out McNamara's orders." It was the only time I've ever seen him get absolutely huffy. But this was a classic example of military versus civilian authority as Paul Nitze saw it, and he was a classic constitutionalist.

I went back to Admiral Sharp and I gave him my view that the CNO [Anderson] was going to be in deep trouble if he reclaimed it [sought reconsideration of a decision]. Sharp went up to see Admiral Anderson and that I believe was kind of the first of the series of events that led McNamara to conclude he was going to get rid of Anderson.[17]

The administration, having crafted a direction to take, had informed Congress and convinced its leaders that the situation did not permit time for further deliberations. The earlier resolution passed by Capitol Hill, barring establishment in Cuba of any external military force that endangered American security, provided a congressional imprimatur upon the policy. JFK also recognized the wisdom of international approval. While Adlai Stevenson could not hope to win the sanction of the Security Council at the UN because the Soviets held a veto, traditional allies like France and Great Britain along with South American countries could be persuaded, particularly through sharing intelligence.

7

RESOLUTION AND
REVERBERATIONS

During the reign of John F. Kennedy, the Central Intelligence Agency, badly wounded by the Bay of Pigs fiasco, recovered and gained in power and prestige. It provided the undeniable proof of the Soviet mischief in Cuba. When its data were coupled with that compiled by the intelligence services of the military, the president was in a position to confront Nikita Khrushchev and to present the case to the world. If need be, the United States would have proceeded on its own, but there was an obvious benefit in winning favorable opinion around the world. Resolution of the missile crisis by a show of military force, however, may have emboldened some American movers and shakers to believe that the same hardball strategy would work even ten thousand miles away, in Southeast Asia.

The White House had planned to cue Western leaders—British prime minister Harold Macmillan, German chancellor Konrad Adenauer, and French president Charles de Gaulle—on the Cuban missile situation at the penultimate moment. The Europeans regarded the intense hostility of Americans toward the Castro government as verging on the paranoid. They tolerated life within range of or even cheek by jowl with communist missiles and legions.

Kennedy and Macmillan spoke on the telephone shortly after the president informed the world of the crisis and the initial steps being taken. The British prime minister was sympathetic but did not take a position on the use of force before attempting UN negotiations. David Ormsby-Gore, the British ambassador to Washington and a Kennedy friend, was far more supportive. Neither de Gaulle nor Adenauer opposed the American policy.

In Moscow, Khrushchev seemed inclined to force the American hand. The president's speech and the letter enraged him. He called the blockade "banditry, the folly of degenerate imperialism,"[1] and ordered Soviet ships approaching the demarcation line of the quarantine to ignore it and maintain their course for Cuba. The first vessels were scheduled to reach the forbidden zone at 10 a.m. two days later, where they would be confronted by U.S. warships with instructions to open fire if the Soviet-flagged transports did not stop. Deputy premier Anastas Mikoyan modified Khrushchev's directive. The captains were told to halt just short of the blockade line, but one freighter, bearing nuclear warheads, had actually had entered a Cuban port five hours before the deadline for the quarantine.

The Monday night address to Americans by their president and the media coverage generated near panic among some, an overflow of patriotism among others. Citizens stocked up on food, gasoline, and other items that might be in short supply should a war erupt. News organizations mobilized reporters for duty as war correspondents. Flags fluttered from municipal buildings and homes while TV, radio, and newspapers interviewed the "man in the street," gathering quotes that expressed bravado about Castro and Cuba as well as anxiety. Overseas, the reactions were mixed.

The Soviet premier insisted the missiles were there purely to defend Cuba against an invasion. Meanwhile, Dean Rusk on October 23 briefed members of the Organization of American States, seeking their backing. The OAS, said Lyndon Johnson scornfully, "couldn't pour piss out of a boot if the instructions were written on the heel,"[2] but its seal of approval would confer legitimacy upon the missile-crisis policy. The delegates, upon instructions from home, almost unanimously awarded a thumbs-up to the plea.

At the United Nations, Adlai Stevenson struck hard at the Soviet Union, earning praise from the president for his advocacy. The Soviet representative sneered at the American position and insisted that the charge of offensive weapons was a lie to cover up U.S. plans for aggression upon Cuba. Fidel Castro, convinced of an imminent strike against his domain, asked the Soviets to launch a preemptive strike at America. Khrushchev may have been irate, but he was not crazy. He cabled Havana that Castro "had failed to understand us correctly. We had installed the missiles not for the purpose of attacking the United States, but to keep the United States from attacking Cuba."[3]

As zero hour for a confrontation at sea approached, the first delicate steps toward negotiation emerged. In 1961, a back-channel connection developed between Georgi Bolshakov, a Soviet military intelligence officer assigned to the Washington embassy, and Robert Kennedy. Through journalists Bolshakov learned that the Americans might trade the missile bases in Italy and Turkey for those in Cuba. RFK surreptitiously slipped into the Soviet offices to talk with Dobrynin. They bickered over the nature of the missiles before the American dangled a tempting morsel, the dismantling of the overseas bases.

When a portion of ExCom gathered on the morning of October 24, John McCone reported twenty-two ships bound for Cuba with hatches large enough to handle missiles. Urgent messages from the Kremlin to the ships notified the captains that henceforth all orders would come from Moscow. Midway through the discussion, McCone received a message saying six vessels, including the two closest to the blockade, had either stopped or reversed course. Worried that an overzealous navy might pursue any ships that came near, the president ordered that a confrontation at sea be avoided if possible. "We want to give that ship a chance to turn around. You don't want to have word going out from Moscow, 'Turn around,' and suddenly we sink their ship."[4]

The president, meeting congressmen, dismissed a summit as "useless." No one complained about the steps taken or projected. Later, the president told Lovett that Fulbright, who had originally backed a surprise airstrike and invasion, now felt the blockade route was "the proper course of action."[5]

United Nations secretary-general U Thant suggested to the president a temporary halt in actions by the parties. "This involves on the one hand the voluntary suspension of all armed shipments to Cuba and also the voluntary suspension of the quarantine measures involving the searching of ships bound for Cuba." It was unacceptable to the White House. JFK told Harold Macmillan, "We'll point out the deficiencies in it—that there's no guarantees against a breach of the quarantine, and also the work on the missile sites will continue and the danger will be greater within two weeks."[6]

That night another testy communication from Khrushchev reached the White House. "You, Mr. President, have challenged us. Who asked you to do this? By what right have you done this? Our relations with the Republic of Cuba . . . concern only the two countries. . . . You, Mr. President, are not declaring quarantines but advancing an ultimatum and threatening that unless we subordinate ourselves to your demands, you will use force." He concluded, "We shall not be simply observers of piratical actions of American ships on the high seas. We will then be forced for our part to take measures which we deem necessary and adequate to protect our rights."[7]

It sounded like a direct challenge to the quarantine, and the administration readied its guns. McNamara, already unhappy with his chief of naval operations, Admiral George Anderson, for his failure to promptly relay information about the turnabout of some Soviet ships, went to the navy flag plot room to obtain the latest information. He interrogated Anderson on the means to hail the oncoming vessels. "In what language—English or Russian?"

"How the hell do I know?" answered Anderson.

"What will you do if they don't understand?"

"I suppose we'll use flags," responded the admiral.

"Well, what if they don't stop?"

"We'll send a shot across the bow," was the reply.

"Then what, if that doesn't work?"

"Then we'll fire into the rudder." McNamara described the admiral as now "clearly very annoyed."

The secretary of defense firmly asserted, "You're not going to fire a single shot at anything without my express permission, is that clear?" Anderson retorted that the navy had been running blockades successfully since John Paul Jones. Even angrier now, McNamara said, "This was not a blockade but a means of communication between Kennedy and Khrushchev," reiterating that no guns should fire without his permission. Asked if he understood, Anderson glumly said yes. If there were any confrontation, McNamara wanted a minute-by-minute account of the interception, and after he consulted with the president the navy would receive its instructions.[8]

Taylor agreed with McNamara. "President Kennedy, very rightly . . . wanted to know where every ship was every morning and to find out just what instructions went to every ship's captain. This appeared to my naval colleagues as being unpardonable intervention in the execution of purely military movements. The argument I made . . . was that this was not really a military situation, but a political situation; it just happened that the power being used by the government were military toys. . . . This was political chess and those ships . . . very properly directed by the master player, the president."[9]

The president rejected the accusations in Khrushchev's letter in a reply that reiterated the U.S. demand that no offensive weapons be installed in Cuba and urged the Soviet leader "to take the necessary action to permit a restoration of the earlier situation." Khrushchev, after the latest communication from Kennedy, began to retreat. The Kremlin leader told the Soviet Presidium that he would offer to remove the missiles in exchange for a U.S. guarantee not to invade Cuba.[10]

Although the USSR had begun to pull back, momentum toward a confrontation steamed forward. The technicians in Cuba worked to complete installations and assemble bombers. The movements of ships and the UN debate occupied ExCom. Major concern that negotiations without a verifiable suspension of progress at the missile sites would give the enemy time to render them operable crackled through the comments. The armed forces prepared for airstrikes and an invasion. State Department experts worked on plans for a post-Castro government.

At the United Nations, Adlai Stevenson scored a stunning blow after the Soviet representative, Valerian Zorin, insisted that only defensive weapons were in Cuba. Stevenson brought out the photographs of the missile sites. Zorin dismissed them as doctored evidence, like that introduced during the Bay of Pigs. Stevenson countered that if a UN team could inspect the sites in Cuba, little doubt would remain about the nature of the disputed ordnance.

However, when Stevenson joined the ExCom meeting on October 26 and defended a moratorium plan initiated by UN secretary-general U Thant, he met withering fire. His remarks that it might be necessary to pledge not to invade Cuba and yield the missile bases in Turkey and Italy drew scorn, although JFK appeared willing to remove the Jupiters overseas.

Another back-channel contact opened a doorway to a peaceful denouement. ABC News State Department correspondent John Scali lunched with a Soviet embassy official who actually served as KGB station chief in Washington. The official urged Scali to advise his "high level friends" of the possibility of a deal that would exchange the missiles for a commitment not to invade Cuba.[11]

On the evening of October 26, the administration began to digest a long communiqué from Khrushchev to the president. The Soviet premier repeated all of his arguments that the weapons in question were purely defensive and the quarantine "piratical." However, he insisted that he would never jeopardize peace. In that vein he wrote, "Let us normalize relations." He referred to U Thant's "proposal . . . that our side should not transport armaments of any kind to Cuba for a certain period of time, while negotiations are being conducted—and we are ready to enter such negotiations—and the other side should not undertake any sort of piratical actions. . . .

"If assurances were given by the President and the government of the United States that the USA itself would not participate in an attack on Cuba and would restrain others from actions of this sort, if you would recall your fleet, this would immediately change everything."

When Kennedy gathered his advisers on the morning of the following day, CIA director McCone reported that work on the missile sites continued at a rapid pace. Approaching the blockade was the tanker *Grozny*, which initially appeared to have missile paraphernalia on its deck. It was a likely candidate for a stop-and-search. Feelers to the Turkish government about the possibility of dismantling the Jupiters evoked a negative attitude from that country's leaders. Replacement with top-of-the-line aircraft, however, would be acceptable. Any weakening of Turkey's military capacity might discourage other countries leaning to the West. However, with the introduction of the Polaris, a nuclear-tipped missile that could be fired from submarines lurking in the Mediterranean or the Black Sea, there was no need for any missiles on the Turko-Soviet border. The Italians evinced no concern if the missiles planted there were removed.

During this session, broadcasts of the text of a statement by Khrushchev started. Although billed as a letter to the president, the content differed radically from the previous one. He proposed, "We agree to remove those weapons from Cuba which you regard as offensive weapons . . . the United States, on its part, bearing in mind the anxiety and concern of the Soviet state, will evacuate its analogous weapons from Turkey." His country would pledge to respect the sovereignty of that country but asked the same position from the United States vis-à-vis Cuba.

The differences in the two messages confused the Americans. Word from the UN in New York said the first statement was confidential and intended to lessen tension but the second one was a substantive proposal. Ultimately, on October 27, the president replied, confirming his understanding that the weapons systems in Cuba would be removed and no new ones imported, with UN supervision as a guarantee. In return, the United States would end the quarantine and commit not to sanction an invasion of Cuba. There was no mention of the missiles in Turkey, but JFK did say that subsequently he would be willing to discuss arrangement on "other armaments" and "détente affecting NATO and the Warsaw Pact."[12]

That evening, the president gathered some of his top advisers to provide fodder for a meeting between Robert F. Kennedy and Soviet ambassador Dobrynin later that night. At Dean Rusk's suggestion, all agreed that RFK would say that while there would be no immediate deal on the Jupiters in Turkey, the president would remove them once the Cuban crisis ended. Because of the political damage this might inflict, the bargain must be kept secret by both sides.

When Dobrynin came to the Justice Department for his talk with Robert Kennedy, the latter reviewed the situation. He said that it was imperative to remove the offending missile bases. The alternative would be dead Americans and dead Russians (to say nothing of the many more dead

Cubans). He vowed that if the Soviets did their part, the United States would not move against the Castro regime. In a memorandum to Rusk, the attorney general wrote, "He then asked me about Khrushchev's other proposal . . . removal of the missiles from Turkey. I replied that there could be no *quid pro quo*. . . . This was a matter that had to be considered by NATO." However, he added, "If some time elapsed . . . I mentioned 4 or 5 months— I said I was sure that these matters could be resolved satisfactorily."[13]

The Joint Chiefs drafted a recommendation for a series of massive airstrikes beginning on October 28 or the following day while readying the amphibious and airborne forces for an assault. At sea, the *Grozny* plowed through the water, headed toward a rendezvous with U.S. warships. Low-level reconnaissance flights returned to their bases reporting that ground gunners had fired on them. Further bad news revealed that a U-2 plane had been shot down by a SAM in Cuba and the pilot, Major Rudolph Anderson, killed. Unbeknownst to the White House, the SAM that brought down the U-2 had been fired by the local air defense officers without permission from the Soviet generals in Havana or Moscow. The event delighted Castro but infuriated Khrushchev, who issued a direct order: "No independent initiatives. Everything is hanging by a thread as it is."[14]

When Curtis LeMay heard of the shoot-down of the U-2 he immediately directed that jet fighter-bombers equipped with rockets take out the SAMs readied for an attack. McNamara, realizing that a standing order for retaliation against a firing SAM site existed, told LeMay not to launch the planes without direct orders from his commander in chief. The general could not contain his disgust, growling, "He chickened out again."[15]

JFK telephoned his three living predecessors, Herbert Hoover, Harry Truman, and Dwight Eisenhower. He lied to all three, indicated that he had either rejected any deal involving Turkey or else that the Soviets had taken that issue off the table.[16]

On Monday, October 29, the crisis dissolved. The *Grozny* stopped dead in the water, short of the quarantine zone. Radio Moscow broadcast a long statement from Khrushchev in which he said that the Soviet government would dismantle and remove its missiles from Cuba. He spoke of Kennedy's vow that no attack would be made upon Cuba from the United States or any other country in the Western Hemisphere. The subject of missiles in Turkey was not mentioned.

In his reply, the president welcomed the efforts of his opposite number in the Kremlin. He agreed that through the United Nations, the first steps toward resolution could move ahead. In regard to a U-2 that had intruded upon Soviet airspace over Siberia, he explained that this aircraft had been engaged in an "air sampling mission in connection with your nuclear tests. Its course was directed from Eielson Air Force Base in Alaska to the North Pole and return. In turning south, the pilot made a serious naviga-tion error which carried him over Soviet territory."

In Washington, the Joint Chiefs characterized the news as a ploy to delay the necessary action by the United States. They recommended that the president approve airstrikes the next day, then an invasion, unless there was "irrefutable evidence" of the dismantling at the missile bases.

About 5 p.m. on October 28, Soviet technicians in Cuba began to dis-mantle the missile bases. The next morning, a Soviet official met with U Thant to arrange for UN representatives to perform on-site inspections in Cuba. An interdepartmental task force convened at the U.S. State Department to formulate plans for the withdrawal of the Jupiters from Turkey. At the same time, the White House insisted that the surveillance flights continue, and the president even reviewed with the Joint Chiefs the scenario for the invasion of Cuba. But it was all over. At ExCom the following day, the president appointed a Coordinating Committee "to give full-time attention to the matters involved in the conclusion of the Cuban crisis."

When the president learned that the CIA continued to sponsor sabo-tage missions inside Cuba he angrily ordered McCone to terminate the program. He instructed McNamara to begin the process of pulling out the Jupiter missiles in Turkey, over the resistance of some military leaders. Robert Kennedy reaffirmed to Dobrynin that they would be gone within a few months. However, this provision remained secret for roughly twenty-five years.

Within months, the CIA resumed efforts to destroy the Castro gov-ernment through sabotage and propaganda. Operation Mongoose, somno-lent during the missile crisis, reawakened. The Soviets shipped to Cuba a brigade of soldiers, a sop to Castro, who had vilified Khrushchev as a "son-of-a-bitch, bastard, asshole" when he heard the missiles would be taken away.[17]

The resolution of the crisis brought cheers from the press and the pub-lic, as the administration was perceived to have stood up to the commu-nists and forced them to back down. The administration celebrated its toughness, its ability to win at hardball. They congratulated themselves on their wisdom for managing the crisis in total secrecy. They believed such matters were too fraught with danger to involve members of Congress. Only after a decision on strategy and tactics was reached would the legislators get an opportunity to voice their opinions. The Cuban Missile Crisis thus helped establish a pattern for future commanders in chief of freezing out Capitol Hill.

As time passed, revisionists had an opportunity for an investigation into what happened. Among those was Major Alexander M. Haig Jr., who was deeply imbued with the credo of Douglas MacArthur: "There is no substitute for victory." After serving on a team assigned to draft an analytical study of the events from a military viewpoint, Haig said that the risks of a nuclear war were exaggerated. "No rational Soviet leader, and Nikita Khrushchev was eminently rational . . . would have contemplated a nuclear exchange with the United States." He quoted the Soviet leader as having later admitted that if the United States had started a war then, his country was not adequately prepared to attack it.

What truly annoyed Haig and other critics was the credit accorded the Kennedy administration. "The crisis was resolved not as folklore would have it by a steely display of presidential will and courage, but by a secret deal between Kennedy and Khrushchev in which the United States gave up at least as much as it gained," referring to the swap of the Cuban missiles for the ones in Turkey and Italy. "The Jupiters had been targeted on the Soviet Union and on Soviet installations inside the Iron Curtain and had been regarded as an important element in the Western deterrent. There were no plans to replace them with comparable weapons."

As a consequence, the members of NATO might think twice about relying on the United States to protect them. "If we would not defend Turkey, would we defend West Germany or France?" Haig said he was told that he should regard the Jupiters as being withdrawn "in an unconnected action justified in its own right." The documents and recordings from the time refute that position. He and his colleagues submitted their paper for approval by the Joint Chiefs, which said "the possibility that what was described as a coincidence could easily be interpreted as a secret arrangement." Haig recalled that after reading the treatise, Taylor "slammed it down on the table, and said that he would never approve it for transmittal to the President. Our paper disappeared."[18]

On the value of the missiles, however, Haig would seem off the mark. While Curtis LeMay agreed with Haig, the weapons systems extracted by the United States were increasingly of less value, both because of obsolescence and their vulnerability, Taylor had called them "a sterile asset"; "fixed and without mobility," they were "stationary bulls-eyes."[19] Jupiters were soon phased out everywhere. Most military experts, including Eisenhower, discounted them as anything more than a temporary measure. The

Polaris missiles that replaced the Jupiters were a ready and more effective tool. Furthermore, Haig and his compatriots do not seem to have considered that while the Soviets would have refrained from a nuclear response, they might well have overrun Berlin, where, short of using nuclear weapons, the West could have done little.

The president in his messages to Khrushchev had indicated his willingness to agree not to invade Cuba or permit such an action from elsewhere in the hemisphere. However, that aspect became an element in the bargaining over UN inspectors who would certify the elimination of Soviet-built bombers from Cuba. These negotiations never reached a full agreement, and as a result the United States never formally promised not to invade. Still, there was an implicit acceptance of Cuba's sovereignty. What had been trumpeted as a total victory of U.S. strength in the face of communist aggression now appears to have been a settlement on missiles and nothing else.

On another front, the war in Vietnam ground on. When Kennedy was inaugurated some two thousand American servicemen were in Vietnam. That figure climbed steadily during his presidency. Originally there as advisers or technicians to service and maintain equipment, they had begun to support missions by South Vietnamese troops, taking casualties. The historian Arthur Schlesinger said Washington was misled by its representatives in Saigon. General Paul Harkins and Ambassador Frederick Nolting claimed that the leader of South Vietnam, Ngo Dinh Diem, was irreplaceable and the suppression of the Vietcong guerrilla movement was on the verge of success. Harkins told McNamara, "There is no doubt we are on the winning side. If our programs continue we can expect Vietcong actions to decline." The secretary of defense believed the general, and it was announced, "We have turned the corner in Vietnam." Harkins predicted victory within a year.[20]

Journalists on the scene painted a much more gloomy landscape. They discredited the body counts of killed guerrillas and disputed the regime's reports of success in establishing strategic hamlets. They characterized Diem as a despot, a Roman Catholic vindictive toward the majority Buddhist population of the area he controlled, and reported that his brother, Ngo Dinh Nhu, and his beautiful wife, Madame Nhu, used their position for personal gain. To the reporters, the communiqués from Nolting and Harkins consisted of distortions or flat-out lies. For their part, the officials regarded the newspapermen as unpatriotic, hurting U.S. interests. Admiral Harry Felt scolded the Associated Press's Malcolm Browne: "Why don't you get on the team."[21]

Washington denied the accuracy of the correspondents, and so did some media outlets. *Time* magazine, with a passionate anticommunist orientation, wholeheartedly endorsed the regime of Diem, refusing to print stringer Merton Perry's account, which backed up critics. Others in officialdom, however, agreed that the war was not going well.[22]

In the Kennedy administration, those who believed in a military solution predominated. Secretary of State Rusk bought the package presented by Nolting and Harkins. He praised the strategic hamlet program, noting progress in the effort to develop a constitutional system. He agreed that the Vietcong were on the ropes. W. Averell Harriman, a roving ambassador, dissented from the cheery optimism. Brigadier General Edwin Lansdale, the expert on guerrilla warfare, warned that unless the people in a country believed in their government, they would not resist the communists.

In late May Diem trampled the individual rights of the Buddhists by forbidding them to celebrate the Buddha's 2,587th birthday in Hue. When the worshipers defied the order and gathered, soldiers fired indiscriminately into the crowd, killing and wounding many. A round of demonstrations followed. Americans from the president to the casual newspaper buyer were appalled as photographs showed protesting monks immolating themselves after dousing their bodies in gasoline. Madame Nhu earned the nickname of "the Dragon Lady" for her expression of delight whenever a bonze "barbecued" himself.

Diem remained adamant in his oppression of the Buddhists, and the administration recognized that in spite of what their chief representatives in Saigon reported, the war for hearts and minds was being lost. The president decided to replace Ambassador Nolting with former Massachusetts senator Henry Cabot Lodge. At the same time he tried to reassure Diem of U.S. support. He talked of the difficulty of establishing independence in a land where war had dragged on for twenty years. "In my opinion for us to withdraw from that effort would mean a collapse not only of South Vietnam but Southeast Asia."[23] He believed the Vietcong were an arm of international expansionist communism rather than nationalists with a limited goal.

Although Diem had told Nolting he would refrain from further attacks on the Buddhists, as soon as Nolting left, South Vietnamese troops invaded many pagodas and jailed hundreds of monks, assaults that Madame Nhu called "the happiest day of my life since we crushed the Binh Xuyen [a warlord faction] in 1955."

Some in the administration feared that Lodge's background meant he would back the entrenched establishment. However, he confounded his doubters by forwarding to Washington word from top Vietnamese generals that they had neither been involved in the Buddhist temple attacks nor did they condone them. Roger Hilsman Jr., who succeeded Harriman as assistant secretary of state for Far Eastern affairs, a West Point graduate who fought with guerrillas in the China-Burma-India Theater during World War II, concluded that victory was impossible if Diem remained. He and his associates drafted a cable to Lodge that said the United States would no longer support Diem if he continued to repress the Buddhists and reign as an autocrat. If the South Vietnamese leader refused to change he might have to go. While the United States would not involve itself in a coup, it could be expected to work with a new anticommunist government. "Currently . . . Ambassador and country team should urgently examine all possible alternative leadership and make detailed plans as to how we might bring about Diem's replacement if this should become necessary."[24] The message could certainly be read as encouraging a coup.

Because of August vacations, neither CIA head McCone, Dean Rusk, nor Robert McNamara saw the message before it went to the president, who was sojourning on Cape Cod. Undersecretary of State for Political Affairs Harriman, however, approved the cable. Hilsman contacted Undersecretary of State George Ball, who related the message to Kennedy, and the president was agreeable to transmission of the cable if other top advisers approved. Ball spoke to Rusk by telephone in New York and reported the president's position. Rusk tepidly endorsed the cable. With McCone unavailable, Harriman checked with the CIA's deputy director for plans, Richard Helms. He expressed misgivings but said McNamara "went along because the President had already done so." In place of McNamara at Defense, Roswell Gilpatrick, his deputy, wrestled with the import of the cable before reluctantly signing off. He dispatched a copy to Taylor, who was shocked by an almost casually decided major shift in Vietnam policy.

When JFK returned to Washington he regretted the cable to Lodge. Robert F. Kennedy explained, "He passed it off too quickly over the weekend at the Cape—he had thought it was cleared by McNamara and Taylor and everyone at State. In fact it was Harriman, Hilsman and Mike Forrestal [National Security Council staffer for Southeast Asia] . . . and they were the ones who were strongly for a coup."[25]

Moves to overthrow Diem were temporarily derailed, and the South Vietnamese leader and his brother, confident they had prevailed, embarked on a new series of raids and arrests. Alarmed by the ruler's callous disregard for human rights and worried about the progress of the war, the president sent two more representatives for a firsthand inspection. One was

General Victor H. Krulak of the marines, who had previously spent time in Vietnam; the other was Joseph Mendenhall, a member of the Foreign Service who also knew the terrain. When they returned the pair delivered diametrically opposing views. Krulak thought the war was progressing wonderfully well and that Diem enjoyed the confidence and affection of his people. Mendenhall argued that the South Vietnam government was teetering on the edge of total collapse and that at least Diem needed to be removed. The president could only ask, "Were you two gentlemen in the same country?"[26]

At the Hyannis Port family compound on Cape Cod, CBS-TV's Walter Cronkite questioned the president, who voiced his policy. "In the final analysis, it is their [the South Vietnamese's] war. They are the ones who have to win it or lose it. We can help them, we can give them equipment, we can send our men out there as advisers, but they have to win it, the people of Vietnam, against the Communists. . . . All we can do is help, and we are making it very clear, but I don't agree with those who say we should withdraw. That would be a great mistake."

Unfortunately, at this moment the "advisers" were increasingly becoming combatants, flying helicopters or even going on ground missions. Anthony Lake, who had arrived in South Vietnam as a special assistant to the ambassador, said, "There was blood on the flag."[27]

Lodge grew increasingly unhappy with the lack of response to him by the Saigon government. He cabled Washington that it might be wise to suspend all aid. In one more attempt for an accurate diagnosis, the commander in chief dispatched McNamara and Taylor to the war-torn country, and in Saigon Harkins and Lodge argued their findings, with the latter finally convincing the secretary of defense that reform of the political situation overshadowed the military program. When McNamara returned home, he seemed persuaded that Diem would not survive but that the war was still going well enough that by the end of 1963 the first thousand American "advisers" could be withdrawn, with the remainder leaving by the end of 1965.[28] In his book In Retrospect, McNamara recalled a statement by the president on October 2, 1963, that he expected the training mission to be completed by 1965 and that he would begin withdrawing U.S. training forces within ninety days of that time (that is, by December 31, 1963).

In the first years of the U.S. involvement in Vietnam, the unanimity of intelligence that had governed the missile crisis broke down. Most of the military leadership argued that the rebels could be defeated with American troops aided by those of the South Vietnamese government.

Some civilian investigators worried that only with political and social reform could Saigon maintain rule. Few of any stripe were willing to accept that a victory by the Vietcong would not be a terrible loss to the United States. In the halls of Congress and the White House and in the media, there was a fatal lack of understanding of the indigenous culture and how little Western concepts of democracy meant.

8

LBJ, PART OF THE WAY

Westerners are fond of characterizing Asians as devoted to "saving face." But president after president, starting with Kennedy, would invoke the specter of U.S. prestige at stake when contemplating whether to retreat from a situation. The falling domino metaphor, first uttered by Dwight Eisenhower, dominated foreign relations. The obsession with preventing any further tilt toward communism by nations around the world biased analyses of intelligence and blinded American officials to the weaknesses of the governments they supported.

The criticisms and threats by U.S. officials to cut him off may have persuaded Diem of a need to modify his actions. But before he could act, on November 1, 1963, the generals struck, murdering the Diem brothers. Washington rejected any suggestion of complicity. Arthur Schlesinger described the president as "somber and shaken" when he heard of the assassinations. A new government was recognized by the United States. Three weeks later John F. Kennedy himself lay dying from an assassin's bullets.

Lyndon Baines Johnson, made commander in chief by the assassin's bullets on November 22, 1963, was a far different creature from his predecessor. Bred in hardscrabble Texas, he had worked, clawed, and schemed his way into the corridors of power. His was a quixotic personality honed by his experiences in politics and as a son of dirt-poor Texans. He could be petulant, querulous, suspicious, sentimental, a bully, a flatterer, magnanimous, and visionary. He too had a fondness for women that went unreported, and he often laced his talk with down-home wit. As majority leader in the Senate he grabbed individuals by the lapels or literally put the arm on recalcitrants to cajole, wheedle, compromise, and threaten.

Johnson had known the sting of defeat, lost elections, and seen his abortive try for the Democratic nomination in 1960 won by his younger rival. While Kennedy had no problem accepting advice from others and even adopting their proposals as his own, that was far more difficult for Johnson. In the guise of soliciting counsel he often came across as telling people how he thought and what he had decided. He was not hesitant to use the power of his office.

When Lyndon Baines Johnson ascended to the role of commander in chief, there were more than sixteen thousand U.S. advisers in South Vietnam, and seventy-eight Americans had already been killed in combat. Amid the turmoil generated by the murder of JFK, the sometimes violent conflicts of the civil rights movement, the tendentious relations with the USSR, and the demands of ordinary government business, Johnson confronted the volatile situation in Southeast Asia.

LBJ said that as Air Force One flew him back to Washington from Dallas on November 23, 1963, he vowed, "I would devote every hour of every day during the remainder of John Kennedy's unfulfilled term to achieving the goals he had set. That meant seeing through in Vietnam."[1] He made his intentions public at a joint session of Congress, five days after being sworn in. "We will keep our commitments from South Vietnam to West Berlin."

It is Robert McNamara's contention that John F. Kennedy "would have eventually gotten out of Vietnam rather than move more deeply in."[2] "Eventually" hardly conveys any exactitude in terms of a specific date or even a period of years. Furthermore, the statements of JFK on the subject provide no substance to support the former secretary of defense. Quite apart from Kennedy's public utterances on his desire to prevent South Vietnam from falling to the Vietcong, there were more private comments that indicated domestic political danger in a retreat. He told Senator Mike Mansfield in 1962, "If I tried to pull out completely now from Vietnam, we would have another Red scare on our hands." In 1963, he told reporters in an off-the-record press conference, "We don't have a prayer of staying in Vietnam. But I can't give up a piece of territory like that to the Communists and get the American people to reelect me."[3]

Decisions that meant war, death, and destruction for Americans as well as foreigners hinged on how the issues played to voters. As a consequence, the Johnson administration and that which followed often conflicted with the media's coverage of events in Indochina. The battle for control of the region would be the most freely reported war ever. Correspondents filed their accounts without censorship, moved freely, and had great influence on public perceptions.

LBJ was not an ideologue. He was foremost a practical politician, but even pragmatists base their actions upon their perceptions of reality. Like so many, he reflected an obsession with the alleged lessons of Munich: unless one stood firm, aggressors not only reaped rewards but would be encouraged to gobble up more territory. He explained to McNamara that retreat in Vietnam meant "the dominoes would fall and a part of the world would go to the Communists."[4]

As the enemy forces increased in number and areas of control, McNamara and Taylor traveled to Vietnam for a fresh assessment, where General Nguyen Khanh stood atop a volatile heap of military and civilian groups. The pair reported to the president and the National Security Council worsening conditions, with deteriorating security, morale, and political effectiveness. They spoke of North Vietnam's increasing involvement in the guerrilla war. Johnson quoted McNamara: "The U.S. at all levels must continue to make it emphatically clear that we are prepared to furnish assistance and support *for as long* [italics added] as it takes to bring the insurgency under control."[5]

The secretary of defense wanted to increase military aid and training significantly, and "his final recommendation was that we be ready to carry out, on three days' notice, certain border control actions as well as retaliation against North Vietnam. We should also be in a position, he said, to conduct a program of graduated military pressure against the North on a month's notice."[6] Whatever he said later, in March 1964 he sounded determined to stay the course.

The Joint Chiefs disdained the kind of incremental steps outlined by McNamara. In particular, General Wallace Greene, Marine Corps commandant, and Curtis LeMay objected. Greene argued that if the nation were to stay and win in South Vietnam, it should apply its full concentrated power. According to McNamara, he did not spell out what that meant. The always truculent LeMay wanted to immediately bomb North Vietnamese logistical bases that supplied the Vietcong as well as the routes through Laos and Cambodia.[7]

With Dean Rusk and other National Security Council representatives backing the defense secretary, LBJ adopted his proposals. The commander in chief recalled that he feared any steps that might provoke a strong response from the enemy because South Vietnam lacked the capacity to resist. He also worried about any agreement between North Vietnam and the Chinese or Soviets that would cause them to plunge more heavily into the conflict. The rejection of the recommendations from the hard-line military leaders brought complaints that Johnson preferred to keep a low light under Vietnam to avoid that subject from overheating before the coming elections in November.

Senate Majority Leader Mike Mansfield of Montana introduced a dissenting note. He recommended that the administration seek a neutral Southeast Asia, one in which neither the United States nor the communist countries try to dominate the indigenous people. The president asked Rusk, Bundy, and McNamara for their reactions. They rejected the idea, arguing that U.S. disengagement would only encourage aggression and weaken resolve to suppress "wars of liberation." In hindsight McNamara said they did not properly investigate the political, military, financial, and human costs of trying to contain insurgency movements by military force.

The steps taken after the visit of McNamara and Taylor to South Vietnam notwithstanding, the insurgency encroached ever farther upon the areas controlled by the Saigon government. Hard-pressed General Khanh, unable to reverse the tide, now urged his American allies to open a bombing campaign against the Hanoi regime. Subsequently, Khanh reversed himself on his appeal for airstrikes against North Vietnam. Ambassador Lodge, however, vehemently urged quick strikes to shut down the infiltration of men and supplies south. Lodge even talked about yet another coup, stunning McNamara with the remark that "the U.S. should be prepared to run the country, possibly from Cam Ranh Bay [a huge base near Saigon]."[8]

The Johnson administration secretly enlarged the American participation in Southeast Asia with airpower in Laos. That country's neutrally inclined premier, Souvanna Phouma, ousted in a bloodless coup by right-wing generals, had been restored with some backroom manipulation by the State Department. Still, the communist Pathet Lao threatened to extend its domination beyond an area guaranteed it at Geneva in 1962. Johnson authorized American air reconnaissance of the group. He temporarily permitted U.S. civilian pilots to fly Laotian air force fighters against enemy targets, an arrangement similar to that of the American Volunteer Group, or Flying Tigers, of World War II. After the Pathet Lao shot down a recon aircraft, armed escorts from the U.S. Air Force accompanied the surveillance flights. Push had come to shove, and punch quickly followed with strikes at antiaircraft batteries and Pathet Lao installations. The watchdogs of Congress dozed while this partially surreptitious campaign sputtered ahead.

By the summer of 1964, with the campaign to halt the Vietcong flagging, partisan politics began to play a role. During a telephone call with Senator Richard Russell, Johnson countered a warning about becoming bogged down in Southeast Asia. "All the senators are all saying, 'Let's move, let's go into the North.' They'd impeach a president that would run out. . . . Run and let the dominoes start falling over. God Almighty, what they said about us leaving China would just be warming up." He cited two rivals for the presidency, former vice president Richard Nixon and Arizona senator Barry Goldwater, as among his principal attackers.[9]

That July, the Republicans nominated Goldwater, a fierce anticommunist conservative. Before Goldwater had entered the primaries he had called for withdrawal of recognition of the Soviet Union and freedom for local commanders to use atomic weapons against the USSR—"Let's lob one into the men's room of the Kremlin."[10] He immediately accused the Johnson administration of insufficient resolve to preserve South Vietnam.

On the morning of August 2, the duty officer at the White House received a high-priority message saying that North Vietnamese torpedo boats had attacked the destroyer *Maddox* in the Gulf of Tonkin, which washes Vietnam and the southernmost shore of China. The report stated that three PT craft opened fire on the warship while it patrolled an area thirty miles off the North Vietnamese coast. The *Maddox* retaliated with its five-inch guns and called for air support from the nearby carrier *Ticonderoga*. Jet fighters subsequently strafed the torpedo boats, leaving one dead in the water and the other two fleeing for home.

Admiral Ulysses Grant Sharp Jr., commander of the Pacific Fleet, claimed that the *Maddox* was steering a course eight nautical miles off the North Vietnamese coast. However, he admitted, "The *Maddox* was directed to not approach *islands* [his emphasis] in the Gulf closer than four miles, thus keeping outside of our territorially recognized waters. . . . She picked up some patrol craft that generally paralleled her course and stayed out of range. The afternoon of the second of August [Tonkin Gulf time] she was approached by these craft at high speed and took them under fire when they approached in a threatening manner."[11] While the United States believed sovereignty extended only three miles, the North Vietnamese claimed five miles.

The commander in chief described the *Maddox*'s mission as a "DESOTO patrol," a type of mission whose purpose was to detect evidence of the infiltration of men and supplies via the sea to the insurgents in South Vietnam and to collect electronic intelligence. LBJ said the destroyer was well beyond even the twelve-mile boundary that some claimed marked international waters. With his top advisers he concluded that "an overeager North Vietnamese boat commander might have been at fault or that a shore station had miscalculated. So we decided against retaliation, but I

ordered the Navy to continue the patrol, add another destroyer and provide air cover."[12]

Two days later a second destroyer, *Turner Joy*, which also patrolled the
Gulf of Tonkin, and the *Maddox* reported that their radar had detected
hostile ships that appeared intent on an "ambush." The two American
vessels changed their courses but still were forced to dodge twenty torpedoes. The Defense Department reported that the U.S. warships observed
tin fish wakes, searchlights, automatic weapons fire, and radar and sonar
contacts, and returned fire. The department said the American vessels had
been sixty-five miles from the nearest land.

CIA director McCone wondered whether the North Vietnamese were
reacting defensively to U.S. attacks on their offshore islands. He remarked
that the attack "is a signal that the North Vietnamese have the will and
determination to continue the war. They are raising the ante."[13] Johnson
seems to have interpreted the action by the North Vietnamese as equivalent to knocking the chip off the American shoulder. "The unanimous
view of . . . advisers was that we could not ignore this second provocation
and that the attack required retaliation. I agreed. We decided on air
strikes against North Vietnamese PT boats and their bases plus a strike on
one oil depot."[14] Admiral Sharp confirmed the details of the incident as
reported by the president.

The commander in chief said, "I was determined . . . to seek the fullest
support of Congress for any major action that I took, whether in foreign
affairs or in the domestic field. I believed that President Truman's one
mistake in courageously going to the defense of South Korea in 1950 had
been his failure to ask Congress for an expression of its backing."[15]

Nine senators and seven congressmen, a bipartisan group of heavy-
weights on foreign relations and defense, listened to a briefing from
McNamara. LBJ informed them he would address Americans that evening
and explain the nature of a limited response. It did not include bombing
North Vietnamese cities. "I went around the table asking each . . . for his
frank opinion," remembered Johnson. "Each expressed his whole hearted
endorsement of the course of action and of the proposed resolution."[16]
Goldwater said, "We cannot let the American flag be shot at anywhere on
earth if we are to retain our respect and prestige."[17] On August 6, American aircraft roared off to hit targets. Two planes were lost as four enemy
bases were bombed and twenty-five patrol boats reported hit.

On August 7, Congress ratified the Southeast Asia Resolution, more
familiarly known as the Gulf of Tonkin Resolution. It stated: "That the

Congress approves and supports the determination of the President, as Commander-in-Chief, to take all necessary measures to repel any armed attack against the forces of the United States and to prevent further aggression." At the end it noted that the resolution would expire either when the president determined peace and security in the area were assured or when it was terminated by a new and open-ended resolution from Congress.

What the president and his legislative partners had wrought was the overture to a greatly expanded conflict in Southeast Asia, the clichéd slippery slope, one that eventually slid across borders into other countries and ultimately engaged more than two million members of the U.S. military. The enthusiasm of Congress was dampened by only two dissenters, Senators Wayne Morse and Ernest Gruening. Some legislators recognized the full import of the resolution. During the floor debate, Senator John Sherman Cooper questioned Fulbright: "Are we now giving the President advance authority to take whatever action he may deem necessary respecting South Vietnam and its defense, or with respect to the defense of any other country included in the [SEATO] treaty?" After Fulbright answered in the affirmative, Cooper concluded, "Then looking ahead, if the President decided that it was necessary to use such force as could lead into war, we will give that authority by this resolution?" Fulbright said that is how he would interpret it.[18]

Gruening begged for a full inquiry before endorsing such a drastic resolution, characterizing the proposed legislation as a "predated declaration of war." Morse argued that passage meant "subverting and circumventing the Constitution . . . handing the chief executive "war-making powers in the absence of war." He questioned the wisdom of relying on the discretion of an individual who happened to be president in putting men in harm's way.[19]

Louisiana senator Allen Ellender asked Fulbright about possible provocations. The Arkansas senator reassured him that both McNamara and Rusk denied any operations of American or South Vietnamese vessels in the disputed area. Russell warned his colleagues, "Our national honor is at stake. We cannot and we will not shrink from defending it."[20]

Freshman senator George McGovern had some doubts about the resolution. In 1963 he had said, "The current dilemma in Vietnam is a clear demonstration of the limitations of military power. This is scarcely a policy of 'victory'; it is not even a policy of 'stalemate.' It is a policy of moral debacle and political defeat. It is a policy that demonstrates that our expenditures for more and more 'special forces' [now regarded as a key element in counterinsurgency] are as useless and dangerous as our expenditures for more and more nuclear capability."

McGovern later commented, "The Gulf of Tonkin alleged attack was largely a fraud. The commander of one of the two destroyers realized the administration was overreacting but his voice wasn't heard. Morse had a pipeline into the Pentagon although he never said he did. Some source there told him it wasn't a significant attack. Fulbright as the floor leader told me that Johnson just wanted it [the resolution] because he was taking heat from Goldwater but it didn't mean a thing; it was harmless. At that stage Congress was more willing to go along, unanimously in the House. We were already involved. It was a clear violation [of the right of Congress to declare war]. Morse and Gruening gave strong statements on the floor. There's not much excuse for the rest of us to say we were in the dark. That was the single vote I most regret from my entire career." McGovern has said that he learned from the Gulf of Tonkin vote to "never trade what I see as the truth for a winking assurance in a back room."[21]

According to McNamara, "Fulbright . . . came to feel that he had been misled—and indeed he had. He had received definite assurances from Dean [Rusk] at the August 6, 1964, hearing (and I believe privately from LBJ as well) that the president would not use the vast power granted him without full congressional consultation."[22] Fulbright would not be the last legislator gulled into a blank-check option. The founding fathers, unwilling to trust in good faith or intentions, had sought through checks and balances to prevent an individual from plunging the nation into perilous adventures. The Tonkin Gulf Resolution ignored the precepts of the constitutional framers.

LBJ won no surcease from criticism by Goldwater. A few days after the resolution passed, the Arizona senator thundered that the nation "must prosecute the war in Vietnam with the object of ending it." He sneered at the retaliation after the clash in the Gulf of Tonkin, calling the air attacks "a response, an incident, not a program or a new policy, a tactical reaction, not a new winning strategy." He charged that guerrilla war would never have been started had the enemy really believed the United States would act.[23]

The most controversial aspects of the Gulf of Tonkin affair were the facts of what occurred and what was told to Congress and the American people. Not in dispute was the existence of Plan 34A, CIA operations that used boats and aircraft to deposit South Vietnamese agents in North Vietnam, where they committed acts of sabotage and gathered intelligence. A second task force deployed high-speed patrol boats "manned by

South Vietnamese or foreign mercenary crews" to launch hit-and-run raids against North Vietnamese installations on the mainland and two small islands nearby. The DESOTO missions were a separate program resembling the deployment of intelligence trawlers by the Soviets off the U.S. coast and elsewhere. Sharp said the *Maddox* had explicit instructions to keep clear of the 34A operations.

McNamara wrote, "Long before the August events in the Tonkin Gulf, many of us who knew about the 34A operations had concluded they are essentially worthless. Most of the South Vietnamese agents . . . were either captured or killed, and the seaborne attacks amounted to little more than pinpricks." Nevertheless, 34A sorties continued "as a relatively low-cost means of harassing North Vietnam,"[24] a rather casual write-off of human lives.

As a member of McNamara's staff in 1964, Alexander Haig noted that the report on the Tonkin Gulf incident went first to the National Security Agency and the president before it reached the Pentagon. "At the time," he said, "I felt there was a genuine attack. McNamara assigned his counsel to make an investigation. He drafted a report but all of the copies were scooped up before anyone could see it. McNamara locked the report up in his safe. There was no attack. It was an anomaly. Electronic devices picked up the thump of engines and these were mistaken for torpedoes. Johnson had warned the North Vietnamese that if they continued to blow up hotels in South Vietnam, there would be retaliation, but what happened in the Gulf of Tonkin was a bad example to use."[25]

Four years beyond passage of the resolution, after a retiring Secretary of Defense McNamara testified before a senate committee, Wayne Morse, now better informed than when he objected to the resolution, rose on the Senate floor and said, "I am satisfied that the transcripts of the Record [congressional] both on August 6, 1964, and February 20, 1968, show that the Secretary of Defense sought to do a snow job on the committee." Morse referred to the alleged second attack on the *Maddox* and *Turner Joy*. "The first question . . . is: Was Congress and were the American people aware that in August 1964 the *Maddox* was a ship engaged in electronic surveillance? Were they aware that one of its assigned missions was to stimulate radar and other shore installations of North Vietnam? Were they aware that the *Maddox* conducted operations as close as 4 to 8 miles off the coast of North Vietnam . . . a country which had not engaged in any aggressive actions whatsoever against the United States?

". . . In view of the fact that we were also involved in the bombardments of these islands and of the mainland, these instructions [to stimulate electronic reaction from the enemy] constituted, under international law, an act of constructive aggression on the part of the Government of the United States." From the viewpoint of the enemy, the American warships had violated North Vietnamese territorial waters and engaged in highly provocative activities.

Morse said the administration had concealed the fact that before the first attack on the American warship, "the *Maddox* proceeded in the direction of Hon Me and Hon Nieu [the two islands] coming within 4 miles of those islands before turning southward. This patrol, was, therefore, off the islands which had been attacked only 40 hours earlier by American-supplied vessels, operated by South Vietnamese. How did the North Vietnamese know whether or not our attacks were over? By what right do we assume that the North Vietnamese, having been bombarded and then having this destroyer that close to their shore, with the destroyer stimulating electronically the electronic defensive instruments in North Vietnam, how could they not assume that there was not going to be additional bombardment? They had every right to take such course of action as they thought necessary to protect their sovereignty."

Morse roundly condemned the administration. "We are being treated to an undeclared war, and therefore an unconstitutional war, and slaughtering increasing hundreds of American boys in that illegal act." He reiterated his accusation that because of the provocations by the United States and its "implication in the bombing" (by South Vietnamese boats), the North Vietnamese had decided they were dealing not only with their southern countrymen but also with the United States.

Senator Morse then examined the details of the first attack. He accepted that under the circumstances, Captain John Herrick, skipper of the *Maddox*, and his crew were "jittery." He remarked, "No wonder their initial reports showed 22 torpedoes coming from two non-torpedo carrying Swatows [gunboats without torpedoes] and one PT boat. . . . One thing that I believe is perfectly clear is that for Captain Herrick to seek to [tell] his Government and his superiors that 22 torpedoes were fired is just plainly fantastic, when a PT boat carries only two torpedoes. There was no flotilla of PT boats sent against the *Maddox*. I happen to think that a torpedo was fired. Perhaps more than one, but . . . there could not have been more than an exceedingly small number."[26]

Curiously, six hours after the *Maddox* radioed of being under attack on August 4 and sent messages about more than twenty torpedoes, Captain Herrick sent a "flash" message to his superiors. "Review of action makes any reported contacts and torpedoes fired appear doubtful. Freak weather effects on radar and overeager sonar men may have accounted for many reports. No actual visual sighting by *Maddox*. Suggest complete evaluation before any further action taken."

Some forty minutes later, Admiral Sharp telephoned General David Burchinal and advised that no matter what Herrick had said, he had no doubt that this second attack was genuine. Herrick himself about an hour later changed his mind, radioing, "Certain that original ambush was bonafide." McNamara personally telephoned Sharp, who insisted the attacks had occurred but believed that the number of torpedoes was exaggerated, and when the secretary of defense pressed him admitted there was a slight possibility that no ambush had occurred.[27]

Sharp, who was in contact with the two destroyers, said they deliberately tried to avoid contact with the enemy and were sixty miles off the coast when "they reported the enemy boats were at a range of about 6,000 yards from the *Maddox* . . . radar tracking indicated that the contact turned away. They then heard torpedo noises on the *Maddox*'s sonar. The *Maddox* passed this word to the *Turner Joy*, and both ships took evasive action. Personnel aboard the *Turner Joy* reported they sighted a torpedo wake passing abeam of the *Turner Joy* about 300 yards to port. One target was taken under fire by the *Turner Joy* and numerous hits were observed and they said it disappeared from all radars. The commanding officer and other . . . personnel said they observed a thick column of black smoke from this target. . . . Both *Maddox* and *Turner Joy* reported that torpedoes had been fired at them. *Turner Joy* reported . . . that she was turning to ram one of the North Vietnamese boats which would indicate that the boat was quite close aboard."[28]

On the other hand, one of the pilots from the *Ticonderoga*, James B. Stockdale, who would later endure eight years in a Hanoi prison camp, receive a Medal of Honor, and after retirement run for vice president with Ross Perot and the Independence Party in 1992, flew over the destroyers. He believed there was no attack. "I had the best seat in the house to watch the event," he later said, "and our destroyers were just shooting at phantom targets—there were no PT boats there . . . there was nothing there but black water and American fire power."

Admiral Thomas Moorer, who would ascend to chairman of the Joint Chiefs of Staff but at the time served with the Seventh Fleet, noted, "In the Tonkin Gulf incident, we still had destroyers that had hand decoding equipment. They had two ensigns there trying to decode these top secret messages that the Secretary of Defense was sending direct to this destroyer.

He was asking questions at the rate of about one every thirty minutes and if he didn't get an answer he would send them another one . . . why haven't you answered my question? . . . when it comes in in code you don't know what the hell is in it, so these ensigns were about three days behind in decoding all these messages. The Tonkin Gulf was long over before they got the questions."[29]

Even the commander in chief, whose long service in Congress had made him skeptical of military leaders, wondered about the authenticity of the incidents. In September 1964, while meeting with McNamara, he ruminated on the Gulf of Tonkin affair. After voicing a fear that error might "make us very vulnerable if we conclude that these people are attacking us and we were merely responding and it develops that that just wasn't true at all . . . I sure want more caution on the part of these admirals and destroyer commanders . . . about whether they are being fired on or not." Reverting to his "good ol' boy" persona, the president continued, "I don't want them just being some change-o'-life woman running up and saying that, by God, she was being *raped* just because a man walks in the *room!* [his emphasis]

". . . I've been listening to these stories for thirty years before the Armed Services Committee, and we are always sure we've been attacked. Then in a day or two, we are *not* so damned sure. And then in a day or two more, we're sure it didn't happen at *all!*"[30]

The revelation that the State Department had drafted a resolution that would allow expansion of U.S. military action in Indochina more than two months *before* the alleged incidents off the coast of North Vietnam reinforced accusations that the administration faked the reports. Few can doubt that Johnson and company eagerly snapped up a seeming casus belli. At best they mistook wisps of smoke for an inferno. It seemed a divine opportunity to declare the nation steadfast in its opposition to the perceived communist threat, simultaneously shut up the carping of domestic partisans, and boost the morale of the government of South Vietnam. The precipitous approval by Congress, a pitifully short forty-minute debate, and a total absence of any independent investigation of the events by both the legislators and the media demonstrated an appalling retreat from responsibilities.

Richard Holbrooke, a junior State Department officer in Saigon then, said in 2004, "I don't believe the second incident ever happened. I think the first one was simply that the North Vietnamese thought this was just another 34A operation and reacted against it. The administration exploited the alleged events to get the resolution, which Bill Bundy had drafted several months before. If they had not gotten the resolution I believe they would still have enlarged the war."[31]

In 1999, McNamara, who had previously insisted that the attacks were genuine and originated with the communist leadership in Hanoi, accepted that he had erred. He had met with the North Vietnamese defense minister, General Vo Nguyen Giap, who said the local commander, not the North Vietnamese, ordered the August 2 torpedo boat strike against the *Maddox* in retaliation for U.S.-backed raids by South Vietnamese commandos. Giap and other sources flatly denied that any second attack ever occurred. Concluded McNamara, "It appears that on August 4 the appearance of an attack may have been derived from poor visibility, anxious U.S. sonar operators and mistaken analyses of intercept data from North Vietnamese communications."[32]

The public and the press appeared to approve the actions taken after whatever happened in the Gulf of Tonkin that August. The bellicose Goldwater could not find favor with his harder line and insinuations that he favored using nukes. He frightened voters with talk of making Social Security voluntary, sneers at welfare recipients, opposition to civil rights legislation, and calls for elimination of the graduated income tax. In the 1964 election, the civil rights, War on Poverty president easily routed his challenger.

Senator Russell, who had been a mentor to the young Johnson when he entered the Senate, spoke with LBJ a week after the election. In May Russell had told the president that Vietnam was "just one of those places where you can't win." He now said, "You've got the majority to get anything you want. All you've got to do is keep your good judgment and your head on your shoulders." Johnson asked what he should do about Vietnam. Russell, a notable hawk when it came to resisting the expansion of communist-controlled territory, responded, "I wish we could figure some way to get *out* of that, Mr. President. I think if we get in there and get messing around with those Chinese, we could be in there for the next ten years. But I don't know how we can get *out*. I told John McCone he ought to get somebody to run that country [who] didn't want us in there. . . . Then . . . we could get out with good grace. But he didn't take me very seriously. It would have been a whole lot better than putting in this Khanh and all that crowd."[33]

After the confrontation in August LBJ had discussed options with his chief advisers. George Ball was one who strongly suggested consideration of attempts at a political settlement, a negotiation aimed at preserving the autonomy of South Vietnam. While several officials agreed that the objective was highly desirable, they saw no way to achieve it. To withdraw the iron fist of military force meant a collapse of resistance to the communists. Said McNamara, "We saw a world where the Hanoi-supported Pathet Lao continued to push forward in Laos, where Sukarno appeared to be moving Indonesia ever closer to the Communist orbit, where Malaysia faced immense supported insurgents, where China had just detonated its first atomic device and continued to trumpet violent revolution, where Khrushchev and his successors in the Kremlin continued to make bellicose statements against the West. In light of all those threats, we viewed unconditional withdrawal as clearly unacceptable."[34] Most vociferous in their rejection of lessening or eliminating military force were the generals and admirals of the Joint Chiefs.

As Lyndon Johnson entered his first full term in the White House, the momentum to plunge ever deeper into Vietnam gained strength. The available intelligence did not reveal the errors drawn by assumptions about the enemy or the viability of the South Vietnamese officials. Media currents and public opinion supported a heavier investment of assets. There was no effective political opposition. Congress dropped the reins and the commander in chief felt no obligation to seek formal approval.

9

DOWN THE SLOPE

T
he ability of Truman, Eisenhower, Kennedy, and Johnson to either evade the need for congressional approval or else steamroller the legislators into acquiescence set a tone that would persist until the blowback—unexpected consequences—overwhelmed even the more browbeaten residents of Capitol Hill. But that turnaround would not come until the 1970s. Well before that, in the final months of his White House years, LBJ increasingly accepted the premise of victory through force, even while naysayers in Congress and the media offered evidence that this was a bankrupt policy.

As he continued his presidency in 1965, LBJ created a working group to once more assess the problems and propose solutions for that far-off region. The team stated, "We cannot guarantee to maintain a non-Communist South Vietnam short of committing ourselves to whatever degree of military action would be required to defeat North Vietnam and probably Communist China militarily. Such a commitment would involve high risks of major conflict in Asia, which could not be confined to air and naval action but would almost inevitably involve a Korean-scale ground action and possibly even the use of nuclear weapons at some point."

McNamara had said the heads of the armed forces discounted the risks as better than the consequences of a retreat from Southeast Asia. "The president and I were shocked by the almost cavalier way in which the chiefs and their associates, on this and other occasions referred to, and accepted the risks of, the possible use of nuclear weapons."[1]

The working group presented the commander in chief with three alternatives. First, the United States could continue its present course of limited support to the incumbent government of South Vietnam, which had little hope of success. Second, American airpower could start an intense bombing campaign of targets in the north with an eye to forcing Hanoi to end support for the Vietcong and perhaps encourage the start of negotiations. Third, the United States could begin a graduated campaign of bombing, which carried a lesser risk of enlargement of the war. The air force and the marines were much more enthusiastic about the efficacy of airplanes than the army or navy. The CIA expressed only limited approval of air assaults, correctly noting that agricultural, decentralized North Vietnam was not terribly vulnerable to a bombing campaign.

The president ordered General Maxwell Taylor to Saigon, where he would insist that the clique of generals set their house in order. His mission ended in failure; the military leaders continued to squabble and even carried out still another coup. Taylor, who had always been a hawk, became so frustrated that he talked about pulling out, leaving the GVN (Government of South Vietnam) to see if it could survive for any period of time without the United States. Soon, however, he recanted his heresy. He doubted that the war could be satisfactorily ended through aerial assault and warned that defeat of the Vietcong on the ground would require a massive investment of soldiers.

The enemy had the effrontery to attack a U.S. officers' billet in Saigon, and in January their irregulars thrashed two South Vietnamese divisions. The president agonized over his predicament. He groused that "all the [military] chiefs did was come in every morning and tell him, 'Bomb, bomb, bomb,' and in the afternoon come back and tell him again, 'Bomb, bomb, bomb.'" He sat with columnist Walter Lippmann, hardly an appeaser, who said the only sensible course lay in a negotiated withdrawal of American forces from an unwinnable war. "But this is a commitment I inherited," complained Johnson. "I don't like it, but how can I pull out?" When Lippmann pointed out that French president Charles de Gaulle had told him not even a million U.S. troops in Vietnam could achieve lasting victory, the president was not persuaded.

In contrast to Lippmann, columnist Joseph Alsop regularly branded the president as pursuing a weak strategy. He wrote that LBJ was "consciously prepared to accept defeat here [Saigon]," which in Alsop's eyes would "be his defeat as well as a defeat for the American people." Alsop pierced Johnson's most sensitive spot when he compared Vietnam with the Cuban Missile Crisis. "If Mr. Johnson ducks the challenge we shall learn by experience about what it would have been like if Kennedy had ducked the challenge in October 1962."[2]

Any invidious comparison with his glamorized predecessor enraged the president. He believed the chorus of criticism for his gingerly moves in Southeast Asia from conservatives not only reflected their blind anticommunist fervor but also their way of aborting his Great Society plans.

"They hate this stuff, they don't want to help the poor and the Negroes but they're afraid to be against it at a time like this when there's been all this prosperity. But the war, oh, they'll like the war."[3] Polls indicated that a substantial plurality of Americans favored military action against the Vietcong and perhaps their North Vietnamese allies.

Another strike by the guerrillas on February 6, 1965, battered South Vietnamese Army headquarters and the American air base near Pleiku, 240 miles north of Saigon. They killed eight U.S. servicemen and wounded more than a hundred. Johnson convened members of the National Security Council along with congressional leaders. Almost everyone advocated bombing runs on Hanoi, including even George Ball, the erstwhile proponent of negotiations. However, Senator Mike Mansfield remarked that the success of the Vietcong should have "opened many eyes. The local populace in South Vietnam is not behind us, or else the Vietcong could not have carried out their surprise attack." He cautioned LBJ against a reprisal, warning that the country would no longer be "in a penny ante game."[4]

Having heard out the single naysayer, the president ordered an airstrike, relying on the authority granted by him in the Gulf of Tonkin Resolution. McGeorge Bundy returned from Saigon with a bleak picture. The Vietnamese could not carry the burden of their own self-defense. Short of strong U.S. action, the independence of South Vietnam seemed doomed. Bundy warned of the risk to American prestige abroad and claimed negotiation meant surrender. Vice President Hubert Humphrey proposed to the president that they seek a negotiated solution. LBJ banished him from meaningful conversations about Southeast Asia.

The president again drew together the usual cast of "wisemen," including Dwight Eisenhower. The former commander in chief told the current one it was his duty to stop communism in Southeast Asia. He believed a more sustained bombing program of the north might help but accepted the suggestion that as many as eight divisions of American troops might be required. If the Soviet Union or the Chinese threatened to interfere, "We should pass the word back to them to take care lest dire results [i.e., nuclear strikes] occur to them."[5] Ike recalled that when he became president he sent secret messages to the North Koreans and the Chinese indicating that unless a satisfactory armistice was promptly signed, he intended to remove the "limits we were observing as to the area of combat and the weapons employed."[6]

The president agreed to begin with pressure from the air and so began Operation Rolling Thunder, a series of attacks upon North Vietnam. The planes flew out of bases like Da Nang, but Vietcong freely moving about the countryside menaced the airfields. General William Westmoreland, the Commander, U.S. Military Assistance Command, Vietnam (COMUS-MACV), requested two marine battalions to provide a defensive perimeter. Taylor, who had replaced Lodge as ambassador to South Vietnam, thought the introduction of ground forces a bad idea, that it paved the way for further investment of soldiers. But protection for the bases seemed common sense to the secretary of defense and the marines took up station.

The interdiction campaign from the air, aimed at bases, headquarters, supply points, and trails for infiltration of men and equipment, suffered from breakdowns in security. B-52 raids originated from Guam or U-Tapao in Thailand. "Oftentimes, by the time the airplanes were taxiing [for take-off], their bombing destinations were known," said Russell Dougherty, the air force deputy for operations. "We would get some radio intercepts. We would determine where their headquarters were. We could go after that headquarters . . . the orders came out the night before. You loaded the bombs. You took off the next morning, and the headquarters moved because they knew they had been [targeted]."

Dougherty commented that interdiction on the Ho Chi Minh Trail could not stop the flow, only attrit it. "We destroyed a lot, but there was a failure . . . to appreciate how much was coming in. The Soviet resupply of Vietnam was unbelievably large. You could destroy trucks by the thousands and the trucks kept coming . . . in the aftermath of an attack . . . you don't really know what you have gotten . . . you go in there and put a hell of a lot of bombs down and you think you have destroyed all the trucks, and 50 percent of them will come out without a scratch. . . . A hell of a lot of smoke comes up from the bomb dropped, and it looks like you blew hell out of them. You find out if you are 150 feet off . . . you don't do a thing but shake it up."[7]

There have been accusations of fake documents, two sets of books, to hide the raids in Cambodia. Admiral Moorer, chairman of the Joint Chiefs, insisted that "the record wasn't falsified. . . . We had a computer printout that went to everybody . . . everyone responsible for buying gasoline, buying bombs, shipping bombs . . . this listed the number of hours the aircraft of all services flew and from where, point A to point B. What we did, when they went into Cambodia, we put in fictitious targets. This report wasn't made out for the benefit of Congress. It was made out for the computer printout and we had to keep [that] unclassified."[8] His defense seems disingenuous since there were no notifications to Congress or the public of where the B-52s flew.

The tons of ordnance dumped on North and South Vietnam had not slowed the advance of the enemy in the south. The commander in chief summoned his army chief of staff, General Harold K. Johnson, and gave him the mission of an on-site investigation of the situation. Johnson made a brief tour of still secure areas and conferred with Westmoreland and Taylor in Saigon. From them he heard the discouraging words on the inadequacy of the forces resisting the Vietcong. They were unable to achieve a numerical superiority of even five to one over the insurgents, and experiences in the Philippines and Malaya suggested that success required an advantage of from ten to twenty times the guerrilla numbers.

On his return Harold Johnson recommended an immediate and substantial increase in the ground forces even as the air war was expanded. The general suggested that a multinational force might patrol the border between the north and south to halt infiltration—an idea with no chance of acceptance by the international community or North Vietnam. He confounded the civilians and even the other Joint Chiefs when he estimated that the war could only be won with the infusion of five hundred thousand American soldiers geared for a five-year struggle.

Alexander Haig, an aide to McNamara at the Pentagon, recalled that he and a fellow officer received an assignment from General Johnson to work up a list of every possible action open to the United States. Haig said they prepared a memorandum in which they spelled out recommendations for shoring up the existing effort and introducing a larger American presence in South Vietnam. Below this they detailed "possible actions based entirely on the military and strategic realities of the situation. These included full mobilization; the movement of several ready fighting divisions on full alert to the West Coast of the United Sates and to strategic bases in the Pacific; the creation of an amphibious force capable of invading North Vietnam; the deployment of major naval and air units capable of carrying out a sustained bombing campaign against the North, including the mining of harbors and the interdiction of supplies through attacks on shipping."

Haig believed that the United States mistakenly applied gradual escalation. "We were using tentative, piecemeal incrementation, a philosophy started in the Pentagon during the 1960s when a bunch of educators, professors from the Northeast, became involved in war planning. They created poodle blankets for Berlin, which was not the way to conduct crisis management. It is too easy for the other side to then up the ante until finally someone knocks the stick off your shoulder and you have a war. We did not win in Vietnam because of the restraints on going to the source. We should have gone to Russia and told them we won't tolerate what was happening. We should have told them we'll take Hanoi out and they would have backed off."[9] When General Johnson delivered his report to the president, the lower half of the research done by the two officers had been scissored off, recalled Haig, leading to a "timorous pattern of action . . . it also meant conceding sanctuary to the North Vietnamese in their own territory and Cambodia."[10]

Haig, like most of his fellow officers, believed a military solution of "victory" was the only means to arrive at an acceptable political resolution. He argued that the defects of the government under Diem were not critical to success; what counted was American determination. He disdained the notions of containment and limited war. "The Army realized that the war could not be fought and won under the terms laid down by the doctrine of incrementalism."

In Haig's view, the Kennedy-Johnson policies rested on "the same errors that produced such suffering and needless loss in Korea." As a champion of the domino theory he would insist that the Americans in Vietnam were fighting against the USSR, and "had we been willing to mobilize for a full scale war in Vietnam—a minimum of one million soldiers according to the thesis of ten to one for every fighting guerrilla—we could have crushed the insurgency." At the same time, the United States would have signaled the Soviets to quit the game because "as the power behind the war, [they] would not be immune from American action." Haig insisted that the probable reaction of the Kremlin would have been communist restraint in Vietnam, some threatening gestures in Berlin with little likelihood of a nuclear confrontation because of "overwhelming nuclear superiority then enjoyed by the United States.[11]

The demands for a greater military presence in Vietnam grew. After an April 1, 1965, White House discussion, the president, while balking at a request from the Chiefs for two combat divisions, agreed not only to the deployment of the two marine battalions but even broadened their mission significantly. They would not only be responsible for base security but also could engage in active combat. It was a tipping point for the Johnson approach to Vietnam.

During this period the United Nations attempted to arrange a ceasefire and use diplomacy to bring peace to the region, to no avail. Both sides would set conditions or else reject out of hand proposals to work toward an agreement. The president artfully pretended to consult with Congress, but in essence he only would inform the legislators of his decisions rather than heed their counsel, much less accept direction. The White House tapes of the time frequently reveal LBJ's unhappiness with his growing band of critics in Congress. Adding to his discomfit was the nascent antiwar movement. Many people of all ages had begun to have their doubts about the policy in Vietnam. Although FBI director J. Edgar Hoover stoked LBJ's imagination with images of communists and extreme left-wingers behind the demonstrators, Richard Helms, CIA deputy director in 1965–1966 and then director, to the disappointment of the president could not find proof that Moscow or Beijing was orchestrating the antiwar movement.[12]

At high schools and college campuses, the nation's youths, restless under the authority assumed by their elders and aware that their segment of the population would be the ones expected to fight and die in Vietnam, had begun to openly take issue with the administration as well as other institutions. Deepening the winters of discontent, the civil rights movement stormed the barricades of discrimination, while feminists sought to change the habits of the workplace, the inequality of the laws, and roles in the family.

The commander in chief, in dealing with Southeast Asia, tried to have it both ways. To the hawks he emphasized his stepped-up bombing program, additions of U.S. forces, and his unwillingness to compromise South Vietnam's independence. To the doves he argued that only he blocked the seemingly wild-eyed demands of Curtis LeMay and his ilk—"bomb them back to the stone age"—for a strategic bombing campaign that would smash Hanoi and Beijing. His youthful aide Bill Moyers detected more than the usual touch of paranoia that often afflicts those in power, as well as bouts of depression as Johnson wrestled with the decisions about Vietnam. Richard Goodwin, another White House aide, used the word "paranoic."[13]

The disagreements among his advisers, the rants and hurrahs from congressmen, the pro-and-con media coverage, percolated in the brain of a commander in chief with an overweening desire to be regarded as a great statesman, a president worthy of the best who ever occupied the office. He subscribed to the notion that war is too important to be left in the hands of the generals, boasting that he personally controlled the selection of bombing targets and the rules of engagement. That attitude enabled military leaders to complain that they were denied success because the White House limited their options. Not that there was unanimity on war policy within the Joint Chiefs. The army and air force often did not agree.

Smack in the middle of the confusion over South Vietnam, the commander in chief wrestled with a Latin American eruption. In 1961, the thirty-one-year reign of the Dominican Republic's dictator, Rafael Trujillo, ended with a bloody assassination. The Dominicans elected Juan Bosch as president, but a military junta deposed him after only seven months. In Washington Bosch was considered far too accommodating to the extreme left wing and to resemble Fidel Castro.

Constitutionalist elements staged their own coup. Dominican military leaders and the insurgents faced off for several days before the rebels appeared on the brink of victory. Alarmed that Bosch might return, Ambassador Tapley Bennett cabled the State Department on April 28 of the danger from "Castro-type elements." Tales of Dominicans climbing the walls of the embassy and threatening the lives of Americans reached Washington.

The president met with congressional leaders and stressed the danger to American interests. To reporters he spoke of fifteen hundred people brutally murdered and six embassies invaded. Thousands of individuals had crowded into a hotel to avoid the bloodshed. Bullets whistled through the windows of the embassy, forcing the ambassador to cower underneath his desk. Johnson ordered marines to the Dominican Republic for the protection of the U.S. citizens. LBJ, allowing that Bosch was not a communist, said the CIA had reported that he had been shunted aside and it was now a "Castro operation."[14] Nearly twenty thousand U.S. troops occupied Santo Domingo.

The Organization of American States installed a peacekeeping force, which included U.S. troops. In an election Bosch lost to Joaquin Balaguer, making for a government friendly to the United States. J. William Fulbright said that the main reason the United States interfered in Santo Domingo lay in "faulty advice"—bad intelligence—given the president. But he added that LBJ's claim that he acted to save American lives "was more a pretext than a reason for the massive U.S. intervention."[15]

Vietnam, of course, could not move to a back burner simply because the Dominican situation had boiled over. A conference in Honolulu that included Ambassador Taylor, General Westmoreland, McNamara, Admiral Sharp, and others concluded that the bombing program alone could not halt the aid from Hanoi to the Vietcong. They took their cue from Taylor. "Hanoi must be convinced that the VC cannot win here. Oley Sharp and Westmoreland requested two more divisions and two brigades, a total of about 60,000 men." McNamara and Taylor pared down the figures, but the increases would boost the American presence from 33,000 to 82,000.[16]

The secretary of defense said he urged LBJ to advise the congressional leadership of the added deployments, which would inevitably mean higher casualties and greater public scrutiny. But LBJ clutched his cards tighter to his breast. Additions would be announced as each unit deployed, a trickle-out of news rather than a big splash. However, to fund operations, the commander in chief asked Congress for $700 million in supplemental appropriations to cover Vietnam and the Dominican Republic. To ensure passage he recruited Vice President Humphrey for private conversations with potentially opposed congressmen. LBJ coached his emissary, "Let's watch anybody else that might cause trouble. . . . To deny or to delay this request means you're not giving a man ammunition he needs for his gun. You're not giving him gas he needs for his helicopter. You got him standing out nekkid and letting people shoot at him. And we don't want to do that."[17] Similar rhetoric, thirty-nine years later, peppered the 2004 presidential race.

LBJ's message to Capitol Hill stated, "This is not a routine appropriation. . . . Each member of Congress who supports this request is also voting to persist in our effort to halt communist aggression in South Vietnam." His choice of language labeled those who would reject the request as unwilling to stop the march of communism. He did not note that other considerations might be in order or the wisdom of the effort questioned. Lest there remain any doubt about his intentions, the president issued a second message later in the day that emphasized that the funds were more than a routine expenditure and specifically noted that there was no guarantee he would not ask for further money to ensure the safety of South Vietnam. A thoroughly cowed Congress passed the bill 408 to 7 in the House and 88 to 3 in the Senate. Mike Mansfield, who earlier had questioned if not opposed escalation, said, "There is not a Senator who would not prefer, with the President, that a decent peace might be achieved quickly in Vietnam. But we will vote for this measure because there is not one member of this body who does not desire to uphold the President and those who are risking their lives."[18]

The commander in chief bragged of going the extra mile by giving Congress an opportunity to express its wishes through the vote. To Representative George Mahon, the president smugly declared, "I've [already] got a vote of confidence. Five hundred and two to two on the August thing which says 'Prevent any aggression anywhere and protect armed troops anywhere.' I thought this would be a masterstroke with Congress to show them I was frank and candid. . . . I would put it right in their belly, and if they didn't want to give it to me, they'd say so. And if they gave it to me, why, they'd say, 'We can trust the guy. Although he's got authority, he didn't write his check. He let us in on it."[19] To reporters he reiterated his belief that the

August 1964 congressional resolution gave him the power to do what he saw fit in Vietnam.

While Johnson briefly relished his fiscal triumph, the news from Vietnam could not help but depress the administration. A weeklong pause in bombing, intended to entice North Vietnam to the bargaining table, met stony rejection, and the aircraft renewed their attacks. Yet another coup in the south installed General Nguyen Van Thieu as head of state and a flamboyant air force officer, General Nguyen Cao Ky, as prime minister. A dandy in a black flight suit accessorized with twin pearl-handled revolvers à la George Patton, Ky startled Americans, saying he admired Adolf Hitler and "we need four or five Hitlers in Vietnam." Later, he revised his remarks, saying he meant only in terms of the German dictator's ability to organize people. While Washington digested this turn of events, Westmoreland cabled the Pentagon to advise that the South Vietnamese Army (ARVN) appeared unable to cope with the increased capability of the Vietcong, that the desertion rates ran inordinately high and battle losses went beyond the expected. "ARVN troops are beginning to show signs of reluctance to assume the offensive and in some cases their steadfastness under fire is coming into doubt." He wanted to boost the American garrison from 82,000 to 175,000. "Of the thousands of cables I received during my seven years in the Defense Department," said McNamara, "this one disturbed me most."[20]

Westmoreland now hoped to shift the strategy from one that merely supported the ARVN or took a defensive posture in favor of an offensive stance, using the additional Americans to carry the war to the enemy. When McNamara visited the general, the latter made it clear that while he wanted 175,000 soldiers by the end of the year, he would require an additional 100,000 in 1966. He anticipated that he could then compel the enemy to openly confront American and ARVN troops, exposing the Vietcong and the North Vietnamese to conventional warfare where U.S. superiority in equipment, armor, and firepower would destroy them.

Still in the hunt for a way to preserve the independence of South Vietnam without immersing the United States in an intractable morass, and mindful of the imperative to keep the country behind him, the president asked the counsel of elder statesmen, ten prominent former officials including Dean Acheson; General Omar Bradley; newspaper publisher John Cowles; Arthur Dean, Eisenhower's chief negotiator during the Korean War; industrialist Paul Hoffman; Truman secretary of defense Robert Lovett; and John McCloy, former high commissioner for Germany. To the astonishment of the White House, these old hands solidly favored strong intervention. Some even criticized the administration as "too restrained."[21] George Ball was appalled by their unthinking endorsement of a wider war. "You goddamned old bastards," he snarled at Acheson. "You remind me of nothing so much as a bunch of buzzards sitting on a fence and letting the young men die. You don't know a goddamned thing about what you're talking about. . . . You just sit there and say these irresponsible things!"[22]

LBJ kept his demons at bay and with the president's men in tow, except for George Ball, schussed farther downslope. Bolstered by opinion polls that approved of his handling of the war, he announced at a news conference that 75,000 American soldiers would shortly be in Vietnam. Behind the scenes, McNamara asked the president to increase the forces in South Vietnam to well over 175,000 while summoning 235,000 in the reserves. Ball complained that once the threshold of 100,000 was passed the limitations upon U.S. involvement would be shattered and it would easily escalate to 300,000 or 400,000. Johnson himself was not unmindful of the danger that a substantial investment might lead to an even greater commitment.

The downward spiral of fortune in Vietnam bankrupted the honeymoon between Congress and the president. The chorus of naysayers to the actions taken by the administration swelled slowly, but enlisted the president's former ally, Fulbright. LBJ for his part recruited Republicans like House Republican leader Gerald Ford. By December 1965, the Defense Department counted 184,300 troops in South Vietnam and the killed in action had mounted to 1,594.

The assumptions of Westmoreland and the airpower proponents proved incorrect. The foe refused to abandon effective guerrilla tactics and the bombing neither reduced the infiltration of men and supplies from the north nor weakened the resolve of Hanoi. Frustrated by the lack of progress, the Joint Chiefs urged air raids to strike at vital areas in North Vietnam, Hanoi, and the port of Haiphong. Mines laid off Haiphong could reduce imports, but if they sank a Soviet ship the repercussions could include military responses. McNamara and others deflected the proposals because the North Vietnamese seemed even less willing to talk while bombs fell on their country.

To Johnson's despair, McNamara advised him that it seemed likely that U.S. troop strength in Vietnam would need to increase to 400,000 in 1966 and as many as 600,000 the following year. Even with this vast infusion of combat soldiers, the secretary of defense could not guarantee victory and predicted casualties as high as a thousand a month, an underestimate.

Tactically, it was feasible to adjust the bombing campaign, ratcheting it up or down when it served policy. The ground war differed. Here the enemy often took the offensive and a purely defensive stance could allow them to seize larger portions of real estate and establish strongholds. Because the war from the air could be managed, the administration intruded into decisions about targets on the grounds, asserting that they could better judge what would have more influence upon the foe's thinking. The ebb and flow, with pauses that might entice the North Vietnamese into peace talks, became a prime target for those dissatisfied with the entire approach.

Within the administration were those who maintained that without genuine reform in the government of South Vietnam there was scant hope for a viable country. A new mantra, "pacification," infatuated a handful of individuals, including Lodge, who returned to Saigon as ambassador, Edwin Lansdale, the antiguerrilla expert now working for the CIA, and John Paul Vann, a former army officer with combat experience in Vietnam. Lieutenant General Krulak, commander of the marines in the Pacific, said he reaffirmed constantly to the military leaders that "they were aiming at the wrong target in Vietnam and that the best thing for them to do would be to address the attention of ourselves and/or our allies to the protection of the people . . . spreading security outward from the areas where the people lived and the rice would grow."[23] A moderate effort, the Hamlet Evaluation System, followed but never garnered full support. Under relentless pressure from the enemy and indifference of the South Vietnamese leaders, the administration and the top echelons of the armed forces thought largely in terms of a military solution.

From Saigon came encouraging messages. The pacification program, carving out areas free of Vietcong, supposedly was succeeding. The military pointed to ever-climbing body counts, and while at home opposition to the war grew louder, polls of the public generally indicated support for the policies. The media in Vietnam filed less happy news. An infuriated Johnson woke Dr. Frank Stanton, the CBS president, after the network broadcast a story by Morley Safer that showed a marine torching a Vietnamese hut with his cigarette lighter. LBJ lashed out at Safer as a Canadian, accused him of being a communist, and called CBS "unpatriotic . . . to put on enemy film like this."[24] The commander in chief perceived the media as an enemy. He railed that network news was slanted against him. He expressed contempt for Lippmann, scourged James Reston, even accused David Halberstam of having killed Diem. Throughout his incumbency he never eased efforts to convert doubters or use reporters to spin his version of the situation.

In mid-October 1965, the commander in chief embarked on a whirl-wind trip to win support from Asian nations. From Manila, he sneaked in a quick visit to Cam Ranh Bay, one of the major Vietnamese military bases. Air force general Thomas Weschler, a key logistics coordinator, heard the president speak. "The thing that came across to me from his talk was that he was thinking in terms of victory in Vietnam, far beyond any capability of the forces there to achieve. That's where he used the expression, 'And we'll come back with that coonskin on the wall.' I think to the commanders, who recognized what kind of war we were in—going after just the VC, rather than going after North Vietnam, and how diffi-cult that was, and how partial the victory was likely to be, it just seemed completely off key." Said Weschler, LBJ "inspired the troops. It was a won-derful thing to get everybody up and going, and saying, 'By golly, we can lick 'em.'"[25]

After consultations with people from within and without his adminis-tration, LBJ agreed to a bombing pause that began on Christmas Eve 1965. In conjunction, he solicited the help of leaders in a number of other countries and the United Nations in getting the North Vietnamese to enter negotiations. Hanoi was unimpressed and insisted that before it would meet with the United States, all American troops must be with-drawn and the political arm of the Vietcong be recognized as the "sole genuine representative of the people of South Vietnam." Altogether nine complete and seven partial halts in bombing occurred between 1965 and 1968, when Johnson ended his presidency.

Not only did the bombing pause make no difference to the North Vietnamese, it failed to assuage his congressional detractors. Doves Ful-bright and Mansfield called for an extended moratorium on airstrikes, while Senator Everett Dirksen told LBJ to "do what is necessary to win." Richard Russell lectured, "For God's sake, don't start the bombing halfway. Let them know they are in a war. We killed civilians in World War II and nobody opposed. I'd rather kill them than have American boys die. Please, Mr. President, don't get one foot back in it. Go all the way."[26]

Neither point of view gratified the commander in chief. Those who argued for a solution by throwing in more American air assets struck him as unrealistic. He shared the fears of Fulbright that the conflict might pre-cipitate a confrontation with China, but he foresaw that giving up on South Vietnam exposed him to the deadly label of an appeaser. Increas-ingly, the president hardened himself against those who preached for get-ting out as soon as possible, even if on unfavorable terms. The pace down the slippery slope accelerated.

The bombing resumed. Bowing to the arguments of the Joint Chiefs, the administration authorized more ambitious strikes that targeted petroleum dumps near Haiphong, but the North Vietnamese quickly took steps to mitigate the damage. Between 1965 and 1967, the combined air forces of the U.S. and South Vietnam dropped more than a million tons of explosives in the south and half that much in the north. McNamara publicly disagreed with Chairman of the Joint Chiefs Earle "Bus" Wheeler about the efficacy of the program. The secretary of defense said he did not believe it significantly reduced the flow of men and materials southward, while Wheeler insisted that the campaign achieved results.

The ever-mounting number of KIA devastated Johnson. Of all of the commanders in chief after World War II, he seemed to be the only one who agonized over the casualties that resulted from his decisions. He was heard to comment, "I lost 320 of my boys this week."[27] He was also tormented by the intensity of the antiwar dissent, and was astute enough to see that the events in Vietnam obscured all of his achievements in civil rights and other social legislation. At times he seemed to search for a truce. He named Averell Harriman "ambassador for peace" with the mission to promote negotiations. He told Lodge to pursue rumors of contacts between the two halves of Vietnam. However, the emphasis stayed upon military force rather than talk.

Like Truman in Korea, LBJ was mired in an intractable conflict, unable to advance or retreat. Whichever direction he chose, partisans would denounce him. The accretion of executive power was of no use in finding a solution. With Congress unwilling to challenge the president's role in making war and achieving peace, the only means of escape would seem to be through a change in the leadership.

10

TOWARD PEACE
WITH HONOR

The Lyndon Johnson era lurched toward its end. His approval rating with the public sank below 30 percent. He attributed the growing opposition to the use of U.S. troops in Vietnam to biased reporting and warned that the antiwar movement hurt the morale of the men under fire and helped the enemy. (Thirty-five years later, as the polls showed a steep decline of favorable opinion for George W. Bush, the same complaints about discouraging words came from the administration and supporters of the 2003 invasion of Iraq.) The Vietnam stalemate revealed the innate flaw that afflicted a president who engaged the nation in a war. Once the shooting began, as the dead and wounded piled up, the hubris that went with the role of commander in chief prevented any admission of error and a reversal of policy.

The intelligence Johnson received depended upon the assumptions of its sources and their commitment to the policy. LBJ clung to the wishful thinking of the CIA and his generals and admirals. Earle Wheeler, after another visit to Saigon in early 1967, reported that "the VC/NVA [Vietcong/North Vietnamese Army] can no longer hope to win militarily in South Vietnam." But less than six weeks later, Westmoreland requested an additional 200,000 troops above the total 470,000 already in country. The general also proposed expanding ground operations into Laos and Cambodia while intensifying the bombing upon the north. He even spoke of an amphibious invasion of North Vietnam, which was increasingly committing its armed forces to the conflict. American forces had become so stretched that when North Korea seized a U.S. Navy ship off its coast, the administration opted for a diplomatic solution rather than take military action (see more on this starting on page 141).

Historian and columnist Max Boot pointed to a fatal flaw in West-moreland's approach. He refused to shift the military operation into counterguerrilla forces. Instead he continued to organize large-unit search-and-destroy missions. He wanted a "well balanced, hard-hitting force de-signed to fight in sustained combat and just grind away against the enemy on a sustained basis." It was another case of the generals fighting the cur-rent war on the concepts of the last one, in this case Korea. After the war ended, North Vietnam's General Giap explained, "We were not strong enough to drive out a half-million American troops but that wasn't our aim. Our intention was to break the will of the American Government to continue the war." Boot noted, "Hanoi had accurately concluded that the war's center of gravity was American public opinion."[1]

On March 11, 1967, B-52 bombers operating from an air base in Thai-land struck at the Thainguyen iron and steel works about thirty-eight miles north of Hanoi. The air war was no longer confined to infiltration routes. In succeeding months, planes hit targets ever closer to the major population centers and eventually within Hanoi. The North Vietnamese announced that many civilians died from these raids. The resistance to American air power included MIG fighters and skilled antiaircraft artillery. A statement issued by the Senate Preparedness Investigating Subcommit-tee called for the bombing of the airfields of North Vietnam, and within a few weeks, American aircraft began dumping tons of explosives upon the bases that housed MIGs.

Simultaneously, Westmoreland addressed newspaper executives and said criticisms by antiwar individuals were convincing "the enemy to believe he can win politically what he cannot win militarily." Congres-sional dissenters McGovern, Fulbright, Robert Kennedy, and Frank Church returned fire, McGovern recalling that "most of our best generals" had warned against setting "the stage for a larger and bloodier war on the Asian mainland. . . . The glittering military solutions of the war hawks have proved to be wrong." He chided the hawks for blaming failures upon the critics.[2]

When RFK reinforced McGovern, he noted that a source of his in the Soviet Union claimed that although for some years the USSR and China had been undergoing a bitter divorce, the escalation of the war in Viet-nam was "accomplishing what we thought was impossible, because you are bringing Communist China and Russia back together again." Senators Russell Long of Louisiana and Spessard Holland of Florida defended West-moreland's position, and Frank Lausche of Ohio even urged a greater intensification of the military assaults.[3] The optimism of Lodge, West-moreland, and Wheeler infected LBJ. He denounced Robert Kennedy, now associated with the antiwar faction. "I will destroy you and everyone of your dove friends in six months," he shouted. "You'll be dead politically in six months."[4]

Johnson relied on the official intelligence fed him. Amid the rosy re-ports from Lodge and Westmoreland came disturbing word that the strength of the Vietcong battalions should be revised upward. That did not square with the picture from Saigon. The command in South Vietnam insisted it had not padded statistics or cooked the books to harmonize with their views. Body counts, infiltration numbers, bombing damage—all tended to be immersed in doubt. Post–Vietnam War research indicates that the atmosphere created by command headquarters caused many in the field as well as upper echelons to report what they believed their superiors wanted to hear. A dozen experts assembled at an isolated facility in Virginia with the task of developing an effective formula to provide reliable, usable data on war gains. They wrestled with the problem but never could come up with the means to measure data on body counts, weapons captured, or what could truly be called a pacified or unpacified area. McNamara and others have assured that no one tried to hide damaging information from the administration. But for whatever reasons, the commander in chief pro-ceeded on the basis of uncertain intelligence.

General Victor H. Krulak, who had arrived in Vietnam with the first contingents of marines, saw the nature of the war change. "When the United States first put ground forces in Vietnam in '62, the problem was one of subversive insurgency, dominated from Hanoi, but subversive insur-gency within South Vietnam. It was South Vietnamese versus Viet Cong. . . . There was no Viet Cong functional entity as big as a battalion. Then battalions began to appear in the Viet Cong lines. We came to Vietnam in 1965 and the North Vietnamese were there . . . a very good case can be made that they preceded us. . . . We began to be faced with something more than burp guns and plastic explosives . . . it gradually changed in '67, '68 and '69 where the enemy had lots of artillery and all sorts of exotic equipment [Soviet Katyusha rockets]. . . . The battle against subver-sive insurgency became a battle against two enemies, the North Vietnam-ese invasion, which was a very substantial invasion with strong logistic ties and subversive insurgency on the other. . . . It became a dual type of war. Our reaction was a standard military reaction. We weren't ready to fight the first type of war, we were reluctant to shift our gears to fight the second. But as we shifted to fight the second [the North Vietnamese invasion], our tendency was to forget the first."[5]

Command and control within Vietnam sputtered due to differences on strategy among the branches of U.S. services plus the attitudes of the South Vietnamese military. Westmoreland was known as the man in charge but actually he served under Admiral Ulysses Grant Sharp Jr., commander in chief of the Pacific Fleet. While Sharp knew enough not to interfere with ground forces, the arrangement added a speed bump for major decisions. David Jones, named deputy commander for Vietnam operations by the air force, said of the diverse forces, "Each tended to fight its own war. . . . People say things change when you get in a war and everything works out. That wasn't true in Vietnam. We had just as many roles and missions problems . . . control of air never got resolved. A Band-Aid was put over it as to who controlled what air. . . . It was papered over as though the problem had been solved; it certainly had not.

"We fought five air wars there. In the north, we divided the country down—east portion Navy, west portion out of CINCPACFLT [Sharp's fleet command], western Vietnam out of Pacific Air Forces, B-52s out of SAC [Strategic Air Command], Marines by the Marine commander . . . Seventh Air Force under MACV [Military Assistance Command Vietnam], Sixth Air Force being the Vietnamese Air Force." Jones remarked that it was not a matter of personalities but procedures and fear of setting precedents that would impact elsewhere.[6]

Krulak commented on the proliferation of intelligence. "Everybody had his G-2 and nobody's G-2 talked with complete candor with anybody else's G-2. Whether it be the Vietnamese intelligence or the Central Intelligence Agency or the National Security Agency or the MACV or 7th Air Force Intelligence or II Corps Intelligence . . . or our embassy, or the Vietnamese government or their CIA, there were so many intelligence agencies . . . and so little intelligence coordination . . . that ours was a famine of plenty."[7]

Above all there were the twelve-thousand-mile tethers that stretched from the White House and the Pentagon, with the commander in chief and the secretary of defense yanking the strings. While acutely aware of political ramifications, neither knew military tactics, strategy, or equipment.

The rules of engagement frustrated the warriors. Jones recalled, "When you went to some of the passes up north, right on the border of North Vietnam and Laos, you could bomb on the Laotian side. You could go over and hit on the [North] Vietnamese side only if they had fired first.

We did some trolling. An O-2 [observation plane] would be fired at and there would be no air power around at that point and there wasn't any way to counterattack. . . . We would have an O-2 do a little trolling up there when fighters were right over the rise and zap! We almost called the lawyers in to see if this was legal . . . the civilians were imposing restrictions. They didn't understand the impact or what it really meant."[8]

Admiral Harry D. Train, executive assistant to Moorer during his stints as chief of naval operations and chairman of the Joint Chiefs of Staff, recalled, "McNamara tended to make rather simplistic decisions, based on advice he'd get from fairly inexperienced military people. An example was his conviction that it was dangerous to fly high in a Vigilante [North American A-5, a carrier-based bomber converted for photo recon] making a reconnaissance run over a target after you've attacked the target. Therefore, you had to do all your bomb damage assessment runs below a thousand feet . . . below 500 feet as a matter of fact. We had some of those Vigilantes shot right out of the sky flying below ridge lines. They were getting shot at by people with small arms. . . . It just drove the operators crazy to be getting that type of direction."[9]

Admiral Sharp talked of the frustration among the commanders on the scene. "Rolling Thunder was . . . a limited campaign designed by Washington to place enough military pressure on North Vietnam to halt their support of insurgents in South Vietnam and Laos . . . the strike day was specified and it was mandatory that the Vietnamese air force participate, the number of sorties on each target was specified, and you couldn't vary from this without prior justification. Only the primary target or one or two alternates would be attacked, pre-strike reconnaissance was prohibited, maximum feasible damage had to be achieved by a single strike. You could not recycle your aircraft . . . send them back to land and take on fuel and ammo and come back. Bomb damage assessment aircraft had to accompany strike aircraft, and then subsequent bomb damage assessment had to be accomplished without escort . . . and there could be no armed reconnaissance.

"As Rolling Thunder went on, and in accord with repeated requests . . . we gradually gained operational flexibility to some degree. I repeatedly had to inform the JCS that their restrictions were denying the full benefit that operations might achieve . . . the JCS knew this full well, but they were being held down by higher authority in Washington."[10]

The president's popularity sagged. He stuck to his policy, however, as CIA assessments depicted a battle-weary North Vietnam. He attributed the rising fever of the antiwar movement to communist instigators. On one occasion, increasingly intemperate when questioned about Vietnam by several reporters in a private meeting, according to United Nations ambassador Arthur Goldberg, "LBJ unzipped his fly, drew out his substantial organ, and declared, 'This is why.'"[11] He chastised a reporter, "What kind of chicken-shit question is that to ask the leader of the free world!"

In spite of the reports of gains, the president remained vexed by what was being seen as a stalemate. By this time, McNamara's doubts had morphed him into a dove. He recommended capping the ground forces at 525,000, halting the bombing, and transferring responsibilities for combat to the South Vietnamese. The strategy obviously portended an exit. The break with the direction of the administration led to McNamara's departure to become head of the World Bank.

Significantly, Johnson replaced McNamara with Clark Clifford, whom he knew to have doubts about the strategy of deploying U.S. military force to preserve the integrity of South Vietnam. Soon after he became secretary of defense, Clifford questioned requests from Saigon and the Joint Chiefs for further infusions of Americans. The president accepted Clifford's stance.

As his approval rating for handling Vietnam sank into the low 30s, the president took steps to boost his standing. The administration touted a "withdrawal strategy" predicated upon an escalation of force that would lead to "peace with honor." In his eyes, that required a guaranteed noncommunist South Vietnam. He told interviewer David Brinkley, who asked why the United States couldn't just leave, "I'm not going to be the first American President to lose a war."[12]

On January 23, 1968, a confrontation with North Korea erupted as the Pyongyang regime seized the USS *Pueblo*, an intelligence ship plying the waters off Korea. One sailor was killed when he resisted the boarding party, and the other eighty-two members of the crew were taken prisoner. The commander in chief immediately authorized the call-up of fourteen thousand reservists from the navy and air force, a move that did not divert assets from the Vietnam theater.

The U.S. Navy insisted the *Pueblo* had been operating in international waters, beyond the twelve-mile limit, while the North Koreans claimed the intelligence vessel had trespassed. Although the mission orders to the American ship specified it should approach no closer to the limit than one mile, it is quite possible that either side could have been mistaken. Precise determination of distance offshore is a tricky matter. The North Koreans, after capturing the *Pueblo*, published what they said were the navigation charts, clearly showing the ship in their space, but the validity of this proof could never be ascertained. The crew, when ultimately released, insisted they were outside the territorial waters of North Korea.

The White House reacted with great restraint at what some described as an act of piracy on the high seas. When the North Koreans announced that they would try the crew as criminals, the commander in chief said, "We could not allow our indignation to dictate our response, even though that is the course many Americans would have preferred. Some members of Congress were also demanding strong action."[13]

Had the *Pueblo* incident occurred before the Tonkin Gulf events, said Admiral Moorer, "We would have been fighting in North Korea instead of Vietnam. But Johnson and McNamara just couldn't bring themselves to take them both on at once in light of the public attitude at that time when the country was damned near in a state of anarchy. I used to look out [the] window and see Washington burning and people lying down in front of cars, throwing rocks at the FBI building and throwing pig blood at the Pentagon steps . . . and a hundred thousand gathering around the Washington monument."[14] While the nation's capital saw its share of anti-war demonstrations and several riots, it was hardly in the constant state of anarchy that Moorer implied.

LBJ justified his attempts to resolve the *Pueblo* contretemps through diplomatic means because he wanted to bring the crew home alive and avoid "dead bodies." Eventually the Soviet Union agreed to use its influence for a peaceful resolution. The sailors of the *Pueblo* would suffer eleven months of harsh treatment before coming home in December 1968. To gain their freedom, the United States issued an apology to North Korea for intruding upon its domain. However, once the men were freed, the statement was retracted.

Rumors of a big offensive by the enemy in early 1968 encouraged the military to hope for the type of showdown in which American firepower would inflict a decisive defeat. But instead of focusing on the base at Khe Sanh, as predicted, during the Tet religious holiday, the Vietcong and North Vietnamese forces struck at thirty-six of the South Vietnamese provincial capitals and five of its biggest cities, including Saigon. They hit the U.S. embassy, the huge Tan Son Nhut Air Base, and the presidential palace. The troops in the Saigon area broke the offensive there, but the ancient citadel of Hue fell and it required almost four weeks of counterattacks to oust the enemy.

The Tet offensive was actually a major military defeat for the Vietcong and North Vietnamese. Their estimated dead ranged from thirty-three thousand to fifty-eight thousand, with tens of thousands more wounded or captured. During the two-month period from the onset the American dead added up to four thousand, with five thousand South Vietnamese KIA. The insurgent forces also murdered many civilians. The vast deployment of the foe's forces, far beyond what intelligence believed available, stunned the White House. The battles also shocked the American public, which had been led to believe that the enemy had been reduced to hit-and-run operations.

The commander in chief, while calling Tet a military debacle for the enemy, said, "But the defeat the Communists suffered did not have the telling effect it should have had largely because of what we did to our-selves."[15] He attributed much of the blame for the loss of American resolve to the "emotional and exaggerated reporting" of the media and "the cho-rus of defeatism" warbled by senatorial critics and opponents of the war effort.

Undaunted by the lack of progress, unresponsive to the antipathy to the war, and ignoring the congressional hearings that unmasked the facts behind the alleged 1964 incidents in the Gulf of Tonkin, Westmoreland importuned the White House for another two hundred thousand soldiers. Fulbright, in full retreat from his role four years earlier, declared the Gulf of Tonkin Resolution "null and void," like "any contract based on misrep-resentation." He apologized to his colleagues for his role in shepherding the legislation through the Senate.[16]

In March 1968 it had become apparent to the commander in chief that, in the words of McNamara, "He had . . . seen the pursuit of military victory in Vietnam for what it was—an illusion."[17] In the historic tele-vised speech where he announced he would not seek reelection, he said he would grant only a token increase in the numbers of the American military in South Vietnam. He clearly rejected the requests of the Joint Chiefs and their commanders for major reinforcements, and he proposed to expand the South Vietnamese forces, making the war their responsibil-ity. He would order a halt to the bombing of North Vietnam in hopes of jump-starting a peace process. North Vietnam agreed to begin talks in Paris with American representatives.

The controversy over the right direction for the United States in Southeast Asia, which erupted in the streets and disrupted campuses, the ever-mounting casualties, the need to raise taxes to finance the war, and a backlash over Johnson's civil rights legislation ripped the Democratic Party apart. Senator Eugene McCarthy from Minnesota, a strong opponent of continuance of the war, emerged as a challenger for the nomination to suc-ceed Johnson. The assassination of Robert Kennedy, who belatedly decided to seek his party's favor, gave the Democratic nomination to Vice President Humphrey, a reluctant supporter of LBJ's Vietnam policy.

Richard M. Nixon, perceived as a callow Red-baiter while a congressman, then an inconsequential vice president to Eisenhower, a loser in his quest for the presidency against John F. Kennedy, followed by a crushing defeat in a 1962 try to become governor of California, had resurrected himself. He came back to a Republican Party anxious to avoid another humiliating rebuke from the voters after their firm rejection of the perceived extremism of Barry Goldwater.

Like Johnson, Nixon sprang from humble beginnings, growing up poor during the Great Depression. But he lifted himself up to become a naval lieutenant during World War II, and graduated from Duke Law School before entering Congress, helped by a smear campaign against his opponent. Although he resented the eastern establishment, the New England patricians and their Ivy League backgrounds, he stifled his dislike sufficiently to join a Wall Street law firm while out of office.

He was an intelligent, well-read student of world history, and although an ardent anticommunist, a pragmatist rather than an ideologue. That inclination to rely on whatever worked instead of blind adherence to principles, coupled with a touch of the paranoia that hurt his predecessor, tempted him into machinations that eventually wrought his downfall.

Nixon entered the race for the White House with a reputation as an inflexible hawk. As vice president under Eisenhower he had urged the use of American military force against the insurgency in French Indochina. As he began his self-rehabilitation project in 1965 he still preached the gospel of armed resistance to ensure a secure and independent South Vietnam. But in 1968 he saw a public dispirited by the ongoing conflict. He artfully played the issue from both sides, criticizing the Johnson administration's frittering away the country's military power by the policy of gradualism and claiming that an all-out exercise of military strength "could have ended it [the war] with far less than we are now using." That of course was purely an opinion with no evidence to back it up. In the same speech, he called for stronger diplomatic efforts, in tacit recognition that military action would no longer achieve the desired ends.[18] While he never said he had a "secret plan to end the war," he did vow to end it and win the peace.

Hubert Humphrey's campaign underwent severe buffeting from the commander in chief he hoped to succeed. The Paris peace talks broke down and the president renewed the bombing, based upon reports of an imminent offensive by the North Vietnamese. The decision undercut the vice president's promotion of a negotiated settlement. At the Chicago convention, a furious struggle that spilled into the streets fractured the Democratic Party, and a minority led by McGovern and Eugene McCarthy battled the majority obedient to the will of LBJ. The hard-liners defeated a proposal for an immediate cessation of bombing, a mutual withdrawal of all U.S. and North Vietnamese forces from South Vietnam, and a negotiated settlement.

On election day, Nixon became commander in chief–elect. As the Democrats surrendered the White House, the U.S. killed in action in Vietnam reached 30,568, ninety-nine percent of whom died during the period from 1964 to 1968.

Nixon chose Dr. Henry Kissinger to serve as his national security adviser. A refugee from Austria who served in army intelligence during World War II, a Harvard academic, and most recently a tutor to Nelson Rockefeller on foreign policy, Kissinger, judging by his writings, admired Austria-Hungary's Crown Prince Metternich. Metternich had presided over the Congress of Vienna in 1814–1815 and in Kissinger's view brought nearly fifty years of peace to Europe with his balance-of-power negotiations that preserved the dominance of Austria-Hungary. That the arrangement oppressed millions and sowed the seeds of World War I did not disturb Kissinger. Like his new boss, he brought a broad knowledge of foreign affairs and a duplicity that Machiavelli would have envied. Throughout his career he wooed the media with self-deprecating jibes.

I interviewed the new national security adviser several months after he took up station in the White House basement. During our talks he criticized the civil disobedience of young people opposed to the war in Vietnam, saying that civil disobedience should be reserved only for issues of the "highest moral order." When we spoke of campus disturbances, specifically at Harvard, where some students barred entrance to the buildings, he expressed outrage. "That is fascism!" Considering that Cambridge saw one of the mildest protests and the war involved the killing of human beings, I was confused about what he thought was an issue of the highest moral order.

Lyndon Johnson justly earned a reputation for manipulation and shading the truth, qualities in fact common to many presidents. Nixon was no less adept at such management of people and facts. However, he also sought by devious means to tweak minds. "He believed there was advantage in persuading adversaries, foreign and domestic, that there was something irrational about him, that he was a dangerous man capable of any retaliation, up to and including the use of nuclear weapons."[19] He encouraged others to believe in what he termed "the madman theory." He told H. R. Haldeman, his chief of staff, "I want the North Vietnamese to believe I've reached the point where I might do *anything* [his emphasis] to stop the war. We'll just slip the word to them that, 'for God's sake, you know Nixon is obsessed about Communism. We can't restrain him when he's angry—and he has his hand on the nuclear button'—and Ho Chi Minh himself will be in Paris in two days begging for peace."[20] Ho Chi Minh missed the point; it would be five years before negotiations ended U.S. participation, and no one begged for peace.

However, Richard Nixon was anything but irrational. Moorer, who chaired the Joint Chiefs during both the Johnson and Nixon administrations, said that under the latter the National Security Council functioned like the board of a corporation, with subcommittees that met regularly, Kissinger always in the chairman's seat. "If there [was] 100 percent agreement over the issue . . . then authority was granted by the President to go ahead and take action. If there were differences of opinion between Defense and State, for instance, then it was taken up by the National Security Council. The President would open the meeting and he would turn it over to Kissinger [who] would state the issue. . . . Then the President would canvass the people in the room . . . I never saw him make a decision on the spot. He would thank everybody and return to the Oval Office. Some time during the day you would get a NSCDM—National Security Council Decision Memorandum. It would start out, 'The President has decided we're going to do such and such.'"[21]

An issue even before Nixon officially took office concerned Cambodia, along the five-hundred-mile-long western border of Vietnam. Back in 1965, Westmoreland, supported by Ambassador Lodge, had requested authorization for U.S. and South Vietnamese soldiers to cross the border with Cambodia and destroy enemy sanctuaries from which it was claimed hit-and-run attacks came. The State Department, with LBJ's concurrence, refused permission. Americans could shoot into Cambodia only if fired upon from across the border. However, they could enter the country in self-defense. Reporters on the scene thought they detected a new policy with the term "self-defense," a stance that clearly opened the border to trespass. The administration hastily affirmed its policy to respect the sovereignty of Cambodia. At the time, December 1965, the press revealed that American aircraft had been engaged in defoliation raids on the Ho Chi Minh Trail in Laos and B-52s had struck the infiltration routes in that country.

U.S. Special Forces, the counterinsurgency warfare experts expanded in the time of John F. Kennedy, had since 1967 undertaken reconnaissance missions to find the bases in Cambodia and Laos. The teams, code-named Daniel Boone, included several Americans, as well as local mercenaries. Inserted by helicopter, they pierced Cambodia along its five-hundred-mile-long border and confirmed the existence of hard-surfaced roads, bunkers, and large camps for the enemy.

General Creighton Abrams, a tank commander during World War II, had succeeded Westmoreland as the commander of the forces in South Vietnam. Abrams said the North Vietnamese shipped supplies directly to Laos but materials from China, Russia, and Eastern Europe arrived in Cambodia's Sihanoukville for offloading and then traveled to the front in South Vietnam. In the final years of the Johnson presidency, air force planes routinely bombed Laos, even during the planned pauses of strikes at North Vietnam, in an attempt to interdict supply lines. Abrams credited the campaign with drying up the enemy's resources. However, he said, "The enemy is getting more through this year than last year. The results of air action are higher this year than last year, because the enemy has more trucks in the system and we have more gunships which are great truck killers." He also remarked that the foe was in better shape this year. "All of the North Vietnam logistical structure was in good shape. He had moved his supplies to the border in readiness, had his fuel storage areas ready, and had taken all necessary actions to get started when the roads opened." It was an admission (secret when given) that the bombing campaign against North Vietnam had not degraded the country's military potential.[22]

Abrams believed that Cambodia housed a headquarters that directed the North Vietnamese and Vietcong fighting across the border. After carrying out attacks in South Vietnam, bands of black-pajama-clad troops, according to U.S. intelligence, escaped into the thickly canopied jungles of Cambodia. Furthermore, the Ho Chi Minh Trail supply line from the north led through Laos and then into Cambodia before soldiers and supplies moved into South Vietnam.

Abrams asked for massive B-52 raids upon the sanctuaries. Rogers and Kissinger debated the wisdom and timing of Operation Menu, a secret attack (insofar as the American public and other countries would be concerned). The secretaries of state and defense opposed widening the war and arousing opposition in Congress and the media. Nixon vacillated until March 15, 1970, when he notified Kissinger that he was ordering B-52s from Guam to raid Cambodia.

Only on the following day did Nixon discuss with Secretary of State William Rogers, Secretary of Defense Melvin Laird, and Joint Chiefs chairman Earle Wheeler whether or not to bomb Cambodia. He spoke of the more than one thousand Americans killed during the previous three weeks of enemy offensives and he called the meetings of diplomats in Paris "completely sterile."[23] He explained that short of a resumption of bombing North Vietnam, this was the only means to reinvigorate the peace talks. Laird objected only to the insistence that Menu be kept secret. He did not believe it possible to conceal such a venture. Wheeler endorsed the raids. Rogers remained adamant that the operation would damage the prospects for peace talks.

Nixon did not tell his audience that even as they discussed the matter, the bombers were already on their way. Congress was not consulted. To hide the action further, an elaborate scheme faked the paperwork detailing the targeting of the objectives. The purpose of the secrecy was not only to prevent criticism by Congress and avoid feeding fresh fodder to the antiwar movement but also to protect Cambodian ruler Prince Norodom Sihanouk from the need to protest the violation of his country's neutrality. Sihanouk resented the use of his territory by the North Vietnamese but was in no position to object. Kissinger scoffed at the notion of Menu as breaching the wall that defines a neutral state. He asserted that as many as four North Vietnamese divisions operated from within that country with impunity.

The national security adviser claimed intelligence indicated that the indigenous Cambodians were either sparse in number or were excluded entirely from the areas used by the enemy. In fact, three of the identified sanctuary areas held such sizable concentrations of civilians around them that they were not recommended for attacks. Well over a thousand people lived near several sites that were hit. Kissinger said Abrams reported that the headquarters location lay at least a kilometer distant from any known Cambodian hamlets. A thousand yards or so hardly provides a substantial enough margin to avoid drops by high-altitude B-52s.

Sixty B-52s dumped tons of ordnance upon Cambodia, Laos, and the Ho Chi Minh Trail, arousing exuberance in Kissinger. Although the new commander in chief had pledged to change the approach, his record and comments reveal an unambiguous belief in war as usual. "During the first months of the administration," said Nixon, "despite the Communist offensive in February and despite the stalemate at the Paris talks, I remained convinced that the combined effect of the military pressure from the secret bombing and the public pressure from my repeated invitations to negotiate would force the Communists to respond. In March I confidently told the Cabinet that I expected the war to be over in a year."[24]

Nixon, in his memoirs, said that following the attacks on Cambodia, the pace of action by the enemy declined significantly. But at the same time the operation became the overture for a series of ugly acts to halt leaks. *New York Times* correspondent William Beecher had heard a theory that attacks on the enemy installations in Cambodia might lead to a way out of Vietnam. When the Defense Department issued reports of bombing near the border, he realized that no military targets lay in that area and pursued the notion that the real objectives lay in Cambodia. His stories, first printed at the end of March and then in detail on May 9, infuriated Kissinger and Nixon. FBI director J. Edgar Hoover was asked to find Beecher's sources, using illegal wiretaps. Kissinger said he and the president were outraged by Beecher's scoop because "press leaks of military operations were needlessly jeopardizing American lives."[25] Certainly, it was not news to the North Vietnamese and the Cambodians that aircraft were raining bombs on them. In what way the stories put Americans any further in harm's way he never explained.

On April 15, 1969, North Korean MIGs shot down a navy intelligence-gathering plane with thirty-one men aboard off the North Korean coast. When the North Koreans had captured the *Pueblo* a year earlier, Nixon in full political attack mode had scolded the Johnson administration for failure to retaliate. "When . . . a fourth rate military power like Korea will seize an American naval vessel on the high seas, it's time for new leadership to restore respect for the United States." With the shoot-down of the navy aircraft, however, as president, Nixon had responsibilities far beyond that of an opposition candidate. According to Alexander Haig, now an NSC staffer, Nixon's first reaction was that "force must be met with force."[26] Kissinger was equally belligerent, arguing that if the commander in chief did not act, "They will think you a weakling."[27]

Both Laird and Rogers, the secretaries of defense and state, and their aides objected to precipitous action. They ridiculed the national security adviser's description of a "surgical strike," a favorite locution by armchair militarists who have no concept of the lack of precision with even the smartest of bombs and the attendant collateral damage. They cautioned that an attack upon the offender might trigger a renewed war between the Koreas. Monitoring of electronic intelligence indicated the *Pueblo* incident to have been a carefully planned operation, but this time the National Security Agency radio intercepts, provided to the president only, suggested the shoot-down might have been a mistake when a pilot fired due to communications errors with his controllers.[28] None of this calmed the commander in chief, who wanted to smite the North Koreans but gave up when he learned it would require five days to ready an airstrike.

In his memoirs, Nixon made no mention of intelligence intercepts but said he was convinced that this was not the moment to act because of the huge involvement in Vietnam. "If . . . we suddenly found ourselves at war in Korea . . . we simply did not have the resources or public support for another war in another place."[29]

In Paris, where the first attempts to find a peaceful solution had begun in May 1968, the Vietcong representatives publicly declared their terms for a settlement. These specified the total evacuation of all U.S. forces, free elections, a new constitution, and a coalition government that included them. The president rejected the proposal but countered with his own blueprint. He suggested a cease-fire followed by a mutually agreed-upon phased reduction in South Vietnam of the armed forces from both sides. Although he refused to accept unilateral withdrawal of the U.S. troops, the commander in chief indicated a drawdown of the American military, with the substitution of South Vietnamese forces on the fighting fronts.

While the posture hinted at a revision in approach, in fact the president's terms provided no compromise. The ground war in South Vietnam raged on, with appalling casualties. In Paris, McGovern met representatives of North Vietnam and the National Liberation Front, the political arm of the insurgents. He reported to the Senate that their basic prerequisites for peace required unconditional withdrawal of all American forces from Vietnam. They would not accept a mutual withdrawal since they considered only the U.S. military foreigners. Said McGovern, "I have no doubt . . . that if we began withdrawing our troops while moving toward a defensive, cease-fire strategy, the other side would quickly respond by easing off their military pressure." He had been assured that rather than a bloodbath after an American retreat, the killing would stop.[30]

In July 1969, while Kissinger secretly engaged in talks with North Vietnam's Xuan Thuy, the president, on an around-the-world trip, spoke to reporters on Guam. He enunciated what later became known as the "Nixon Doctrine." Acknowledging that previously the United States had committed armed forces, money, and matériel to protect other countries against communism, henceforth nations would be required to furnish their own troops.

The president still clung to a position that had more in common with the hawks than the doves. In September 1969 he told a delegation of

Republican congressmen, "I am approaching the whole question with only two operating principles: I won't make it hard for the North Vietnamese if they genuinely want a settlement; but I will not be the first President of the United States to lose a war,"[31] a perfect replica of the sentiments of his predecessor.

Nixon and Kissinger, upon whom he increasingly relied, strove to achieve peace with honor by overt and covert actions. Laird promoted the notion of "Vietnamization," in which the indigenous people would gradually assume the military tasks filled by Americans, while Rogers stressed the idea of advancing the Paris peace talks. Kissinger, however, preached the gospel of the iron fist. "He felt that if we backed off," Nixon recalled, "the Communists would become totally convinced that they could control our foreign policy through public opinion."[32]

In June the commander in chief, after a meeting with Nguyen Van Thieu, the South Vietnamese president, announced that twenty-five thousand U.S. troops would be brought home in August. Nixon invited North Vietnam to follow suit. The gesture provoked no encouragement from the enemy. It was a mere 5 percent reduction. At most it bought the president a bit of time from those wavering in support for the war. He also hoped to dampen some of the antiwar ardor by calling for an all-volunteer military, which would come to pass in 1971.

In fact, Nixon threatened to escalate the war beyond previous levels. Through a French emissary, on July 15, he sent a personal message to Ho Chi Minh in which he said, "Unless some serious breakthrough had been achieved by the November 1 deadline, I would regretfully find myself obliged to have recourse to measures of great consequence and force." It was what he called a "go for broke" strategy. "I would attempt to end the war one way or another, either by negotiated agreement or by an increased use of force."[33]

The "measures of great consequence and force" described Operation Duck Hook, "a massive series of air raids upon Hanoi, Haiphong, and other industrial areas plus mining of harbors and rivers." The plan drawn up on instructions from Kissinger plotted destruction of North Vietnam's dike system, flooding the countryside, and possibly an invasion in which tactical nuclear weapons would not be excluded. Kissinger, in fact, had written a book espousing "limited nuclear war instead of the John Foster Dulles doctrine of massive retaliation."

To follow up on his message to Ho, the president dispatched Kissinger to Paris for an attempt at secret negotiations, the kind of task that the national security adviser relished. However, the North Vietnamese representative, Xuan Thuy, obdurately refused anything less than the departure of the American forces and the removal of Thieu and Ky as South Vietnam's heads of state. It was an impasse, and with the monsoon season ending, the guerrillas intensified their attacks. Kissinger observed, "The most generous interpretation could not avoid the conclusion that Hanoi did not believe in gestures, negotiation, goodwill or reciprocity."[34]

On September 4, Ho Chi Minh died, but not before he firmly rebuffed the feelers extended by the president. Pham Van Dong, the new premier, showed no inclination to change the policies of his predecessor. Despite the tumult in the streets and on the campuses, the president still bathed in approval by a majority of the people. His withdrawal of the twenty-five thousand men and the bombing pauses, instituted by Johnson, seemed to mark progress toward peace. However, at the same time, he had charted a much more vigorous application of force. The change at the top had not diminished the expanded power of the chief executive.

11

PIECES OF PEACE

U nable to bring North Vietnam to its knees or at least lessen its resolve amid truce talks, the Nixon-Kissinger administration looked to widen the war, increasing the pressure on the enemy by striking at previously immune assets. The commander in chief rebuffed attempts by Congress to challenge his authority for the stepped-up use of force and invasions of Laos and Cambodia. In fact, the inability to restrain the chief executive emboldened him to wield his power elsewhere. The White House shrugged off evidence of misconduct and atrocities by Americans in Vietnam. At the same time, the CIA extended its proactive operations into Chile.

The recalcitrance of Hanoi coupled with his promises to draw down the American military presence in Vietnam caught Nixon in a bind. Renewed offensive operations would unleash an avalanche of criticism from members of Congress and in the streets. Even Republicans questioned the American deployment. However, he had threatened the North Vietnamese with serious consequences if they did not engage in negotiations. If he did not follow through, the chances of what he considered an honorable peace were nonexistent.

The commander in chief tried to hedge his bets. He postponed the Kissinger-sponsored Duck Hook offensive and announced that another sixty thousand Americans would leave Vietnam by December 15. That enabled the suspension of draft calls for the final two months of the year. But the doves were on the hunt and they unsheathed the major weapon of Congress—control of the purse. Representative Charles Goodell introduced an amendment to a foreign assistance bill that would deny further funds for the war. A trickle of similar bills would drop into the hopper.

Kissinger confided to the commander in chief, "I am not optimistic about the ability of the South Vietnamese armed forces to assume a larger part of the burden than current MACV [Military Assistance Command

Vietnam] plans allow."[1] Meanwhile, Fulbright and McGovern spearheaded the mounting criticism of the administration for the lack of progress in ending the war. Massive demonstrations, demanding a moratorium on American involvement, climaxed on October 15, 1969, choking the streets in a number of cities across the country. A quarter of a million people invaded the nation's capital.

To counter the antiwar tide and simultaneously signal to North Vietnam that he did not intend to buckle, on November 3 Nixon delivered an historic speech. He invoked the "silent majority," the vast segment of the public that he believed supported him but were being drowned out by the noise of the minority. Explaining his policy, he flat-out lied with a claim that in 1965 he had opposed LBJ's deployment of troops to South Vietnam. "There are some who urged that I end the war at once. This would have been a popular and easy course to follow"—a rhetorical flourish that established him as a leader who does not rely on the vagaries of opinion, but at the same time his disdain for "a popular and easy course" implied he did not have a silent majority behind him. Like his predecessors and successors he raised the specter of national prestige. "The first defeat in our nation's history would result in a collapse of confidence in American leadership, not only in Asia but throughout the world." It was a successful performance. A poll showed Nixon's approval rating up from 52 percent before Moratorium Day to 68 percent.[2]

Placating the public and stamping out the brushfires of opposition in Congress constantly demanded Nixon's attention. A bitter internecine war raged between his national security adviser and his secretaries of defense and state. Rogers often evaluated military actions from the effects upon relationships with other countries. Kissinger and Laird frequently played soldiers, advocating operations for their strategic value as well as their influence upon enemy thinking.

In all wars, on both sides, omnipresent fear, a kill-or-be-killed ambience, the agonizing spectacles of deaths of friends breed atrocities. With the battle for hearts and minds in the United States raging as fiercely as in country, the commander in chief coped with horror stories. The image of a marine captain torching a hut—"We had to destroy the village to save it"—paled alongside revelations of premeditated murder by American forces.

Rumors of possible gross misconduct by Green Berets surfaced in August, and on September 19, 1969, the New York Times ran a story that the army planned to court-martial six of the Special Forces troops including a decorated West Point graduate, Colonel Robert Rheault, commander of the forty-five hundred Green Berets in South Vietnam. Allegedly the

Americans had discovered an interpreter was a double agent. Unable to obtain a confession, the Green Berets, on Rheault's orders, checked with CIA headquarters in Saigon. According to the troops, the intelligence operatives unofficially offered three options: fire the suspect, restore him to duty, or "get rid of him." The Special Forces chose the last solution and a captain shot the man dead. Within hours, Theodore Shackley, the CIA station chief, called Rheault to warn against "termination with extreme prejudice," the CIA lingo for assassination.

With the corpse of the accused already dumped in the South China Sea, Rheault answered that he couldn't contact him because he was on a mission. Shackley did not believe him and informed Creighton Abrams and Ambassador Ellsworth Bunker. Abrams summoned the head of the Green Berets, who insisted he knew nothing about the missing translator. Abrams subsequently labeled him a liar and ordered a court-martial on charges of murder.

At the White House, Pat Buchanan, who prepared daily news summaries, flagged the story as trouble for the administration, the U.S. Army, the Special Forces, and the policy in Vietnam. The Americans had hired civilian attorneys from the United States for their defense, and one of them, Henry Rothblatt, indicated he would subpoena top officials. The president told Kissinger to persuade Secretary of the Army Stanley Resor and Abrams to drop the matter. They refused. Resor said, "The CIA and the U.S. Army simply do not do business as the men in this case did. Spies are not taken out and killed without due process of law."[3]

Congress stepped into the matter. Albert Watson of South Carolina wrote a private letter to Melvin Laird arguing that all charges should be dropped. "If these brave soldiers continue to be held, the morale of the American fighting man, not only in Vietnam today, but for generations to come, will be irreparably damaged." A group of legislators sent a letter to Resor protesting the way in which the Military Assistance Command had handled the affair. Laird, Westmoreland as army chief of staff, Wheeler as chairman of the Joint Chiefs, Deputy Secretary of Defense David Packard, and the director of the CIA, Richard Helms, all wanted the case to disappear.[4]

Ultimately, the administration quashed the case through Helms. The president instructed Haldeman to obtain a letter from Helms in which the spymaster said the agency would refuse to provide any witnesses on the grounds of executive privilege involving national security.

No amount of behind the scenes arm-twisting, however, could conceal another ghastly story. During the 1968 Tet offensive, which occurred on

LBJ's watch, an army platoon, led by Lieutenant William L. Calley Jr., entered a village known as My Lai 4. The soldiers opened fire, killing an undetermined number of villagers, including women and children. Accounts in the army newspaper *Stars and Stripes* and the *New York Times* had claimed the soldiers had surrounded enemy troops and killed 128. After a soldier who observed the incident reported what actually happened, an army investigation discovered that some women had been raped before being shot.

On November 17, a piece by *Times* reporter Seymour Hersh about the court-martial of Calley, charging 567 had died, greatly disturbed Nixon. He had been made aware of the plan to try Calley and approved. But the immense publicity that now surrounded the case, coming while he was beset by the antiwar adherents, drove him into a tirade that included the remark, "It's those dirty rotten New York Jews."[5] George McGovern became an unlikely defender of the lieutenant, describing Calley as a scapegoat for circumstances that invited such deeds. McGovern, recalling his World War II experience as a bomber pilot, compared what happened to My Lai with air raids or artillery shells that destroyed villages and cities. The trial dragged on until March 1970, when Calley received a life sentence to hard labor in prison.

The *New York Times* quoted James M. Gavin, the highly decorated commander of the 82nd Airborne during World War II and a Kennedy adviser: "[The conviction is] devastating in its implications for the morale of the Army. Junior officers are bound to feel that they're carrying the terrible burden of the war. That the buck stops with them."[6]

Moorer, now chairman of the Joint Chiefs, said, "I personally felt that the Army over-reacted in an effort to come clean . . . that was the nature of the national attitude in those days. . . . My Lai, in my view, was inevitable in the way the war was being fought . . . the national policy was that we were not going to invade North Vietnam. That automatically meant that all the American boys were going to have to fight . . . where it was almost impossible to distinguish friend from foe. You never knew what a woman had, a hand grenade in her brassiere or in a baby's diaper."[7]

After leaving office, Nixon wrote, "Calley's crime was inexcusable. But I felt that many of the commentators and congressmen who professed outrage about My Lai were not really as interested in the moral questions raised by the Calley case as they were interested in using it to make political attacks against the Vietnam war." He complained that atrocities by the enemy did not receive the same attention or censure. He used his authority as commander in chief to release Calley from the stockade and confine him to quarters, pending his appeal.

Amid these dramatic distractions, the battle for control of South Vietnam staggered on. Vietnamization equipped an indigenous army of more than one million with an impressive array of the latest weapons. Unfortunately, no matter how many wore the uniform and carried the best tools for war, the South Vietnamese Army just couldn't fight that well. In January 1970, shortly before one of the frustrating sessions with the enemy in Paris, Kissinger warned, "We have not seen proof that ARVN [the South Vietnamese Army] has really improved."[8] Although the U.S. troops' numbers were shrinking, the bulk of the combat still involved them.

The critics, aware of the deficiencies of Vietnamization through leaks from junior officials in Southeast Asia and Washington and from the accounts by journalists on the scene, suspected that instead of winding down the conflict, the administration intended to expand the scope of the war into Laos with the aim of halting North Vietnamese exploitation there, abetted by the communist Pathet Lao. American planes from Thailand and bases within Laos struck at the NVA and Pathet Lao, who were staging forces and moving supplies through the country. Actually, Americans, sometimes in uniform and sometimes not, had fought in Laos since the days of John F. Kennedy, trying to prop up an independent government friendly to the United States. A CIA subsidiary, Air America, with a hundred and fifty aircraft and six hundred pilots, flew missions in Laos.

Rumors of American ground forces operating in Laos sprang up, and the commander in chief flatly denied the charge. On March 6, he said, "There are no American combat troops in Laos. . . . No American stationed in Laos has ever been killed in ground combat operations"—statements absent from his subsequent memoirs. At the time, there were already a considerable number of U.S. and South Vietnamese soldiers rupturing the borders in hundreds of operations designed to interdict the enemy's flow of men and equipment. Two days after he spoke, a *Los Angeles Times* story reported the combat death of Captain Joseph Bush during a skirmish with Pathet Lao guerrillas a year earlier. Unable to maintain the lie, the Defense Department soon admitted that the unfortunate captain was but one of twenty-seven KIA in Laos during the past year.[9] The commander in chief now acknowledged the presence of four hundred "advisers" in Laos. The distinction between an "adviser" and a combat soldier was a highly transparent fig leaf.

The furor over American involvement in Laos faded quickly as civil disorder racked Phnom Penh, the capital of Cambodia. For a number of years, Prince Norodom Sihanouk, the Cambodian chief of state, had tried to play a neutral hand. His military was too weak to prevent the North

Vietnamese from using his country for bases and as a route south, but he allowed South Vietnamese and American aircraft to attack their enemies in his nation. On March 11, 1970, Sihanouk was en route to Moscow and Beijing. In his absence, the prime minister, General Lon Nol, considered by U.S. intelligence as friendly, ordered all sixty thousand North Vietnamese soldiers in Cambodia to leave. Hanoi ignored the demand. Within a week, the Cambodian legislature voted no confidence in Sihanouk. The coup caught the prince in Moscow. With the authority to recognize a government, granted him by the nation's constitution, Nixon immediately threw U.S. support behind Lon Nol. He also okayed Kissinger's request for additional air raids in Laos.

The pressure to intervene in Cambodia increased. Fuming over congressional rejection of two judges nominated to the Supreme Court and a vote by the Senate Foreign Relations Committee to repeal the Gulf of Tonkin Resolution, the commander in chief snarled to Kissinger, "Those senators think they can push me around, but I'll show them who's tough. The liberals are waiting to see Nixon let Cambodia go down the drain just the way Eisenhower let Cuba go down the drain."[10] Laird and Rogers opposed introduction of any troops into Cambodia initially and then restricted their caveats to the use of Americans. They foresaw heavy casualties and political trouble at home. Most analysts regarded the introduction of American ground forces into Cambodia, and perhaps even the airstrikes by U.S.-piloted planes, as contrary to the assertions of the Nixon Doctrine uttered in 1969, which said that in the future the locals must provide the armed forces.

Alarmed by the confirmation of U.S. soldiers operating in Laos and the threat of a spread into Cambodia, Fulbright preached heresy. He told his colleagues, "The master myth of Vietnam . . . is the greatly inflamed importance which has been attached to it. From the standpoint of American security and interests, the central fact about Indochina, including Vietnam, is that it does not matter very much who rules in those small and backward lands." He said the origins of this perception lay in "that hoariest, hardiest, most indestructible myth of the international Communist conspiracy." Fulbright argued that North Vietnam was an independent, underdeveloped nation with the strength neither to carry out imperialist aims nor to threaten U.S. security.[11]

In Saigon, General Abrams, encouraged by General Westmoreland, had long urged an incursion into Cambodia. He produced an ambitious plan to hit supply routes and "progressive escalation in U.S. participation, coupled with continuing ARVN cross border operations . . . use of U.S.

gunship, artillery and tacair in Cambodia . . . selective application of military force against selected military targets in North Vietnam."[12]

Chaos enveloped portions of Cambodia. The North Vietnamese garrisons, beset by the bombing raids of Operation Menu, had retreated westward, away from the South Vietnamese border. They easily overcame any resistance by Cambodian soldiers and then issued weapons to some of the Vietnamese in residence—there were some four hundred thousand of them in the country—to protect themselves against the local people. In an ethnic cleansing spasm, civilians and military massacred the foreigners. A hitherto relatively small communist element, known as the Khmer Rouge, allied itself with the North Vietnamese and sought to wrest power away from Lon Nol.

New York Times reporter William Beecher broke a tiny scoop, the provision of captured communist rifles to the Cambodian government. A rather trivial piece of news, it triggered a monumental meltdown by the president. According to Kissinger, that leak caused Nixon to telephone him at least ten times on April 23. He barked orders to fire several individuals and directed that a CIA team immediately fly to Phnom Penh where everyone with access to the information would be subject to a lie detector. But as members of the administration had learned, if they did not immediately act on his outbursts, the president soon forgot what he had demanded.

Haldeman informed the White House staff of the assault into Cambodia. "Only the President has all the facts in this situation. He must act in what he considers to be the best interest of our country and our troops."[13] The commander in chief's aide foreclosed discussion and debate in a democratic society through one of the hoarier and more absurd shibboleths. Donald Rumsfeld, then head of the Office of Economic Opportunity, protested to Kissinger that it was not credible to say this was not an expansion of the war. The national security adviser snapped back that "the North Vietnamese have 40,000 troops marching on the capital of Cambodia, and a lousy 50 U.S. advisers go in . . . and you hear Senators say we're the ones who are escalating."[14]

The president announced on television on April 30, 1970, Operation Shoemaker, which put U.S. and ARVN forces into Cambodia. Ignoring the heavy air raids that had pummeled portions of the country for several months, he began with a lie, claiming that the United States had "scrupulously respected" the neutrality of Cambodia during the previous five years. Kissinger also spread this fabrication among the media in his background briefings. The chief executive claimed there was no intent to widen the conflict but only to aid Cambodia's right to neutrality, and that it had the purpose of winding down the war. "This is not an invasion of Cambodia. The area in which these attacks will be launched are completely occupied and controlled by North Vietnamese forces."

Nixon contended that the size of the enemy forces in these sanctuaries presaged massive attacks on the U.S. and ARVN soldiers inside South Vietnam. What he had ordered was a thrust against an imminent threat, a preemptive action. Furthermore, a failure to move would destroy U.S. credibility around the world.

Alexander Haig himself had no problem with the attack into Cambodia. "When the Cambodian government collapsed, they asked us to help. When the business in Cambodia started, we were having four hundred casualties a week. In War Zone C it was a constant cat-and-mouse game. They were conducting offensives from Cambodia, crossing the border and then retreating behind it. Washington directed no shooting over the border and we could not fire into Cambodia.

"We had meetings with leaders in the House and Senate and told them about the B-52 raids and the ground incursions. They said do it. Russell and [Senator Carl] Vinson were guys who thought of the country instead of themselves. We got a consensus which they'd deliver to their committees. Some chose not to speak about it, but it wasn't a secret war. The legislators were informed. The left wing of Congress painted it as a criminal act. But there is nothing in the Constitution that said we don't have the right to defend ourselves."[15]

Touted to the world and the media as predominantly a South Vietnamese campaign, the invasion included more than thirty-one thousand U.S. soldiers and forty-three thousand South Vietnamese. Kissinger had but a few days before sneered about outrage for a mere fifty advisers crossing the border. Misinformation was the order of the day. In Cambodia, the American ambassador informed Lon Nol that the public figure for Americans was five thousand. In an effort to conceal the facts, the State Department dutifully directed Saigon to avoid making this sound like a major operation, and there would be an attempt to prevent correspondents from accompanying the troops. Lon Nol agreed to limit the opportunities for the media inside Cambodia to get to the major combat areas.

Haig said the sweep produced great results. "It attacked twelve enemy bases, locating and disrupting the mobile COSVN headquarters," locating enough small arms, ammunition, and food to have satisfied "six or seven enemy infantry divisions." The New York Times carried a story that the invaders had penetrated twenty miles inside Cambodia without encountering significant numbers of the enemy. British reporter William Shawcross said, in spite of Haig's comment about a "mobile headquarters," that "COSVN was never discovered." Towns and villages were destroyed; the South Vietnamese soldiers "plunged into Cambodia raping, looting, burning in retaliation for the murder of Vietnamese in Cambodia a month earlier."[16]

Admiral Moorer, the chairman of the Joint Chiefs of Staff, justified the thrust into Cambodia as within international law on the grounds that if a sovereign state cannot prevent a warring nation from using its territory to fight the war, then the nation on the receiving end has the right to protect itself. But the absence of any vast number of enemy near the border belied the rationale that the invasion preempted an imminent invasion from Cambodia by the North Vietnamese.

Moorer attributed the depth penetrated to a casual remark by the president at a press conference. "Nixon was asked, 'How deep are you going into Cambodia?' He said, 'Twenty miles.' That's because all presidents feel that they have to know everything. No one had ever discussed twenty miles . . . certainly the Joint Chiefs of staff didn't know about it. . . . The media drew a line and if one soldier had gone past the 20 miles, the headline in the *Washington Post* would have said, 'The President has lied.' Laird was calling me on the intercom all the time saying, 'Be sure they don't go any further than that. Be sure they don't go in too deep.'

"The point was that in some of those sanctuaries if we had gone twenty-five miles, it would have been worth twice as much. . . . [It was] Washington that put a major restraint on this operation. We should have gone forty miles . . . but twenty miles is the magic number and . . . once the President makes a statement, he'll never retract it. He should have kept his mouth shut and said, 'This is a military matter. We'll look and see how the operation goes.'"[17]

While the White House preened over a flood of congratulatory messages from the public, Congress expressed outrage. Capitol Hill had not been consulted about the plans. At most, the leaders received briefings on military aid proposed to prop up Lon Nol's government. A few hours before the troops jumped off, the president had called to inform Congress that Americans and South Vietnamese would be crossing the border at a point known as Fish Hook. Instead of having a say in matters of war, the legislators again were simply slapped with a fait accompli.

On the very day of this announcement, a demonstration at Kent State University in Ohio confronted National Guardsmen, who opened fire, killing four students. Within a week, more than four hundred colleges and universities shut their doors because of fears of destructive demonstrations.

National Guard units prowled the campuses of twenty-one institutions of higher learning. Flag-waving, pipe-wielding, fist-swinging hard hats pitched into a Manhattan crowd of war protesters. Americans, jolted by the violence spreading through the land, read in influential newspapers and magazines like *Time* and *Newsweek*, ordinarily supportive of the administration, that the Cambodian venture had profited little and provoked considerable harm to the body public.

In the Senate, debate over the Cooper-Church amendment to a bill on foreign military sales threatened to shut off the money for Vietnam. Defenders of the administration, like John Stennis, argued against denying funds while battles in Cambodia still raged. Although the president had not deigned to seek the imprimatur of Congress upon Operation Shoemaker, several days after it commenced he assigned Assistant Attorney General William Rehnquist to justify the action.

Rehnquist, a forty-five-year-old lawyer from Arizona, whom Nixon called "the clown" because he wore bright pink shirts, garish neckties, and sported scraggly sideburns, drafted a fourteen-page document. He described the mantle of commander in chief as "a grant of substantive authority" enabling presidents to deploy troops for "conflict with foreign powers on their own initiative" and even to use the armed forces "outside of the United States on occasion in a way which invited hostile retaliation." He asserted that Congress had approved such presidential initiatives and the courts had affirmed the commander in chief's rights. He argued that what had happened in Indochina fell within the Tonkin Gulf Resolution. The president had taken the war into Cambodia in order to safeguard U.S. forces. Rehnquist labeled the operation "precisely the sort of tactical decision traditionally confided to the Commander-in-Chief in the conduct of an armed conflict."[18]

Historian Arthur Schlesinger scoffed at Rehnquist's legal scholarship. The precedents marshaled by Rehnquist did not match the situation of a sovereign Cambodia. To insist that the Constitution's simple statement naming the president as head of the army and navy included the authority to commit troops for war with other countries on his own initiative was a stretch of the imagination beyond what even the most activist judge might have decreed. (Rehnquist, who eventually became the Supreme Court's chief justice, was supposed to be a strict constructionist.) That a president, even during wartime, could march into a neutral country because of his gut feeling that they posed a potential threat to Americans across the border hardly met the test of the law. Under this doctrine, had Nixon felt China and the Soviet Union posed a threat, the commander in chief could have attacked those nations.[19] Absent from the rationale for invading Cambodia was the doctrine of hot pursuit—chasing interlopers who had just crossed into South Vietnam.

The Rehnquist brief changed no minds and the politicos maneuvered to limit the Cambodian adventure yet avoid an outright rejection of the administration's attempt to achieve "peace with honor." Since Nixon had said he would remove American forces from Cambodia by June 30, the Cooper-Church amendment was rewritten to make the congressional demand for withdrawal from Cambodia in harmony with administration policy. The Tonkin Gulf Resolution was repealed, seemingly foreclosing the use of that statute as a device to expand military actions. Nixon reaffirmed his right "to use American air power any place in North Vietnam or Southeast Asia where I found that it would be necessary for the purpose of protecting American forces."[20]

Kissinger said, "Cambodia was *not* [his italics] a moral issue . . . what we faced was an essentially tactical choice; whether the use of American troops to neutralize the sanctuaries for a period of eight weeks was the best way to maintain the established pace and security of our exit from Vietnam and prevent Hanoi from overrunning Indochina."[21] But the argument of the opponents concerned not morality but legal authority, which the erstwhile Harvard professor never challenged. Furthermore, as the participants in Shoemaker found, the North Vietnamese and their allies were nowhere near the border or in a position to hamper a safe American exodus.

In his accommodation with Cooper-Church, an important distinction lay in the commander in chief's word that he would rely on air attacks. As Kissinger commuted to Paris, haggling with his opposite number, Le Duc Tho, the administration renewed the bombing campaign in Cambodia. The aerial campaign in Cambodia and threats to hit North Vietnam all seem to have been calculated to drive the enemy to concessions at the bargaining table.

Cooper-Church fell short of what doves desired. McGovern and Senator Mark Hatfield, a Republican opposed to the administration's policies in Southeast Asia, introduced their own amendment that required an irreversible, time-limited pullout by American forces in place of the vague promises of the White House for a withdrawal. But legislators refused to line up behind McGovern-Hatfield because, in a long-standing tradition, they could not bring themselves to cut off funding for the men in the field. McGovern recalled colleagues who said, "It's up to the Commander-in-Chief to make these decisions, these military judgments. We don't have the information to do this."[22]

One of the most bald-faced presentations of that point of view came from Barry Goldwater. The Arizona senator orated on the president as commander in chief. "Just why the founding fathers saw fit to confer this title on him and to invest him with these powers, I've never quite been able to understand; but I have a growing feeling that they recognized and [in the] infinite wisdom of the founding fathers, they realized that a single man with these powers who would not be disturbed by the politics of the moment would use them more wisely than a Congress which is constantly looking toward the political results." Goldwater claimed that the framers of the Constitution in their wisdom saw fit that "the power of war and peace might better be vested in a single man."[23] It was a breathtakingly upside-down view of the founding fathers, who had divided war powers specifically to prevent a lone individual, a George III or the feared "man on horseback," from having the sole authority to engage the nation in war.

Although polls indicated a majority of Americans favored Hatfield-McGovern, the amendment lost in the Senate by fifty-five votes to thirty-nine. An even larger margin of defeat would have marked a House vote, and even if passed, its advocates could never have rounded up enough votes to override a presidential veto. That did not soothe administration rancor. Kissinger fulminated at what he viewed as the undermining of the peace talks. "Hanoi could only be encouraged to stall, waiting to harvest the results of our domestic dissent."

Away from Vietnam were the covert actions against groups or governments deemed hostile to the United States. Following the National Security Act of 1947 that created both the National Security Council and the CIA, a series of administrations had established procedures to regulate covert action. In the time of Eisenhower the "5412" Committee reviewed and supervised clandestine operations. The 5412 became the "303" under Johnson and then the "40" for the Nixon White House. All basically studied a proposal for covert action, and if approved, the president through the NSC issued a directive. The role of Congress, which eventually appropriated funds, depended upon personal relationships of senior members and CIA directors.

In Chile, the CIA engaged in a covert operation aimed at the ouster of leftist Salvador Allende Gossens, who had led all candidates for the presidency with a plurality that amounted to 36.2 percent of the vote. The Chilean constitution specified that if no candidate won a majority, the country's congress would decide who would be the leader. There seemed little doubt that the legislators would anoint Allende. Ambassador Edward Korry advised Kissinger, "Chile voted calmly to have a Marxist-Leninist state, the first nation in the world to make this choice freely and knowingly." Korry emphasized Allende's tiny margin of victory and warned that this could have a "profound effect on Latin America and beyond." When the report reached the president, he underlined the sentences dealing with the repercussions in other lands.[24]

Kissinger regarded the Allende government as a "challenge to our national interest. We did not find it easy to reconcile ourselves to a second Communist state in the Western Hemisphere. We were persuaded that it would soon be inciting anti-American policies, attacking hemisphere solidarity, making common cause with Cuba, and . . . establishing closer relations with the Soviet Union." Kissinger made the case that Allende intended to establish a totalitarian state.

"In these circumstances it was neither morally nor politically unjustified for the United States to support those internal political forces seeking to maintain a democratic counterweight to radical dominance." Kissinger described the president as "beside himself" when Allende won the election because for years he had denounced the Democrats for permitting the establishment of communist power in Cuba. (Actually, Fidel Castro took power during the Republican administration of Dwight D. Eisenhower.) Nixon ordered a major effort by CIA director Richard Helms to see how to forestall Allende's ascension. The president said, according to Kissinger, that if there was one chance in ten it should be tried and if it required $10 million, he would provide the money.[25] Usurpation of the Allende regime became the task of the CIA, with guidance from the 40 Committee. Kissinger was not joking when he told them, "I don't see why we have to let a country go Marxist just because its people are irresponsible."[26]

The 40 Committee authorized Korry to approach Chilean military leaders to intervene, forcing a new election where U.S. economic and military aid might leverage an alternative for head of state. As the Chilean congress appeared about to affirm Allende as president, the White House pressured the Chilean military with promises of continued military assistance if they acted. The CIA explored schemes to kidnap the country's army chief of staff, General René Schneider, a coup opponent, and two attempts were bungled. The intelligence officials supposedly now abandoned the notion. However, the locals recruited for the abduction either never heard of the cancellation or else decided to go ahead on their own. When they tried to snatch the general, he drew his pistol and one of the kidnappers fatally wounded him. A Senate committee concluded that the United States had never plotted to assassinate Schneider. But CIA agents in Chile had supplied submachine guns to the conspirators for the earlier tries.

Two days after the death of the general, the Chilean congress voted Allende into office. The official policy of the Nixon administration was to avoid confrontation and maintain a correct but distant posture. The national security adviser would insist that when Allende was later overthrown, "It was by his own incompetence and intransigence; military leaders without consulting us moved against him on their own initiative because they were convinced that he was intent on taking over total power and about to organize his own coup to that end."[27]

Throughout these struggles, the U.S. Congress stayed mute, removed from what was being done in the name of the country. While the machinations to change the government of Chile did not involve the use of military force, the gross interference in a sovereign nation fell between a cold war of propaganda and diplomatic maneuvers and a hot shooting war. From how far up the chain of command came the orders for coups, financial support for opposition political groups, and even armed assistance to insurgencies seems to muddy the waters when snorkeling for responsibility. But ultimately, as President Harry Truman said, "The buck stops here."

The bucks to carry out covert actions required a congressional bill. As allegations of U.S. tampering in the affairs of Chile surfaced, the legislators decided to formalize agreements for cloak-and-dagger operations, since they could be construed as acts of war. The Hughes-Ryan amendment to the Foreign Assistance Act of 1974 provided that no money could be expended by the CIA for any purpose other than obtaining necessary intelligence, "unless and until the President finds that each such operation is important to the national security of the United States." Henceforth, a president would need to draft a "finding" that notified the appropriate committees of Congress of the desirability of covert efforts beyond merely gathering information. The congressional bodies were those with oversight for such matters as intelligence and defense. The presumption was that they would not divulge the secret operations, but all administrations regarded the senators, representatives, and their staffs as leaky vessels. In 1991 the provisions were refined with a more formal standard that the covert action must be "necessary to support identifiable foreign policy objectives" and also must be "important to the national security of the United States."[28]

The covert machinations of the CIA in Chile provoked no public outcry, but the casualty lists from South Vietnam fueled dissent. The voices in the street and politicians that questioned his authority infuriated the president. The private Nixon when angered was an intemperate man, and his reactions boded ill for his ability to govern or to use wisely the war powers defaulted by Congress.

12

THE BITTER END

The passions of his critics on the streets, on the campuses, and in the capital ignited the smoldering paranoia of the president. Even as Kissinger poured his own fury at dissenters into the chief executive's ears, he observed a "point of exhaustion [in Nixon] that caused his advisers deep concern."[1] To his associates Nixon complained that communist elements fueled the dissenters. He ordered a public relations campaign around the motif of "support the troops." He angrily deplored information damaging to the administration about events in Vietnam and decision-making at home, and tried to persuade the country that Vietnamization, the development of the indigenous military, would allow Americans to withdraw gracefully. While presidents from Truman through Nixon had bruised the Constitution, it remained the national charter. A commander in chief who overstepped his bounds, particularly on the domestic front, remained subject to the checks a Congress could impose.

Bile poisoned reason. Nixon lost faith in the FBI, even as it followed his orders and installed illegal electronic surveillance of officials and reporters. The White House formed its own posse to collect evidence unlawfully and assassinate the character of its enemies.

As the commander in chief took the offensive at home, he carefully cozened those wavering in their war support. He promoted the Vietnamization plan as on target and reduced the ground forces in Southeast Asia. He offered a cease-fire that sounded like a genuine step toward peace but with conditions unacceptable to the North Vietnamese. He cultivated the image of a president coping with disreputable protesters prone to violence, and he exploited the unhappiness of Americans who thought the civil rights movement had gone too far, too fast and were repelled by media-manufactured images of a nation of pot-smoking, sexually promiscuous youths with no regard for their elders or legitimate authority.

Although congressional war opponents increased, Nixon could still count on sufficient backers for his policy, drawn from both sides of the aisle. Resolute in the belief that a political solution depended upon military force, he approved a major offensive, Dewey Canyon II, a three-tined attack within South Vietnam, Laos, and Cambodia. American ground troops advanced in central South Vietnam toward the old base of Khe Sanh to forestall an expected enemy offensive. Meanwhile, on February 8, 1971, twenty thousand South Vietnamese soldiers, girded with American airpower and artillery, penetrated Laos with the objective of clamping down the Ho Chi Minh Trail. The Laotian prime minister condemned the incursion, but the State Department retorted that it was North Vietnam that constantly violated its neighbor.

A contingent of troops entered Cambodia with the same objective. American ground troops supposedly did not participate. The actions appeared to demonstrate Vietnamization, but they seemed to widen the war rather than narrow it. The White House publicized the campaign as a major success and created expectations that Dewey Canyon would assure withdrawal of all American forces. But it was a fiasco, as the North Vietnamese routed the invaders and punished the American support, damaging 604 helicopters and shooting down 104.[2]

Hatfield-McGovern, with a few new wrinkles, surfaced again in June 1971, but the administration rallied its allies and the amendment gained only a few new votes. McGovern drew comfort in defeat: "This must be the only time in American history that [more than] 40 senators have stood up in the middle of a war and told the commander-in-chief to end it."[3] *Newsweek* reported that an unidentified Republican insider confided, "The Senate doesn't want to assume responsibility for the war and its aftermath. The senators want a time-table, but they don't want to set it themselves."[4]

After the courts refused to bar publication of the extensive Defense Department documents on Vietnam, known as the Pentagon Papers, the crew organized within the White House to plug leaks and win hearts and minds turned into desperadoes. Their shenanigans eventually led to a break-in at the offices of the Democratic National Committee in Washington's Watergate Hotel during the 1972 election campaign. The commander in chief had hinted that Americans might be out of Vietnam by election day. He and Kissinger said they had contacted the North Vietnamese and offered to remove all U.S. troops as soon as the enemy released some four hundred men believed held prisoner. The announcement ignored the fine print of the proposal—who left the country and when. McGovern ran as the Democratic candidate and Nixon easily won reelection. He had defused the Vietnam issue with the steady reductions in the U.S. presence, and McGovern's domestic agenda was not acceptable to many Americans.

North Vietnam, undoubtedly dismayed at a new rapprochement between the United States and its two main supporters, the USSR and China, regrouped and, to the chagrin of Americans, launched a massive offensive into South Vietnam with as many as 120,000 soldiers. Predictably, the antiwar people said it was time to get out as quickly as possible and let the South Vietnamese determine their own fate. The commander in chief refused to buckle. "The bastards have never been bombed like they're going to be bombed this time."[5] U.S. airstrikes pounded targets above the demilitarized zone, including Hanoi and Haiphong. Several Soviet ships in the harbor were hit and sailors aboard them killed. While ground troops continued to depart, navy and air units added nearly 30,000 personnel, mostly engaged in intensive bombing raids.

While attempting to extricate the U.S. armed forces from South Vietnam, the president and his national security adviser hoped to preserve the independence of the Thieu-led government. But the South Vietnamese leader balked at the apparent acceptance by the United States of a presence of North Vietnamese troops in his domain. The White House tried to reassure him of its firm commitment to sovereignty both through heavy air raids north of the border and by building up Thieu's own air force to a point where it qualified as the fourth largest in the world.

During the following months, the commander in chief whittled away the numbers of Americans in the country, and the figure dropped to only 49,000 from a peak of 550,000 at the time he set up housekeeping at 1600 Pennsylvania Avenue. But the reductions did not lessen the desire to restrict use of the armed forces. The War Powers bill, drafted by dovish Republican Jacob Javits of New York, and chastened hawk John Stennis, contained a number of provisions to check the warmaking authority assumed by presidents after World War II. Other previously hard-line legislators appeared to have changed their plumage. The Senate majority whip, Robert Byrd, spoke for a growing number as he said, "The actual power to initiate war . . . has practically speaking, shifted since World War II from Congress to the Executive. The power of Congress must be reasserted in no uncertain terms." Herman Talmadge echoed Byrd: "The President, acting virtually alone, has determined whether we follow a course of war or peace. The decision is too great for one man to make, no matter how thick his hide or how broad his shoulders."[6]

While the factions within Congress debated the provisions for the War Powers bill the jaw-jaw of peace negotiations without progress exhausted Nixon's patience. He ordered a massive new round of bombing raids and harbor mining, with the campaign beginning on December 18, 1972, and lasting for eleven days. The ordnance wrought extensive devastation, albeit at a high cost in American planes, including fifteen B-52s. The damage and the growing unwillingness of the USSR to continue to finance and equip North Vietnam led to a return to the Paris peace table.

One week after Nixon's second inauguration, on January 27, 1973, the United States, South Vietnam, North Vietnam, and the "Provisional Revolutionary Government of South Vietnam" (the Vietcong) signed an agreement to end the war. While it temporarily halted the shooting, it brought no peace to Indochina. The document did not cover either Laos or Cambodia. The Pathet Lao were willing to enter into a cease-fire, but in Cambodia the Khmer Rouge no longer accepted the dictate of the North Vietnamese in their war on the government of Lon Nol.

In a message to South Vietnam's Thieu, Nixon said that if he did not accept the agreement, all American economic and military assistance would be terminated. Having pressured Thieu he continued, "I will make it emphatically clear that the United States recognizes your government as the only legal government of South Vietnam; that we do not recognize the right of any foreign troops to be present on South Vietnamese territory; that we will react strongly in the event the agreement is violated." Given the U.S. political situation and public opinion against continued involvement in Southeast Asia, it was an empty promise.

Chief of Staff H. R. Haldeman recalled Nixon's statement to his cabinet. "He said we have a cease-fire for Vietnam, possibly in Laos and Cambodia. We have peace with honor, the POWs are back, the supervised cease-fire, and the right of South Vietnam to determine their own future. It's been long, painful, and difficult for all of us. This is not Johnson's war or Kennedy's war. They did start it [rather than communist expansionism] and they did handle it badly, but the United States was involved. We have now achieved our goals—peace for Vietnam, the right of the South Vietnamese to determine their future without an imposed Communist government. The fact that we have stood firm as a country was responsible and has had a decisive effect on the world. If the United States did not prove to be responsible in Vietnam, if this had ended in defeat and surrender, the Chinese and the Russians would have no interest in talking

to us. Europe wouldn't consider us as a reliable ally, in spite of their bitch-
ing about the war."[7]

The situation in South Vietnam deteriorated, with the communist elements and North Vietnamese troops obviously gaining control. The president realized he lacked the political backing to reinsert ground forces into
the country or try to strike at North Vietnam from the air. But because
Cambodia did not fall within the bounds of the Paris agreement, he could
order an air campaign in support of Lon Nol. Congress had other ideas,
and in June, legislation denied funds for any American combat actions in
either Laos or Cambodia. The president vetoed the bill. "After more than
ten arduous years of suffering and sacrifice . . . it would be nothing short
of tragic if this great accomplishment, bought with the blood of so many
Asians and Americans, were to be undone now by congressional action."[8]
While the House sustained Nixon, Mike Mansfield warned that the legislation would be introduced again and again until it prevailed. Although
the bombers continued their missions, the commander in chief recognized
the futility of further military efforts in Cambodia. He grudgingly agreed
to a halt by August 15. His appetite for confrontation with his foes about
Vietnam sharply diminished as he pivoted to ward off the growing threat
of the Watergate investigation.

Approximately thirty-three thousand Americans had been killed in
Vietnam by January 1969, with 99 percent of the casualties accumulated
during the Johnson years. Another twenty-five thousand died while the
Nixon White House wrangled with their opposite numbers from North
Vietnam. The losses among the Vietnamese probably mounted toward a
million. Nearly five years of sparring, beginning in 1969 and changing
nothing in Southeast Asia other than to add devastation in Cambodia,
earned truce negotiators Henry Kissinger and Le Duc Tho Nobel Prizes for
Peace.

As the conflict in Vietnam wound down, the War Powers bill passed
through the various committees until it was deemed ready for presentation
to Congress. The ultimate language in Section 2. (a) announced that its
purpose was to "insure that the collective judgement of both the Congress
and the President will apply to the introduction of United States Armed
Forces into hostilities, or into situations where imminent involvement in
hostilities is clearly indicated by the circumstances and to the continued
use of such forces in hostilities or in such situations."

Section 2. (c) said, "The constitutional powers of the President as
Commander-in-Chief to introduce United States Armed Forces into hostilities or into situations where imminent involvement in hostilities is

clearly indicated by circumstances, are exercised only pursuant to (1) a declaration of war, (2) specific statutory authorization, or (3) a national emergency created by attack upon the United States, its territories or possessions, or its armed forces."

On the surface the legislation restored the exclusive authority for declaration of war to Congress, but the language of 2. (c) also accepted "specific statutory authorization," which covered the string of resolutions that had either plunged the United States into combat or presaged a war. The War Powers bill required that the president "in every possible instance shall consult with Congress before introducing United States Armed Forces into hostilities or into situations where imminent involvement in hostilities is clearly indicated by the circumstances."

In the absence of a declaration of war by Congress but where the armed forces were either in combat or on the verge, the president was obliged to report to Congress on the status of the action and the expected scope and duration. Once the chief executive submitted the report, unless Congress declared war or specifically authorized further involvement of the armed forces, the military must be withdrawn within sixty to ninety days. One significant omission was the paramilitary actions taken by the CIA, almost always covert. Interference in elections and attempts to destabilize regimes and support insurgencies that might lead to fuller involvement of the armed forces were not covered.

The administration fiercely resisted the bill, perceiving it as a slap at the current resident of 1600 Pennsylvania Avenue as well as his predecessors. The White House and its supporters insisted the War Powers bill was an unconstitutional restriction on the president's authority, but it passed the Senate and House by huge margins. President Nixon exercised his veto but Congress mustered the two-thirds vote to override his rejection.

Ten months later, exposed for his role in the cover-up of the crimes committed by those he deputized to plug leaks and destroy the opposition, Richard Nixon in August 1974 resigned from the presidency and Vice President Gerald Ford became commander in chief.

While the peace accord had been signed, spasms of violence convulsed Southeast Asia. Prince Norodom Sihanouk, disliked by the Nixon administration, and having been deposed by Lon Nol, found a temporary home and support in Beijing, seeking to present himself to both the Chinese and the Americans as a suitable alternative to either Lon Nol or the Khmer Rouge. As president, Gerald Ford had chosen to retain Henry Kissinger as his secretary of state. There was nothing he could do about Laos, now wholly controlled by the Pathet Lao and hostile to the United

States, but there was an opportunity to work with Sihanouk toward a neutral government in Cambodia.

For the United States, such an arrangement meant cooperation with the Chinese and the Khmer Rouge communists while dumping Lon Nol, whom Washington had championed ever since 1970. To complicate matters further, the United Nations had recognized Lon Nol's faction as the legitimate government of Cambodia. The effort collapsed basically because neither the Chinese nor the Americans trusted one another sufficiently to guarantee their interests.

The Khmer Rouge renewed their attacks with vigor, bolstered by weapons and ammunition from North Vietnam. Lon Nol's troops fought bravely, but the communist forces almost completely surrounded Phnom Penh. The best that Washington could offer was airlifts of vital supplies to the besieged capital. Since the Cooper-Church amendment forbade direct military aid, a "private" company, Bird Air, flew the materials from Thailand to Cambodia. The aircraft were lent by the air force with their official markings painted over, and many of the pilots were reservists recruited by Bird Air. The most important result was humanitarian; the rice shipped to Cambodia saved many from malnutrition, but thousands may still have died from food shortages.

President Ford, counseled by Secretary of State Kissinger, urged Congress to support an ally. The administration asked for the authority to supply Lon Nol the stuff of war and went so far as to invite a number of legislators to visit Phnom Penh. The journalist William Shawcross said they "were visibly shocked by what they saw of the suffering on the government side and, in most cases, by what they heard of the brutality of the Khmer Rouge."[9] But as appalled as they were, the congressmen could not see how additional military aid could do anything more than delay the inevitable.

On April 12, 1975, the United States officially abandoned Cambodia. Helicopters with several hundred fully armed marines landed near the embassy and evacuated the staff of 82, plus 182 Cambodians and 35 other foreign nationals. Two days later the Khmer Rouge entered Phnom Penh. For a brief period, Sihanouk served as a figurehead for the new government, an increasingly vicious regime that established brutal reeducation camps and plowed huge killing fields under the leadership of the infamous Pol Pot.

By April 1975, the hoped-for independence of South Vietnam, the "peace with honor" supposedly achieved in the Paris agreements, had fallen apart. Without the U.S. troops and airplanes, the stuff of war diminishing, the government of Thieu and Ky could not deny the Vietcong and

North Vietnamese. Ford had asked Congress for $1.4 billion in military aid but the actual money amounted to only half that. "With adequate United States military assistance, they can hold their own," Ford said to the legislators. "We cannot turn our backs on these embattled countries."[10] Aping his predecessors, the commander in chief warned that if the United States did not stand up to aggression, it would lose credibility around the world.

Antigovernment forces occupied a number of cities on a march toward Saigon, and Ford sent a special mission to South Vietnam headed by Army Chief of Staff General Frederick C. Weyand to evaluate the situation. He also asked David Kennerly, a former *Time* magazine photographer who had covered the war in Southeast Asia, to go along and provide an unofficial report. When Weyand returned he said that with a quick $722 million in supplies, the South Vietnamese might be able to stabilize matters sufficiently to encourage a political solution. Kennerly, however, met Ford privately and according to the president said, "Cambodia is gone and I don't care what the generals tell you; they're bullshitting you if they said that Vietnam has got more than three or four weeks left. There's no question about it. It's just not gonna last."[11]

Kissinger advised Ford to address the American people and lay the blame for the debacle in Southeast Asia squarely upon Congress. Ford instead asked Congress for nearly $1 billion in military and humanitarian aid. His appeal fell on deaf ears. Members of the Senate Foreign Relations Committee listened to Kissinger, Secretary of Defense James Schlesinger, and General Brent Scowcroft from the National Security Council. They adamantly refused to vote for any military aid, only funds for evacuation. Ford stubbornly insisted that the United States could not "cut and run."

Toward the end of March, evacuation of U.S. personnel plus thousands of Vietnamese refugees began by air and by sea. As Admiral Harry Train reported:

> We lost only two people in the crew of a plane-guard helicopter that had an operational crash. . . . The Air Force . . . and Marine helicopters all went in and picked up the security force. They took them into the defense attaché's compound and then . . . overland to the embassy. The Marine security force was actually at the embassy for the evacuation . . . from the roof of the embassy itself. It just went on endlessly. We just started feeding Vietnamese [and foreign nationals] into the helicopters instead of U.S. citizens.
>
> Schlesinger called me. "How many more helicopters will it take to get just the U.S. out of the embassy?"

I said, "Nineteen."

He said, "Call CinCPac [Commander in Chief Pacific Fleet] and tell him that the President says that there are to be only 19 more helicopters and that Ambassador Graham Martin must be on the very last helicopter."

. . . CinPac reported that the 19th and last helicopter had departed and Graham Martin was on board. Bill Clements [deputy secretary of defense] . . . called Kissinger and reported this. . . . Kissinger was acting as spokesman at the White House and Kissinger said, "Fine, I will have the President announce it."

Bill Clements said, "No, I don't think you ought to do that yet, because I'm not sure we've got all the people out."

Kissinger was on a speaker and he said, "Well, you told them to send 19 helicopters and have Graham Martin on the last helicopter."

Clements said, "Yes, but we didn't say to have all the people out."

At that point Kissinger said, "Well, I'm going to announce it."

. . . CincPac then . . . said, "We've still got the 187-man Marine security force on the roof of the embassy and would you get the President's permission to send more helicopters?"

"Permission, hell, send more helicopters!" They send additional helicopters in, and they send the wrong kind first. They sent great big H-53s that couldn't land on the roof and couldn't pick up the Marines. They inserted the H-46s again and the Marines got off just as the Vietnamese were breaking through onto the roof.[12]

In those last minutes of the evacuation, frightened Vietnamese desperately climbed the embassy walls seeking a ticket out. Some grabbed the skids of the helicopters in a pitiful attempt to escape. Ford wrote that in a sixteen-hour period, "We managed to rescue 6,500 U.S. and South Vietnamese personnel without sustaining significant casualties. . . . I felt deep satisfaction and relief that the evacuation had been a success."[13] But in truth, the United States had cut and run.

The last of the Americans in Saigon had hardly left the country before President Ford faced a serious confrontation. On May 12, 1975, it was reported to the president that an American cargo vessel, the SS Mayaguez, while in international waters had been seized by the Cambodians. Sketchy information indicated the ship under tow to a Cambodian port and the crew taken prisoner. When the commander in chief convened the National Security Council, Kissinger urged a forceful reaction. "The issues at stake went far beyond the seizure of the ship, he said; they extended to international perceptions of U.S. resolve and will. If we failed to respond to the challenge, it would be a serious blow to our prestige around the world. 'At some point,' he continued, 'the United States must draw the line. This is not our idea of the best such situation. It is not our choice. But we must act upon it now, and act firmly.'" This was a familiar Kissinger aria. Secretary of Defense James Schlesinger remarked, "Henry was an incorrigible signal-sender, even when it might have been dangerous."[14]

The president ordered an aircraft carrier and destroyers to steam to the scene, for the Joint Chiefs to prepare for air attacks and a rescue mission. While the State Department issued a strong statement demanding the immediate release of the crew and ship, a major problem lay in the absence of contact with those now governing Cambodia, precluding diplomatic negotiations.

As President Ford and his counselors digested the news, on May 13, little more than twenty-four hours since the seizure of the Mayaguez, reconnaissance from the air located the Mayaguez steaming toward the mainland port of Kompong Som. A covey of U.S. fighters appeared and expertly strafed the water ahead of the ship, shrapnel from their 20-mm cannons ripping across the deck. The Cambodians now in control of the vessel halted dead in the water near the island of Koh Tang and transferred the Americans to a fishing trawler. One of the low-flying pilots observed Caucasians on the deck of the fifty-foot boat and they were identified as the American sailors. The Cambodian craft tied up at a pier on Koh Tang from where heavy antiaircraft fire menaced the aircraft. Through the Joint Chiefs of Staff, the commander in chief directed that aircraft intercept all boats traveling to and from Koh Tang.

Before additional troops could reach the area, Seventh Air Force commander General John J. Burns in Thailand launched a rescue effort with volunteers from an air rescue and recovery squadron and a special operations squadron from Nakhon Phanom, Thailand. The plan called for helicopters to stage from U-Tapao and then land atop the containers on the Mayaguez's deck. Minutes after the flight rose from Nakhon Phanom the rotor system on one chopper malfunctioned and the helicopter plummeted to earth, killing all twenty-three aboard. Shaken by the crash and with confusion on the whereabouts of the crew from the captured ship, the command reviewed the mission. The teams from the Seventh Air Force were ordered to stand down.

According to Ford, when his NSC convened on the afternoon of May 14, the information on the location of the sailors remained fragmented. "Some crewmen, we had to assume, remained aboard ship. Some may have been on the island [Koh Tang], while others had been taken to the mainland." In the discussion, Kissinger championed an aggressive stance, one that prevented any reinforcement of Koh Tang and which included punishing airstrikes at the mainland. Secretary of Defense Schlesinger called for a more moderate approach. "He was far less eager to use *Mayaguez* as an example for Asia and the world."[15]

A voice from the back of the room interrupted the conversations. Photographer Kennerly, after taking pictures, and now packing up his gear, asked, "Has anyone considered that this might be the act of a local Cambodian commander who has just taken it into his own hands to halt any ship that comes by? Has anyone stopped to think that he might not have gotten his orders from Phnom Penh? If that's what has happened . . . you can blow the whole place away and it's not gonna make any difference. Everyone here has been talking about Cambodia as if it were a traditional government. Like France. We have trouble with France, we just pick up the telephone and call. We know who to talk to. But I was in Cambodia just two weeks ago, and it's not that kind of government at all. We don't even know who the leadership is."[16]

Ford said he was glad to hear this unsolicited, sensible view. Yet, the expression of such good sense seems hardly to have made a significant impression upon those in the room, for they quickly agreed to proceed with an ambitious series of operations that included four carrier-based attacks. The only alteration was to cancel a proposed massive raid by B-52s. The destroyer *Holt* received orders to haul a contingent of marines who would board and secure the freighter. Marines would storm ashore on Koh Tang and rescue crew members. Navy fighter-bombers would strike at the military facilities around Kompong Som.

Ford said he consulted with Congress before sending the U.S. military into action, fulfilling the requirements of the War Powers Act. In fact, he interpreted "consultation" as simply briefing Congress on the actions already ordered, rather than actually involving them in the decision-making process. Senator Mike Mansfield expressed deep concern, apprehension, and uneasiness about the plans. However, Senator James O. Eastland mumbled, "Blow the hell out of 'em."[17] The moment that the commander in chief began to inform the congressmen, the choppers received clearance for takeoff.

A tragedy of errors followed. The marines assigned to simultaneously capture the *Mayaguez* and liberate the crew during an assault on Koh Tang relied on intelligence gathered by aerial reconnaissance of the island and a former naval officer who had served there. The garrison was estimated at twenty to thirty Khmer Rouge. The planners ignored the level of antiaircraft fire, which suggested a stronger force in residence.

Harry Train, director of the staff for the Joint Chiefs, said, "The Marines got there and mated with Air Force helicopters that they had never seen before. The Marines . . . had loaded their helicopters in a non-optimized way. They had all the radios in the first helicopter. The first helicopter was shot down going in, so they had no radios. They had little hand held Motorolas [equivalents of walkie-talkies] on the ground trying to get air support."[18]

Immediately streams of tracers poured from the green foliage beyond the seaside strand. A second helicopter about to settle down radioed "Hot LZ" and the door gunners returned fire. Instead of the two dozen or so defenders, the marines faced as many as two hundred entrenched soldiers who pinned the invaders down, lobbing mortar shells onto the beachhead. The Cambodians knocked three helicopters out of the sky. According to the plan, 175 marines would participate, but because of the torrid ground fire only about 110 landed.

Out to sea, the destroyer *Holt*, with marines at the ready and machine guns on deck, inched toward the *Mayaguez*. A pair of jets roared over the freighter dropping tear gas, which enveloped the ship. The warship closed the distance, bumped against the side, and the first two marines leaped onto the *Mayaguez*. The two ships parted momentarily but then came together again and a full squad of marines crossed to the other deck. They found no one aboard.

While the leathernecks were securing the *Mayaguez* and the invaders of Koh Tang battled for their lives in the early evening of May 14, the official radio in Phnom Penh announced that the ship would be released. In Washington, however, the commander in chief and Kissinger decided not to halt the operations unless the Cambodians also freed the crew. When the first wave of navy fighter-bombers arrived over the targets on the Cambodian mainland, the president instructed the Pentagon to delay the strike until they could fully evaluate the meaning of the announcement from Phnom Penh on the *Mayaguez*. After about twenty minutes of discussion, Ford decided to go ahead with the bombing.[19]

The captured sailors were not on Koh Tang but nearby Rong Sam Lem island. An hour after Phnom Penh radio declared its intentions to release the ship, the crew sailed on a fishing boat manned by Thais. Their Cambodian guards and an accompanying gunboat returned to the harbor. The destroyer *Wilson* picked up the Americans as they neared the *Mayaguez*.

During this action, the president, attending a state dinner, excused himself several times for an update from the Pentagon. Train reported, "The White House was running every piece of the operation from the White House situation room. We really started getting concerned about how to get them off of there. We still didn't know where the crew of the

Mayaguez was. It became obvious those Marines were in a real firefight and that they needed all that combat air support, and it wasn't being very effective.

"In the course of looking for the crew and destroying all the boats that were around, the White House said, 'Before the aircraft attack a boat, you have to make a low pass and ensure that there are no Caucasians on the boat, because you may be attacking the boat with the crew in it.' So A-7s [Corsair II jet bombers] were making low passes, reporting back that there were no Caucasians aboard. Could they attack? The NMCC [National Military Command Center] would relay the information to the White House situation room, and they'd come back and say, 'Yes, you can attack.' That was perhaps the most 'over control' I ever experienced."[20]

In the midst of a miasma of depression over early news of fierce fire-fights on Koh Tang, about 11 p.m. James Schlesinger called with word that the *Wilson* had retrieved the crewmen and the ship itself was in American hands. Ford recalled, "I dropped the phone into its cradle and let my emotions show. 'They're all safe,' I said. 'We got them all out. Thank God. It went perfectly. It went just great.' Kissinger, Rumsfeld and the others erupted with whoops of joy."

By this moment, with three more waves of bombers in the air and bound for Cambodian sites, it was clear that both the *Mayaguez* and its crew had been liberated. Brent Scowcroft asked if there was any reason not to disengage. Everyone now knew that the assault upon Koh Tang had been unnecessary because none of the Americans were hostages there. Kissinger insisted, "Tell them to bomb the mainland. Let's look ferocious. Otherwise they'll attack us as the ship leaves. Kissinger still wanted to be in charge, wanted to give orders, and he certainly knew the Cambodians had no viable means with which to mount a counterattack from the coast."[21] The commander in chief agreed with his secretary of state.

The second and third strikes pounded installations around Kompong Som. The fourth flight was diverted to Koh Tang to provide tactical support for the marines, now being evacuated from the island. Train said, "In a withdrawal, you have to maintain a certain size [security] force that won't collapse before you can get the whole force out. You have to take that last group out really fast before their perimeter collapses and they're overrun. We dropped what we call a commando vault, or BLU-82 on the islands. It's a 15,000-pound fuel-air mixture bomb that had the stated purpose of clearing helicopter landing zones in the jungle. But it really is a big bang. That created enough of a distraction for us to make the last snatch."[22]

The president jubilantly issued a statement: "At my direction, the United States forces tonight boarded the American merchant ship SS *Mayaguez* and landed at the Island of Koh Tang for the purpose of rescuing the crew and the ship, which had been illegally seized by Cambodian forces. They also conducted supporting strikes against nearby military installations. I have now received information that the vessel has been recovered intact and the entire crew has been rescued. The forces that have successfully accomplished this mission are still under hostile fire but are preparing to disengage." Before retiring for the night, he wrote to House and Senate leaders, explaining all that had happened since the seizure of the *Mayaguez* sixty-five hours earlier. These letters, he said, fulfilled the requirements of the War Powers Act.

Ford's announcement did not mention that the Cambodians had voluntarily released the crew and abandoned the ship. He did not know the casualties for the venture at the moment, but the rescue of forty men cost forty-one dead, including those in the helicopter crash in Thailand, and forty-nine wounded. Yet to many, still hungover from Vietnam, the affair was a smashing success.

Barry Goldwater exulted, "It was wonderful, it shows we've still got balls in this country." Columnist C. L. Sulzberger in the *New York Times* described Ford as moving "from the doldrums of Hooverdom toward the vigor of Harry Truman." Secretary of State Kissinger preened, "The impact ought to be made clear that there are limits beyond which the United States cannot be pushed."[23] Ford later remarked that his actions ignited confidence in the White House and the American public. Indeed his standing in the polls rose eleven points.

There were naysayers. Sulzberger's colleague on the *Times*, Anthony Lewis, wrote, "Once again an American government shows that the only way it knows how to deal with frustration is by force." Mansfield and others argued that the president had subverted the War Powers Act, having merely told them what he was doing rather than truly consulting.

Ford exulted over what he listed as his most significant foreign policy decision. "*Mayaguez* provided us with a shot in the arm as a nation when we really needed it. It convinced some of our adversaries we were not a paper tiger."[24] But there is no evidence that any country trembled over a bungle-packed demonstration of force against a puny state.

Harry Train disagreed with his president. "We got the crew back, but it was at great cost, and the cost exceeded the merits of the political objective."[25]

The fade-out of the *Mayaguez* affair signaled an end to the ordeal in Southeast Asia. Politicians, statesmen, and the American public added a new and cautionary parable to their primer, "the lessons of Vietnam," which would occupy a place next to "the lessons of Munich." They could point to historian George Santayana's warning that those who failed to understand history are condemned to repeat the mistakes of the past. In a bumper-sticker mentality, no one counseled a corollary of that warning, of the danger of comparing events of long ago with current situations where the culture, the dynamics of the relationships, and the geography might be hugely dissimilar. The end of the Vietnam agony did not resolve the question of how to balance the demands of national security while keeping presidential authority within the prescribed limits.

13

IRAN, AFGHANISTAN,
AND LEBANON

The painful experience of Vietnam discouraged further adventures on behalf of national security in that part of the world. Nevertheless, no one believed in a return to isolationism. The United States would continue to promote an agenda overseas in support of friendly governments or political movements. The focus shifted from Southeast Asia to Latin America and the Middle East as potentially more hospitable arenas for U.S. action and exercise of executive power.

The high-testosterone years, from the Kennedy presidency in 1961 through Johnson and Nixon, ebbed with Gerald Ford in the White House, although Secretary of State Kissinger sought to inject Ford with a bit of the old moxie. While the *Mayaguez* incident boosted Ford's presidential stock, when the 1976 elections came he could not overcome a deficit created by his pardon for his predecessor and a perception of weak leadership. His successor, Democrat Jimmy Carter, a former Georgia governor, peanut farmer, and Naval Academy grad, entered the White House as an antidote to foreign adventurism. Carter signaled a break with his predecessors at Notre Dame's 1977 commencement ceremonies: "We are now free of that inordinate fear of communism which once led us to embrace any dictator who joined us in that fear."

The new president championed an agreement that returned the Panama Canal Zone to Panama. The treaty squeaked through the Senate. Ronald Reagan tried to exploit the misgivings about the transfer with the mantra, "We bought it, we paid for it, it's ours and we're going to keep it."[1] Flags waved, listeners clapped, but the arrangement was irreversible.

Among those who placed democracy and individual freedom at the top of goals for U.S. foreign policy, Carter earned some high marks. A military junta that ruled Argentina after a coup ousted a civilian government drew censure for human rights violations. The administration upbraided Chilean dictator Augusto Pinochet, who took charge after the machinations of the CIA helped overthrow Salvador Allende. Both of the totalitarian South American countries had tortured, murdered, and "disappeared" thousands of citizens. In February 1977, National Security Adviser Zbigniew Brzezinski approved an initiative that curtailed shipping arms to those labeled "egregious human-rights violators."[2]

Brzezinski supported his commander in chief's emphasis upon human rights. The son of a Polish diplomat, he and his family had suffered the pain of forced exile, first from the Nazi invasion of Poland, then from the harsh Soviet occupation of the country. Unlike his predecessor, Kissinger, who had ignored tyranny if practiced by friendly despots such as Pinochet, Anastasio Somoza in Nicaragua, and the China of Mao Tse-tung, Brzezinski saw human rights not only as a moral issue but also as a weapon with which to whack the Soviet conduct in Eastern Europe. Early in the first year of the Carter presidency, one of Brzezinski's regular advisories to his boss noted, "Some in Congress are using human rights as an excuse to block aid or attach restrictions. . . . I believe the human-rights idea is morally justified and historically relevant. It must be a broad concept . . . encompassing social and economic existence as well as political liberty."[3]

In 1979, Carter suddenly faced the collapse of the government of Iran. That country had been a key part of the 1969–1970 Nixon Doctrine. Originally known as the Guam Doctrine but later spun with a new title that promoted its putative author, it postulated a world system in which the United States would create strong regional actors to secure their own and American interests in their respective neighborhoods. The theory fitted neatly into the kind of geopolitical structure that Kissinger had frequently urged while still an academic and found an enthusiastic advocate in Nixon. Iran was chosen as the anchor for the Middle East. In pursuit of the doctrine, Nixon promised to sell the shah conventional weapons systems, bypassing the usual interagency arms deals scrutiny. The policy also favored trade with Iran to provide economic stability. Little attention was paid by either the Nixon or Ford regimes to the massive corruption encouraged by American largesse and the iron-fisted squeeze on the people by the shah and his coterie. Carter inherited the situation.

The program to strengthen Mohammed Reza Pahlavi in Iran had wrought one of the cruelest betrayals in U.S. diplomatic history. The minority Kurds, revolting against Iran's enemy, Iraq, had been promised by Nixon and Kissinger $16 million in arms. During the Ford presidency, Iran and Iraq agreed upon a truce. As part of the agreement, the United States halted the shipment of the tools of war to the Kurds beset by Iraq's Saddam Hussein. Mustafa Barzani, the Kurdish leader, pleaded with the secretary of state to restore the arms, but Kissinger did not even reply.

When he appeared before a closed-door investigation by a congressional committee, Kissinger, never a zealot when it came to other people's freedom, explained the reversal of policy toward the Kurds in their struggle for freedom: "Covert action should not be confused with missionary work."[4] Later he expressed some regret for the shabby treatment of the Kurds, but that unfortunate people seemed destined to suffer from U.S. infidelity. As a direct result of the new policy, Saddam Hussein butchered thousands of them.

In spite of his mantle as an advocate of freedom and democracy, in November 1977 Carter invited the Iranian leader to Washington for an official state visit. The president pledged his support to the shah, praising him as a "strong leader . . . we look upon Iran as a very stabilizing force in the world at large."[5] In a private conversation, Carter appealed for reform on human rights, but the shah refused to bend. The president endorsed all military and economic requests from Iran.

The rancor and disorder in Iran mounted, and the shah, determined to quash any movements he saw as "subversive/communist," responded with even harsher rule. In other Middle Eastern countries the antigovernment forces had extreme left-wing elements, but in Iran the strongest opposition issued from radical Islamists, dismayed more by the secularism, corruption, and "immorality" of the regime than by a lack of democratic institutions. Many more individuals, while not devout Muslims, followed the religious leaders because they represented the best hope of ousting the shah. By 1979, revolution threatened to overthrow the government. In a country where the CIA had enjoyed its first success, getting rid of Mossadegh, the intelligence community failed miserably. "Our political intelligence indicated continuity in Iran," said Brzezinski, "and later still, by the end of October, [William] Sullivan [U.S. ambassador to Tehran] was reporting that 'our destiny is to work with the Shah' in a controlled transition. Yet within ten days we in Washington were confronted with sudden report of a serious crisis, with the Shah said to be considering abdication."[6] Unfortunately, the Iranian rebels regarded the twenty-five years since Mossadegh as a period fraught with overweening U.S. influence.

Beset by uncontrollable mobs in the streets of Tehran and other major cities, with the military no longer able to guarantee his security and the flames of revolution fanned by the rhetoric of newly returned exile Ayatollah Ruhollah Khomeini, the shah, suffering from cancer and gallstones, chose exile, departing Iran on January 16, 1979. A man without a country, he wandered from Egypt to Morocco to Mexico, hoping he might somehow be restored to power.

"Fuck the Shah," said the president. "He's just as well off playing tennis in Acapulco as he is in California."[7] Subsequently, Carter offered him humanitarian entry to the country for medical treatment. Angry Iranians demanded that his protectors turn him over for trial. After the White House refused, on November 4, 1979, a mob in Tehran overran the American embassy, taking sixty-six hostages. A number were released on various grounds, but fifty-two settled in for an anxiety-riddled stay. Khomeini turned out to be a prophet of fire, brimstone, and death.

The president shook his fist. He sent a pair of aircraft carriers to the area, but this was not a nineteenth-century case of Caribbean pirates or a warlord to be frightened by a show of the flag. He halted all oil purchases from Iran and froze that country's assets. The World Court and the United Nations Security Council condemned the hostage-taking, but the Iranians ignored the international criticism. Frustrated Americans tied yellow ribbons on their mailboxes in memory of the imprisoned and wore T-shirts emblazoned with vulgar suggestions to the ayatollah and his countrymen. For its part the Khomeini government embarked on a campaign of executions against anyone deemed subversive, heightening fears for the safety of the incarcerated.

After five months of failed diplomatic efforts, Carter resorted to a high-risk military venture aimed at liberating the hostages. At zero hour for the launch, the commander in chief summoned congressional leaders, but they were advised, not consulted, about a military operation already under way.

Admiral Train, in command of the Sixth Fleet, remembered, "My helicopters were used, and Gen. Dave Jones [chairman of the Joint Chiefs] didn't tell me what they were going to use the helicopters for. I had sent two intact squadrons of helicopters . . . not knowing that my crews were going to be taken off those helicopters and replaced with Marine crews and that my maintenance people would be replaced by Marine maintenance people. The people we had planning [the mission] couldn't make contact with any of our people, couldn't tap into any of the knowledge regarding that type of helicopter operations. No one was sensitive to the fact that to take an RH-53 that is designed to fly low and slow with high drag and to make it fly high, fast, for extended ranges through sandstorms isn't necessarily the best utilization of an asset."[8]

A half dozen C-130 transports flew ninety commandos to a remote airstrip in the Iranian desert. From there the eight helicopters would carry them to the embassy, where they would overcome the guards, load the hostages on the choppers, and escape before the Iranians could mount a defense. Unfortunately, only six helicopters reached the rendezvous site and one developed mechanical problems. The commander on the scene realized the remaining aircraft could not carry out the mission and received permission from the White House to abort. Disaster struck as a helicopter collided with a C-130 while it refueled. A fiery explosion killed eight servicemen and badly burned four others. The survivors fled Iran in the remaining aircraft.

A blizzard of criticisms enveloped the commander in chief. He was taken to task for acting too late, for not deploying sufficient resources, and for approving such a high-risk scheme. What would have occurred in Tehran if the army Rangers had descended on the embassy area as planned is unknown. But the commander in chief, while giving his imprimatur to the expedition, had left its execution entirely to the military experts.

General Jones attributed much of the blame to the lack of experience of the services in working together. "We couldn't find any base to operate out of except an aircraft carrier. The Navy had to be involved. We didn't find any way to operate with other helicopters. The best . . . were the Marines' minesweeping helicopters. They had the range, the size. There were Marine pilots as well as Navy pilots available. The only thing to assault the Embassy was the Delta team, Army. We needed the air refueling and the transports from the Air Force to put all this together. . . . Security was overriding; there was no way to run a total dress rehearsal and not tip the hand."

Jones said he worked closely with General John Vogt, who was in charge of the mission, and the Joint Chiefs also spent considerable time on the plans. "President Carter was unfairly criticized . . . as though he got in and monkeyed with everything. He did not get in and tinker." At a final meeting with the president, Jones reported that Carter said, "I want to make sure this is very clear. No one will speak for me. I will be available."

Jones arranged that he would be the sole contact with Vogt and his instructions would come either from the commander in chief or Secretary of Defense Harold Brown. "I told President Carter that as I got information I would inform him. Sometimes an hour or two would go by and we would get no information. I would not bug Vogt. The President didn't bug me. . . . We had determined that under certain conditions we would abort. We told the President it was best to decide these things ahead of time where the pressure of going ahead wasn't so great. When we got down to the too few helicopters, we got word that people in the desert recommended aborting. General Vogt recommended aborting. When they told me, I recommended we abort. I called the President, and he said, 'I agree.'"[9] Carter accepted full responsibility for the disaster. But much of the public refused to excuse him for bad luck or mistakes by those involved in the rescue effort. Instead he earned a reputation for incompetence.

Another South Asian nation, Afghanistan, surfaced as a battleground, forcing the Carter administration to choose sides. While the Islamic religion predominated there, a sectarian stew, limited arable land, poverty, and the absence of a strong central government fertilized revolution. In the twentieth century a dozen leaders had lost their power by assassinations, executions, or bloody usurpations. In April 1978, communist elements seized control.

The communists fared little better than their predecessors at governing the fractious nation. They began a campaign of terror against religious and secular individuals whom they believed antagonistic to their rule. Like the Americans dealing with Iran, the Soviets and their Afghan counterparts badly underestimated the growing strength of conservative Islamism. An uprising against the local communists and their mentors in Herat slaughtered a dozen Russian political advisers. In revenge, Soviet pilots flew bombers that pounded Herat into rubble, killing as many as twenty thousand. The pulverization of Herat inflamed Afghans. Troops mutinied against their commanders; whole units defected to the rebels and murdered their foreign advisers. The loyalists struck back with another massacre and a full-fledged jihad ignited.

At the White House, the president considered proposals from the CIA for covert aid to the anticommunist rebels. Not only would the Soviets and their allies in Afghanistan be forced to expend resources dealing with the opposition, but by aligning itself with the insurgents the United States might deflect some of the antagonism of Middle East Muslims, whipped up by the Iranian militants and burnished by American support for Israel. Most of the intelligence analysts believed that while the Soviets would increase their shipments of arms and send more advisers, they would not directly intervene in the civil war.

Late in June, Brzezinski, acting on the suggestions of a committee considering options, recommended that the commander in chief authorize "non-lethal" covert support for the rebels.[10] On July 3, 1979, Carter signed a presidential finding as required by the Hughes-Ryan amendment. The finding enabled the CIA to invest half a million dollars in propaganda, psychological operations, ship radio equipment, medical supplies, and cash to the rebels.

At the time the president issued his finding, CIA analysts largely agreed that the Soviet premier, Yuri Andropov, a former KGB head and hardly bashful about savage repression, would not intervene in the civil war. But not only did the mujahideen threaten to seize power, the Soviet-friendly establishment in Kabul had fallen apart. Unwilling to lose control of Afghanistan, on December 26, 1979, a month after the Iranian mob overran the U.S. embassy in Tehran, Soviet troops entered the country and installed a new puppet.

The president, who had begun his term saying the policy of containment no longer automatically prevailed, was forced to tell the nation on January 4, 1980, "Soviet-occupied Afghanistan threatens both Iran and Pakistan and is a stepping stone to possible control over much of the world's oil supplies." He invoked the specter of history: "that aggression, unopposed becomes a contagious disease." He labeled the Soviet intervention in Afghanistan as (possibly) "the most serious threat to peace since the Second World War," a stretch in light of the Korean conflict, the threats to Taiwan, the missile crisis, and the war in Vietnam.

In 1998, Brzezinski boasted to a reporter for a French journal, "According to the official version of history, CIA aid to the mujahideen began during 1980 . . . after the Soviet army invaded Afghanistan. But the reality, kept secret until now, is completely different." Citing the finding by the president, Brzezinski said, "I explained that in my opinion this aid would lead to a Soviet intervention." Expressing no regrets, he continued, "The secret operation was an excellent idea. It drew the Russians into the Afghan trap and you want me to regret it? On the day that the Soviets officially crossed the border, I wrote to President Carter, saying in essence: 'We now have the opportunity of giving to the USSR its Vietnam War.'"[11]

Brzezinski made no such perspicacious claim in his book *Power and Principle*, published in 1983, nor did he even mention his recommendation for clandestine support to his commander in chief. In fact, the day after Christmas 1979, as Soviet tanks rumbled across the border, Brzezinski sent a memo to the commander in chief: "We should not be too sanguine about Afghanistan becoming a Soviet Vietnam. The guerrillas are badly organized and poorly led. They have no sanctuary, no organized army and no central government—all of which North Vietnam had." Like most generals as well as civilian experts, the national security adviser mistakenly thought in terms of the previous war, instead of looking at the current situation.

For the next ten years, including the Ronald Reagan presidency, U.S. policy supported and supplied its surrogates, the mujahideen, but put no boots on the ground, other than perhaps CIA agents. In aiding the anti-Soviet forces, the United States risked no adverse reactions in the Middle East. Every Muslim country, almost all nondemocratic, quickly denounced the Soviet invasion. Communist China, in further demonstration that not all Reds traveled together, supported the mujahideen for fear that a Moscow-dominated Afghanistan threatened its neighbor Pakistan.

As the 1980 presidential campaign loomed, the hostage situation in Tehran dragged on. A man on horseback rode out of the West to infatuate the voters. Erstwhile silver-screen cowboy Ronald Wilson Reagan, parlaying a middling career in Hollywood and his stints as president of the Screen Actors Guild and as the public face for General Electric, with the help of his wife Nancy and devoted friends had transformed himself from a Democrat into the Republican governor of California. His best biographer, Lou Cannon, subtitled his book *The Role of a Lifetime*, an exceedingly apt description of a man who so wondrously personified the image of the presidency and values that Americans believed in, even when both behaved quite differently.

The Carter White House had intensified its diplomatic efforts to liberate the Iran hostages during the months before the election as both candidates realized that their safe return could swing the vote. Gary Sick, who served under Brzezinski and later on the Reagan National Security Council, wrote that Reagan's campaign manager, William Casey, through connections with the CIA secretly met with an Iranian representative of Ayatollah Khomeini in Madrid. Casey promised delivery of arms—something Carter to date had refused—and an end to the freeze on Iranian assets under U.S. control, if release of the hostages could be postponed until after the election. The deal was approved by the Iranians.[12] Negotiations now stalled until after the defeat of the incumbent. Not until the day of Ronald Reagan's inauguration on January 20, 1981, did the hostages board a plane that flew them to freedom.

In the White House, Reagan articulated a vague vision—America as the shining city on the hill and the destruction of the USSR, the "evil empire," a *Star Wars* moniker. He believed wholeheartedly that wherever communism reared its ugly head, the seed and the feed flowed from Moscow. Interviewed by the *Wall Street Journal* five months before his election, he said, "The Soviet Union underlies all the unrest that is going on. If they weren't engaged in this game of dominoes, there wouldn't be any hot spots in the world."[13] That grinding poverty, corruption, totalitarian governments, religious and ethnic persecution, or nationalism might inflame "hot spots" did not seem to cross his mind.

Official documents and schedules painted him as a conscientious chief executive, but in fact he worked roughly nine to five, catnaps during cabinet meetings included, with afternoons off on Wednesdays and sometimes Fridays. Critics called him "lazy," but he accepted gibes with good humor, aware that his strongest asset lay in his invincible portrayal of a president. Unlike Kennedy, Johnson, Nixon, Carter, and to a lesser extent Gerald Ford, he presided above the battle, leaving his subordinates to fill in the details, which often wound up becoming policy. Closest to him was a coterie that included Michael Deaver, a California public relations executive who served as deputy chief of staff, onetime California prosecutor Edwin Meese in the attorney general's seat, and Texas lawyer James Baker serving as chief of staff. First Lady Nancy Reagan played an important role, not in making policy, but with her fierce determination to protect her husband's health, well-being, and reputation.

Commander in chief Reagan brought a cast of characters to the executive branch of the government that varied not a whit from their predecessors in geopolitical philosophy. They were all resolutely anticommunist and believed that mischief mainly emanated from Moscow. However, along with their leader, the men and women who drove the policies differed in personality from the earlier incarnations of their offices. They were not academic or business intellectuals. For the most part, they had earned their spurs fighting in the economic trenches. The initial recruits, Chief of Staff James Baker, Secretary of Defense Caspar Weinberger, Treasury Secretary Donald Regan, Ambassador to the United Nations Jeane Kirkpatrick (an exception, who did have a professorial background), National Security Adviser Richard Allen, and CIA director William Casey, were, like their leader, individuals supremely confident of their knowledge and skills. None were given to the type of hissy fits that occasionally afflicted Kissinger.

The one appointee who did not fit neatly with the incoming administration was the secretary of state, Alexander Haig. Age had not withered his ego nor custom staled his assertiveness. Kissinger had never liked him, perhaps because he refused to suppress his own opinions, even when they ran counter to those of his superior. Haig would complain that the Reagan style denied the secretary of state the sort of privileged access to the commander in chief that enabled State to manage foreign affairs. Both Edwin Meese and Michael Deaver acted as filters for the president. They were offended by what they considered the imperious manner of the secretary of state. Haig bridled at insults to his status, such as when, for example, Deaver assigned him to a compartment on Air Force One that placed him farther from the president than he desired; on another occasion he was denied a seat on the presidential helicopter.

The detached style of Reagan's governance worked fairly smoothly on the domestic front. His general policy of lower taxes, cuts in domestic spending, and heavier investment in the armed forces did not encroach upon congressional prerogatives. However, abroad, the pervasive thrust of anticommunism meant covert actions and commitment of the military. As Lou Cannon pointed out, to fulfill his broad foreign policy outlines his deputies engaged in actions that went well beyond the accepted scope of the White House. The arrangement baffled Al Haig, whose previous service in Washington during the Johnson and Nixon administrations had led him to believe that foreign policy and its execution were visible in the precincts of the secretary of state, the Defense Department, and the National Security Council. "To me," wrote Haig later, "the White House was as mysterious as a ghost ship; you heard the creak of the rigging and the groan of the timbers and sometimes even glimpsed the crew on deck. But which of the crew had the helm? Was it Meese, was it Baker, was it someone else?"[14]

Haig spoke more pithily about the situation to Cannon. "Do you think I gave a shit about guerrilla warfare with a bunch of second-rate hambones in the White House? For Christ sake, I've lived through more guerrilla warfare in my lifetime than anybody I know."[15]

The Reagan regime inherited the ongoing campaign to promote a noncommunist Afghanistan by funding and supplying the guerrillas battling Soviet troops. Early in 1981, the president renewed the Jimmy Carter finding that authorized the CIA to arm and fund the anticommunist guerrillas. The agency bought hundreds of thousands of surplus single-shot British-made Lee Enfield rifles and thousands of rocket-propelled grenade launchers from Greece, India, Egypt, and even China (which was resolutely opposed to the USSR) and shipped them through Pakistan.[16]

William Casey, the CIA chief, uncertain about the operations in Afghanistan initially, became an enthusiastic supporter, twisting arms to double CIA appropriations and inveigling Saudi Arabia to contribute. The Saudis regarded Muslim fundamentalism, properly monitored, as a lever to suppress democratic, or worse, communist, elements in their midst. The cost to the Soviets so delighted Casey that he ultimately would sponsor Islamic guerrillas inside the borders of the Soviet Union. That military action obviously went way beyond anything contemplated in the findings and transgressed upon the authority of Congress to make war.

Another hallmark of the Reagan administration, the intervention of the United States in Central America, thought by many to have been a creation of the Reagan regime, actually had its origins in the Carter presidency. When the Marxist Sandinistas, named for the 1920s revolutionary Sandino, overthrew the murderous dictatorship of Anastasio Somoza in 1979, the White House supplied $125 million in economic aid, even as some in Congress such as North Carolina Republican Jesse Helms warned that the Sandinistas were a carbon copy of the Castroites. In El Salvador, leftist insurgents increased the bloodshed in guerrilla warfare against a pro-U.S. government. A week before Reagan's inauguration, Carter suspended the economic aid to Nicaragua and dispatched nineteen U.S. military advisers to aid the embattled Salvadoran government.[17]

Although Haig appears not to have been involved in the covert actions in Afghanistan, he grabbed the cudgels to swat communist influences in Latin America. During the first National Security Council meetings attended by the president, the secretary of state argued for an aggressive defense of the centrist José Napoleon Duarte government of El Salvador. But the best he could persuade the White House to do was to increase the military advisers from the original nineteen to fifty-five and send additional armaments. Even that relatively modest program drew criticism from Congress. However, Reagan sounded the alarm with an interview in the March 27, 1981, *Washington Post*, labeling the Salvadoran insurgents terrorists and representatives of "revolution being exported to the Americas, to Central America and further south." He credited the genesis of their insurrection to the USSR and Cuba. The rebels were beaten back. After leftists boycotted elections, the right wing won a majority and chose for president Roberto D'Aubuisson, who at best cast a benign eye upon death squads that murdered anyone in opposition.

Haig tried to organize a strategy to evict Fidel Castro. But the group put together by State's legal counsel, Robert "Bud" McFarlane, could not come up with a practical means to overthrow the Cuban dictator. McFarlane later told Cannon that when he informed Haig of their findings, Haig snarled, "This is just rash, limp-wristed, traditional cookie-pushing bullshit."[18] Overt and covert U.S. involvement in the armed struggles of Central America would steadily deepen, albeit without the issue of conventional U.S. forces on the ground and planes in the air.

Haig said he was uncomfortable with clandestine machinations against unfriendly nations. "I think covert action is a copout. It means you're not willing to share decisions with the people. I am not against covert operations for little things, but it should be rejected for major policy. That was totally ignored by Reagan. He loved Bill Casey. I kept asking him to bring things to the 40 Committee [a policy review group] but it wasn't done."[19]

The American contribution to the struggle in Afghanistan percolated smoothly without stress to the Reagan administration. However, the chronic sickness of the Middle East took a turn for the worse in June 1982 when Israel responded to an assassination attempt on its British ambassador with an air raid that blew up an empty grandstand and an ammunition dump in Beirut. Members of the Palestine Liberation Organization, composed of refugee Arabs displaced by the 1967 and 1973 wars, then fired shells from inside Lebanon at towns in the Galilee. On June 6, Israeli troops poured over the border into Lebanon, crushing the PLO and Syrian forces. The Israeli forces paused for a few days but then began to bombard West Beirut.

While American diplomats tried to broker a cease-fire that would include removal of all foreign armed parties in Lebanon—the PLO, as well as Israeli and Syrian units—the commander in chief secretly agreed to participation of the United States in a United Nations peacekeeping force. The decision irked the military leaders. General John W. Vessey, newly installed as chairman of the Joint Chiefs, wrote a memo to Caspar Weinberger saying it would "be very unwise for the U.S. to find itself in a position where it had to put its forces between the Israelis and the Arabs."[20]

Haig, although his resignation had been accepted, thought he had arranged for international peacekeepers to enter Beirut after the withdrawal of the PLO. Then the Israeli and Syrian forces would depart. "Under my direction," said Haig, "Phil Habib put it together. Then King Khalid of Saudi Arabia died. Cap Weinberger and George Bush went to the Saudi palace [a condolence mission] and said Haig did not speak for the U.S. That ended the agreement."[21]

On August 25, eight hundred U.S. Marines joined French and Italian contingents as part of the peacekeeping brigades. All seemed to go well as the PLO evacuated positions in Beirut, and a Reagan Plan to bring resolution of the disputes drew encouragement from moderate Arab leaders and grudging acceptance from Israeli prime minister Menachem Begin. A fortnight after they had arrived, the marines departed. The secretary of defense and the chairman of the Joint Chiefs convinced the commander in chief that the mission was accomplished. The new secretary of state, George Shultz, and Philip Habib, the special envoy to the Middle East, sharply disagreed with the decision. The French and Italians took their cue from the United States and withdrew.

Four days after the marines shipped out, a huge explosion at the head-quarters of the Phalangist Party killed the Christian leader, Bashir Gemayel. Within twenty-four hours, Israeli troops poured into West Beirut, in vio-lation of the agreement under which the PLO had been evacuated. Begin and his armed forces commander, General Ariel Sharon, claimed they acted to protect civilians from reprisals by Gemayel's militia. But while the Israelis stood by, that militia invaded two Palestinian refugee camps and slaughtered at least seven hundred people. Any semblance of govern-ment vanished in Lebanon. Violence prowled the Beirut streets and civil strife threatened to engulf the entire country. The president, against the wishes of Weinberger and the Joint Chiefs, promoted a new multinational force as a means to recharge the peace process. Reagan indicated a limited time period, sixty days, but that stretched out for nearly a year.

For some six months Lebanon's violence diminished enough to drop out of the headlines but on April 18, 1983, a delivery truck packed with explosives blew up in the yard of the Beirut U.S. embassy, killing sixty-three people, including seventeen Americans. Among the dead were eight CIA agents, providers of vital intelligence as well as key links in the efforts to cobble together a government friendly or at least neutral. When George Shultz could not achieve an agreement that evacuated both the Israeli and Syrian forces from Lebanon, Weinberger intensified his opposi-tion to the stationing of marines in Beirut.

Weinberger told Lou Cannon that Shultz and Bud McFarlane lobbied the commander in chief on the grounds of patriotism. "He was being told all this stuff. Marines don't cut and run. Americans don't run when the going gets tough. Americans don't pull down the flag. I said, 'Nonsense, they're not doing any good over there.'"[22] But those who wooed the president with notions of patriotism knew their man. In an August 23 Seattle speech, he bugled, "As a nation, we've closed the books on a long dark period of fail-ure and self-doubt and set a new course. . . . Our military forces are back on their feet and standing tall." Placement of troops thus hinged on the prideful concept of international prestige, a principle responsible for almost as much death and destruction as battles over religion. Anti-American fac-tions fired rockets and mortars at marines stationed at the Beirut airport. Warring partisans occupied the flank of the leathernecks.

The commander in chief authorized U.S. Navy warships to support the Lebanese army. Still, the marines took more casualties, and now congres-sional voices raised the War Powers Act, which required the removal of the armed forces after ninety days. Working with the House Speaker,

Democrat Tip O'Neill, the president persuaded the legislators to draft a resolution that permitted the marines to remain another eighteen months. Weinberger adamantly opposed the policy, but his was the only dissenting voice in the president's inner circle. The Joint Chiefs, also against the deployment, fed memos through Weinberger, but according to Cannon the president probably never read them. Chief of Naval Operations James Watkins undermined their position in testimony before Congress: "It is the opinion of the Joint Chiefs of Staff that withdrawal of the multinational forces at this time probably would have devastating effect and could plunge Lebanon into anarchy."[23] Later, General Vessey admitted, "None of us marched in and told the president that the U.S. is going to face disaster if the Marines didn't withdraw."[24]

Reagan had entered the White House as an antidote to a president who spoke of an American "malaise." He determined to announce that no one should regard the United States as weak, and apparently believed that a show of armed force would persuade those who doubted American resolve or the inference that its chief executive had lost his power. However, it was no longer a world where the sight of a few warships or the proverbial whiff of grapeshot deterred those inspired by ideology and with access to deadly weapons.

14

BEIRUT, CENTRAL
AMERICA, AND IRAN

The enemies of the United States were not cowed by the presence of American armed forces. But instead of a direct confrontation they resorted to what would become the chief terrorist weapon, the suicide bomber. A frustrated Goliath, with no obvious target for retaliation, could only demonstrate its power with a war against a puny island in the Caribbean and vigorous covert actions against presumed foes in Latin America. The Reagan White House, which wielded human rights as a club against the Soviet Union's "evil empire," ignored them when it came to Chile, El Salvador, and Nicaragua.

At 6:22 a.m. on Sunday, October 23, 1983, the disaster predicted by General Vessey erupted. A Mercedes truck stuffed with six tons of TNT roared through the parking lot of the four-story, reinforced-concrete headquarters of the First Battalion, Eighth Marine Regiment. "The truck drove over the barbed and concertina wire obstacle, passed between two Marine guard posts without being engaged by fire, entered an open gate, passed around one sewer pipe barrier and between two others, flattened the Sergeant of the Guard's sandbagged booth at the building's entrance, penetrated the lobby of the building and detonated while the majority of the occupants slept. The force of the explosion ripped the building from its foundation. The building then imploded upon itself. Almost all the occupants were crushed or trapped inside the wreckage."[1] Altogether, 241 marines died from the blast, while many more were severely wounded. A few miles away, a slightly less devastating bomb blew up the barracks of French paratroopers, killing 58.

That same weekend, the State Department had received a plea from the Organization of Eastern Caribbean States, a small, loose confederation of former British colonies. The group appealed for intervention in Grenada, one of their number. There, members of his own party had kidnapped, then murdered left-wing prime minister Maurice Bishop. A military council had proclaimed itself the legitimate government. Of particular concern to the White House were some one thousand Americans, mainly students at the medical school. Some envisioned a replay of the Iranian hostage situation.

Even before the killing of Bishop, Vice President George H. W. Bush had been tasked with the formation of a contingency plan for dealing with Grenada, where Cuban laborers and some soldiers were building a new airport. There were fears that Fidel Castro would dominate the island. When George Shultz and Bud McFarlane briefed the president, telling him that the chaos jeopardized the lives of the thousand Americans there, he immediately authorized an invasion, under the code name Urgent Fury. "He was very unequivocal. He couldn't wait."[2]

Secretary of Defense Weinberger had no problem with an invasion of Grenada. "It was a war in which we were asked. They were seeking help in an anarchical situation. Prime Minister [Eugenia] Charles [of Dominica] was very persuasive. We wouldn't have gone unless asked. We certainly did not need approval from the UN or NATO." Weinberger added, "The UN is incapable of fighting a war. Procedurally, two or three countries can block an action." He cited the Revolutionary War as a parallel example. "Washington had a terrible time because the Continental Congress wanted to direct military action."[3] His analogy was not applicable.

The request from the OECS, signed by Prime Minister Charles, enabled Reagan to claim he had no choice but to intervene, despite the fact that the United States did not belong to the OECS and had no treaty connections with it. Future Supreme Court chief justice John G. Roberts, at the time an assistant White House counsel, rebuffed questions on the authority to send in the troops. "This has been recognized at least since the time President Jefferson sent the Marines to the shores of Tripoli. While there is no clear line separating what the president may do on his own and what requires a formal declaration of war, the Grenada mission seems to be clearly acceptable as an exercise of executive authority . . . when it is recalled that neither the Korean nor Vietnamese conflicts were declared war."[4] But the marines went to Tripoli because freebooters had robbed and ransomed Americans, which was not the case in Grenada. Truman never had the authority to fight North Korea, and the earliest U.S. armed forces in Vietnam came by invitation from South Vietnam. Later, LBJ had obtained the enabling Tonkin Gulf Resolution. Absent a declaration of war or permissive resolution from Congress, Roberts's opinion lacked any genuine precedents.

On October 24 the first paratroopers from what was ultimately an attacking force of five thousand touched down. They met some resistance from the eight hundred Cubans working at the airport, and casualties for the Americans added up to 19 dead, 115 wounded. But after two days, Grenada had been secured. The American students apparently had never been in serious danger.

Subsequently, some critics, such as former Colorado Democratic senator Gary Hart, doubted the justification for the invasion. "I personally never understood the necessity for the Grenada invasion. I don't recall any briefing about American lives at risk. It was a kind of a Monroe Doctrine thing, a show of force to demonstrate American resolve and strength."[5]

In fact, the commander in chief deliberately refused to alert Congress ahead of time about Urgent Fury. "If word of the rescue mission leaked out in advance, we'd hear this from some in Congress. 'Sure it's starting small, but once you make that first commitment, Grenada's going to become another Vietnam.'"[6] Some may have been naïve enough to believe this assertion, but it's difficult to compare the tiny island and small population in the Caribbean, on America's doorstep, to Vietnam, twelve thousand miles from Washington and in the backyards of the two big communist powers.

Several hours after the start of Urgent Fury, McFarlane broke the news to the president of the carnage inflicted on the marines in Beirut. Shocked and grieving over the deaths of the leathernecks, the president angrily denounced the attack on the barracks, but no one could suggest a target for retaliation. He was buffeted in the media and in Congress for the Beirut disaster.

Others wondered whether the Grenada affair was a public relations attempt to overcome the negative reactions to Lebanon. Tip O'Neill said, "Grenada was really about Lebanon." Cannon argued that the plan to invade Grenada pre-dated the bombing in Beirut and therefore could not have been designed to restore the White House's image.[7] On the other hand, the president himself drew a connection between the two places. In an October 27 speech to the country, he said, "The events in Lebanon and Grenada, though oceans apart, are closely related. Not only has Moscow assisted and encouraged the violence in both countries, but it provides direct support through a network of surrogates and terrorists." He cited the presence on the island of Soviet advisers and the Cubans and talked of national security concerns, "which can be threatened in faraway places. It's up to all of us to be aware of the strategic importance of such places and to be able to identify them."

George Shultz called the Grenada invasion "a shot heard round the world," similar to the 1981 British decision to fight for retention of the Falkland Islands against Argentina. Shultz claimed the two events demonstrated that "some Western democracies were again ready to use military strength . . . in defense of their principles and interests,"[8] a genteel replay of the explanation for U.S. troops in Vietnam that Lyndon Johnson gave to Arthur Goldberg.

While a case might be made for Grenada in the Caribbean as a potential security issue, hardly the same could have been said for Beirut. Only in terms of Middle East instability could Lebanon have been an issue of national security. In any case, in neither instance did Congress get to exercise anything resembling its power to declare war. The marines went to Lebanon on the basis of an agreement for a multinational peacekeeping force, reached by Philip Habib and approved by the White House. Congress never had an opportunity to draft an authorizing resolution vote until after the marines were already there.

Haig remarked, "Bill Clark [the national security adviser], the biggest jerk in Washington, put the force in Beirut. The marines there had been told not to load their weapons. They were defenseless. When the bomb blew up the barracks, the battalion commander was relieved. No one else was held responsible."[9]

The commander in chief's first reaction to the deaths of so many of his troops in Beirut had been one of deep sorrow. That emotion gave way to a desire to retaliate. He threw a wild punch, one that would not strike those directly responsible for the devastation of the marine barracks but would remind sponsors of the consequences. With the halfhearted support of Weinberger and the Joint Chiefs, an airstrike from flattops blasted targets at Baalbek in the Bekaa Valley that housed the alleged sources of the Beirut bombing, Iranian Revolutionary Guards and anti-American Lebanese Shiites. Syrian gunners knocked down two planes.

Weinberger said, "I approved the first insertion of troops in Lebanon. It was a specific job and a multinational operation to lift the PLO out of Beirut. I agreed to the bombing of Baalbek. No congressional approval was necessary. I don't think the president gave formal notice, not that he had to, there was no War Powers Act invoked." Weinberger had resisted the stationing of the marines in Beirut. "The second time we went in, I opposed. We had no mission. We were a bull's-eye. The rules of engagement restricted our ability to protect the hard ground in front of the airport; our flank was exposed and we were too lightly armed. The first time was with the consent of the Lebanese government with some thirty-one countries involved."[10]

In the wake of the Beirut terrorism, the Americans briefly questioned their infatuation with Reagan. More than 250 American servicemen had died on his watch, dwarfing the handful killed during Carter's failed Iranian rescue attempt. But somehow the Gipper escaped opprobrium, even though the responsibility for the debacle clearly lay on his doorstep. The success in Grenada, heralded as a mighty blow against the expansion of the "evil empire," restored his approval ratings. A Pentagon investigation of what happened in Lebanon noted the failure of the United States to appreciate political conditions in the area and reliance on its military power, but attention focused on the security lapses at the marine installation rather than the posting of troops there.

Unwilling to "cut and run," the White House dragged out the process of evacuating the marines in Lebanon while the situation deteriorated further. Even McFarlane and Shultz, who originally favored stationing troops in Lebanon, wavered. Questioned about Tip O'Neill's assertion that the House would pass a resolution calling for removal of the American forces, the commander in chief chose a military term: "He may be ready to surrender, but I'm not. As long as there is a chance for peace the mission remains the same."[11]

According to Professor Jeffrey Record, during the seventeen months following the redeployment of the marines to Beirut, the commander in chief and his minions "cited at least a dozen different political objectives, some incompatible with one another and others clearly beyond the reach of the intervention forces and their rules of engagement."[12] The rationalizations included guarding the Beirut airport, protecting Lebanese, enabling the local army to suppress insurgency, creating a democratic and unified Lebanon (nation-building, ordinarily scorned by Republicans), advancing the Arab-Israeli peace process, preventing domination of Lebanon by either Syria or the Soviet Union, and the traditional "we will not be intimidated by terrorists."

Although Reagan protested, like Lord Byron's reluctantly compliant maiden, saying "I'll ne'er consent, [he] consented." The White House said it would support the government of Lebanon—which was almost nonexistent—with ships and planes while it redeployed the troops, a patently transparent euphemism for withdrawal.

Reagan's regime advanced a total of $600 million to Afghanistan, compared to $30 million under Carter. In 1986 the United States shipped

Stingers, handheld antiaircraft missiles deadly against helicopter gunships, which would later show up in the hands of the Taliban and other anti-Americans after the Soviets withdrew from Afghanistan. The events in that far-off land became known as a prime example of "blowback," the unforeseen consequences of a policy.

Much closer to home, the Reagan presidency vigorously opposed any left-winged, communist-tinged movements or governments in Latin America. In the Kennedy-Johnson, Nixon-Ford mode, the president justified the policy as trying to stop this destabilizing force of terrorism and guerrilla warfare and revolution from being exported. "The Soviet Union had violated the Monroe Doctrine and gotten away with it twice, first in Cuba, then in Nicaragua. . . . We captured secret papers on Grenada that documented how the USSR and Cuba were acting in concert to make the Caribbean a Communist Lake."[13] No such documents were ever verified.

However much the commander in chief detested the uprisings or establishment of anti-U.S., Marxist-dominated governments in Latin America and elsewhere, he understood that his devoted public could quickly turn on him if he immersed the country in anything that might resemble the bloody muck of a Vietnam. Columnist Charles Krauthammer dubbed the approach the Reagan Doctrine. With the enthusiastic aid of Casey and the CIA, the basic principle was not a direct confrontation with the USSR or its surrogates but to undermine the "evil empire," aiding rebels in Afghanistan or Nicaragua while supporting those, as in El Salvador, trying to liberate their nation from communists or withstand a left-wing insurgency.

In Nicaragua, where the Carter administration had halted loans to the Somoza government, a Marxist Sandinista government in 1979 had replaced the brutal dictatorship of Somoza. Alarms rang early at the CIA. Director Casey persuaded the president to sign a finding authorizing $19 million to fund the first Contras, a five-hundred-man anti-Sandinista force trained by Argentinians in Honduras. At the same time, as the White House embarked on a program to support the Contras opposing the Sandinistas of Nicaragua, it continued to work with the government in El Salvador to suppress its guerrilla insurgency. The latter involved no Americans inside the country and required no congressional backing. The right to meddle in Nicaragua, a sovereign state under a recognized government, even if no U.S. military forces participated, was a far different matter.

The American support for the regime in El Salvador began in the Carter years even after José Napoleon Duarte, a conservative moderate, was supplanted by an extreme right-winger, Roberto D'Aubuisson. In March

1980, gunmen assassinated Archbishop Oscar Arnulfo Romero and in December of the same year, thugs murdered four American nuns. Mystery cloaked the authors of the two events, but suggestions that right-wing extremists orchestrated the killings caused the Carter administration to temporarily suspend aid. A week before he vacated the White House, the president not only reinstated the funding but also, for the first time, supplied weapons.

Robert White, the ambassador to El Salvàdor, blamed government security forces for the deaths of thousands of people holding left-wing attitudes or even suspected of sympathy to that point of view. But immediately after the new administration moved into their offices, a campaign to vilify the dead and protect their murderers began. Jeane Kirkpatrick asserted, "The nuns were not just nuns. The nuns were also political activists . . . on behalf of the [opposition] Frente and somebody who is using violence to oppose the Frente killed these nuns." Haig muddied the waters further. "The vehicle that the nuns were riding in may have tried to run a roadblock or may have accidentally been perceived to have been doing so, and there may have been an exchange of fire."[14] Eleven months into the Reagan White House, Deane Hinton, in Haig's words, "more tough-minded," "courageous and a very able professional," became the American ambassador. That notwithstanding, Hinton advised Washington that the murder of Archbishop Romero had been planned under the aegis of D'Aubuisson.

Accusations of terrorism by the rebels justified the unwavering U.S. support for the Salvadoran government. Acting secretary of state John Bushnell informed the Senate Foreign Relations Committee in 1981 that "the number [of civilians] killed by unauthorized activities of the security forces . . . are certainly not as great as the number that are killed by the forces of the left."[15] The statement begged the question of what fell under the category of "unauthorized," since statistics on death squads compiled by three human rights groups sharply contradicted Bushnell.

Indeed, an evaluation of the activities of the Salvadoran military by Pentagon officers found that their subjects showed no qualms about the use of excessive force or violence. Brigadier General Fred E. Woerner, who signed the report, wrote, "Unabated terror from the right and continued tolerance of institutional violence could dangerously erode popular support to the point where the armed forces could be viewed not as the protector of society, but as an army of occupation."[16] Several Democratic congressmen pushed through a statute that required the administration to certify improvements in matters of human rights and democratic ideals.

At best because of poor intelligence, or more likely in order to prop up the Salvadoran government, the White House and its officials "certified" untruths about the situation. On January 28, 1982, the president duly advised Congress, "The Government of El Salvador is making a concerted and significant effort to comply with internationally recognized human rights." He cited a decline in violence and alleged abuses during the year while excusing some casualties on the grounds that noncombatants who accompanied guerrillas frequently entered the crossfire of the armed forces.

The rebel broadcast station, Radio Venceremos, had been advising listeners of a mass killing in Morazán, a province in eastern El Salvador, where leftist leaders had issued a plea to human rights organizations and the media to investigate the "genocide" of more than nine hundred Salvadorans. By happenstance, two days before the president spoke to the legislators, Raymond Bonner of the *New York Times* and Alma Guillermoprieto of the *Washington Post* both wrote stories of a December slaughter of civilians around the village of El Mozote in a sector controlled by guerrillas. Photographs taken by Susan Meiselas, who accompanied the reporters, depicted bodies and devastation.

Todd Greentree, a State Department official, and Major John McKay, a military attaché, dispatched by the embassy, visited the area. They never actually reached the immediate site of the alleged massacre because their escorts from the Salvadoran army refused to expose themselves to possible attacks, but they were able to interview indigenous people from the region, who talked of events in the most guarded of terms, possibly nervous because of the presence of the soldiers. The Americans, unable to document what happened, left the scene. McKay said he had the feeling "something horrible happened." Greenwood thought "there had probably been a massacre."[17]

Ambassador Hinton drafted a report cabled to Washington: "Civilians did die during Operacion Rescate but no evidence could be found to confirm that the Government forces systematically massacred civilians in the operation zone, nor that the number of civilians killed even remotely approached number being cited in other reports circulating internationally."[18]

Assistant Secretary of State Thomas Enders dismissed reports by the Human Rights Commission and Amnesty International and the Meiselas photos that offered eyewitness testimony on the mass murders. The U.S. ambassador to Honduras, John Negroponte, notified his superiors that his own investigation lent credibility to the newspaper descriptions. Elliott Abrams, assistant secretary for human rights, tried to discredit the negative accounts by falsely insisting that the entire population of El Mozote was less than half the seven hundred to nine hundred victims claimed. However, the newspaper stories had clearly said the killings took place in several villages, not just El Mozote. Abrams finished his misleading statement to Congress with, "It appears to be an incident which is at least being significantly misused, at the very best, by the guerrillas."[19]

The public could not help but be confused. The *Wall Street Journal*, a classic case of a split personality, with excellent reporting from its news staff but a cartoonish obeisance to conservatism on its editorial pages, trashed the press coverage of the El Mozote affair, labeling Bonner and Guillermoprieto as being "overly credulous" of the peasant eyewitnesses. The editorial ignored the corpses seen by the reporters and the Meiselas photographs. The *Times* replaced Bonner with a reporter deemed less hostile to the Reagan administration.[20]

The administration's campaign of obstruction and deception succeeded in quelling the furor over El Mozote. If anything, El Salvador became an even more fertile killing ground. Said Lou Cannon, "The death squads, never fully under control in the best of circumstances, became even busier."[21] However, after the Constituent Assembly, exploiting a boycott of elections by opposition parties, endorsed D'Aubuisson as president, the Reagan administration, aware that his reputation could derail support, blocked his accession.

In Washington, Congress muted its complaints and continued to support the White House program. Elliott Abrams told the journalist Mark Danner, "If Congress felt so strongly about human-rights abuses, it could simply cut off aid. But Congress didn't cut off aid, because it didn't want to risk being blamed, if the guerrillas won as a result, for 'losing' El Salvador." Deane Hinton said criticism was "a way for the congress . . . to be for and against something at the same time."[22] More than thirty years after Mao Tse-tung and his comrades took power in China, the legislators remembered the devastating campaign against Democrats for having "lost" China. Hard-liners had also stung members of Congress with the charge that defeat in Vietnam was the fault of those who shut off the money. No one wanted to be smeared with losing El Salvador.

Ultimately, when the war in El Salvador officially ended with a peace agreement in 1992, seventy-five thousand Salvadorans lay dead and the United States had spent $4 billion funding the civil war. The Catholic archdiocese in El Salvador compiled the death toll for acts of terrorism by insurgents and the extralegal killings under government auspices for the ten years. It attributed to the supposedly bloodthirsty rebels 776 killings and to the government 41,048, an excess of almost 5,500 percent.[23] That is not to say, however, that the elements of the FMLN did not resort to murder and assassination, but only to note a difference in degree.

The question of what happened around El Mozote was settled by a Salvadoran Truth Commission in 1992. It uncovered the remains of more than five hundred humans, including women and children. Forensic investigation revealed that every bullet, except one, came from a U.S.-made M-16 rifle. In 1993, former assistant secretary of state Thomas Enders admitted, "I now know that the materials that we and the embassy passed on to Congress were wrong."[24]

Nicaragua presented the Reagan administration with an exact opposite to El Salvador. The Sandinista government that had replaced Somoza, a hated dictator friendly to the United States, exhibited the hallmarks of a left-wing authoritarian state eager to reach out to friends in Cuba and the Soviet Union. Haig had proposed a blockade of Cuba to shut down the shipment of arms to rebels in El Salvador and the Sandinistas in Managua, but the Joint Chiefs and their boss Cap Weinberger rejected the tactic as ineffective and requiring the use of assets required elsewhere.

Haig bitterly decried the failure to apply military resources to gain the advantage in Central America. Weinberger had come to roughly the same conclusions as Haig about the Southeast Asia defeat. In a speech to the National Press Club, he said he thought the failure lay in the "gradualist, incremental approach." He went on to state what became known as the Weinberger Doctrine—that U.S. troops should be deployed only on matters vital to U.S. interests, only when there was "reasonable assurance" that the commitment would have public support, and only as a last resort. In Vietnam, not only were the American people doubtful, but there was no "exit strategy."[25] There had to be a clear intention of victory—another Haig prescription. The troops should enter combat only on the basis of clearly defined political and military objectives and only with the understanding that "the relationship between our objectives and the forces we have committed . . . must be continually reassessed and readjusted if necessary."[26] The use of marines in Beirut had not met the standard for clearly defined political and military objectives.

Weinberger explained further, "We had daily meetings with John Vessey [chairman of the Joint Chiefs]. Plans were made and the forces needed discussed. I intervened only when I thought the force was not adequate and I generally doubled what the Joint Chiefs asked for. I was criticized for that but it made Grenada, for example, a very easy matter. Carter made a big mistake with the helicopter rescue of the Iran hostages. They did not understand that helicopters are extremely fragile. They did not use sufficient force."[27] Those directly involved in that operation countered that a larger force would have jeopardized security.

The secretary of defense did not view military intervention in El Salvador or Nicaragua as amenable to widespread public support or justifiable as a last resort. Nor did he believe a blockade would be effective. George Shultz, at the State Department, and as strongly opposed to communism as Weinberger, was often more willing to deploy military force. Shultz pointed to the role of Congress and the conflict in Vietnam as the real obstruction to use of American strength: "We had a Congress whose most active members saw the specter of another Vietnam and seemed determined to prevent such an outcome by denying the United States the ability to use any aspect of national power to deal with Communist advance in Central America."[28]

The White House had no intention of risking negative public opinion with a potentially dismal outcome in Nicaragua. However, the commander in chief believed Americans would support him if he openly backed surrogates, "freedom fighters," to liberate Nicaragua, which lay "two days' driving time from Harlingen, Texas" (one heckuva road trip and utter nonsense in terms of a military unit of any size). His closest advisers were not as sanguine about the reaction of voters and the attitude of Congress to entanglement in a Central American nation.

There was evidence that "outsiders" were aiding those perceived as inimical to U.S. interests in El Salvador and Nicaragua. The rebels in the former had received shipments of small arms, rifles, and submachine guns from the Sandinista regime in Nicaragua, as well as from Cuba.[29] The government in Managua bolstered its forces with direct infusions of weapons from the USSR.

Assisting the rebels in Nicaragua, known as Contras, presented a trickier situation than aid to El Salvador. Nicaragua's leaders operated a sovereign nation. The support given by the Reagan White House to the Contras based in neighboring Honduras troubled members of Congress, who regarded such action as potentially the first tentative step down the slippery slope of another Vietnam and as beyond the authority of a president. Edward Boland, a quiet Massachusetts Democrat with thirty years in the House, threw up a roadblock to the White House program. He proposed an amendment to an intelligence bill that would prohibit the CIA or the Defense Department from furnishing military equipment, military training, or advice or other support "for the purpose of overthrowing the Government of Nicaragua." It became law in December 1982.

While the president signed the bills into law and publicly declaimed he would not violate it, his CIA director, William Casey, ignored the ban. The Sandinistas in early 1984 complained that the United States was secretly mining Nicaragua's harbors. The charges passed without much notice until March 21, when a mine seriously damaged a Soviet tanker in Managua harbor. Vessels flying other flags also exploded mines, subsequently discovered to be planted by CIA agents using ships and helicopters. Even U.S. Navy SEALs participated in the campaign, although Secretary of Defense Weinberger declared, "The United States is not mining the harbors of Nicaragua."[30]

The revelations of what qualified as acts of war outraged some members of the congressional oversight committees who at first blush said they had never been told. In fact, Casey had given them a single almost incoherent sentence that indicated what the CIA was doing, and the watchdogs without due diligence had appropriated $21 million that covered the program. Barry Goldwater considered the evasion so dishonorable that he attempted to read the CIA's classified account to his comrades, but the Committee on Intelligence snuffed his intemperate outburst shortly after he began and all references were expunged from the *Congressional Record*. A new statute proscribed mining of ports or territorial waters of Nicaragua.

Because of confusion about the original language, a second Boland amendment specifically barred money from the CIA, the Department of Defense, or any other agency or entity involved in "intelligence activities" to "support directly or indirectly military or paramilitary operations in Nicaragua by any nation, group, organization, movement, or individual."

The president strongly defended private assistance to the Contras, referring to a "tradition"—the (largely communist) brigade of Americans who fought in the Spanish civil war. He also cited the American Volunteer Group—the Flying Tigers—who were recruited by the Chinese to fight the Japanese prior to American involvement in World War II. His analogies neglected to note that in both instances the groups had supported existing governments battling rebel Fascists in Spain and the Nipponese invasion of China. He referred to aid to Contras as "the right thing to do." Cannon wrote, "He had no interest whatever in the legal restrictions that Congress believed it had imposed on him and on the executive branch by passing Boland II." McFarlane said, "His judgments were often formed by simply what he thought [was] the right thing to do with no more institutional, legal or other framework than that."[31]

As the chief executive and with a tunnel vision of anticommunism, Reagan approved extreme measures designed to thwart left-wing or genuine communist elements. The Cannon and McFarlane analyses explain the Reagan administration's descent into a netherworld of shady deals, obfuscation, lies, and outright violations of the Constitution. What was new to the expansion of executive power was the intensive employment of the offices of the National Security Agency and the CIA in acts of war.

15

IRAN-CONTRA

Reagan and his associates, who felt that the war against communism in Latin America superseded all other considerations, were not about to yield to narrow definitions of the law. If that meant defiance of Congress they were not deterred. Nor did they regard trading with an avowed enemy like Iran out of bounds, so long as some advantage accrued to the United States. The president also felt it behooved him to rescue Americans taken hostage in Lebanon.

The harbor-mining scandal and the second Boland amendment appeared to put the kibosh on further CIA machinations on behalf of the Contras. A total of $24 million appropriated by Congress in fiscal 1985 petered out, and the legislators appeared resolute against further contributions to the war against the Sandinistas. Undeterred, the president directed his staff to find a way to keep the Contras, "body and soul," together. He considered the Boland amendments unconstitutional interference with his right to conduct foreign affairs. Opponents argued that engaging in a war, even through surrogates, went beyond the powers of a president.

White House aides detected a chink in the wall erected by Congress. The organizations affected by the statutes did not specifically include a domestic office, the National Security Council. Bretton G. Sciaroni, counsel to the President's Intelligence Oversight Board, wrote a memorandum in September 1985 in which he concluded the NSC fell outside the strictures of the amendment. Sciaroni's analysis never reached Congress, where it undoubtedly would have been attacked as a violation of the spirit of the law if not the language, since the NSC clearly held a responsibility for intelligence through its connection with the CIA.

Armed with this erroneous imprimatur, a self-appointed sheriff, William Casey, recruited a posse. Lieutenant Colonel Oliver North, an NSC staffer, NSC adviser Robert "Bud" McFarlane, and his deputy, Vice Admiral John Poindexter, all accepted the chance to serve as vigilantes.

North, raised in small-town upstate New York, had struggled back from a nearly crippling accident to graduate from the U.S. Naval Academy. As a marine lieutenant in Vietnam, he picked up two wounds, a Silver Star and Bronze Star for valor, and a reputation for bravado. Marine lieutenant general Victor H. Krulak wrote of North, "His combat exploits in Vietnam are romanticized, like the Sunday-supplement tale of his valiant single-handed midnight forays across the DMZ to capture and bring back a North Vietnamese prisoner. It is an exciting story, but like many others it never happened."[1] During his tour of duty with the NSC, North inflated his intimacy with the top people. A private tête-à-tête with the president was actually a large group meeting. He spoke of a dinner discussion with Jeane Kirkpatrick, but she denied ever sharing a meal with him.

Robert McFarlane, son of a Texas Democratic congressman, graduated from the Naval Academy with a commission in the marines. He led the first marine combat unit into Vietnam in 1965 and subsequently returned to the war for a second tour. With a master's degree in international relations, he was chosen as Kissinger's military assistant in the waning days of the Nixon White House and then became executive assistant to Brent Scowcroft, Gerald Ford's national security adviser. Alexander Haig chose McFarlane as a counselor for his State Department, and subsequently the retired lieutenant colonel ascended to the chair of national security adviser. Unlike Oliver North, he was a reticent, disciplined individual.

For eighteen months, the coterie from the NSC defied Boland II, secretly raising $34 million from other countries and $2.7 million from private contributors to preserve the Contras' bodies and souls. Assistant Secretary of State Langhorne Motley lied to Congress, assuring the legislators that the administration was not "soliciting and/or encouraging third countries" to finance the Nicaraguan rebels (Boland prohibited such requests).[2]

Initially, the money went directly to bank accounts controlled by the Contras, but in July 1985 North assumed control of the funds, enabling direct covert payments on behalf of the Contras. To facilitate activities, North, retired air force major general Richard Secord, and businessman Albert Hakim set up a Swiss bank account and two private organizations, Lake Resources and "the Enterprise." The latter employed planes, pilots, and an airfield.

The conspirators also had begun clandestine deals to sell arms to Iran, which was officially barred from such goods by an embargo because of its war with Iraq, not to mention the animosity toward Tehran on the part of both Washington and the public due to memories of the embassy hostage crisis. Furthermore, as a presidential commission later said, "Some time in July 1982, the United States became aware of evidence suggesting that Iran was supporting terrorist groups, including groups like Hezbollah, engaged in hostage-taking."[3] Between March 1984 and the summer of 1985, eight U.S. citizens had been seized in Beirut. One escaped in 1985, but the others remained in captivity. The Reagan White House vowed it would not pay ransom for the hostages nor would it sell arms to either Iran or Iraq.

Casey and his cohorts believed that they might gain influence in Iran while obtaining freedom for the hostages despite the fact that within the administration both Shultz and Weinberger strenuously opposed any dealings with Iran. However, in August 1985 the president decided that the United States would sell arms to Iran. The decision also reversed a policy against making concessions to ransom hostages. The shift was made so casually that it never was written down. Reagan, fifteen months later, could not recall it, and neither Shultz nor Weinberger were told about it.[4]

To achieve the twin objectives the Americans schemed with shadowy Middle Eastern wheeler-dealers to use Israel as a middleman, avoiding both congressional strictures and giving President Reagan plausible deniability on the charge of trading arms for hostages. A series of secret meetings arranged for the transfer of TOW antitank missiles from Israel, which would receive replacements. The Iranians surrendered a single hostage for some thirteen hundred missiles and demanded more and better ordnance before freeing more individuals.

Even the most covert operations of this sort required paperwork and permissions within the administration. A Defense Department expert's memorandum advised Lieutenant General Colin Powell, military assistant to Caspar Weinberger, of problems. By law, Iran remained ineligible for direct sales from the United States, and at the very least the indirect route through Israel required notification of Congress (which, however, remained out of the loop). Furthermore, even if arms were sold to Iran they could only be used for self-defense, a promise Iran would not give. The questions of legality were brushed aside.

Bud McFarlane, dubious about the propriety of the operations and distressed by the collapse of the first arms-for-hostages attempts, quit his post. The president named McFarlane's deputy, Admiral John Poindexter, as national security adviser. According to Lou Cannon, "Rarely has such an intelligent and unassuming man been so poorly suited for the high position he inherited."[5] Unlike his predecessor, Poindexter lacked knowledge of world affairs and disdained politics although his was a highly political position. He isolated himself from Congress, the media, and his contemporaries in the administration. His background, personality, and lack of understanding of the rules in American government led Poindexter to ignore statutory limitations of a public official.

Word of the secret sales inspired a frantic cover-your-backside in Washington. CIA deputy director John McMahon, upon hearing of his agency's involvement several days after the fact, ordered the house counsel to prepare a Covert Action Finding to provide a presidential authorization for the CIA's past and future support of the Iran dealings. This ex post facto finding would absolve the agency from violations of Hughes-Ryan. Said the Tower Commission Report on Iran-Contra, "A Finding was drafted and delivered to VADM Poindexter, but the evidence suggests it was never signed by the President."[6]

Although the first try to ransom the hostages had produced minimal results, initiatives to liberate them, motivated by the president's concern for those held, percolated within some areas of the administration. There were warnings, vouchsafed by Oliver North, that unless Iran received arms, hostages would be executed. North and Poindexter, backed by Casey, pursued a fresh deal. The new national security adviser obtained a finding, signed by the president, permitting the arms sales. However, Poindexter said he made no copies for distribution to the appropriate agencies such as the CIA, and later when the Iran-Contra scandal broke he destroyed the original.

During the negotiations with the Israelis, as an official from that country jotted down in his handwritten notes, the idea arose of using profits from the swap of missiles for hostages to pay for operations in Nicaragua. Whatever North told the Israelis, when the commander in chief brought to the White House Shultz, Weinberger, John McMahon (representing Casey, who was out of town), McFarlane, and Poindexter, the two secretaries vigorously opposed any weapons for Iran. They argued that the initiative would negate the public position against deals with terrorists and shake the confidence of moderate Arabs seeking to deflect radicals. Weinberger spoke forcefully about the illegality and McMahon disparaged claims of moderates within Iran or that the leaders might become more friendly to the United States.

Shultz recalled that the president remarked, "'Well, the American people will never forgive me if I fail to get these hostages out over this legal question' or something like that."[7] McFarlane, however dubious of the intermediaries, and Poindexter still pushed for the program.

In January 1986 Poindexter persuaded Reagan to endorse an expanded finding. Rather than use Israel as a beard for the sales of arms to Iran, the CIA would acquire weapons from the Defense Department and sell them to

Lake Resources, which would act as a commercial cutout. It would siphon off money from the payments for use in Nicaragua. The finding included language that instructed the CIA not to notify Congress of the covert activity. It was implied that the legislators would be informed at some future, unspecified date, perhaps after the release of the hostages.

Arms sales went on for several months without serious progress in liberating the Americans, but the resources flowed through the new pipeline to aid the Contras. A mission to Tehran by North collapsed as the Iranians demanded more missiles before freeing a single person. They also complained of price-gouging. Three more Americans in Beirut disappeared into the Hezbollah warrens. One hostage, Father Lawrence Jenco, was released.

In Washington, for the first time, the Joint Chiefs heard of the arms deals. Admiral William J. Crowe Jr., the JCS chairman, with forty years in uniform, was "startled" because it was "contrary to our policy." He approached his boss, Weinberger, and asked why the Joint Chiefs had not been consulted. The secretary of defense answered that the decision emanated from the commander in chief: "He can do what he wants to do," and "consultation with others below the Commander in Chief level would not have perhaps been very fruitful."[8] In 2004, Weinberger qualified his comment about the presidential prerogatives as applying to the context of the moment rather than a blanket omnipotence.[9]

Crowe's concern had less to do with the rupture of policy than with questions on the strategic balance in the Middle East. As the congressional committees that later looked into Iran-Contra noted, before any sales of weaponry were authorized, the military should have been asked if the arms affected the interests of the U.S. armed forces.

North led renewed negotiations with an Iranian representative, who included freedom for Da'wa, radical Muslims held in Kuwait, in their wish list. In dramatic pieces of fiction, North described to the Iranians a meeting with the president at which Reagan thumped a table while pronouncing that he wanted to end the war between Iran and Iraq. North added a vignette in which the president, having returned from a weekend of prayer for guidance on whether to authorize North to declare American acceptance of the Islamic Revolution, as a gift inscribed in a Bible, "This is a promise that God gave to Abraham. Who am I to say that we should not do this?"[10] Actually, North himself had suggested to the president that he inscribe that message in a Bible. More arms, at a lower price, reached Iran, but although the kidnappers turned over hospital administrator David Jacobsen, Terry Waite, a special envoy from Britain's archbishop of Canterbury, disappeared.

Things began to fall apart when the Lebanese magazine *Al-Shiraa* printed an account of business done through secret meetings of Americans and Iranians. Shultz, appalled already by both the policy and the publicity, was shocked when he learned of the plans bandied about by North and an Iranian representative, and he sought out the president, who he said gave no indication that he was familiar with it but "reacted like he had been kicked in the belly." In particular, the proposal concerning the Da'wa in Kuwaiti custody aroused great indignation. "The President was astonished, and I have never seen him so mad. He is a very genial, pleasant man. . . . But his jaws set and his eyes flashed . . . in that meeting I finally felt that the President understands that something is radically wrong here."[11] Reagan directed Shultz to tell Iran that the United States repudiated any plans arrived at by North and no longer would sell arms to Tehran. The effort to ransom the hostages ended. Discomfit over revelations of unsavory intrigues involving Iran and the hostages was heightened by the disclosures of the diversion of funds for the Contras.

Some of the so-called residuals had enabled "the Enterprise" to construct an airfield in Costa Rica in early 1986. Lewis Tambs, the American ambassador, pledged it would not be used to aid the Contras, but on October 5 a Sandinista SAM missile struck an Enterprise plane carrying ten thousand pounds of ammunition and gear for the Contras. Two American pilots and a Nicaraguan Democratic Force (FDN) soldier died but crew member Eugene Hasenfus survived. The Sandinistas produced him and he confessed to the mission of his aircraft. The press and several government agencies, including the FBI, opened investigations.

A host of officials including Undersecretary of State Elliott Abrams, Poindexter, and North attempted to conceal U.S. involvement, and a flurry of denials greeted a *New York Times* report that said the administration had asked the rebels to accept full responsibility. Although individuals at the highest levels, including Vice President George H. W. Bush, had been alerted to the possible involvement of North, the president firmly announced to the press, "There is no government connection with that at all. We are aware that there are private groups and private citizens that have been trying to help the Contras—to that extent—but we did not know the exact particulars of what they're doing."[12] The administration tried a wall of silence to shut off critics and investigations. It crumbled under official, media, and public pressure for an accounting.

On November 12, the eve of a presidential address to the nation, the commander in chief met with congressional leaders concerned with national security and with Bush, Shultz, Weinberger, Attorney General Edwin Meese,

Donald Regan, Casey, and Poindexter, plus some staff. Reagan began the session with a statement that declared no laws were broken, no ransom paid for hostages, and no officials or agencies within the U.S. government bypassed, at best white lies and at worst whoppers. Poindexter, who conducted the briefing, continued to omit and mislead.[13]

When the president spoke to his fellow citizens he claimed that he had authorized shipments of small amounts of defensive weapons and spare parts that "taken together could easily fit into a single cargo plane." He asserted that the initiative fully complied with the law and condemned "the wildly speculative false stories about arms for hostages and alleged ransom payments." Not only did he not admit to green-lighting the trade of weapons for those in captivity but his interpretation of the legality of the arms sales was dubious.

At a press conference on November 19, the commander in chief again misstated the facts. He denied involvement of a third country, Israel, on the grounds that the United States had nothing to do with transactions by other countries and Iran. Actually, the January 17, 1985, finding, which he signed, clearly noted the Israeli participation. Furthermore, Shultz later said that prior to this press conference, the president said he knew of the shipment of HAWK missiles to Iran by Israel. Reagan repeated the falsehood that shipments were limited to one or two that would not even fill the space of a single cargo plane. He explained the confusion of arms for hostages by noting that it was not Iran that held the Americans. Donald Regan blamed the inaccuracies upon Poindexter's many-faceted briefings that "sort of confused the Presidential mind as to what he could say and couldn't say and what he should say and shouldn't say."[14]

Late November 1986 witnessed a messy attempt by the conspirators to cover up the business of hostage ransom and the sub rosa financing for the Contras. Poindexter lied to congressional committees about what the president knew and when he knew of the arms shipments to Iran. Casey floated a fake story that the CIA believed it had been asked to transport oil-drilling equipment by NSC staff, only to learn later the cargo consisted of missiles. North lied to Meese about running his own investigation in hopes of protecting the president.

Both Poindexter and North destroyed a pile of documents, including four of the five memoranda North wrote about diversion of profits, as well as phone logs and notebooks. They altered other items in a clumsy attempt to absolve the NSC of charges its staff fractured Boland and other laws. North's secretary, Fawn Hall, smuggled documents out of North's offices by stuffing them in her boots and clothing.

The chiefs of the palace guard, Meese and Regan, commenced damage control. They forced Poindexter to resign. The admiral apologized to Reagan for not shutting down the diversion. "I knew it would hurt the Contras, and the way those guys on the Hill [Congress] are jerking around . . . so I didn't look into it."[15] Ollie North's head also went on the chopping block. Since he was not a presidential appointee he could simply be reassigned in the Marine Corps.

On November 25, the president with Don Regan, Meese, Shultz, and Casey briefed congressional leaders. Meese laid it all off on North and perhaps one or two others on the NSC staff. House Majority Leader Jim Wright, a Texas Democrat, pointedly asked if others in the government knew or approved of the diversion. Meese said Poindexter was aware of the funds going to the Contras but played no role. Wright also inquired whether the CIA knew of the diversion and Casey lied, "No, I didn't."[16]

On November 25, the commander in chief informed the press of the departures of Poindexter and North from the administration. He said he was "deeply troubled that the implementation of a policy aimed at resolving a truly tragic situation in the Middle East has resulted in such controversy." While he believed "our policy goals to be well founded," he added, "information brought to my attention yesterday convinced me that in one aspect implementation of that policy was seriously flawed." He insisted he had not made a mistake in sending arms to Iran and then took no more questions.[17]

Besmirched by the revelations, the president reserved his opprobrium for the media. After telling Time's Hugh Sidey that North was "a national hero," he continued, "this whole thing boils down to great irresponsibility on the part of the press. . . . I have to say that there is bitter bile in my throat these days. I've never seen the sharks circling like they are now with blood in the water. What is driving me up the wall is that this wasn't a failure until the press got a tip from the rag in Beirut and began to play it up."[18]

Congress created a joint committee to dig into the Iran-Contra affair and determine what happened and who was responsible. When the connection between the arms transactions and aid to the Contras became public, the profits were pegged at $16.1 million. Of this at least $3.8 million went for assistance to the rebels. That left a balance of more than $12 million. In the grand scheme of things, Casey and his chief henchman, Oliver North, had envisioned wider use of the money that accrued from the arms deals than just support for the Contras. The pair had discussed "off-the-shelf, self-generating activities" that involved other areas of the world.

None of the findings signed by the commander in chief, whether they involved buying freedom for the hostages or for aiding the Contras, ever authorized diversion of money from the Iran program for activities in Nicaragua. Poindexter testified that he withheld that scheme to preserve the president's "deniability." However, he asserted that he believed the president would have approved of the diversion as an "implementation" of his policies.[19]

When Oliver North appeared before the congressional committee that investigated the affair he gave a bravura performance. He wore his marine uniform replete with medals. He announced that he would be willing to take on terrorist Abu Nidal mano a mano because Nidal had supposedly threatened him and his family. Confronted by the law he showed less courage, with a demand for immunity against self-incrimination. He admitted that he lied to Congress, speechifying, "It is very important for the American people to understand that this is a dangerous world; that we live at risk and that this nation is at risk in a dangerous world. And that they ought to be led to believe, as a consequence of these hearings, that the nation cannot or should not conduct covert operations. By their very nature, covert operations or special activities are a lie. There is great deceit, deception practiced in the conduct of special operations. They are at essence a lie."

Having parsed the meaning of lies and covert operations, North confessed to shredding documents after CIA director Casey told him to "clean things up." He had lied to Congress because the legislators could not be trusted to keep a secret. He reiterated the absurd claim that Boland's ban on weapons to the Contras, while it applied to the CIA, did not cover the NSC.[20]

In contrast, the meticulous, scientifically oriented Poindexter astonished his listeners by memory malfunctions that prevented him 184 times from recall of events. He said he had endorsed the scheme to aid the Contras as logical in light of the president's policy. He believed that had he asked the commander in chief for approval of the diversion, he would have received it. However, he testified he never requested such consent because "the buck stops here with me."[21] It was an assumption of authority that belied Harry Truman's insistence that such critical decisions belonged to the president. Those who refused to see anything untoward in the Iran-Contra business treated the admiral as hero. When he lunched at the Army-Navy Club in Washington, he received a standing ovation.

The majority report by the committee tagged "a small group of senior officials [who] believed that they alone knew what was right. They viewed knowledge of their actions by others in the Government as a threat to their objectives. They told neither the Secretary of State, the Congress nor the American people of their actions. When exposure was threatened, they destroyed documents and lied to Cabinet officials, to the public, and to elected representatives in Congress. They testified that they even with-held key facts from the President."[22] The committee indicted North, McFarlane, and Poindexter as the three chief culprits for the "secrecy, deception and disdain for the law." The report said Casey "encouraged North, gave him direction and promoted the concept of an extra-legal covert organization."

Because of legal questions about the separation of powers, the congres-sional committee did not attempt to get the president to testify. It acknowl-edged that Reagan had publicly stated he was unaware of the diversion. North had never told him but assumed Poindexter had informed him. However, the admiral testified that he had not. "Nevertheless, the ulti-mate responsibility for the events in the Iran-Contra Affair must rest with the President. If the President did not know what his National Security Advisers were doing, he should have. It is his responsibility to communi-cate unambiguously to his subordinates that they must keep him advised of important actions they take for the Administration. The Constitution re-quires the President to 'take care that the laws be faithfully executed.' . . . Members of the NSC appeared to believe that their actions were consis-tent with the President's desires. It was the President's policy—not an iso-lated decision by North or Poindexter—to sell arms secretly to Iran and to maintain the Contras 'body and soul.'"[23]

That Ronald Reagan failed to "communicate unambiguously" was ironic in light of his reputation as "the great communicator." The atmo-sphere he created could be interpreted as a wink and a nudge for those gung ho to push objectives regardless of constitutional and congressional mandates. The expressed desire to overthrow the Sandinistas carried a whiff of Shakespeare's assassins in *Richard II*, who take their cue from their sovereign—"Have I no friend will rid me of this living fear?"—and when the deed is done are disowned by him.

The congressional investigating committee's report was split along party lines. The minority Republicans, characterizing the majority statement as "hysterical conclusions," said, "The bottom line . . . is that the mistakes of the Iran-Contra Affair were just that—mistakes in judgment and nothing more. There was no constitutional crisis, no systematic disrespect for the 'rule of law,' no grand conspiracy, and no Administration-wide dishonesty or coverup."

The president named his own special review board. Led by Senator John Tower, former senator and Carter secretary of state Edmund Muskie, and Lieutenant General Brent Scowcroft, the Tower Commission in its report ascribed the scandal to "the perils of policy pursued outside the constraints of orderly process." The investigators bluntly labeled the Iran initiative as directly counter to the administration's own policies on terrorism, the Iran-Iraq war, and military support to Iran. The commission pointed out a fundamental contradiction in the belief that arms to Iran would curry favor with the moderates and bring home the hostages when in fact it was the radical elements that supported the kidnappers. As was quickly obvious, the strategic advances to the Iranian government never achieved any traction and the operations were entirely based upon a ransom for the captives.[24]

The Tower Commission defended its creator. Noting that he must take responsibility for National Security Council actions, it said, "President Reagan's personal management style [hands-off] places an especially heavy responsibility on his key advisers . . . they should have been particularly mindful of the need for special attention in which this arms sale initiative developed and proceeded."[25]

When the Tower Commission first asked the commander in chief about the HAWK deal, he claimed he did not remember how the shipment came about. He said he objected to it and as a result the missiles were returned to Israel. In a second meeting with the commission, Reagan said neither he nor Don Regan could recall any conversation about the subject.

His recall contradicted McFarlane's assurance to George Shultz that he had "cleared it with the President." Lou Cannon subsequently interviewed Don Regan and asked if McFarlane okayed the arrangements with the president. "Sure he got approval from him," said Regan. "Did Ronald Reagan approve shipment of HAWK missiles to Iran in 1985? Definitely yes."[26]

George McGovern, who had completed his Senate service in 1980, expressed the anger of those who felt betrayed. "The actions of the Reagan Administration in Central America were outrageous, right through the Irangate scandal, selling arms to generate money for the Contras. These can be construed as acts of war, done in secret, despite the Boland amendment to block it. Boland was not a screaming left-winger but he just thought it flagrantly violated proper action. The only way Congress can control this is by cutting off funding, the ultimate control."[27]

Brent Scowcroft, a member of the Tower Commission, was more forgiving. "Certainly Congress can forbid aid going somewhere they don't

want it to go. The president can then veto that. The Boland amendment—there were several of them attached to other bills—and the constitutional issues here were never adjudicated. The whole issue was imprecise.
Congress was sloppy in the way it drafted the legislation. It gave the administration enough pause to not do it openly. But it was clearly a violation of the spirit of the Boland amendments."[28]

"One thing that contributed to my resignation," said Haig, "was Bill
Casey conducted a war in Nicaragua without any discussion before the 40
Committee. Iran-Contra was never discussed. Much of it was done in the
vice president's [George H. W. Bush's] office but he never got nailed for it.
When I left the White House, I was convinced it was headed for trouble.
While I was against the Boland amendment because you cannot legislate
morality, you do need a formal procedural system to make policy. Eisenhower, as an old military hand, had such an arrangement and he made
damn few mistakes. Nixon had, with slight modification, formal committees. The only problem was Henry [Kissinger] got the president to put him
in the chairman's seat in every one. The system meant recommendations
. . . instead of typical mush, we had people giving options, pro and con,
up, down, and in the middle. The president heard dissenting voices."[29]

The Reagan administration had also smudged the limits on its use of
military force in confrontations with Muammar Gadhafi, the prickly dictator of Libya. The White House reported on March 24, 1986, that Libya had
launched half a dozen surface-to-air missiles at a group of U.S. Navy aircraft
accompanying warships in the Gulf of Sidra. The Americans, acting in
self-defense, had returned fire, sinking three Libyan patrol boats. On April
14, the commander in chief ordered a range of airstrikes at Libya, hitting a
number of military installations and a compound that housed Gadhafi. He
escaped but one of his children died. This operation was labeled retaliation
for the bombing by Libyan terrorists of a West Berlin disco that killed one
American and wounded fifty other servicemen. This too was justified as a
measure of self-defense under the UN Charter. Congressional leaders only
learned of the raids as the bombers neared Libya. Public opinion supported
the president in what was seen as a blow at terrorism.

The fiasco of Iran-Contra could not mar the Teflon coat over Ronald
Reagan's reputation. He did not emerge from the muck of an embarrassing
episode; he flew above it. He escaped opprobrium in large part because his
minders were careful to shield him from the details although the circum-
stantial evidence indicated he was much more culpable than the investigations admitted. However, the blatant circumvention of restrictions on
presidential prerogatives sounded a cautionary note for future officials.

16

BUSH ONE

Iran-Contra shook public confidence in the Reagan administration, but left the prime figure intact. Meanwhile, a series of infarcts in the heart of the evil empire left the Soviet Union gasping for breath. Reagan struck up a relationship with General Secretary Mikhail Gorbachev, while the Kremlin leader tried to resuscitate the dying communist government. The American commander in chief, confident that he had rebuilt the U.S. military to a dominant position, could bargain from strength. When he retired from the White House in 1988, Reagan bequeathed his successor, George H. W. Bush, a world where communism no longer threatened but perils for national security on the national doorstep and in the Middle East waxed hotter. Exercise of the role of commander in chief once again became critical.

Even before Gorbachev assumed office, Reagan had begun to negotiate a lessening of tension and a moderation of the cold war. With Gorbachev as his opposite number, Reagan's foreign policy initiative blossomed, albeit with a few fits, stops, and starts. Thus the two superpowers agreed upon a reduction in their nuclear arsenals and ballistic missiles. Reagan enhanced his standing with a tour of Europe. At the Brandenburg Gate, hard by the infamous wall that separated the two Berlins, he delivered one of his most celebrated speeches when he passionately urged, "General Secretary Gorbachev, if you seek peace, if you seek prosperity for the Soviet Union and Eastern Europe, if you seek liberalization: Come here to this gate! Mr. Gorbachev, open this gate! Mr. Gorbachev, tear down this wall!" It was a high point in the redemption of Ronald Reagan as a world leader. When he left office on January 20, 1989, he enjoyed a higher public approval rating than any other modern president.

His successor as commander in chief, George Herbert Walker Bush, entered the White House with the widest experience in foreign affairs of any modern president. He had served as an ambassador, headed the CIA, been a congressman, and as vice president during the Reagan administration sat in on NSC meetings. His national security adviser, Brent Scowcroft, was aware of the ongoing disputes about presidential power. "I guess I think the Constitution's language on the role of the president and Congress in making war, is, as one Constitutional scholar said, 'an invitation to struggle.' Different people interpret it in different ways. An act of war is not the same as war. When the Constitution, as it does, says Congress had the right to 'declare war,' that is not the same as to make war [a distinction made by the authors of the Constitution]. If you don't declare it, it is not a war."[1] Certainly, an act of war can bring resistance or retaliation, and if the other side responds with force, the situation adds up to war. An "undeclared" war sounds like a semantic distinction to avoid congressional approval.

During the first months of his presidency, George H. W. Bush had little need to don his commander in chief hat. Except for the covert aid to the Afghan rebels battling the communist government and the Soviet troops inside the country, the decline in the fortunes of the USSR and its ability to fund governments and insurgents hostile to the United States reduced the urgency for intervention on the scale practiced by previous regimes. The ineptitude of the Nicaraguan Sandinistas inspired resistance beyond the Contras. Nicaraguan leader Daniel Ortega mistakenly believed he might legitimize his control over the country. Instead, the people voted the Reds out and a more democratic regime in. The civil wars of El Salvador abated. Fidel Castro still fulminated against Yanqui imperialism, but without infusions of money from Moscow the Maximum Leader could no longer afford to try to sow his revolutionary seeds in Africa and Latin America. Pinochet remained firmly in command in Argentina, and altogether the threat of communism in the Western Hemisphere faded. In Europe, country after country broke away from Soviet control and the USSR disintegrated into independent nations.

In 1989, Panama became a hot spot. Manuel Noriega, head of the secret police and a former CIA agent, ran the country. The United States had indicted him for drug trafficking but attempts to nudge him out the door with displays of military strength, economic sanctions, mediation by other nations, and a coup failed. On December 15, 1989, Noriega's puppet National Assembly declared that "the Republic of Panama is in a state of war while there is aggression against the people of Panama." While the White House mulled the spectacle of a mosquito attacking an elephant, a Marine Corps lieutenant in mufti was killed and a naval officer detained while soldiers sexually abused his wife. Although the local military did not strike at any U.S. installations, the incidents and the declaration qualified to Washington as an attack on the United States. Bush, when previously chided for timidity about confronting Noriega, had said, "We've got a lot of hawks out there; a lot of macho guys out there that want me to send somebody else's kid into battle. . . . We're not going to imprudently use the force of the United States."[2]

With Panama having initiated the state of war and Bush's secretary of state, James Baker, claiming intelligence—admittedly unverified—indicated that Noriega might attack some thirty-five thousand U.S. citizens there, the president became commander in chief without need for authorization by Congress. The Bush administration moved swiftly and in Operation Just Cause an invasion force of twenty-four thousand fell upon Panama. Casualties were light: twenty-four Americans dead. Noriega was captured, and a court in Miami sentenced him to a long prison sentence.

Representative Charles Rangel said, "As much as I'd like to get rid of that bum, I don't see the legal authority for use of the military." Tom Foley, the Democrat Speaker, said, "Under the circumstances the decision is justified," while Senator Claiborne Pell weighed in against unilateralism: "I would have preferred that the President had only taken such action in concert with neighboring Latin American countries." Mexico and other Latin American nations condemned the invasion.

Against largely negative worldwide reaction, the House passed a resolution applauding Operation Just Cause. The president had acted "decisively and appropriately in ordering United States forces to intervene in Panama after making substantial efforts to resolve the crisis in Panama by political, economic and diplomatic means . . . to avoid resorting to military action."[3]

In Afghanistan, where the United States had been helping the insurgents, nearly fifteen thousand Soviet troops had been killed and tens of thousands wounded in a futile attempt to prop up a puppet government. With its satellite countries breaking away, the economy in near free fall, and the public bitterly opposed to further losses, the USSR in 1991 sought to end its military involvement in Afghanistan. James Baker on behalf of Bush and Soviet foreign minister Boris Pankin pledged a mutual cutoff of arms to the chief indigenous factions. But withdrawal of American aid convinced the Afghani rebels that the United States never really wanted to create an independent country but only to bleed the Soviets through surrogates. Warlords intent on preserving their duchies, groups genuinely interested in a less authoritarian government, and jihadists of the most radical Islamic stripe battled for control. The extremist Taliban emerged as victors.

In the early 1980s, the United States had begun to court Iraq as a balance against the virulently anti-Western Islamic Shiite regime in Iran. The minority Sunnis there, led by Saddam Hussein, governed the country. France and Germany sold billions in arms to Iraq, which was viewed as a secular outpost in the Middle East, and the American government, while restrained by Congress and avoiding direct military aid, gave billions in credit for foodstuffs, enabling Saddam to allocate resources to weaponry. Under Ronald Reagan, the United States removed the country from the list of states sponsoring terrorism and opened the way for a resumption of diplomatic relations.

Scowcroft said, "The Persian Gulf had not been among our major concerns early in the Administration. Despite a number of sometimes exasperating differences with Iraq, developments in the region had begun to return to normal following the 1980–88 Iran-Iraq conflict." Bush continued the tilt in favor of Iraq, even though the White House recognized Hussein as a "tough, ruthless, and even paranoid dictator."[4] Over the objections of many in Congress, the administration tried to increase trade. However, Scowcroft said that in 1990 he detected ominous changes in Saddam's attitude. The Iraqi leader denounced the United States as a member of a conspiracy with Israel and Great Britain aimed at him. There was mounting evidence of Iraq's hunger for newer and more powerful weapons.

In 1990, a group of senators, led by Robert Dole and Alan Simpson, journeyed to Baghdad. Dole assured Saddam that the president would resist sanctions, and Simpson publicly ascribed Saddam's problems in the United States to "the Western media and not with the U.S. government." He labeled the American press as "haughty and pampered." Howard Metzenbaum said, "I am now aware that you are a strong and intelligent man and that you want peace."[5]

Saddam pushed harder, fixating upon Kuwait, his smaller, oil-rich neighbor. He disputed the borders and complained that its overproduction of oil depressed the market, that its adjacent fields drained Iraqi oil reserves. Furthermore, Iraq still owed Kuwait $30 billion for aid rendered during the war with Iran. In July 1991, Iraq posted two Republican Guard divisions on its Kuwait frontier and mobilized more troops. U.S. ambassador April Glaspie met with Saddam, where in her view he offered a conciliatory tone for a diplomatic solution. No U.S. official notes of their discussion exist, but Glaspie said, according to a transcript released by the Iraqis, "We have no opinion on Arab-Arab conflicts, like your border dispute with Kuwait."[6] Bush later criticized Congress for misconstruing Glaspie's statement when legislators berated her for giving Saddam a green light to invade. Bush said the Iraqi leader lied to the ambassador and had no intention of participating in a diplomatic effort.[7] However, Glaspie subsequently admitted to reporter Elaine Sciolino that she along with others in the State Department believed some border adjustments at the expense of Kuwait might have been a reasonable solution.[8]

Saddam's armies on the border increased to a hundred thousand and a July 31 conference in Jidda broke down over the Iraq demands. A day later, Iraqi forces poured into Kuwait. Absent a request for help from either Kuwait or Saudi Arabia, the president could only order warships to steam to the Persian Gulf. By midmorning, the Security Council at the UN had adopted UNSC Resolution 660, condemning Iraq's aggression and demanding the troops leave Kuwait. Bush was encouraged by Soviet Union and Arab League support for the resolution.

Of the first session of the National Security Council, Scowcroft said, "I was frankly appalled at the undertone of the discussion, which suggested resignation to the invasion and even adaptation to a *fait accompli*. There was a huge gap between those who saw what was happening as the major crisis of our time and those who treated it as the crisis *du jour*." He commented that most seemed to be concerned with the price of oil and the turmoil in the Middle East, and he sensed a belief that the events halfway around the world were too difficult for any serious intervention. Scowcroft expressed his disappointment to Bush, who agreed with him about "the absolute intolerability of that invasion to U.S. interests."[9] The national security adviser would appear to have put the matter within the context of oil, rather than a question of human rights or the sovereignty of Kuwait.

When Bush contacted Egyptian president Hosni Mubarak and King Hussein of Jordan he learned that both rulers wanted to settle the matter through Arab diplomacy. But the Americans worried that what Scowcroft called "an Arab solution" might end in a compromise with negative aspects for the United States but which could not be rejected. A major problem lay in the region's dislike of the Kuwaiti government because it frequently pumped more oil than the quota decreed by the Organization of the Petroleum Exporting Countries (OPEC). The president talked with Saudi Arabia's King Fahd, who, while resentful of Saddam's machinations, thought an agreement might be reached. Fahd rejected an offer to base an F-15 squadron inside Saudi Arabia.[10]

CIA intelligence indicated that Saddam intended to stay in Kuwait. He would control the second and third largest proven oil reserves in the world, backed by his military, the fourth largest army in the world, and the immense wealth of Kuwait. Colin Powell, chairman of the Joint Chiefs, briefed the NSC on the military effort to deter invasion of Saudi Arabia and evict Iraq from Kuwait. Said Powell, "This is harder than Panama or Libya. This would be the NFL, not a scrimmage. It would mean a major confrontation."[11]

Because bases in Saudi Arabia would be critical to success of any military effort by the United States, the White House invited Saudi ambassador Prince Bandar to Scowcroft's office. The ambassador indicated that the reluctance of his country to accept American forces stemmed from a perception of unreliability. Scowcroft pledged that if the troops were accepted they would not cut and run, upon which Bandar's attitude changed and he asked if he could be briefed on "our defense plans." With the approval of Secretary of Defense Dick Cheney, the envoy was shown the war plan for Iraq, developed by General Norman Schwarzkopf with the Joint Chiefs of Staff.

Great Britain, Turkey, Egypt, France, Germany, Japan, and the Soviet Union, heretofore considered a major backer of Iraq, lined up in favor of a strong stand against Saddam. The administration also wooed support from Middle Eastern countries through deals on textile tariffs involving Turkey and concessions on the debt owed by Egypt to the United States. In other circumstances these would be labeled bribes. Powell informed the NSC of a refined plan that would defend Saudi Arabia and lay the foundation for a thrust into Kuwait. Scowcroft quoted him: "It is difficult but doable. It will be enormously expensive to project and sustain a force of this size."[12]

Schwarzkopf warned that on paper Iraq fielded formidable assets—more than eleven hundred planes (a figure revised later to about seven hundred). The army numbered nine hundred thousand, with nearly six thousand tanks. However, Iraqis' weapons were not top caliber and they lacked self-propelled artillery. SAMs (surface-to-air missiles) ringed their major cities and installations. Iraq had previously employed chemical weapons. Following Schwarzkopf's presentation, Powell ventured that Saddam probably did not want to confront the United States but that it was necessary to show the flag in Saudi Arabia. The president agreed. "I'm inclined to feel that a small U.S. military presence and an air option will do it." Schwarzkopf projected as many as twenty thousand casualties by Coalition forces.[13]

King Fahd still temporized over the offer to bring in the American military. The president tried to persuade him that delay increased the vulnerability of Saudi Arabia. Meanwhile, sanctions that included an embargo on trade with Iraq became the first coordinated international response. Saddam was seen on the verge of officially annexing Kuwait. On August 5, five days after the invasion, Bush told reporters, "This will not stand, this aggression against Kuwait."[14] To Powell it sounded like a declaration of war. He would express astonishment that the chief executive had not consulted with him in his capacity as chairman of the Joint Chiefs nor convened the NSC before setting the nation on a course to war.[15]

Cheney met with Fahd in Riyadh on August 6 and told the monarch that if invited, the American military would come but would leave when asked to go home. To help persuade Fahd, Schwarzkopf showed photographs of Iraqi tanks and troops on the border. The royal court preferred further talk and perhaps a payoff to Saddam, but the king accepted the American offer. Many Saudi officials distrusted the American claims that they sought no long-term presence in the kingdom, and the more religious leaders feared the influence of the U.S. military on the indigenous culture. Osama bin Laden, a son of one of the wealthiest and most prominent families in Saudi Arabia, who had fought in Afghanistan against the infidel Soviet forces, had approached Crown Prince Abdullah with an offer to mobilize a hundred thousand mujahideen, veterans of the war in Afghanistan, arguing that use of his troops would make it unnecessary to bring in the westerners. Abdullah rebuffed his offer, thereby stoking bin Laden's anger against the House of Saud and his paranoia about foreign troops. Considering that Iraq's forces included aircraft, armor, and artillery and the logistical difficulty of mustering a hundred thousand men with light armament from Afghanistan, Abdullah's rejection of bin Laden was a sound military decision.

The UN Security Council passed additional resolutions that implemented economic sanctions. Saddam responded by announcing the internment of all foreign nationals in Iraq and Kuwait, 2.3 million people of all ages from at least fifty countries, but most critically, some ten thousand westerners. He expressed his pain for the internment but blamed the governments preparing for "aggression" against Iraq. He damaged his cause further when he brought the children of the alien nations into Baghdad under his personal custody for their "safety." Tales of atrocities by Iraqi occupiers, a few of which were fabrications or exaggerations, circulated.

With the go-ahead from King Fahd, Bush ordered the deployment of U.S. forces to Saudi Arabia, and Fahd also invited other nations to station troops on the kingdom's soil. As the first tens of thousands of Coalition forces arrived at the theater of operations, the president called for "the immediate, unconditional, and complete withdrawal of all Iraqi forces from

Kuwait." But he did not threaten Saddam. He spoke of protecting Saudi Arabia, "which is of vital interest to the United States," and said that "[the] mission of our troops is wholly defensive. . . . They will not initiate hostilities . . . to drive the Iraqis out of Kuwait . . . is not the mission."[16]

The almost worldwide sanctions against Iraq, coupled with enforcement by U.S. Navy ships, all but shut down Iraq's economy. But the Iraqi forces remained in Kuwait as Saddam simply cinched the belts of his countrymen tighter. Perhaps sanctions stretched over years might have changed the dictator's mind, but his capacity to endure suffering by the Iraqi people seemed unlimited. As weeks dragged into months, the attitude of the White House changed. Instead of limiting the objective to safeguarding Saudi Arabia, gradually the mission morphed into a drive to evict Iraq from Kuwait, the destruction of the Iraqi armed forces, and the toppling of Saddam Hussein himself. In November 1990, the president doubled the American troop levels in the Middle East, providing the strength for offensive action. What had begun as a defense of Saudi Arabia and became a plan to liberate Kuwait now escalated toward destruction of the Iraqi armed forces with their nuclear, chemical, and biological weapons, and even regime change.

Congress believed that it ought to be involved in any decision on the use of military force. But when Cheney went before the Senate Armed Services Committee on December 3, 1990, he denied that the president required any additional authorization from the legislators. The House insisted otherwise, adopting a resolution that insisted the president get authorization from Congress unless Americans were endangered. The proposal passed, 177 to 37.

Bush has claimed, "I wanted to find a way to get Congress on board with an unmistakable show of that support for what we were doing and what we might have to do. I had asked Boyden Gray [his White House counsel] to look into how Lyndon Johnson had handled Congress at the time of the Gulf of Tonkin Resolution of 1964."[17]

In fact, Scowcroft, the national security adviser, said he believed the president did not need approval from Congress, that it was within his constitutional authority as commander in chief to carry out the policy toward the Iraqi aggression. "I was reluctant to ask for congressional approval because if the Congress said no, then we were really in a mess." However, said Scowcroft, his president referred to Lyndon Johnson's maxim, "Don't undertake an activity without the support of Congress." Bush did not argue with Scowcroft that he was wrong, that it was not within his power to act, but rather that the backing of Congress was politically necessary. "Early on," recalled Scowcroft, "we debated whether we needed a casus belli—what would justify the use of force by the president. To resolve that we needed to get UN authority. If we didn't get that [which the Security Council had given] it would have been much more difficult to go to Congress."[18]

The situation with Iraq evoked both the images of the consequences of the Munich appeasement and the quagmire of Vietnam. In Congress, many warned that the policy would inflame anti-Americanism in the Middle East. During a contentious meeting at the White House, Representative Tom Foley advised, "Mr. President, be cautious before you lead the country to war." Senator Sam Nunn, considered a proponent of a strong military, noted that massive deployment tended to skew toward a shooting war rather than diplomatic resolution. A heavy investment of troops can be sustained for only a short period of time before resort to force or withdrawal. Congress voted in favor of resolutions that supported the administration's policies while urging a diplomatic solution.

President Bush exploited his bully pulpit to promote his actions. In a speech in Hawaii he recalled, "In World War II, the world paid dearly for appeasing an aggressor who could have been stopped. Appeasement only leads to further aggression and ultimately to war." A few weeks later he addressed the Vietnam syndrome, insisting that he would not take the country into another quagmire.

Although he believed war inevitable, on November 30 Bush announced his willingness to travel "an extra mile for peace" and offered direct talks between the United States and Iraq. Hawkish elements charged appeasement. Kissinger remarked that compromise meant "aggression is rewarded," while Richard Perle sneered at "Bush's tendency to buckle under pressure."[19] Saddam Hussein, navigating with his own compass, interpreted the meetings as submission to him. He released his hostages but refused to yield an inch of Kuwaiti soil. UN secretary-general Javier Pérez de Cuéllar flew to Baghdad and achieved no promises of a withdrawal after listening to a lecture on American-Zionist conspiracies.

While Congress had passed resolutions that approved the administration's diplomatic efforts and approved limited military deployments in the Middle East, there was no authorization by the legislators for war against Iraq. At a small White House dinner, Vice President Dan Quayle, Scowcroft, Cheney, Powell, and Baker's deputy, Lawrence Eagleburger, debated with the commander in chief about whether to ask Congress for its imprimatur to launch an attack. Cheney argued that it was unnecessary to risk a confrontation with Capitol Hill. Harry Truman had established a precedent when he dispatched the armed forces to Korea on the basis of a UN resolution and without any congressional vote.[20] Although Cheney was correct on his facts, Truman's decision lacked legal weight. When it approved the UN Charter, Congress only did so after being assured that nothing the international body did abrogated its powers, including that of declaring war.

The commander in chief received the authority, by a wide margin in the House, and a narrow one in the Senate, to use force in the event a diplomatic solution could not be reached. On January 16, 1991, the first explosions rocked Baghdad as Tomahawk missiles launched from sea and conventional bombs dropped from F-117 and B-52 bombers fell upon Iraq to begin Operation Desert Storm.

After a monthlong aerial preparation for the ground campaign, General Schwarzkopf reported that by the end of January all known nuclear reactor facilities had been destroyed and the research center reduced to rubble. Damage assessments also claimed almost total reduction of the two other types of weapons of mass destruction, chemical and biological.[21] These results were questioned by others. A UN report said postwar inspection found huge stores of loaded chemical bombs, shells, and missiles and three uranium/hydrogen bomb component factories.[22] The capacity of Saddam to restore or reconstitute these would become a contentious issue a decade later.

As the bombers and missiles began to run out of targets, pressure for start of the land war increased. At the penultimate moment, Saddam appeared to waver, agreeing to a Soviet plan that included some concessions to Iraq if it evacuated Kuwait. However, at the same time, the Iraqis blew up or ignited hundreds of oil wells and apparently executed some Kuwaiti citizens. A twenty-four-hour ultimatum deadline passed without the start of a withdrawal. On February 24, President Bush announced that the Coalition forces in Saudi Arabia had been instructed to start the ground campaign.

The Coalition completely controlled the air. The Iraqi air force, which included about seven hundred planes, with sixty French-made Mirage jet fighters, had offered only token resistance. The Coalition shot down thirty-five without a single plane lost in air-to-air combat. One hundred and twenty-two of Saddam's aircraft fled to Iran and the remainder were destroyed or badly damaged. After two days of ground combat, while some of Saddam's forces tried to fight, the Iraqi army had collapsed and began to flee. The road from Kuwait to Basra, choked with vehicles and men in full retreat, became known as the "Highway to Hell" or "Highway of

Death" as jets, tanks, and artillery zeroed in on hapless Iraqis. Schwarzkopf and a representative of Saudi Arabia arranged a cease-fire. Iraqi troops killed in combat numbered between eight and thirty-five thousand. American casualties added up to 148 dead, 467 wounded in action, with perhaps 25 percent due to friendly fire, and 45 missing.

The terms imposed upon Iraq included the total liberation of Kuwait, a promise not to develop WMDs (with UN inspections to prevent illegal activity), and the right of the Coalition to fly surveillance missions. The United States and Great Britain, not the UN, imposed a ban on Iraqi aircraft over certain territory. Still, Saddam remained in power. Postwar critiques focused upon whether or not the Coalition forces should have gone all the way to Baghdad and taken him prisoner.

Secretary of Defense Cheney, interviewed on BBC radio, said, "If we'd gone to Baghdad and got rid of Saddam Hussein—assuming we could have found him—we'd have had to put a lot of forces in and run him to ground some place. He would not have been easy to capture. Then you've got to put a new government in his place and then you're faced with the question of what kind of government are you going to establish in Iraq? Is it going to be a Kurdish government or a Shia government or Sunni government? How many forces are you going to have to leave there to keep it propped up, how many casualties are you going to take through the course of this operation?"[23] As vice president in 2001, Cheney ignored every reservation he had expressed in 1991.

Bush insisted, "I firmly believed we should not march into Baghdad. Our stated mission, as codified in UN resolutions, was a simple one—end the aggression, knock Iraq's forces out of Kuwait and restore Kuwait's leaders."[24] He remarked that he hoped the Iraqi people and military would depose Saddam because of the devastation he had brought to the country. Secretary of State Baker guessed that Saddam would not last six months after his humiliating defeat.

Brent Scowcroft recalled, "There was not much talk [in the administration] of going to Baghdad. This was partly on practical grounds, rather than constitutional ones. The UN authorization was only to drive Iraqi forces out of Kuwait. Had we gone to Baghdad, our Arab allies would have deserted us." He added that George H. W. Bush, having served as an ambassador to the UN, had a great perspective on how other countries looked at us and was sensitive to world opinion.[25]

The rout of Saddam's armies encouraged the Kurds, a distinct ethnic group from the Iraqis who lived in the northern area of the country, to seek more autonomy for themselves. That worried the Turks, who had their own large Kurdish minority and feared the creation of an independent state. President Bush had called on Iraqis to get rid of Saddam, "to take matters into their own hands." But when the Kurds in the north and some Shiites in the south attempted to rebel, the administration adopted a neutral stance. Saddam slaughtered Kurds and Shiites, in a replay of the massacres of Kurds during the Reagan years, when the United States had also refused to intervene.

The commander in chief was not happy with the media. "The Iraqis went to great lengths to take the CNN people [still in Baghdad] to orchestrated events, where the journalists duly recorded whatever they were being told. I was irritated by the argument that the media in general were only impartial observers, and that all this was only part of looking at two warring parties. I questioned the logic of this position. These were people covering a war in which, as Americans, they had a stake. I had an awful feeling that they were hoping to prove the Pentagon wrong. . . . While I knew the correspondents were trying to do their jobs, I thought the American people saw the selective emphasis in much of their reporting as prejudicial to U.S. interests. I know I did."[26] Saddam Hussein did try to use CNN feeds as propaganda, showing damage to civilians and nonmilitary targets.

During Desert Storm, journalists, unlike in Vietnam where they roamed without chaperones, traveled at the pleasure of the armed forces and were limited in what they saw and whom they could interview. The tight control reflected the anger of the military over coverage in Southeast Asia that contradicted official accounts and exposed abuses. Bush's argument that American media should perform as cheerleaders rather than objective observers ignored the credibility gap if the press hewed to the party line. The problems of the Vietnam War would never have reached the American people but for correspondents. Like the father, the son in 2005 bemoaned the presentation by journalists in Iraq. Bad news from the battlefront never sits well in the White House.

George H. W. Bush confessed that he never grasped "the vision thing." Unlike Reagan, he could not articulate a prospectus of "the shining city on the hill." Lacking an ability to conjure up an image of a glorious domestic future, he could not build upon the euphoria of the Gulf War victory. But he did realize that a commander in chief was strengthened when Congress backed him. Equally important, he understood that the United States was far better off when it rallied the world around its policies than if it traveled solo. His presidency did not change the dynamic between Congress and the chief executive.

17

NATION-BUILDING AND GENOCIDE

Unfortunately for George H. W. Bush, credibility overseas is not a bankable commodity when it comes to the American public. (That might help explain the cavalier disregard for world opinion by the politically astute administration of his son.) Notwithstanding the apparent stunning success of the 1991 Gulf War, by election time 1992, the popularity of George H. W. Bush had plummeted, largely because of economic doldrums at home. His Democrat rival, former Arkansas governor William Jefferson Clinton, a gifted if long-winded speechmaker, offered a vibrant alternative to a man who confessed a problem with "the vision thing."

Whereas Bush seemed to devote himself to foreign affairs, the new president took office with a 360-degree perspective. He would try to reform health care, welfare, and the stagnant economy while simultaneously pursuing objectives abroad. In his forays as commander in chief, Clinton stretched the definition of the national interest to cover situations that did not directly impinge upon the United States—humanitarian causes in Africa and civil wars in the Balkan hot spot of what formerly had been Yugoslavia. It also fell to Clinton to confront the newest menace, terrorist attacks whose source was not an enemy government.

The Bush regime in its final days actually initiated the effort to alleviate suffering in Africa. In December 1992, the lame-duck administration dispatched nearly twenty-eight thousand troops, as part of a UN effort, to the African nation of Somalia. Racked by civil wars, Somalia faced a famine caused by warlords who used starvation as a weapon to control people and territory.

The first marines debarked in Mogadishu, the capital city, on December 9 under a panoply of television cameras and correspondents, heralding a humanitarian effort by the armed forces. France, Italy, and Canada were also scheduled to land troops in much smaller numbers. Bush said, "Our mission has a limited objective—to open the supply routes, to get the food moving, and to prepare a way for a U.N. peace-keeping force to keep it moving. This operation is not open-ended. We will not stay longer than is absolutely necessary."[1] Colin Powell compared the insertion of U.S. armed forces to the stereotypical cowboys-and-Indians films, with the cavalry riding to the rescue, followed by a transfer of authority to the "marshals"— the UN peacekeepers.

The White House indicated that the Americans would pull out in six weeks, by the time Clinton took the oath of office. There was no enabling resolution requested from Congress, although the potential for the troops getting in harm's way was considerable. Smith Hempstone, ambassador to Kenya, had advised that the administration should think "once, twice, three times" before involving itself in Somalia. He predicted casualties and compared the situation to Lebanon in the early days of the Reagan regime. "If you liked Beirut, you'll love Mogadishu."[2]

Clinton supported the Bush decision to invest American assets in the attempt to ameliorate the starvation and disease that had killed an estimated 350,000 Somalis. Clinton said Scowcroft had told incoming national security adviser Sandy Berger that the troops "would be home before my inauguration."[3] Scowcroft, skeptical of the venture, denied this quote. "I said while we hoped they could be removed, we doubted we could meet that deadline."[4]

During the first six months of Clinton's presidency, the American force dropped to some four thousand, and more UN nations contributed peacekeepers. Though the man-made famine abated, schools and hospitals began to function, and refugees who had fled the combat zones returned, no functioning government ruled the country. Friction between the Somali militias and Colin Powell's "marshals" intensified. Prominent in the quest for power, Mohammed Farrah Aidid controlled a large portion of Mogadishu. His guerrillas, the Habr Gidr clan, on June 24, 1993, murdered twenty-four unarmed Pakistani peacekeepers. The slaughter infuriated UN secretary-general Boutros Boutros-Ghali and his representative for Somalia, retired American admiral Jonathan Howe. Howe and Boutros-Ghali concluded that peace required the arrest and trial of Aidid. Colin Powell, about to retire as chairman of the Joint Chiefs of Staff, said Clinton "came to me with a recommendation that I approve a parallel [to a UN attempt] American effort to capture Aidid, though he thought we had only a 50 percent chance of getting him, with a 25 percent chance of getting him alive. . . . I agreed."[5]

On October 3, a crack team of more than 150 Delta Force and Rangers flew into the battered shambles of Mogadishu aboard Black Hawk helicopters. As they slid down ropes from the choppers, the Americans encountered small-arms fire from Aidid's thugs. Within minutes, matters went from bad to worse: resistance intensified, and two Black Hawks, hit by rocket-propelled grenades, crashed into the rubble-strewn streets. The advance contingent of Rangers fought for their lives while reinforcements, under a gauntlet of fire, struggled to reach their comrades.

The shooting lasted for forty-eight hours and it ended with eighteen Americans dead, dozens wounded, and a Black Hawk pilot captured. More than five hundred Somalis died, a thousand suffered wounds, and about seventy of Aidid's people were seized. The leader of the Habr Gidr escaped. Through the media, Americans witnessed the horrific spectacle of a soldier's body dragged through the Mogadishu streets by jeering Somalis who spat upon and kicked the near-naked corpse. All of the American dead, when eventually retrieved, had been badly mutilated.

Officials quickly manned their barricades. Secretary of Defense Les Aspin and Secretary of State Warren Christopher attempted to explain how a humanitarian mission scheduled to end months earlier had deteriorated into a humiliating and bloody defeat. Senator Robert F. Byrd called for a halt in "these cops-and-robbers operations," while Senator John McCain insisted, "Clinton's got to bring them home."[6] Politicians and pundits accused the administration of catering to the whims of UN secretary-general Boutros-Ghali and of "mission creep," transforming a short-term humanitarian effort into nation-building. (When he ran for office in 2000, George W. Bush vowed not to engage in nation-building, but after he took the country to war in Iraq he flip-flopped.)

Clinton, who had flashed a green light to the original plan to neutralize Aidid, had not been apprised in advance of the October 3 raid. According to author Mark Bowden, in his excellent and detailed account, the president complained that "he had been blindsided." Bowden wrote that Clinton felt betrayed by his military advisers and staff in much the same way that John F. Kennedy believed he had been misled at the time of the Bay of Pigs.[7]

Richard Clarke was among the NSC staff that sat down with the president immediately afterwards. The commander in chief listened to reports and then said, "We are not running away with our tail between our legs. I've already heard from Congress and that's what they all want to do, get out tomorrow. We're staying. We are also not gonna flatten Mogadishu to prove we are the big badass superpower. Everybody in the world knows we could do that. . . .

"We are going to send in more troops, with tanks and aircraft and any-thing else they need. We are going to show force. And we are going to keep delivering the food. If anybody fucks with us, we will respond mas-sively. And we are going to get the UN to finally show up and take over. Tell Boutros he has six months to do that, not one day more. Then . . . we will leave."[8]

Clinton said he chose restraint because "if we went back in and nabbed Aidid, dead or alive, then we, not the UN, would own Somalia, and there was no guarantee that we could put it together politically any better than the UN had."[9] Clinton would have met stiff resistance from Congress if the troops had stayed in Somalia in an attempt to create a functioning government.

After the lone American prisoner had been released and the United States began to withdraw its troops, Congress investigated. Legislators blamed Aspin and Clinton for an ill-conceived, poorly planned, and inad-equately equipped effort. Bowden disputed criticism centering on the absence of heavier firepower from the air and the use of tanks, saying they would have killed more noncombatants and that armor would have taken away the element of surprise and prevented a swift strike. Adversaries of foreign deployments smeared the Mogadishu misadventure as a demon-stration of what happens when U.S. troops fight under UN direction. However, the UN had nothing to do with either the planning or the exe-cution of the Task Force Ranger mission.

Major General William Garrison, the Ranger commander, drafted a letter to his commander in chief in which he insisted that responsibility and accountability for the operation resided with him. "For this particular target, President Clinton and Sec. Aspin need to be taken off the blame line."[10] Said Clinton, "I respected Garrison, and agreed with his letter, except for the last point. There was no way I could, or should be taken off the 'blame line.' I believe the raid was a mistake. . . . In wartime, the risk would have been acceptable. On a peacekeeping mission, they were not, because the value of the prize was not worth the risk of significant casual-ties and the certain consequences of changing the nature of the mission in the eyes of both Somalis and Americans. . . . It was worth doing under the right circumstances, but when I gave my consent to General Powell's rec-ommendation, I should also have required prior approval of the Pentagon and the White House [meaning staff responsible for national security] for any operations of this magnitude."[11]

Somalia, sometimes termed an exercise in "nation-building," repre-sented the first occasion where no direct challenge to U.S. security or interests existed. Absent a more pronounced raison d'être, the public and the Congress possessed a low toleration for casualties. The failure in Mogadishu would influence subsequent actions by a commander in chief.

Well before any of the other Iron Curtain countries stripped themselves of their slavish fealty to the Soviet Union and their communist governments, Yugoslavia, an ersatz country formed of rival ethnic and religious factions after World War I, broke away from Moscow. Once dictator Tito died, Yugoslavia fell apart. It separated in 1989 into a flock of small states—Slovenia, Croatia, Serbia, Macedonia, and Bosnia and Herzegovina. Within this framework, Montenegro was part of a federal union with Serbia that retained the name of Yugoslavia, while Kosovo was listed as an autonomous province within Serbia. There were border disputes among the states and within them. Enclaves of ethnic and religious minorities soon warred with their neighbors.

Ancient hatreds have been cited for the strife, but Richard Holbrooke, with more than thirty years as a State Department official, said, "Yugoslavia's tragedy was not foreordained. It was the product of bad, even criminal, political leaders who encouraged ethnic confrontation for personal, political, and financial gain. Rather than tackle the concrete problems of government in the post-Tito era, they led their people into a war."[12]

The principal villain was Slobodan Milosevic, an ambitious opportunist who in 1989 fired the first oratorical shot with a racist speech to his fellow Serbs. The George H. W. Bush administration, preoccupied with Iraq, avoided involvement in the dissolution of Yugoslavia that began in 1991 when Croatia and Slovenia declared independence. The Serbs, in the name of Yugoslavia, invaded Slovenia. Conflicts between Croats and Serbs, Serbs and Bosnians, and Croats and Bosnians followed. Hundreds of thousands died in an orgy of killing and destruction.

Bush's secretary of state, James Baker, backed by the president, was the architect behind a nonintervention policy. National Security Adviser Brent Scowcroft, who did a tour in Belgrade as a military attaché, said, "Eagleburger [Baker's deputy] and I were most concerned here about Yugoslavia. The President and Baker were furthest on the other side. Baker would say, 'We don't have a dog in this fight.' The President would say to me once a week, 'Tell me what this is all about.'"[13] The problem was viewed as one for Europeans to solve. But as Holbrooke noted, the Bush administration had engaged in the European matter of German reunification.

A Yugoslav-Slovene war flared briefly before Milosevic realized that few Serbs lived in Slovenia and its departure from the republic actually strengthened his hand. In contrast, hundreds of thousands of Serbs lived in Croatia. When Yugoslav troops attacked Croatia, savage guerrilla bands ravaged the land. Combat seemed to end with the recognition of an independent Croatia, and indeed organized fighting ceased, but local Serbs as irregulars continued ethnic cleansing, using the weapons of rape, murder, and forcible removal from many areas as they wiped out countrymen of different faith or ancestry. The UN agreed to deploy 12,500 peacekeepers.

The establishment of Croatia set the stage for bitter campaigns. Bosnia-Herzegovina, as a province of Yugoslavia, had been ruled by a coalition that recognized its diversity. Muslims in the territory constituted about 45 percent of the population, Serbs 30 percent, and Croats about 17 percent. The leading Muslim politico, Alija Izetbegovic, called for full sovereignty as an independent nation. The top Serbian leader, Radovan Karadzic, aligned himself with the government of Milosevic. A national referendum approved of independence, but most Serbs boycotted the vote. The subsequent separation from Yugoslavia brought the worst of the region's wars in 1992 as ethnic cleansing by Serbian paramilitary groups scoured and scarred the land and Milosevic sponsored attacks that focused heavily on civilian populations, notably in Sarajevo and Srebrenica. In addition to air raids and artillery shelling, snipers picked off men, women, and children. Sarajevo would lie under siege for four merciless years.

Although the Bush administration had been reluctant to take a stand, it had urged adoption of a UN measure that imposed economic sanctions on Serbia. The UN also maintained its arms embargo on both sides. That deprived Bosnia of weaponry, but the Serbs already possessed abundant supplies. When he ran for the presidency, Clinton had called for NATO airstrikes to deter the Serbs and an end to the arms embargo to enable the Bosnians to better defend themselves, but once in the White House he found European countries, most particularly the French, less friendly to the Bosnian Muslims. Clinton ascribed the tilt against the Bosnian majority to fear of a Muslim state capable of exporting extremism to Europe. He succeeded in establishing a no-fly zone to thwart use of Serbian airpower. However, he backtracked on ending the embargo, because that might have led to a halt of restrictions upon Haiti, Libya, and Iraq.

Initially, the United States committed to the NATO forces twenty-five fighter aircraft, equipped for combat and ready to fire in self-defense. The president advised Congress that the Americans would not act alone but only in concert with a multilateral force. He would not permit the use of the nation's ground forces. He did not promise to obtain congressional approval for airstrikes but allowed he would "welcome and encourage con-

NATION-BUILDING AND GENOCIDE

gressional authorization of any military involvement in Bosnia."[14] The reaction on Capitol Hill was to dither. Palaver substituted for firm action and members voted for a number of nonbinding statements.

In February 1994, the Balkan strife accelerated. Heavy shelling of a market in Sarajevo killed dozens of people, and NATO, with the blessing of the UN secretary-general, said that if the Serbs did not pull back their artillery from Sarajevo they would be bombed. On February 28, 1994, NATO planes shot down four Serbian aircraft that had violated the no-fly zone. This was the first military action by NATO in its forty-four years of existence. The president informed Congress, "U.S. Armed Forces participate in these operations pursuant to my constitutional authority to conduct U.S. foreign relations and as Commander-in-Chief."[15]

In November of that year, Serbian warplanes based at a field in Udbina attacked Croat and Muslim targets in western Bosnia. Richard Holbrooke, after a brief tenure as ambassador to Germany, had been appointed assistant secretary of state for European and Canadian affairs and was assigned to seek resolution. "I am a liberal interventionist," said Holbrooke. "While I am aware of the abuses of American power in Guatemala, Nicaragua, and Iran, without being a neocon, you must protect national interests. Failure to pursue an interventionist policy means isolationism. George Kennan [a former State Department official and foreign policy expert] argued against this because 'cultural superiority corrupts our morality.' When we intervene to overthrow a dictator like Milosevic, this is positive. When we intervene to keep thugs like Somoza or Mobutu [of Congo] in power, it's wrong."[16]

Holbrooke reacted strongly to this latest breach of the no-fly zone and persuaded Secretary of State Warren Christopher to demand that NATO destroy the Udbina capability. The subsequent raids, trumpeted by NATO as the largest since World War II, actually did little damage. Holbrooke justified the use of air attacks as authorized by NATO under Article 5 of the North Atlantic Treaty, which calls for individual or collective defense by the signatories in the event of an armed attack against one or more of them in Europe or North America. "It was the same in Yugoslavia as with Truman in Korea and Bush with Desert Storm, under the UN," Holbrooke said.[17] He is correct in his history but wrong about the prerogatives of a president; an okay from NATO or the United Nations does not obviate the limitations of the Constitution. However, he fully recognized the value of congressional support. When he appeared before the Senate for a confirmation hearing to be named assistant secretary of state for European and Canadian affairs, he said, "I told John Ashcroft [then senator from

Missouri] Truman was wrong when he did not get the Congress to pass a resolution on Korea."[18]

Negotiations for a cease-fire among the various warring parties stumbled along with little progress. As Serbs continued to hammer the defenseless residents of Sarajevo and other sites, NATO struck again from the air. The Bosnian Serbs upped the ante considerably, seizing some 350 blue-helmeted UN peacekeepers as "human shields" against further NATO raids. The use of French, British, and Dutch soldiers as hostages both alarmed and infuriated their governments. They feared that further NATO action might lead to murder of the captives.

Holbrooke recommended that Washington issue an ultimatum: "We give the Serbs forty-eight hours to release all hostages unharmed, and tell [them] that if they don't, we will bomb Pale [the Serbian capital of Bosnia]." While aware that those at risk were not Americans, he argued that the world community could not permit the Serbs to defy it.[19] The Serbs released the peacekeepers following a meeting with the top UN commander. Washington never received details of the bargaining, but Milosevic and the Pale leaders claimed that they received assurances of no more UN or NATO airstrikes. The Serbians pressed their military efforts harder and the major contributors to the UN forces trying to stop the war faltered in their resolve. The United States also faced a tough decision. The White House had promised NATO that if the peacekeepers were to be withdrawn, it would commit twenty thousand American soldiers to assist in the evacuation of the NATO forces.

While the Americans debated policy, General Ratko Mladic, the Yugoslav army officer who commanded both regular troops and the brutal bands of irregulars, overplayed his hand. His forces, which had surrounded the enclaves of Srebrenica, Zepa, and Gorazde—designated by the Security Council as "safe areas" and housing small numbers of UN peacekeepers—besieged Srebrenica, swollen with refugees. Mladic's forces captured the town, took hundreds of Dutch soldiers hostages, and unleashed a reign of terror against local Muslims. The ethnic cleansers herded men into a soccer stadium where they shot them. They murdered others seeking escape. The Red Cross listed 7,079 slaughtered in ambushes and mass executions. Srebrenica entered the infamous list of mass atrocities with Lidice, Oradour, Baby Yar, and the Katyn Forest.

The West stood by, impotent because of concerns for the Dutch prisoners and fears that retaliation might expose their own men. However, at a conference in London, Secretary of State Warren Christopher convinced other NATO members to assume a much tougher stance. They "drew a line in the sand" (a deliberate reference to George H. W. Bush's statement before the Gulf War) that protected Gorazde and Sarajevo. Initiatives for military action would now reside with NATO rather than the UN.

Holbrooke led a negotiating team to Belgrade for a showdown with Milosevic. The Americans had hardly begun the diplomatic effort when Bosnian Serbs lobbed a mortar shell into a Sarajevo marketplace, killing thirty-eight and wounding upwards of eighty-five people. Asked what he would recommend, Holbrooke unflinchingly suggested a major airstrike, rather than the mild retaliatory "pinpricks" of the past. As a young Foreign Service officer in Vietnam, Holbrooke said he had opposed the air campaign against North Vietnam as futile. In contrast, he said, Bosnia was different and so were the objectives. The Bosnian Serbs were "poorly trained bullies and criminals" unlikely to stand up to strong NATO airstrikes in the fashion that the "seasoned and indoctrinated Vietcong and North Vietnamese had." He reasoned that Belgrade would not support the Bosnian Serbs as forcefully as Hanoi did the Vietcong.[20]

On August 30 Operation Deliberate Force launched sixty aircraft from bases in Italy and an aircraft carrier. They battered the Serbian positions surrounding Sarajevo. French and British artillery, from the Rapid Reaction Force, part of the UN peacekeepers, shelled the Serb barracks outside of Sarajevo. None in Congress questioned the authority of the United States to engage in the NATO operations. The *New York Times* and *Wall Street Journal* endorsed the intervention.

As diplomats representing the British, French, German, Russian, and U.S. governments shuttled between Belgrade and Zagreb, bombs rained down upon the Serb military installations all over Bosnia. NATO suspended the attacks on September 1 to give Mladic an opportunity to comply with a demand for the end to the Sarajevo siege. When Mladic and Radovan Karadzic resisted acceptance of the NATO proposals, Holbrook told Washington, "If we do not resume the bombing . . . it will be another catastrophe. NATO will again look like a paper tiger . . . you may never take any decision as public officials more important than this one. Give us bombs for peace. Give us a resumption of the bombing by morning."[21] The hard-line advocates won out, bringing on board the chief opponents to air attacks.

The latest missions fired Tomahawk cruise missiles that targeted military centers distant from both Sarajevo and Gorazde. Those opposed to the use of force grumbled about the attacks. Pressure to cease flowed from Moscow, always partial to the Serbs. At a strategy session, Clinton asked, "Has the NATO bombing reached the point of diminishing returns?"

"No, Mr. President," said Holbrooke. "There may come a time when continued bombing would hurt the peace efforts, but we're not there yet." Christopher supported him. Clinton accepted their advice but complained, "I am frustrated that the air campaign is not better coordinated with the diplomatic effort."[22] But ultimately the assaults from the air achieved their purpose. Karadzic and Mladic, unable to rely on full support from Milosevic, caved, agreeing to remove all heavy weapons near Sarajevo, allow the airport to open, and permit free traffic over two land routes. Still Muslims, Serbs, and Croats continued to battle one another in other areas. Atrocities were not confined to Serbs, as Croats and Bosnian Muslims avenged themselves.

The suspension of the NATO flights and the liberation of Sarajevo aside, war continued to rage in the Balkans. The parties to the often heated bargaining brought a mixture of personal animosities, distrust, ambition, provincialism, and idealism. "[Secretary of Defense] Bill Perry," said Clinton, "stated that a peace agreement would require NATO to send troops to Bosnia to enforce it. Moreover, since our responsibility to participate in NATO missions was clear, he did not believe we were required to seek advance approval from Congress. I thought Dole and Gingrich [Newt, the Georgia Republican House majority leader] might be relieved not to have a vote on the Bosnia mission; they were both internationalists who knew what we had to do, but there were many Republicans in both chambers who strongly disagreed."[23]

The American mediators, spearheaded by Holbrooke, proposed, cajoled, and threatened until ultimately all accepted, however grudgingly, boundaries for Serbia, Croatia, and Bosnia and Herzegovina. A strong international military organization, the Implementation Force (IFOR), would see that the terms were fulfilled without violence. An uneasy calm settled on the Balkans.

While some might debate whether turmoil in central Europe involved national security, direct, serious threats to the United States confronted the Clinton administration from the start. Before 2001, few Americans had worried about attacks by terrorists in the United States. A bomb blast at Manhattan's World Trade Center on February 26, 1993, killed six people, but the culprits left an easy trail for the FBI. The swift arrests, trials, and convictions suggested that the threat was manageable. But because of the increased frequency of such acts around the world, Clinton directed his national security team to investigate terrorist organizations and devise ways to protect the nation.

In April 1993, Kuwait security forces arrested about a dozen people and charged them with conspiring to assassinate former president George H. W. Bush while he visited the area. The FBI determined that the Iraqi government had masterminded the plot. "I asked the Pentagon to recommend a course of action," said Clinton, "and General Powell came to me with the missile attack on the intelligence headquarters as both a proportionate response and an effective deterrent." The U.S. fired twenty-three Tomahawk missiles aimed at the proposed target. Several overshot the mark, exploding in a residential neighborhood and killing eight civilians. Clinton actually wanted to hit Iraq harder, but Powell convinced him strikes on presidential palaces probably would not find Saddam Hussein and would likely add more nonmilitary deaths.[24]

After the Gulf War of 1991, the Saudi government had permitted the United States to maintain a military base in the country as a way to quickly deter further adventures by Iraq. In 1995, terrorists in Dhahran blew up a truck bomb outside the security barrier of a military housing complex. Nineteen air force personnel died and almost three hundred more Americans were injured. The government there eventually claimed to have caught those responsible and executed them.

The Saudis had expelled Osama bin Laden for his antagonism to the government's acceptance of a U.S. military base and his religious extremism. From the Sudan, bin Laden in 1996 issued a fatwa, a declaration that called for attacks on Americans abroad and at home. The U.S. effort to combat terrorism applied economic sanctions, which induced Sudan to take action against some of its violent resident extremists. The Sudanese claimed they offered to ship bin Laden to the United States, but several investigations found no reliable evidence to support their assertion. The Clinton administration did not ask for him to be placed in U.S. custody.[25] Nevertheless, the Sudanese forced bin Laden and his al-Qaeda organization to relocate to Afghanistan, where his politics, religious views, and fatwa were all embraced by Mullah Omar, head of the Taliban, Muslim fundamentalists who ruled Afghanistan. American intelligence experts did not identify al-Qaeda as a threat until 1997, and not until 1999 was it designated as a foreign terrorist group.

Clinton claimed his counterterrorists blocked several plots by al-Qaeda to overthrow governments and blow up commercial aircraft. However, after bombs exploded at the doors of the U.S. embassies in Tanzania and Kenya, murdering 257 people, including a dozen Americans, and wounding five thousand, the CIA created a station exclusively devoted to that organization within its Counterterrorism Center. In August 1996, the CIA advised the president that bin Laden and his top staff planned to meet at a camp in Afghanistan. The commander in chief consulted with Sandy Berger, national security adviser, about a military strike against the al-Qaeda chief. While international law bars military action as revenge or punishment, the rules for self-defense permit an attack to prevent or thwart future raids.

Politics intruded upon the situation. From the start of his presidency, Clinton had been a target for partisan attacks. Questions about the dismantling of the White House Travel Office, accusations of illegality in a real estate venture in Arkansas known as Whitewater, the suicide of Vincent Foster, a White House counsel staff member, and Clinton's sexual peccadilloes, which resulted in his lying under oath, fueled a savage inquisition. When the commander in chief considered military strikes at sites in Sudan and Afghanistan, he was aware that some of his opponents would charge him with an attempt to divert public attention from his possible impeachment.

Whatever the domestic tempests howling about the commander in chief, he gave the orders for the attacks. Missiles fired from ships in the Arabian Sea and the Red Sea blasted a chemical plant in Sudan and the camps in Afghanistan. The Sudanese government claimed the destroyed factory manufactured no dangerous chemicals, but CIA intelligence said otherwise. The seventy-five Tomahawks targeted on Afghanistan killed more than twenty jihadists, al-Qaeda agents, but the intended victim, bin Laden, was not there.

Briefed in advance by new defense secretary William Cohen, the leaders of Congress applauded what they viewed as a proper defensive response to attacks on U.S. interests. Clinton asked General Hugh Shelton, chairman of the Joint Chiefs of Staff, and Richard Clarke of the National Security Council to draw up plans for commando raids against al-Qaeda in Afghanistan. That option never achieved support. "It was clear," wrote Clinton, "that the senior military didn't want to do this, perhaps because of Somalia, perhaps because they would have to send in the Special Forces without knowing for certain where bin Laden was, or whether we could get our troops back out to safety."[26]

In addition to the station created by the CIA exclusively devoted to bin Laden and his people, Clarke at the NSC now began to organize the collection of information on terrorist groups like al-Qaeda and how to deal with attacks that used chemical or biological weapons. Economic sanctions were imposed upon bin Laden and his organization, with a similar embargo subsequently applied to the Taliban hosting the terrorists. Clinton signed "Memoranda of Notification," documents similar to a finding that authorized the CIA to use lethal force against bin Laden and his top associates. "Our plans," said Cohen, "were to try to, quote, capture and/or kill . . . capture or kill bin Laden."[27] Lacking paramilitary capability within it, the agency contracted with local Afghan warlords to carry out the hits.

The Taliban rejected overtures to expel or curb bin Laden, and neighboring Pakistan, home to a large number of citizens who favored the Taliban, refused to make an issue of al-Qaeda with Afghanistan. This was a new type of enemy, one not identified with a single nation-state, one without cities or fixed installations that could be raided. It was less vulnerable to military force and the belief that it could be defeated by killing its leader was a fallacy. And once again, a situation freighted with politics and ideology was treated as if there were a military solution.

The sad result of Mogadishu, apart from the continuing suffering of the Somali people, was the reluctance by Congress to put boots on the ground for other humanitarian efforts such as the pogroms of the Hutus against the Tutsi people in Rwanda, the slaughter in Sudan's Darfur region, and the problems of starvation and disease in other areas of Africa. On the credit side of the ledger, Clinton could point to the cessation of ethnic cleansing in the Balkans, achieved through the use of American armed forces in conjunction with members of NATO. While the administration did attempt to strike at the terrorists of al-Qaeda, under the mandate of self-defense, the effort neither hurt the enemy nor discouraged him. Congress supported the attack but did nothing to give the threat a sense of urgency. Commander in Chief Clinton's executive decision to deploy the armed forces in the Balkans furthered presidential power as he created a precedent for future involvements without the authority of Congress.

18

PREVENTION AND RETALIATION

Based on the earlier successes in halting strife among the Serbs, Croats, and Bosnians, Clinton found it relatively easy to enlist the UN and NATO when a vicious new conflict erupted in the remnants of Yugoslavia. He was unable, however, to significantly increase the intensity of efforts to quell terrorism. His administration would turn over that responsibility to the incoming chief executive, George W. Bush, whose administration initially appeared much more concerned with Saddam Hussein, still in power nine years after the president's father had led a coalition that seemingly had emasculated him. It would quickly become evident that the incoming president not only intended to show a mailed fist but that he would not hesitate to use it.

Al-Qaeda easily penetrated the soft defenses against its brand of warfare on September 11, 2001. Even as he rallied the stunned American people and launched a war against the terrorists and those who harbored them, Bush II still eyed Hussein as a target. Because of 9/11 and the awareness that the continental United States was now in the crosshairs, Congress indulged the commander in chief without questioning his agenda or sources of information.

Before 9/11 and during Clinton's final two years in office, terrorism issues simmered on a back burner. The Yugoslavian province of Kosovo, housing Serbs and Albanians, people divided by ethnic heritage and religion, had become a replay of events in Bosnia. Dictator Tito had granted the province, as part of Yugoslavia, the right of self-governance in 1974. Milosevic snatched autonomy away in 1989. Kosovar Albanians rebelled, and by 1998 the Serbs had begun a murderous campaign reminiscent of earlier ethnic cleansing. The UN had imposed an arms embargo and NATO urged a diplomatic solution. U.S. secretary of state Madeleine Albright pressed for a military intervention by the family of nations.

A NATO threat to launch air attacks temporarily halted the oppression, but by the beginning of 1999 the Serbs had returned to the killing fields. While the insurgent Kosovars reluctantly accepted an agreement that included being disarmed, the Serbs rejected the proposal and deployed forty thousand soldiers on the borders of the province. NATO proposed a peacekeeping force that would include U.S. troops, a commitment approved by the Senate and the House.

On March 23, 1999, under the aegis of NATO secretary-general Javier Solana, U.S. general Wesley Clark directed eleven weeks of airstrikes that pounded the Serb positions within Kosovo and in Serbia, including Belgrade. Clinton wooed public opinion in a broadcast that outlined the conflict and described the atrocities attributed to Serbs.

Congresswoman Nita Lowey said, "I believe that prevention of genocide, 'nation-building,' and humanitarian missions are, in many cases, just as important to U.S. national security as other types of military campaigns. In addition to our responsibilities as a signatory to the UN Convention on Genocide, the United States has an interest in preventing the kind of atrocities and rectifying the kind of humanitarian situations around the world that provide haven for terrorists and lead to regional and global instability. While it would be irresponsible to make a blanket statement about all such instances, I believe in theory that these types of missions are critical to national security and thus are acceptable uses of the U.S. armed forces."[1]

Milosevic eventually caved in and agreed to withdraw the troops from Kosovo. Clinton noted, "The success of the air campaign in Kosovo marked a new chapter in military history." He obliquely addressed critics: "I'm also still convinced that fewer civilians died than would have perished if we had put in ground troops, a bridge I would nevertheless have crossed rather than let Milosevic prevail."[2] Yet it seems highly unlikely that Congress and the public would have allowed him even to approach that bridge.

The antiterrorism strategy thwarted a series of plots that fell under the heading of the Millennium Terrorist Alert of December 1999. Using intelligence gathered at home and abroad, law enforcement shut down strikes aimed at the Los Angeles airport and the destroyer USS *Sullivan* visiting the Yemeni port of Aden. Ten months later, an al-Qaeda suicide squad did succeed in exploding a skiff against the destroyer USS *Cole* while the ship was in Aden, killing seventeen sailors.

Osama bin Laden and his terrorist network remained virulent and undeterred. What to do about the threat would now become the responsibility of the incoming commander in chief. The successor to Bill Clinton, George W. Bush, entered the White House with the most meager résumé for foreign affairs of any president since the 1920s. A Texas-bred and -raised preppie, a Skull and Bones member at Yale, he compiled a mediocre record as a businessman, a fellow handed the key to the executive washrooms largely because of who his father was. His major achievement lay in his time as the governor of Texas.

Bush's ebullient personality fitted the bonhomous stereotype of the salesman. Comedians and anti-Bush pundits delighted in repeating his malapropisms, mispronunciations, and occasional factual fumbles, but he was not stupid. Clarke commented, "When he focused, he asked the kind of questions that revealed a results-oriented mind, but he looked for the simple solution, the bumper sticker description of the problem. Once he had that, he could put energy behind a drive to achieve his goal."[3]

Bush had not traveled to foreign lands or served in any capacity that brought him in contact with other nations, except for his Texas gubernatorial duties involving Mexico. He was unabashedly not a great reader of books, magazines, or newspapers. "Nobody needs to tell me what to believe," he said. "But I do need somebody to tell me where Kosovo is."[4]

When I interviewed Brent Scowcroft in the spring of 2004, the former national security adviser for Bush 41 spoke of Bush 43 with what I felt was pain over the difference between the two. "He is unlike his father," remarked Scowcroft. "He does not seem to understand or care about the importance of the attitudes of other nations toward the U.S."[5]

When he was inaugurated in 2001, the new president had his own ideas on how the United States should act. At his side, the president had individuals like Secretary of State Colin Powell, Vice President Dick Cheney, National Security Adviser Condoleezza Rice, and Secretary of Defense Donald Rumsfeld, all of whom were experienced in global politics, including war.

During a meeting in the Oval Office several months after U.S. troops in 2003 swept into Baghdad, Senator Joseph Biden related his concerns about the mounting problems of "winning the peace, the explosive mix of Shiite and Sunni [Biden left out the fractious element of the Kurds], the disbanding of the Iraqi Army and problems securing the oil fields." To his puzzlement, the president looked at him, "unflappingly sure that the United States was on the right course and that all was well. 'Mr. President,' I finally said, 'How can you be so sure when you don't know the facts?'" Bush answered, "My instincts. My instincts." Biden said he shook his head and answered, "Mr. President, your instincts aren't good enough."⁶ The new chief executive explained his decisions as coming after prayer and from his "gut." At a Geneva conference he told world leaders, "Look, I know what I believe, and what I believe is right."⁷

Unlike Richard Nixon, who devoured reports and documents dealing with policy, or Bill Clinton, an equally voracious reader but also a man of great curiosity who never missed an opportunity to quiz someone who might have information, George W. Bush was not a man who thought, but one who knew. He was above all the truest believer of any modern president, an evangelical endowed with the certainty that faith demands.

His predecessor advised the incoming president that "his biggest [national] security problem would be Osama bin Laden" and terrorism. The assault upon the *Cole* emphasized the threat. At the time, however, unable to pinpoint a target for retaliation, the Clinton administration took no action, and its replacements concluded they needed a different type of response. Clinton national security adviser Sandy Berger had warned about bin Laden and al-Qaeda. Outgoing secretary of defense William Cohen had created a bipartisan group headed by former senators Warren Rudman and Gary Hart for a study on national security in the future. Their final report, issued on January 31, 2001, recommended that top priority be assigned to the problem of terrorism. "A direct attack against American citizens on American soil is likely over the next quarter century . . . even excellent intelligence will not prevent all surprises."

Richard A. Clarke, the National Security Council specialist on terrorism, sent a memo to Rice. He described the nature of al-Qaeda, the presence of terrorist cells in forty countries including the United States, and indications of plots for direct attacks on the United States. In the thirteen-page document, Clarke outlined a series of measures to balk al-Qaeda, with particular attention to its Afghanistan headquarters. He proposed "massive support" to anti-Taliban groups as a way "to keep Islamic extremist fighters tied down," hitting the terrorist camps "while classes are in session," intelligence teams to gather "humint," deploying armed drone aircraft to hunt down terrorists, more aggressive tracking of the money that flowed to al-Qaeda, and acceleration of FBI translations and analyses of data gained through surveillance of suspect terrorists in the States. (The report was not declassified and released to the media until February 11, 2005.)

Rice would insist that the paper did not really amount to a plan for dealing with the terrorist network. Whether Clarke's report could be

defined as a "plan" or not, it most certainly clamored for immediate attention and provided talking points for a full-court press against al-Qaeda.
But he was unable to arrange meetings with the president to persuade him
to take more effective action. Others detected a chief executive preoccupied with Saddam. Secretary of the Treasury Paul O'Neill recalled that the
commander in chief talked about removing Iraq's leader less than two
weeks into his presidency.

Before George W. Bush officially assumed the mantle of commander in
chief, outgoing defense secretary William Cohen, a Republican, met with
Bush, Cheney, Rumsfeld, Rice, Powell, and representatives of the Joint
Chiefs at the Pentagon. Cohen said few nations would back a strong military action against Saddam and he doubted that airstrikes would achieve
much. However, he believed the Iraqi strongman was "effectively contained and isolated."[8]

At the CIA, when Director George Tenet delivered a national security
briefing to the incoming president, he named three major threats to U.S.
security. He called Osama bin Laden and his al-Qaeda organization "a
tremendous threat" and an "immediate" one. He cited proliferation of
WMDs, but only tangentially referred to Iraq. Tenet listed the growing
military strength of China as the third worry.

Questions about Iraq's stocks of weapons of mass destruction persisted.
In December 1998, United Nations Special Commission (UNSCOM)
chairman Richard Butler had complained of inadequate cooperation with
inspectors looking for biological and chemical weapons of mass destruction. The matter of nuclear weapons was the responsibility of a separate
agency, the International Atomic Energy Agency (IAEA). Saddam in
turn accused members of UNSCOM of providing intelligence on Iraqi
security. British and American aircraft from December 17 to 21 bombarded radar sites and other air defense installations. The damage was
negligible and Saddam banned all inspectors unless economic sanctions
were removed. Both the United States and Britain urged that the sanctions continue, but the other three members of the Security Council,
China, Russia, and France, sought to lift them. The restrictions on trade
seemed to have achieved little. The dictator had no compunction about
burdening his subjects with the rigors of sanctions, and a UN Oil-for-Food
Program helped ease the pain, while a number of individuals, including
Saddam and some UN officials, enriched themselves.

CIA chief George Tenet had agreed with Clarke's assessment of al-
Qaeda and bin Laden as imminent menaces, but early on in the Bush 43
presidency, leading members of the administration merged terrorism with

Saddam Hussein. When National Security Adviser Rice finally convened a meeting in April 2001 to consider programs aimed at al-Qaeda, Clarke said she downgraded the importance of antiterrorism. Neocon Paul Wolfowitz, deputy secretary of defense, questioned the attention to bin Laden. "We are talking about a network of terrorist organizations called al Qaeda," said Clarke, "that happens to be led by bin Laden, and we are talking about that network because it alone poses an immediate and serious threat to the United States."

Wolfowitz allegedly replied, "Well, there are others that do as well, at least as much, Iraqi terrorism for example."

"I am unaware of any Iraqi-sponsored terrorism directed at the United States, Paul, since 1993, and I think FBI and CIA concur in that judgment."

Wolfowitz persisted. "You give bin Laden too much credit. He could not do all these things like the 1993 attack on New York, not without a state sponsor. Just because the FBI and CIA had failed to find the linkages does not mean they don't exist." The charge of Iraq as behind the 1993 World Trade Center bombing exasperated Clarke, who said investigations had found it totally without foundation.[9]

The major repositories of intelligence on the subject, the FBI, CIA, and NSA, collected sketchy information about agents of al-Qaeda. The CIA and FBI identified some individuals with hostile intentions toward the United States, and the State Department put them on a "watch list," known as TIPOFF, to track their whereabouts. Several were discovered to have traveled to the United States, where they had encountered no difficulty entering the country. Visas were easily obtainable abroad, and the issuing nations paid little attention to who left their shores. Further, U.S. immigration rules, covering millions of visitors, were not geared to winnow out anyone without a public profile. In the United States, no one followed up on the activities of even those on a watch list. The FBI did not maintain a terrorist watch list. The Federal Aviation Administration, concerned with skyjackers, kept its own "no-fly" list. No one coordinated that ban with State's TIPOFF.

President Bush, along with Cheney and Rice, received briefings about possible al-Qaeda ventures as part of the latest intelligence at morning meetings with Tenet. By early summer 2001, the warnings crescendoed with words like "spectacular," "high profile attacks," and "Bin Laden threats are real." However, these referred to Saudi Arabia, Israel, Bahrain, Kuwait, Yemen, and even Rome. Embassies and armed forces overseas went on the alert.

The commander in chief inquired whether any of the suspected attacks might hit the United States. The CIA drafted a paper, the Presidential Daily Brief of August 6, 2001. Headlined, "Bin Ladin Determined to Strike in US," it cited clandestine sources that indicated the terrorist leader wanted to hit inside the United States. The one-and-a-bit-page document—the president had let it be known he preferred such concise reports—quoted some of bin Laden's statements, his long-term planning, and that some members of his organization "have resided in or traveled to the United States for years, and the group apparently maintains a support structure that could aid attacks."

Further on, it said, "We have not been able to corroborate some of the more sensational threat reporting, such as that from a [blanked out] service in 1998 saying that bin Ladin wanted to hijack a US aircraft to gain the release of 'Blind Shaykh' 'Umar [convicted for a role in the 1993 bombing]." The paper concluded with a cover-your-behind sentence: "The FBI is conducting approximately 70 full field investigations throughout the United States that it considers bin Ladin–related." The PDB did not provide credible information of a specific attack inside the country.

Neither Clarke nor the Counterterrorism and Security Group (CSG), which he headed, ever were informed of specific FBI discoveries of al-Qaeda operatives within the United States. Nor did they know of the arrest and investigation of Zacarias Moussaoui because of a visa violation triggered by suspicious behavior at a flight school where he asked to learn only how to control a jet in flight rather than the techniques for taking off and landing. An FBI agent in Phoenix advised of a coordinated effort by Osama bin Laden to enroll "an inordinate number" of people in flight school. The memo never went beyond a field office or to the terrorism experts.

Rice and her deputy, Stephen Hadley, did arrange for a presidential directive dealing with al-Qaeda. They began work around the time of the PDB and expected to review and edit it before submission to the president on September 4. The draft envisioned greater covert action against al-Qaeda and increased aid to the Northern Alliance and other anti-Taliban elements, like the Pashtuns. Unfortunately, even if the commander in chief signed off, there was no money in the till. Congress would need to appropriate funds, which could take weeks or months.

Clarke recalled a meeting of the top echelons as a nonevent. "Tenet and I spoke passionately about the urgency and seriousness of the al Qaeda threat. No one disagreed. Powell laid out an aggressive strategy for putting pressure on Pakistan to side with us against the Taliban and al Qaeda.

Money might be needed, he noted, but there was no plan to find the funds. Rumsfeld, who looked distracted throughout the session, took the Wolfowitz line that there were other terrorist concerns, like Iraq and Iran."[10]

The September 4 meeting accepted a presidential directive that called for added covert activity, use of Predator drone aircraft, and to work out a policy covering Afghanistan and Pakistan that might curb al-Qaeda. It hardly qualified as a full-court press against the terrorists.

One week later, on the morning of Tuesday, September 11, al-Qaeda's suicide skyjackers struck the devastating blows that obliterated the World Trade Center, heavily damaged the Pentagon, and killed nearly three thousand people. When the president addressed Americans that evening, he changed the language of a prepared statement that the United States would not separate those who planned the acts and those who tolerated or encouraged the terrorists. Instead, he said, "We will make no distinction between those who planned these acts and those who harbor them." It was a very broad commitment, made without consulting Cheney, Powell, Rumsfeld, or Congress. Under the circumstances, an attack upon the United States, the commander in chief required no declaration of war from Congress, although after Pearl Harbor, Franklin D. Roosevelt had asked for a formal vote by the legislators. At the same time, NATO invoked Article 5, which declared that the attacks on the United States on September 11 amounted to an attack on all NATO countries.

When those responsible for national security met in the first hours after the towers collapsed, Clarke said he detected a shift in the Defense Department from al-Qaeda, whom the CIA explicitly identified as the source of the attacks, to Iraq. Wolfowitz argued that assaults were too sophisticated for a terrorist group to manage without a state sponsor (Iraq). On Wednesday afternoon, little more than twenty-four hours after the horrors, Rumsfeld, said Clarke, grumbled about the absence of "decent targets for bombing in Afghanistan and that we should consider bombing Iraq, which had better targets." The president did not reject the notion but remarked that instead of blasting Iraq with cruise missiles what was needed there was regime change.

Clarke said he was further discomfited when the commander in chief took him and several others from the NSA aside. "I want you, as soon as you can, to go back over everything, everything. See if Saddam did this. See if he's linked in any way." Clarke protested that this was clearly the work of al-Qaeda and that the intelligence experts could find no real linkages to Iraq, although there were minor connections with Iran, Pakistan, Saudi Arabia, and Yemen.

"'Look into Iraq, Saddam,' the president said testily and left us."[11]

In one of his finer moments, the president traveled to New York City where thousands sifted through the still smoldering rubble of buildings, furnishings, and people. From the charred ruins of a fire truck, he spoke through a bullhorn to the rescue workers. "America today is on bended knee in prayer for the people whose lives were lost here." When someone shouted that he couldn't hear him, Bush put his arm around Bob Beckwith, a retired firefighter, and yelled, "I can hear you. The rest of the world hears you. And the people who knocked these buildings down will hear all of us soon."

However strong the desire to oust Saddam, in Operation Enduring Freedom the Bush administration on September 26, 2001, began its war on al-Qaeda and its host nation, Afghanistan, ruled by the Muslim extremist Taliban. On October 7, working off plans developed in the Clinton administration, the first air raids, using land-based bombers, carrier-based planes, and cruise missiles from American and British vessels, struck. In little more than a month, Mullah Omar, the Taliban chief, abandoned the capital of Kabul and fled to the mountains on the border of Pakistan. Ground troops drove toward the major city of Kandahar, but did not seal the border with Pakistan.

General Tommy Franks, commander in chief of the United States Central Command (CENTCOM), directed the final campaign, Anaconda. From the air-conditioned Joint Operations Center in Tampa, surrounded by an array of consoles humming with a constant feed of electronically conveyed information, Franks watched battle scenes fought in the dusty, mountainous ridges of the ill-defined border between Afghanistan and Pakistan.

According to the general, the enemy had chosen to take their stand in an area where they had defeated Soviet troops in the 1980s. However, he claimed that his forces overran "this last bastion, sealing caves and tunnels—and the enemy inside—with powerful demolition charges, destroying huge caches of ordnance. Our young infantrymen, combat aviators and SOF [Special Operations Forces] troops were killing hundreds of the enemy's best-armed, most highly motivated fighters. . . . I realized we were winning a decisive battle. Before Anaconda ended, the last of the enemy's cohesive, well-armed forces in Afghanistan would be destroyed."[12]

Franks's army may well have won the battle, but hardly the war. When information suggested that bin Laden and Omar might be found in the rugged Tora Bora region, instead of the U.S. forces conducting search-and-destroy missions, the task was parceled out to the local warlords. The latter-day Hessians achieved little, their failure due either to a distaste for risk or perhaps sympathy with the fugitives. German intelligence claimed that the Afghan militias, hired by the United States to hunt down Osama bin Laden, and who knew his whereabouts in 2001, accepted a payoff from the terrorist chief and let him escape.[13]

Five years after issuing his "dead or alive" demand and quoting heavyweight boxing champion Joe Louis—"he can run but he can't hide"—the commander in chief had no coonskin to nail on the Oval Office wall. Both Osama bin Laden and Mullah Omar remained at large. Although they had not hit the United States again, cells associated with al-Qaeda exploded devastating bombs in Madrid, London, and Egypt. (A group claiming affiliation with al-Qaeda would begin deadly operations in Iraq after the United States invaded.)

The invasion had ended the rule of Afghanistan by the Taliban. However, the creation of a democratic government capable of ruling Afghanistan was something else. There would be elections in 2004 and a government in Kabul that promised a free society. But while women no longer lived under the harsh strictures of a theocracy, they were not the equals of male citizens. Nor did the rule of law extend much beyond a few large cities. The Bush administration's reluctance to engage in "nation-building," articulated when he ran for president in 2000, limited aid to the new Afghan government. The Taliban actually resurfaced with new strength.

Demands for postmortems on the failure to prevent the World Trade Center attacks forced acceptance by the administration of a 9/11 Commission, headed by former New Jersey governor Thomas Kean and former representative Lee Hamilton. It found a critical lack of connections among and within the agencies responsible for domestic security. Louis Freeh, director of the FBI, testified that all of the hijackers entered the United States "easily and lawfully from abroad," and the CIA's George Tenet said seventeen of the nineteen were "clean." The facts say otherwise. The 9/11 investigation pointed out that the men who crashed the planes included "known al Qaeda operatives who could have been watchlisted," that they held passports "manipulated in a fraudulent manner," with "suspicious indicators of extremism," "made detectable false statements on their visa applications," "were pulled out of the travel stream for greater scrutiny by border officials," and lied to the border officials. Furthermore, they "violated immigration laws while inside the United States."[14]

Once inside the United States, the hijackers also escaped apprehension because of ineptitude and bureaucratic bungling. Neither the FAA nor other agencies could plead ignorance of the possibility for hijacking. The commission reported that the FAA possessed information claiming that associates of Osama bin Laden in the 1990s were interested in the use of an aircraft as a weapon, although no specific evidence of such a plot existed. The FAA discounted the threat: "Fortunately we have no indica-tion that any group is currently thinking in that direction."[15]

Defenders of the president argued that the administration was ham-strung by a lack of intelligence. Critics said that as commander in chief Bush failed to take the threat seriously enough and it was his responsibil-ity to ensure that the agencies under his control not only gathered the information but also correctly interpreted it. The argument of who should be blamed was one without likely resolution.

What was clear was that the celebrated Operation Enduring Freedom had displaced al-Qaeda but not destroyed it. The George W. Bush admin-istration clutched information tighter to its breast than any White House before it. At the same time, it generated spin that habitually overinflated achievements and concealed defeats. The anxiety generated by 9/11 estab-lished a climate hospitable to the cliché, "The best defense is a good offense," although the target should have been open to debate. As a man who firmly believed he and his minions manufactured reality, Bush was primed to use military force as he saw fit. He was not about to compromise the authority he had given his own presidency. Opposition to his policies melted away. The burial of partial culpability for 9/11 and the fulsome boasts of success in Afghanistan helped pave the road for an advance upon Iraq.

19

BETWEEN IRAQ AND
HARD PLACES

As several eyewitnesses testified, beginning early in 2001, the administration started to paint a bull's-eye on Saddam Hussein. Having falsely announced that Afghanistan could be considered secure from al-Qaeda, the CIA, the State Department, the Pentagon, and of course the White House itself became preoccupied with the question of legitimizing an attack on Iraq. They launched a vigorous effort to provide evidence of a threat through weapons of mass destruction and connections with the terrorists of al-Qaeda. Officials predicted that the Iraqis would welcome a regime change and the resistance would be overcome with a minimum number of troops. Congress, with a few exceptions, dutifully followed the White House lead.

The military campaign in Afghanistan had afforded Defense Secretary Donald Rumsfeld an opportunity to demonstrate the efficacy of his theories on modern warfare. Rumsfeld had denigrated Clinton for his caution as a commander who sought to avoid the use of ground troops and preferred missiles. During his first eight months in office, the defense secretary started to transform the military, which he described as outdated, saying it was equipped, trained, and organized to fight old enemies, mainly the Soviet Union. Rumsfeld prescribed capabilities to defend against missiles, terrorism, and threats against space assets and information systems. He emphasized smaller ground-force units that could move fast and were less encumbered by heavy vehicles and big artillery pieces, and stressed increased reliance upon Special Forces and intensive tactical support from the air.

A collegiate wrestler, onetime navy pilot, and four-term congressman from Chicago's North Shore, Rumsfeld had served in the Nixon administration, been ambassador to NATO, done a tour as Ford's chief of staff and then secretary of defense. He emerged from the gunfire and explosions of Operation Enduring Freedom the hip-hop star of the Bush administration. Unlike dour, growling Cheney, who seemed to regard questions about his activities as vulgar intrusions, Rumsfeld played Delphic oracle— "Absence of evidence is not evidence of absence" (after inspections found no WMDs); "There is the war you see and the war you don't see" (speaking of the progress of the campaign against al-Qaeda). He displayed the indifference of the armchair general removed from harm's way, saying, "You go to war with the army you have," after a soldier in Iraq wondered why vehicles lacked adequate armor. He redefined the nature of a democratic society: "Looting is what you have when people get freedom."

Operation Enduring Freedom had hardly begun when the commander in chief on November 21, 2001, seventy-two days after 9/11, closeted himself with Rumsfeld. "What kind of a war plan do you have for Iraq? How do you feel about the war plan for Iraq?" Bush asked. He then cautioned his defense secretary that he wanted to avoid a leak which would ignite "enormous international angst and domestic speculation. I knew what would happen if people thought we were developing a potential for a war plan for Iraq."[1]

The United Nations in 1999 with Resolution 1284 had preserved sanctions but liberalized the Oil-for-Food Program. It had retooled its agency for scrutinizing Iraq's chemical and biological weapons capability into a new entity, United Nations Monitoring, Verification and Inspection Commission (UNMOVIC), chaired by Hans Blix, a former Swedish diplomat and director of the International Atomic Energy Agency from 1981 to 1997. Diplomats exchanged letters and held dialogues designed to reach an agreement that would permit both UNMOVIC and the IAEA back into Iraq. On several occasions when it seemed the parties had come to terms, the Iraqis suddenly raised issues that halted progress.

On January 28, 2002, President Bush delivered a State of the Union address that indicted Iraq as part of an "axis of evil" along with Iran and North Korea. The commander in chief said, "By seeking weapons of mass destruction these regimes pose a grave and growing danger." He went on to assert, "I will not wait on events while dangers gather," raising the specter of a preemptive war.

In England, Prime Minister Tony Blair reiterated the charges against Hussein. "We know he has stockpiles of major amounts of chemical and biological weapons. We know that he's tried to acquire nuclear capability."[2] Yet Blix commented that two and a half months earlier, Blair's Foreign Office had reported no hard evidence on WMDs. France's president,

Jacques Chirac, advised Blix that his intelligence service had found no "serious evidence" that Iraq possessed WMDs.

A *Washington Post* article by Walter Pincus in April 2002 identified Paul Wolfowitz, deputy secretary of defense, as seeking to discredit inspections because they could "torpedo" plans to oust Saddam by military force. Pincus quoted officials: "The hawks' nightmare is that inspectors will be admitted, will not be terribly vigorous and not find anything. Economic sanctions would be eased, and the U.S. would be unable to act."[3]

At a July 23, 2002, meeting of Blair and members of his cabinet, Sir Richard Dearlove, head of MI6, the CIA equivalent, told of his talks in Washington with Tenet and other senior officials. In what became known as the Downing Street Memo when it was leaked three years later, he reported, "Military action was now seen as inevitable. Bush wanted to remove Saddam, through military action, justified by the conjunction of terrorism and WMD. But the intelligence and facts were being fixed around the policy. The NSC had no patience with the UN route. . . . There was little discussion in Washington of the aftermath after military action."

Foreign Secretary Jack Straw said, "It seemed clear that Bush had made up his mind to take military action, even if the timing was not yet decided. But the case was thin. Saddam was not threatening his neighbors and his WMD capability was less than that of Libya, North Korea or Iran." Straw suggested a UN ultimatum to allow back the weapons inspectors as a way to legally justify use of force. Lord Goldsmith, the attorney general, noted that regime change was not a legal basis for military action. Nor could humanitarian intervention or self-defense qualify. UN Security Council authorization was necessary.

Blair said, "It would be a big difference politically and legally if Saddam refused to allow in the UN inspectors." In its conclusions the Downing Street Memo declared that along with coordinating military plans with the United States, there would be an effort to "discreetly work up an ultimatum to Saddam."[4] While the discussion by the British remained hidden, the White House wasted no time shooting down a front-page story in the *New York Times* that said the Bush administration was focusing on "a major air and ground invasion" of Iraq, probably "early next year," using from 70,000 to 250,000 American troops to drive Saddam Hussein from power.

Senator Russell Feingold, who had held hearings on war powers before his Judiciary Subcommittee, responded, "If the president does plan to take such action, it is time for the administration to initiate meaningful consultations with Congress over the authority that will be needed to launch

such an expansive military campaign, if it should be undertaken at all."
He went on, "While the consultative process and debate may demonstrate
that it may be necessary to take military action to limit Iraqi weapons of
mass destruction, it is also clear that the United States must act from a
strong unified position. The Constitution and the American people demand as much." Feingold noted that Congress had authorized Mr. Bush
"to use appropriate force to respond to the attacks of Sept. 11," but had
emphasized that "absent a clear finding that Iraq participated in, aided or
otherwise provided support for" the attackers, "the president is constitu-
tionally required to seek additional authority to embark on a new major
military undertaking in Iraq."[5]

Initially there was no indication that the administration had any interest in such discussions with Congress. The White House turned away
such matters with evasive and ambiguous comments like spokesman Ari
Fleischer's observation that while the Pentagon had "multiple contingency
plans" for dealing with Iraq, Mr. Bush "has no plan on his desk" to implement military action. Deputy Assistant Attorney General John Yoo insisted,
however, that the president was not bound by the War Powers Act requiring specific congressional approval because of his constitutional powers as
commander in chief. Actually there had been intensive and detailed work
preparing the strategy and tactics to overthrow the Hussein regime. Bob
Woodward's book *Plan of Attack* spells out the meetings, the discussions of
means in which Rumsfeld introduced the commander in chief to the concept of "shock and awe."

Rice led a meeting that drafted a National Security Presidential Directive (NSPD). The paper listed, "U.S. Goal: Free Iraq in order to eliminate
Iraqi weapons of mass destruction, their means of delivery and associated
programs, to prevent Iraq from breaking out of containment and becoming a more dangerous threat to the region and beyond." One item read,
"End Iraqi threats to its neighbors, to stop the Iraqi government's tyran-
nizing of its own population, to cut Iraqi links to and sponsorship of international terrorism . . . liberate the Iraqi people and assist them in creating
a society based on moderation, pluralism and democracy." To achieve
these results, the strategy described "all instruments of national power . . .
diplomacy, the military, the CIA and economic sanctions." Furthermore,
the United States would seek a coalition but if necessary would act alone.[6]

Against the backdrop of the UN negotiations, Brent Scowcroft wrote
in the *Wall Street Journal* cautionary notes on precipitous military action.
While agreeing that the world would be improved when Saddam left the
scene, he said, "Any campaign against Iraq, whatever the strategic costs

and risks, is certain to divert us for some indefinite period from our war against terrorism. Worse, there is a virtual consensus in the world against an attack on Iraq at this time. . . . At a minimum, it would stifle any cooperation on terrorism, and could even swell the ranks of the terrorists.

". . . In any event, we should press the United Nations Security Council to insist on an effective no-notice inspection regime for Iraq. . . . On this point, senior administration officials have opined that Saddam Hussein would never agree to such an inspection regime. But if he did, inspections would serve to keep him off balance and under close observation, even if all his weapons of mass destruction capabilities were not uncovered. And if he refused, his rejection could provide the persuasive casus belli which many claim we do not now have."[7]

Cheney, when head of the oil conglomerate Halliburton a stentorian opponent of sanctions against Iraq during the mid-1990s, vigorously called for military action. On August 26, 2002, he informed a Veterans of Foreign Wars convention, "Simply stated, there is no doubt that Saddam Hussein now has weapons of mass destruction." He dismissed the inspection process as breeding a false sense of safety. "The risks of inaction are far greater than the risk of action."

Kenneth Adelman, a Rumsfeld assistant, Cheney ally, and member of the Defense Policy Board, an unpaid hard-line advisory group, ramped up the war fever in a *Wall Street Journal* piece. He described Saddam as more dangerous than al-Qaeda because billions in oil revenues enabled him to create a huge army, and claimed that the dictator possessed "scores of scientific laboratories and myriad manufacturing plants cranking out weapons of mass destruction." Adelman did not provide sources for his assertion.

Members of the administration banged the drums loudly. Rumsfeld seconded Cheney and Adelman: "We know they have weapons of mass destruction. . . . There isn't any debate about it."[8] Colin Powell during a television interview with Fox News, on September 8, 2002, said, "There is no doubt that he [Saddam Hussein] has chemical weapons stocks." Condoleezza Rice pounced upon photoreconnaissance of a shipment of aluminum tubes that she said "are only really suited for nuclear weapons programs, centrifuge programs."[9]

That same month, Bush conflated 9/11 with the problem of Iraq. "You can't distinguish between al Qaeda and Saddam when you talk about the war on terror."[10] National Security Adviser Condoleezza Rice, in an interview on Public Broadcasting's *News Hour*, vouchsafed "contacts between al Qaeda and Iraq . . . there clearly is testimony that some of the contacts have been important contacts and that there's relationship here."

The certitude of the Americans about WMDs surprised Hans Blix. He noted that Cheney cited information obtained from General Hussein Kamel, a son-in-law of Hussein who in 1995 had fled to Jordan, where intelligence officers debriefed him. Cheney did not mention that Kamel, following the Desert Storm defeat in 1991, had ordered the destruction of all WMDs.

On September 12, UN secretary-general Kofi Annan reaffirmed the effort to obtain compliance by Iraq with Security Council resolutions. "If Iraq's defiance continues, the Security Council must face its responsibilities." Bush followed Annan and spoke of Saddam's evasion and defiance for more than ten years. He asserted, "Right now, Iraq is expanding and improving facilities that were used for the production of biological weapons." He promised to work with the Security Council, but if Iraq did not mend its ways, the world body needed to act. He said nothing of inspections.[11]

On October 7, President Bush, in a nationally televised speech, claimed, "We've also discovered . . . that Iraq had a growing fleet of manned and unmanned aerial vehicles that could be used to disperse chemical and biological weapons across broad areas." He spoke of the program to develop nuclear weapons: "Facing clear evidence of peril, we cannot wait for the final proof, the smoking gun, that could come in the form of a mushroom cloud."

Senators were shown an entire National Intelligence Estimate that concluded, "Saddam probably has stocked at least 100 metric tons and possibly as much as 500 metric tons of CW agents—much of it added in the last year." The paper noted, "We judge Iraq has some lethal and incapacitating BW agents and is capable of quickly producing and weaponizing a variety of such agents." In both instances, the intelligence report, although it said in one section, "Baghdad has chemical and biological weapons," hedged its findings elsewhere, not stating or offering proof that Iraq actually possessed chemical and biological weapons. While laying out *possibilities* for use of these unsubstantiated threats, again the NIE could only speculate. With "moderate confidence," the document admitted, "Iraq does not have a nuclear weapon or sufficient material to make one but is likely to have a weapon by 2007 or 2008." Altogether, 195 representatives and every one of the hundred senators had been invited to White House–orchestrated briefings on Iraq. About 70 percent actually attended.[12]

Intelligence experts at the State Department demurred. An eleven-page statement disagreed with much of the NIE presentation and dismissed the case that Iraq had "an integrated and comprehensive approach to acquire nuclear weapons."[13] Powell still urged the congressional authorization for use of force because without it the Security Council would duck the issue.

The White House circulated a proposal that authorized use of the armed forces "as he [the president] determines to be necessary and appropriate in order to (1) defend the national security of the United States against the continuing threat posed by Iraq; and enforce all relevant United Nations Security Council resolutions regarding Iraq." The only constraint upon "Presidential Determination" was a requirement that "prior to [use of force] as soon thereafter as may be feasible, but no later than 48 hours," he should advise the Speaker of the House and president pro tempore of the Senate that he had made that determination.

Despite the disclaimers attached to the NIE, Congress showed little inclination to oppose the commander in chief. His approval ratings ran high; 9/11 memories were still fresh and few cared to appear soft on a vicious dictator whose attitude and behavior easily replicated that of Osama bin Laden. The House of Representatives granted eight and a half hours for debate on a resolution that would grant the commander in chief the power to deploy the military against Iraq. The text of the House Joint Resolution noted the 1991 agreement in which Iraq agreed it would unequivocally eliminate its nuclear, biological, and chemical weapons programs. Furthermore, it said that "the efforts of international weapons inspectors, United States intelligence agencies, and Iraqi defectors led to the discovery that Iraq had large stockpiles of chemical weapons and a large scale biological weapons program, and that Iraq had an advanced nuclear weapons development program that was much closer to producing a nuclear weapon than intelligence reporting had previously indicated." The resolution cited repression of civilians, use of WMDs against other countries and Iraqis, and the attempt to assassinate George H. W. Bush. Language painted Iraq as a harbor for al-Qaeda, and an aid to international terrorists. This last charge, followed by mention of 9/11, "underscored the gravity of the threat posed by acquisition of weapons of mass destruction by international terrorist organizations."[14]

Illinois representative Henry Hyde, after describing the events of 9/11, declared, "Some may question the connection between Iraq and those terrorists. . . . The President thinks so; and based upon what I have seen, I think so also."

Michigan representative Nick Smith said, "I met with CIA Director George Tenet and National Security Adviser Condoleezza Rice. They related classified information about Saddam Hussein's buildup of chemical and biological and radiological and nuclear weapons."

Florida's Ileana Ros-Lehtinen asserted, "Saddam Hussein's regime trained al Qaeda operatives in bomb making, harbors these terrorists . . . Saddam Hussein's regime is pursuing unmanned aircraft to deliver chemical and biological weapons. . . . The Iraqi regime has dozens of ballistic missiles and is working to extend their range in violations of UN restrictions."

California representative Dana Rohrabacher urged passage, commenting that this was not a war on Iraq but a war to liberate the country. "They will be dancing in the streets, waving American flags." He insisted that rebuilding the country would be easier than the task in Afghanistan because of the enormous resources available within Iraq.

In opposition, representative Donald Payne of New Jersey said, "We in Congress have received no evidence of such an imminent and immediate threat. If in fact the United States is in fact in danger of immediate attack, the President already has the authority under the Constitution, the War Powers Act, the United Nations Charter and international law to defend our nation.

"Only Congress has the authority to declare war. House Joint Resolution 114 is not a declaration of war, but it is a blank check to use force without moral or political authority of the declaration of war."

Representative Ron Paul of Texas condemned the proposed bill. "This not a resolution to declare war. . . . This resolution transfers the responsibility, the authority and the power of the Congress to the President so he can declare war when and if he wants to. He has not even indicated that he wants to go to war or has to . . . but he will make the final decision, not the Congress, not the people through the Congress of this country."

Paul dismissed claims of long-range missiles in Iraq's arsenal and cautioned that UNSCOM inspectors reported that 95 percent of Saddam's chemical and biological weapons capabilities had been destroyed by 1998. He noted that the United States had shipped significant amounts of biological warfare materials to Iraq during the 1980s, covertly aiding Saddam against Iran.

Representative Diana DeGette of Colorado questioned whether Iraq possessed WMDs. "We have seen over the last ten years that Iraq is trying to amass chemical, biological and perhaps even nuclear weapons. But we have seen no evidence of their success and we have seen no evidence of a delivery system."

In the House, the measure passed easily, 296 to 133, a much higher majority than that gained in 1991 for Desert Storm. Nita Lowey, a liberal Democrat from the suburbs of New York City, who had supported the enabling resolution of 1991, explained her yea vote. "In the run-up to the vote on the 2002 resolution," she said, "I attended briefings and meetings with various administration officials and outside experts on the situation. While I believe preemption is necessary in specific circumstances, I do not believe preemption is an acceptable doctrine for carrying out U.S. national security policy. Adopting a blanket doctrine of preemption gives short shrift to the value of diplomacy in securing U.S. interests abroad.

"I made very clear when I voted for the 2002 resolution that I did so because I expected the president to use it as leverage in pressing his case before the international community. I repeatedly urged the president to approach the international community with respect, to listen to and try to address the concerns expressed by our allies and to try in earnest to enlist them in a larger coalition."[15]

In the Senate the resolution met stiffer resistance. Edward M. Kennedy vehemently argued, "The Administration has not made a convincing case that we face such an imminent threat to our national security that a unilateral, preemptive American strike and an immediate war are necessary. Nor has the administration laid out the cost in blood and treasure for this operation." He pointed out that the resolution set a precedent for preemptive military action.[16]

Kennedy's fellow senator from Massachusetts, John Kerry, pledged his vote in favor, on the grounds that Saddam's deadly arsenal of weapons of mass destruction posed "a grave threat to our security." However, Kerry also said he expected the president to seek a new UN resolution. Senator Carl Levin, a Michigan Democrat, attempted to require a second vote by Congress if the president could not build an international coalition to attack Saddam Hussein. His legislative siblings rejected his proposal. The final Senate tally counted seventy-seven ayes to twenty-three nays.

Members of the various intelligence subcommittees had examined confidential findings of the CIA and Pentagon on the evidence of WMDs in Iraq. Whether they were shown the caveats of some analysts is uncertain. Nor did the major media do much more than rely on calculated leaks and not-for-attribution sources within the administration. The *New York Times*, guided by administration leakers, had carried a headline, "U.S. Says Hussein Intensifies Quest for A-Bomb Parts," with a story based upon Iraq's attempt to buy the special aluminum tubes vital to a nuclear weapon. The paper failed to question scientists who could have disputed the charges. Similarly, Condoleezza Rice told CNN the tubes are "only really suited for nuclear weapons programs."

The Tonkin Gulf Resolution in 1964 that enabled Lyndon Johnson to expand U.S. military efforts in the Vietnam War was more open-ended.

In contrast to 2002, the language of the 1964 statute spoke in terms of American forces having been attacked and gave the commander in chief the right to use the armed forces to aid members of the Southeast Asia Collective Defense Treaty, while the 2002 resolution limited the war to Iraq. The latter also differed from that voted in 1990 against Iraq upon request of George H. W. Bush. The permission slip issued to Bush 41 required him to inform Congress that diplomacy had failed *before* he launched military action. The authority to his son allowed him to unleash the dogs of war at his discretion provided he inform Congress within forty-eight hours *after* the start of the campaign.

Blix and his counterpart at the IAEA, the Egyptian Mohamed ElBaradei, had journeyed to Washington to meet with Bush, Cheney, Rice, and Wolfowitz. The hard-liners believed Blix could be manipulated by Saddam. The President accordingly sought to stiffen the Swede's backbone. "You've got to understand, Mr. Blix. You've got the force of the United States behind you. And I'm prepared to use it if need be to enforce this resolution. The decision to go to war will be my decision. Don't ever feel like what you're saying is making the decision."[17]

The Security Council debated a new resolution. All members, including Great Britain, found an American draft too extreme. It would ensure rejection by Iraq and its sponsor shelved the proposal. The final version of Resolution 1441, adopted on November 8, 2002, stated that Iraq was in violation of earlier resolutions but would have one final opportunity to open the gates for full access by the inspectors. Any further "material breach" would lead the council to "consider the situation and the need for compliance." The French and other nations understood 1441 as a precursor to military action and that a second Security Council resolution would be required before approval of the use of force. But the White House regarded breach of 1441 as a green light for an attack without further UN consideration. Grumbling about the terms, Iraq accepted inspectors on November 27. At the same time, the United States began to deploy its armed forces for a possible invasion, with the prospect of one hundred thousand in position to attack by the end of January.

On December 21, the president listened to Deputy CIA director John McLaughlin describe the evidence of Iraq's WMDs. His charts, photos, message intercepts, and accounts from defectors left the commander in chief worried about the ability to sell the public on the threat. He turned to the CIA director, George Tenet, and asked how sure he was. Basketball fan Tenet responded, "Don't worry, it's a slam dunk."[18] The Pentagon's Defense Intelligence Agency, in a secret September 2002 report, had informed Rumsfeld, "There is no reliable information on whether Iraq is producing and stockpiling chemical weapons."[19]

Alarmed at the rapid pace toward war, on January 24, 118 members of Congress signed a letter to the president that said, "We believe the U.S. should make every attempt to achieve Iraq's disarmament through diplomatic means and with full support of our allies, in accordance with the process articulated in UN Security Council resolution 1441." They urged the White House to listen to the coming reports to be delivered by Hans Blix and Mohamed ElBaradei and "weigh future decision regarding Iraq . . . including additional inspection time and resources as appropriate." The plea drew no response from the president.

Blix and ElBaradei reported to the Security Council on January 27, 2003, that there had neither been a denial of access nor smoking guns in the latest round of visits to Iraq. There had been some minor infractions uncovered—missile engines, empty chemical weapons warheads. Blix was aware that the tale of aluminum tubes for nuclear weapons was fiction. The Swedish diplomat said that while nothing new of importance had been discovered, for the time being he agreed with Rumsfeld's oft-quoted pronouncement, "Absence of evidence is not evidence of absence." In fact, his gut feeling in mid-January 2003 was that Iraq indeed retained WMDs. He also said he believed that the buildup of American troops could have a salutary effect on recalcitrant Iraqis who continued to drag their feet on some issues. ElBaradei told the delegates, "We have to date found no evidence that Iraq has revived its nuclear weapons program since its elimination of the program in the 1990s. . . . We should be able within the next few months to provide credible assurance that Iraq has no nuclear program."

In fact, the president had decided in early January that force most likely would be required and February 22 would be Notification Day, when the military force flow would accelerate. In his State of the Union message for the new year, a day after the two disarmament chiefs spoke to the Security Council, the president referred to the contretemps with Iraq. He talked about huge stocks of anthrax and nerve gases that had not been accounted for and said, "The British government has learned that Saddam Hussein recently sought significant quantities of uranium from Africa." That indeed might qualify as the casus belli triggering an invasion. However, State Department intelligence analysts early in 2002 described the sale of uranium from Niger to Iraq as "unlikely." In addition, former U.S. ambassador to Iraq Joseph Wilson had undertaken a special mission to Africa for the CIA and learned that the documents on purchases of uranium from Niger were forgeries. Both reports had been filed before the president spoke.

On January 13, Bush conferred with Tony Blair. According to a summary of the discussion by David Manning, Blair's chief foreign affairs adviser, the president had decided to invade Iraq even though inspectors had failed to find WMDs. The American leader spoke of a subterfuge in which a U.S. spy plane, painted with the UN insignia, would fly over Iraq with fighter cover. If the Iraqis fired on it, that would constitute a breach and justify an attack. Bush also raised the possibilities of a defector who would testify to the existence of WMDs or an assassination of Saddam Hussein as grounds for an invasion.

Manning wrote, "The start date for the military campaign was now penciled in for 10 March." His notes indicate that the two heads of state believed the endeavor would quickly achieve its goal of regime change. Manning reported that the pair agreed it was "unlikely there would be internecine warfare between the different religious and ethnic groups."

On February 5, Colin Powell, badgered by the hawks for his lack of enthusiasm for war, after winnowing through the materials collected by the various agencies addressed the Security Council. He informed the members of message intercepts that were interpreted as orders to hide contraband items from the inspectors. He cited "sources" that reported dispersal of weapons with warheads containing biological elements. He displayed sketches of alleged mobile laboratories to manufacture toxins. (Blix's staff thought the trucks served either as hydrogen producers for weather balloons or else ferried water.) Russian experts who had some experience with mobile laboratories thought the information less than compelling.[20] Apparently aware of its lack of authenticity, Powell omitted mention of the Niger yellowcake deal.

It was a compelling performance, one that won over even liberals dubious of the White House agenda. Much of the U.S. media applauded the secretary of state, even though analysts subsequently pointed out that Powell never identified checkable sources. Other powerful nations, except for Great Britain, remained skeptical or at least wanted more time for inspections and sanctions. When Blix returned to the podium at the Security Council on February 14, he again said that the inspectors had not found any of the proscribed weapons and materials. He criticized Saddam for making the task of discovery difficult and time-consuming. Powell, like a man converted by his own speech, disparaged Blix's statements and said more inspectors would not be the answer. Americans as a whole were also supportive of the policy that ultimately meant war. A poll in

January 2003 found that 72 percent believed it was likely that Saddam Hussein was personally involved in the 9/11 attacks.[21]

Since the Goldwater-Nichols Act of 1986 established the chairman of the Joint Chiefs of Staff as a major player with the power to make decisions rather than simply forward recommendations by the heads of the services, the generals and admirals had been reduced to creating plans rather than participating in deliberations. Army chief of staff General Eric K. Shinseki fell out of favor after he questioned the proposed manpower to win the war and then govern. His figure, "something on the order of several hundred thousand soldiers,"[22] drew the scorn of civilian Wolfowitz as "wildly off the mark." Wolfowitz asserted, "I am reasonably certain that they will greet us as liberators and that will help us keep requirements down." Lawrence Lindsey, the president's chief economic adviser, estimated that the war and reconstruction could cost from $100 to $200 billion.[23] Lindsey left office shortly after he offered his gloomy assessment. Shinseki, while allowed to finish out his term, was shunted aside. Nevertheless, he and his colleagues from the air force, navy, and marines all supported the basic offensive plans.

Within the Pentagon and at the White House, officials sought questions about the amount of forces required for a war in Iraq. "The concept," Rice told the New York Times, "was that we would defeat the army, but the institutions would hold, everything from ministries to police forces. You would be able to bring new leadership but that we were going to keep the body in place."[24] Considering that Saddam Hussein was a ruthless tyrant who demanded total loyalty and killed anyone thought to stray, her belief that the Iraqi "ministries" and "police forces" could be easily converted to serve a new democratic state sounds disingenuous.

Military aides to Rice prepared blueprints covering the requirements for postwar security based on several models. The same ratio as in Kosovo meant 480,000 troops in Iraq. The model for Bosnia indicated 364,000. If Afghanistan served as an example, then only 13,900 would be required. However, while three-quarters of the Iraqis lived in urban areas, and half as many in Kosovo and Bosnia, only 18 percent of the Afghans were city folk. Rumsfeld in a February 14, 2003, speech decried the large number for Kosovo, saying it led to a "culture of dependence," discouraging local people from accepting responsibility for their own country.[25]

The secretary of defense showed little interest in emulating the Balkan nation-building peacekeeping forces. He favored less rather than more. If the senior military advisers thought differently, they kept their mouths shut. Rice said that the commander in chief constantly asked his senior

commanders if sufficient troops would be deployed. "Senior military officers acknowledge they did not press the president for more troops. But
some said they would have been more comfortable with a larger reserve."[26]

A last-ditch effort to stave off invasion came in the form of letters to
Blix and ElBaradei inviting them back to Baghdad to try to speed up the
inspection process. The dictator suddenly on March 16 broadcast a statement that admitted possession of WMDs in the past but again insisted the
country no longer had any. He did not agree to meet "benchmarks" that
would provide standards for the disarmament goals.

The president terminated the war foreplay with a March 18 message
to the top congressional leaders that "based on information available to
me . . . reliance by the United States on further diplomatic and peaceful
means alone will neither (A) adequately protect the national security of the
United States against the continuing threat posed by Iraq nor (B) likely
lead to enforcement of all relevant United Nations Security Council resolutions regarding Iraq." In his three-paragraph statement he said his decision was consistent with taking "necessary actions against international
terrorists and terrorist organizations, including those nations, organizations,
or persons who planned, authorized, or aided the terrorist attacks that
occurred on September 11, 2001." Bush thus continued to merge the
World Trade Center and Pentagon assaults with Iraq as further justification for sending in the troops. He said nothing about relieving the Iraqis
of a cruel tyrant and establishing democracy in his place.

On the morning of March 19 the first commando teams slipped into
Iraq. That evening, based on a tip from a covert agent, and hoping to
decapitate the Iraqi government, F-117 fighter-bombers targeted Dora
Farms, a site where Saddam and his two sons supposedly were staying.
They escaped. At 10:16 that night, the commander in chief informed the
country that the military campaign against Saddam, Operation Iraqi Freedom, had begun.

Many of those who dissented from the direction being taken stifled
themselves once the war began. Opposition when the troops are under fire,
certainly at the onset, is politically perilous. All Americans could only wish
that the war would end quickly with minimum casualties and that a swift
restoration of order would follow. Given the absence of cavils about the
evidence and the confident talk of the administration and its supporters,
public optimism seemed warranted. Presidential war power had ramped up
to its zenith.

20

WINNING THE WAR, FIGHTING ON

I nitially, Operation Iraqi Freedom appeared to be a triumph. The "Shock and Awe" phase that inaugurated the invasion of Iraq demolished the nation's infrastructure, and the retreating remnants of Saddam's army blew up some of the oil industry installations. Within three weeks, at a cost of some two hundred American lives, the troops pushed into Baghdad and pulled down a statue of Saddam, symbolizing the end of his regime. General Franks, who had directed the war in Afghanistan and the invasion of Iraq, arrived in Baghdad about a week later. "He told [his commanders] it was time to make plans to leave. Combat forces should be prepared to start pulling out within sixty days if all went as expected. By September, the more than 140,000 troops in Iraq could be down to little more than a division, about 30,000 troops."[1] Commander in Chief Bush saw his war as justified and preened over its apparent success.

What had not been reckoned with was the depth of antagonism to an invading army and the willingness of people to kill themselves along with their occupiers. Nor was there any recognition of the imperative to replace the governmental vacuum left by Saddam's officials and to maintain an infrastructure that would supply the basics of modern life—electricity, fuel, water, sanitation, education, and an economy that provided paying jobs. Iraq would also add to a growing problem of how to manage a bag of prisoners that included defeated soldiers, guerrillas, and terrorists captured in Iraq and Afghanistan.

Franks's rosy view depended partly upon an administration plan to bring in four foreign divisions, including Arab and NATO forces, to replace the Americans. But the outsiders never materialized. Franks, the White House, and Pentagon policymakers had no understanding that the war had destroyed the indigenous institutions that kept the country afloat.

The thin-stretched Coalition forces were incapable of policing the cities and countryside. Washington seemed unaware that victory needed to be followed by a vast reconstruction that included the creation of a functioning government. As anarchy erupted in the wake of the military victory, Rumsfeld dismissed the lawlessness as the natural afterbirth of democracy. His strategy for lighter military forces that could move swiftly proved inadequate for postwar duty because the smaller number of troops could not maintain order. Colin Powell had cautioned that, like the policy of the Pottery Barn chain, "If you break it, you own it." While he erred in his attribution, his warning was prophetic. The administration now waded chin deep in the muddy waters of nation-building.

Unemployment among Iraqis ran well over 50 percent. Factories and stores were rubble and services like water, electricity, and sewage nonexistent. Their absence, stretched over many months, dug deep wells of resentment. The Bush White House downplayed the wretched conditions. In May 2003, the jaunty commander in chief, dressed in a flight suit, landed aboard the carrier *Abraham Lincoln*, in the superstructure of which someone hung the banner "Mission Accomplished." It provided a photo op, soon to become an icon of irony. A few weeks later Bush scoffed at a possible insurgency with a callous "Bring 'em on." While many Iraqis undoubtedly cheered the destruction of Saddam's Baathist regime, they now began to think of the invaders less as liberators and more as occupiers. The Sunni Muslim minority that under Saddam had controlled Iraq became openly hostile and the seeds of an insurgency sprouted. Jihadists from other countries crossed the borders.

No indigenous armed force to control lawless behavior or rebellion existed. U.S. civilian administrators had almost immediately disbanded the entire army, from generals to privates. That decision, as much a military one as political, was arrived at without a canvass of the Joint Chiefs of Staff for their input. Some 400,000 men went home. Bereft of jobs and paychecks, they carried off small arms, from rifles to grenade launchers and even rockets and mortars, tools for a full-blown guerrilla war against the Coalition. Shootouts in streets and from buildings, bedeviling American troops, began. Improvised explosive devices (IEDs) along roads, rifle grenades, firefights, and suicide truck and car bombers took their toll. By August 2006, more than three years after the invasion, American dead mounted above twenty-four hundred, with more than fifteen thousand wounded. Unable to distinguish insurgents from innocent civilians, the soldiers and marines, backed by helicopters, jet fighter-bombers, and artillery, inevitably killed noncombatant Iraqis, including women, children, grandparents. Among the Iraqis the carnage was horrific; the estimated dead ranged from twenty-five thousand to one hundred thousand.

During the presidential campaign of 2004, the president steadfastly refused to admit any error. He attributed the inability of the invading troops to create order to "catastrophic success," meaning that victory had been so sudden and huge there had been no time to establish a program for disarming insurgents while establishing order. The White House insisted that the size of the military forces was not the problem. The generals obediently seconded the administration line, but as one junior officer in the field put it, "We've got the toys but not the boys."[2] In fact, not all the toys were top-of-the-line. Troops lacked the best body armor, vehicles were not adequately shielded from IEDs, and communications systems sometimes failed.

For their part the insurgents concentrated upon the destruction of water mains, oil pipelines, and electrical generation facilities, deepening the hostility for the occupiers, who seemed unable to cope with that type of warfare. Foreign civilians employed by contractors were kidnapped and murdered. Any Iraqis who cooperated with the Coalition, particularly recruits for the police and army and nascent civil government, became targets, discouraging the people from collaboration. The rebels drove out the United Nations with a devastating bomb and destroyed an International Committee of the Red Cross headquarters, leaving the Americans to bear the brunt of the growing enmity alone. Western media suffered the same deadly treatment as other infidels.

L. Paul Bremer, who took over as proconsul in 2003, said his requests for more boots on the ground went unheeded by both Rumsfeld and Bush. Rumsfeld, when asked why planners had not used a larger armed force for the stabilization of Iraq, blamed the general, asserting that "Franks made a call and he made a judgment that not only would they not be needed and it would not be appropriate, but that it would be ill advised to put that many more, quote 'occupation forces' in." Rumsfield said more troops would provide many more targets, and many more people would have the feeling that the United States was taking over the country rather than liberating it. Considering how Rumsfeld and his associates dominated the Department of Defense, this statement seems disingenuous. Indeed, Thomas E. White, a secretary of the army whom Rumsfeld sacked after a dispute, said, "Rumsfeld just ground Franks down. If you grind away at the military guys long enough, they will finally say, 'Screw it. I'll do the best I can with what I have.'"[3]

As the Coalition forces rumbled through Iraq, they discovered no signs of the WMDs. Lieutenant General James Conway from the First Marine

Expeditionary Force informed reporters, "We've been to virtually every ammunition supply point between the Kuwaiti border and Baghdad but they're simply not there."[4] David Kay, the Bush appointee to find WMDs and skeptical of the work of Blix and ElBaradei, made a report to Congress saying that searchers could not find either chemical or biological weapons. As for the vaunted program to "reconstitute" atomic weapons, Kay said, Iraq's nuclear program languished in "the very most rudimentary" state.[5]

Following the invasion of Iraq, a report issued in July 2004 by the Senate Intelligence Committee said, "Most of the major key judgments in an October 2002 National Intelligence Estimate on Iraq's illicit weapons [a critical document in the debate over the right to disarm Saddam forcibly] were either overstated, or were not supported by the underlying intelligence reporting." In particular, the agency was accused of a chain of failures in its analysis of data.

The CIA offered its own mea culpa. The agency's Iraq WMD Review Group reviewed the collection and analysis of information. It concluded that the critical National Intelligence Estimate (NIE) of 2002 that determined Iraq possessed biological and chemical weapons and was rebuilding its nuclear weapons capacity was not properly double-checked and sources could not confirm some conclusions. The CIA conceded it never advised Powell, before his February 2003 UN appearance, of serious caveats to all of the charges Powell laid on Saddam's doorstep. Powell said, "I looked at the four elements that they [intelligence officials] gave me . . . and they stood behind them. Now it appears not to be the case that it was that solid."[6]

The CIA demolished one of Cheney's favorite themes, the alliance of al-Qaeda and Iraq. In October 2004, the agency concurred with the finding of the 9/11 Commission that no "collaborative relationship" between Saddam and the terrorist network existed. While Cheney still claimed the linkage, Bush himself in September 2003 would say there was "no evidence that Iraq was involved in the September 11 attacks."[7] A major source for the administration charge of ties between al-Qaeda and Iraq was a prisoner held by Egyptians. Later, he recanted, explaining that he fabricated the statements to avoid abuse. Rumsfeld would also later admit he had seen no "strong, hard evidence that links the two."[8] Yet during the 2004 presidential election and afterwards, Bush never wavered in a melisma coupling Iraq and terrorism.

CIA headquarters in Langley, Virginia, had hosted a number of visits by Vice President Cheney, his chief of staff, Lewis Libby, Wolfowitz, and another advocate of military intervention, Douglas Feith, from the Department of Defense. All of them had apparently impressed the intelligence analysts of their interest in demonstrating links between Iraq and al-Qaeda and Saddam's WMDs. Bullying of intelligence analysts by senior administration officials included a tirade by then undersecretary of state for arms control and national security John R. Bolton directed at the State Department's Christian P. Westermann. The latter had cast doubt upon information that Cuba had a program to develop biological weapons. Bolton's outburst so rattled State's intelligence section that Colin Powell felt it necessary to personally reassure the analysts that they should continue to "speak truth to power."[9]

The final report of a presidential intelligence commission issued at the end of March 2005 critiqued the CIA's efforts, as well as those of Pentagon intelligence specialists and the National Security Agency, in the run-up to the invasion of Iraq. Chaired by Republican judge Lawrence Silberman and former U.S. senator Charles Robb, it chose to interview neither the commander in chief nor Vice President Cheney. The report does not attribute any blame to them. However, Robb, during a television interview, did say that the commander in chief was responsible for whatever happened on his watch. This commission described the intelligence community as driven by false assumptions about the retention of WMDs after the 1991 Gulf War. Saddam apparently tried to pretend he still had WMD capability in order to frighten opposition around Iraq, and the U.S. intelligence experts accepted him at face value. They failed to properly assess his boasts and evidence of any stockpiles of horrific weaponry. The commission's report took particular exception to the belief that the dictator possessed an armada of "unmanned aerial vehicles" to deliver the lethal packages. President Bush and Vice President Cheney both asserted this nonexistent threat and Cheney continued to talk about "mobile laboratories" as part of the biological warfare program even though no evidence of such ever existed. The NIE on Iraq, issued a few weeks before the invasion, included footnotes in which some intelligence sources doubted the aluminum tubes were for uranium production or that mobile biological weapons labs existed. Those dissents were ignored by the decision-makers.

Much of the American intelligence was derived from a source known as "Curveball," a dissident Iraqi chemical engineer who left the country in 1998 and subsequently entered into a relationship with the German Federal Intelligence Service. A relative of an aide to Ahmad Chalabi, an Iraqi exile in high repute at the Pentagon, he became a primary source for U.S. intelligence. German intelligence, however, cautioned that Curveball was an alcoholic and not a trustworthy source. Tyler Brumheller, head of the CIA's espionage operations in Europe, said he warned his superiors, orally, of the Germans' low regard for Curveball's credibility.[10] George Tenet and his deputy John McLaughlin denied knowledge of doubts. Others in the CIA insisted they had passed along suspicions about Curveball's veracity. The commission said analysts who questioned the reliability of Curveball were "forced to leave." Indeed, a CIA officer said he was obliged to resign after he advised superiors that an informant in 2001 told him Iran had scuttled its nuclear programs.[11] A secret arrangement sent as many as twenty former Iraqi citizens with ties to individuals known to have worked on WMDs back to Iraq to inquire if they were still engaged in this type of endeavor. Everyone returned to report that all denied they were still involved with development of WMDs. Whether this information reached the president is problematic but certainly none in Congress were advised.

Hans Blix, even before the findings of the commission, said, "Despite finding no smoking gun the United States and the United Kingdom prefer to believe in faith-based intelligence. . . . National intelligence is indispensable, but it must apply critical thinking."[12]

The war in Afghanistan, the invasion of Iraq, and 9/11 created a new class of prisoners, combatants who wore no uniform and represented no recognized government. Labeled as terrorists or guerrilla insurgents, they were suspected of either plotting strikes against the homelands of the Coalition of the Willing or attacks within Afghanistan and Iraq. Interrogators believed the captives could reveal valuable information to prevent attacks at home and in Iraq, and people taken into custody at home and abroad were denied the rights of the accused under U.S. law. The White House claimed that the commander in chief, because of the war against terrorism after 9/11 and the war in Iraq, had the power to suspend those rights.

A large batch of captives from the war against al-Qaeda and the Taliban were flown to an installation built for them at Guantanamo Bay, Cuba. That Gitmo site, outside the continental United States, enabled Pentagon and Justice Department lawyers to claim that these potential sources of information did not qualify for the legal rights granted individuals within the United States whether citizens or not. Nor, said the administration, did they enjoy the rights of POWs as expressed in the Geneva Convention. The Convention requires that a dispute about a prisoner's status should be decided by a "competent tribunal." During the 1991 Gulf War, some captives did have their status decided by such a body. In response to a request from the Pentagon for guidance, Alberto Gonzales, then counsel to the president, wrote a memo that characterized the Geneva protocols as "quaint" and "obsolete," insufficient to cover irregulars or guerrillas taken prisoner.[13] Bush signed an order that labeled al-Qaeda members "unlawful," placing them outside the requirements of Geneva. He said, "The war on terrorism . . . ushered in not by us but by terrorists, requires new thinking in the law of war, but thinking that should nevertheless be consistent with the principles of Geneva." Yet nothing in the Constitution confers upon the commander in chief the authority to suspend the right of habeas corpus, and if anything it is Congress that along with the right to declare war is given the power to "make rules concerning capture on land and water." To buttress its claims, the administration cited Franklin Roosevelt's decision to intern Japanese Americans and the use of secret military tribunals to try some German saboteurs who came ashore from a submarine.[14]

The growing Iraqi insurgency induced the U.S. military to become more aggressive. The troops vacuumed up individuals suspected of opposition as well as people who had committed lesser infractions such as breaking curfew or traveling without proper identification. Thousands seized in raids and in police actions became inmates of Abu Ghraib, an infamous prison from the Saddam regime where an estimated four thousand were executed during his 1984 purge. As many as five thousand Iraqis were soon lodged in Abu Ghraib. They too lacked the usual rights given POWs.

In the wake of questions about the status of prisoners in Guantanamo and Iraq came charges of abuses. The International Red Cross, Amnesty International, and a UN committee related complaints about torture from the inmates. An FBI agent complained that military interrogators posing as bureau investigators used "torture techniques."

Until 9/11, the U.S. military had accepted the Convention against Torture established in Geneva. A mere five days after the terrorist attack, Cheney said, "We also have to work, though, sort of the dark side. A lot of what needs to be done here will have to be done quietly without any discussion, using sources and methods that are available to our intelligence agencies . . . it's going to be vital for us to use any means at our disposal, basically to achieve our objective."[15]

Frustrated by the lack of information from the Gitmo inmates, those responsible for obtaining intelligence asked how far they could turn up the heat. Administration lawyer Jay S. Bybee drafted a memorandum in August 2002 in which he said "cruel, inhuman or degrading" treatment could be used without being classified as torture. To qualify as torture, the abuse must inflict pain "equivalent in intensity to the pain accompanying serious physical injury, as organ failure, impairment of bodily functions or even death."[16] The Justice Department did not specify how an interrogator would know whether a technique would result in grievous physical damage or how to draw a line on what constituted severe mental anguish.

Gradually restrictions on physical and emotional techniques loosened. By December 2002, questions of how far interrogators might go reached Rumsfeld. He signed off on a number of acceptable measures—stressful positions, sustained isolation, hooding, and exploitation of phobias such as aversion to dogs—as well as sexual taunting that greatly offended Muslims. He was quoted on an ABC 20/20 broadcast that an "eight-foot-by-eight-foot cell in beautiful, sunny Cuba is not inhumane." After a navy general counsel objected to the conditions, Rumsfeld seemingly rescinded permission for some extreme techniques, but with several more memos on the subject the defense secretary appeared to have confused his subordinates about what was permissible.

A major scandal broke with the April 2004 publication of photographs in newspapers and on CBS's 60 Minutes broadcast of April 28, 2004, showing maltreatment of detainees at Abu Ghraib. The pictures showed sexual taunting, men bound together, prisoners menaced by attack dogs, a hooded man in a physically painful position with electrodes attached to his genitals. Major General Anthony Taguba had already investigated the conduct of the 800th Military Police Brigade, assigned to Abu Ghraib. He found that enlisted personnel directly involved with the prisoners had been told by military intelligence, "loosen this guy up for us," "make sure he has a bad night," "make sure he gets the treatment." The Taguba report noted that tactics included dogs to frighten and intimidate detainees, beatings with a broom handle and chair, threats of rape, and acts of sodomy. A sergeant told the investigators that it was "assumed that if they were doing things out of the ordinary or outside the guidelines, someone would have said something. Also the wing at Abu [Ghraib] belongs to MI [military intelligence] and it appeared that MI approved of the abuse."[17]

The commander in chief, during a photo op in the Rose Garden on April 30, 2004, insisted, "Their treatment does not reflect the nature of the American people. That's not the way we do things in America. . . . I don't like it one bit." The official story was that a handful of low-ranking soldiers had crossed the line.

Several official inquiries followed. One led by Major General George R. Fay and Lieutenant General Antony R. Jones found at least forty-four cases of abuse between July 2003 and February 2004. The report said interrogation techniques were brought to Iraq from Guantanamo Bay, and detailed one death, an alleged rape, numerous beatings, and instances where prisoners were stripped naked and left for hours in dark, poorly ventilated cells that were stifling hot or freezing. Handlers used dogs to frighten adolescents. A prisoner who returned from hospital treatment for a wound was found by a sergeant naked and bleeding in his cell, with a bagless catheter attached to his body. "There were a few instances when torture was being used."[18]

Rumsfeld picked a civilian panel, headed by a former occupant of his seat, James Schlesinger, to look into the matter. Schlesinger's report indicted the administration for its failure to anticipate the Iraqi insurgency and lack of preparation for the flood of prisoners. Furthermore, it found that the planners did not ship sufficient numbers of well-schooled military police to deal with situations like Abu Ghraib. Many of those assigned there were untrained reservists. Like the Fay report, Schlesinger's said the aggressive, cruel tactics of military interrogators appeared to have originated with Special Operations Forces and the CIA during the Afghanistan war. The panel noted that Major General Geoffrey Miller, who had run the Guantanamo Bay operations, went to Iraq in August 2003 toting the same interrogation rules used on supposedly hard-core al-Qaeda and Taliban for use upon the Iraqis, an overwhelming majority of whom possessed little of intelligence value. The commander in Iraq, Lieutenant General Ricardo Sanchez, who succeeded Franks, had relied on Miller's advice for a dozen "aggressive interrogation techniques."

Having all but accused the commander in chief and his secretary of defense of creating a climate for abusive actions, Schlesinger reversed course and absolved the civilian authorities, blaming Miller and Sanchez along with lesser officers who should have supervised the goings on at Abu Ghraib more closely.[19] In spite of the official reports by the likes of Taguba and Fay, the Rumsfeld-appointed commission, and the Red Cross, the administration blocked deeper investigation. A few enlisted personnel visible in the infamous photographs faced military courts, and General Janis Karpinski, in charge of Abu Ghraib, was relieved of duty.

The report issued under the byline of General Fay mentioned conflict between the CIA and the military, particularly in the intelligence agency's use of Abu Ghraib for "ghost" detainees, individuals incarcerated under false names to hide them, a violation of military rules. In an even more egregious offense, some suspects underwent "extraordinary rendition," in which people captured by Americans were outsourced to other nations for questioning. The practice had begun during the Clinton years but expanded greatly under George W. Bush. More than one hundred individuals seized in countries outside the United States were exported to nations like Saudi Arabia, Jordan, and Syria. That exposed them to treatment potentially far worse than in any U.S.-run facility. CIA officials insisted that the nations who received custody of these suspects pledged not to engage in torture. But with Americans denied on-site oversight, the promise meant little.

In March 2005, investigators for the army and navy issued findings that indicated at least twenty-six prisoners taken in Afghanistan and Iraq were suspected of having been homicide victims while in U.S. custody. Some cases may have involved CIA personnel. A review by army inspector general Lieutenant General Stanley E. Green exonerated the top officers responsible for the handling of prisoners and detainees under army auspices. The findings cleared General Sanchez; his deputy, Major General Walter Wojdakowski; Major General Barbara Fast, who served as chief intelligence officer in Iraq and oversaw Abu Ghraib; and Colonel Mac Warren, the command's chief legal officer.[20] Human rights groups attacked the report as a cover-up.

Experts in the intelligence business argued over the value of torture as a means of gaining information. Many believed that cruel, painful techniques produced little of value. Those undergoing the treatment would say anything simply to end the agony. But at least one specialist claimed that critical data was obtained from some of the first al-Qaeda captives in Afghanistan.

The disclosure of abuses of prisoners drew heavy criticism of the United States around the world, and particularly in Middle Eastern nations. But, traumatized by 9/11, neither the American politicians nor the public protested with any vigor about what happened to foreigners or alleged terrorists. The brutality and cruelty of the Iraqi insurgents with their TV tapes of hostages pleading for their lives, the beheading of noncombatants, the suicide bombers, and the open season on journalists all earned bigger headlines and more airtime than the Gitmo and Abu Ghraib revelations.

The exportation of terrorism to the United States, climaxing on 9/11, had already resulted in sweeps that detained several thousand immigrants, mainly from Muslim countries. An executive order by the president on November 13, 2001, allowed that individuals suspected of terrorist activity could be detained and tried under military authority, where the accused lacks many rights secure in civilian courts. The administration based its power upon a congressional resolution after the 9/11 attacks that authorized the president to use whatever force necessary to prevent a repetition as well as upon his inherent entitlement as commander in chief.

Attorney General John Ashcroft pursued terrorism suspects even before the Patriot Act broadened government power. No al-Qaeda representatives were seized, but about 760 people were held without bail and often lodged in jail cells for months, frequently without contact with family or lawyers. U.S. citizen Jose Padilla was arrested in 2002 after arriving at Chicago's O'Hare Airport from the Middle East. He was charged as part of an al-Qaeda plot to explode a "dirty" radiological bomb in the United States and was held in a South Carolina brig for roughly two years without recourse to a lawyer. A lower court agreed with Ashcroft that the commander in chief had the authority to have Padilla detained without access to a court or any review outside the executive branch. But in February 2005, federal district judge Henry F. Floyd, appointed by Bush, said, "The court finds that the president has no power, neither express nor implied, neither constitutional nor statutory, to hold petitioner as an enemy combatant." The Justice Department appealed. Apparently unwilling to contest the case further in the Supreme Court, the administration downshifted the matter to a state court.

In 2003, a U.S. Court of Appeals accepted the argument by a Pentagon official that the open-ended confinement of an American citizen of Saudi descent, Yasen Esam Hamdi, captured in Afghanistan, fell within the president's constitutional authority as commander in chief.[21] Held in the same South Carolina military brig as Padilla, he eventually also obtained legal counsel and then was deported to Saudi Arabia.

The commander in chief refused to admit to mistakes and insisted things were moving in the right direction. Not until late in 2005 did he agree that intelligence on WMDs was flawed. He issued Medals of Freedom to retired CIA director George Tenet, who had proclaimed questions of WMD "a slam dunk"; to Paul Bremer, who many thought bungled the role of Iraq's civilian administrator; and to General Tommy Franks, whose forces won a swift victory but were not geared for the chaos that followed.

Bush survived the 9/11 Commission, which had indicated dereliction on the part of his administration as well as his predecessors in the face of terrorist threats. In his linkage of 9/11 to Saddam Hussein's Iraq he would add the bombings in Madrid, London, and Egypt. He maintained an image of one who was resolute and proceeding with a plan for a democratic Iraq and surprised many pundits with a comfortable margin of victory for his 2004 reelection. While Americans seemed increasingly dubious of the strategy in Iraq, Bush drew voters more for his alleged ability to forestall terrorism in the United States, as well as concerns about abortion rights, gay marriage, and separation of church and state than for a stagnant economy, soaring health care costs, and environmental issues.

Small indications of more democracy in Egypt and Saudi Arabia, and the cries for Syria to evacuate its forces from Lebanon, were trumpeted as proof that the vision of Iraq as a democratic state in the Middle East had resonance. There were questions about whether the administration's policies truly caused these modest upheavals. Internal politics may have been the strongest influences. In any event, some elections in the Middle East favored extremists, as in Iran and among the Palestinians, where Hamas, classified by the administration as a terrorist organization, overwhelmed the Fatah party. The democratic option the administration had hoped to establish in the Middle East appeared to strengthen antidemocratic elements.

When the Iraqis, in spite of the carnage directed at those who went to the polls, turned out in large numbers for their elections, it was an obvious plus for the administration's policy. A tempestuous conclave of the major groups, based upon the election results, drafted a constitution that failed to unite the factions and left the distinct possibility of a theocratic government with diminished rights for women. Meanwhile, the task of actually governing and bringing sufficient order to enable Coalition forces to leave was far from completed. More than three years after the invasion, some 138,000 America troops were still in Iraq, nearly as many as had originally been dispatched. During the 2004 election campaign, the administration spoke of more than 170 battalions of Iraqi army troops training to assume the roles of the Americans. More than a year later, it was admitted that only one battalion was actually prepared sufficiently to operate independent of U.S. forces. Meanwhile, the original Coalition, which numbered thirty-eight countries, steadily shrank as the Netherlands, Spain, Honduras, Norway, Hungary, and ten others pulled out. Italy and Poland began to drawn down their troops also.

The administration and its supporters blamed the media for a preoccupation with bad news and for ignoring the construction of schools and hospitals and the restoration of infrastructure. However, three years after the president announced the end of major hostilities, oil production and electrical power were below prewar output and unemployment ranged over 30 percent.

Much worse, what had begun as resistance to U.S. occupation forces mushroomed into an insurgency against the still unformed Iraqi government and a brutal struggle between Shias and Sunnis, resulting in casualties in the thousands. Near chaos gripped urban centers. The murders, kidnappings, shootings, bombings, and assassinations bore the hallmarks of a civil war.

While most Iraqis were glad to be rid of the brutal Saddam, they coped with a country in ruins, horrific losses of life, businesses destroyed, homes reduced to rubble. Proponents of the war insisted that the Iraqis and the world were better off. The commander in chief and his followers did not address the question of whether the American people, mourning the more than twenty-four hundred killed and fifteen thousand wounded, burdened with massive national debt traceable to administration tax policy, the costs of Iraq, and the ravages of hurricanes, were better off. Unanswered was whether continued inspections and sanctions might ultimately have brought Saddam down. Since embargoes pinch slowly at best, how long it might have taken is unknown. But obviously, this commander in chief was unwilling to wait. He was governed by his perceptions, based upon the faulty intelligence that his attitude helped generate. The Bush White House had said it created its own reality. Whether that one was desirable increasingly became dubious.

With the complicity of Congress, the White House exploited the fear of terrorism and installed the Patriot Act. The legislation gave the commander in chief added dominion over domestic affairs, with a potential for abuse of civil liberties, to an extent not seen since Lincoln suspended habeas corpus. Feeble efforts by legislators and muted public demonstrations were unlikely to restrain the runaway war power wielded by the White House.

In December 2005, leaks to newspapers revealed that the administration had sanctioned warrantless electronic eavesdropping on communications between the United States and other countries. The Bush administration insisted that the commander in chief, based upon Article II of the Constitution, has the inherent right to examine foreign communications. The Bush administration also claimed that the resolution covering the response to 9/11 also entitled the president to use any means he determined proper to wage that war. In fact, the language of Article II, Section 2 simply says, "The President shall be commander in chief of the army and navy of the United States, and of the militia of the several states when called into . . . service." As Alexander Hamilton in number 74 of the *Federalist Papers* had explained, the designation of commander in chief was necessary because management of a war required "exercise of power by a single head." In number 69 he said that the commander in chief's powers "would amount to nothing more than the supreme command and direction of the military and naval forces, as first general and admiral of the confederacy." The aim was only to ensure that a civilian should always have charge of the armed forces, whether in peacetime or wartime, in contrast to the British kings.

"Command and direction" are of course inexact terms, but they do not imply a power to ignore the basic rights of individuals under the Constitution whether we are at war or not. During the Korean War, in 1952, that was made plain in the case of *Youngstown Co. v. Sawyer.* Supreme Court justice Hugo Black, writing for the majority and referring to the language of the Constitution, said, "The order cannot properly be sustained as an exercise of the president's military power as commander in chief of the armed forces. The government attempts to do so by citing a number of cases upholding broad powers in military commanders engaged in day-to-day fighting in a theater of war. . . . Even though 'theater of war' can be an expanding concept, we cannot with faithfulness to our constitutional system hold that the commander in chief of the armed forces has the ultimate power as such to take possession of private property . . . that is a job for the nation's lawmakers, not for its military authorities."

The decision concerned preservation of private property but would seem applicable for other constitutional guarantees concerning search and seizure and habeas corpus. Justice Robert H. Jackson in his 1952 concurring opinion noted a "zone of twilight" wherein in absence of a congressional denial of authority the president and Congress "may have concurrent authority in which its distribution is uncertain." But Congress, with its 1978 Foreign Intelligence Surveillance Act, clearly spelled out the requirement of a warrant from the special FISA court with a provision of a seventy-two-hour grace period for emergency wiretaps, obliterating any "zone of twilight."

It is ironic that the administration chooses to evade the FISA courts, whose judges were appointed by the late Supreme Court chief justice William Rehnquist. As assistant attorney general during the Nixon years, Rehnquist enthusiastically plumped for the commander in chief's inherent right to wiretap within the United States without warrants because of threats to domestic security. The Supremes in 1972 by an eight-to-zero ruling (Rehnquist, now on the bench, abstained) said the government could not listen in without prior judicial approval unless it could show evidence of foreign intelligence links. Congress specifically addressed that loophole of foreign intelligence links when it passed FISA.

The president and his supporters have claimed that only al-Qaeda agents or their connections are overheard by the big ear. But who decides who is al-Qaeda and who is simply opposed to U.S. policy, whether at home or abroad? Vice President Cheney assured Americans that plots had been thwarted by the eavesdrops, but neither he nor other adherents could provide instances. Nor could they demonstrate that the seventy-two-hour waiver was insufficient for the purpose.

Without a court to adjudicate evidence of a terrorist connection we are left in the position of Damon Runyon's crapshooters up against the feared gangster Big Jule. He would appear at a dice game, pick up the cubes, advise the gamblers to place their bets against him. Then he would roll the dice in his hat, peer in, and announce his point. After a few rolls he would look and announce he'd made his point, sweep up the money, and leave. Americans, like the losers to Big Jule, are being asked to take Mr. Bush's word that he made his point, just as he and his cohorts asserted that Saddam had WMDs, that the Iraqis would greet us with flowers, and that we had ample troops to occupy the country.

21

POWER AND ABDICATION

B y the middle of 2006, bad news dominated the reports from Iraq. Although the administration talked up the number of schools that had reopened, the restoration of oil production, and the development of electric power, at best the rebuilding only replaced what had been destroyed in the war. Senator Chuck Hagel, a onetime supporter of the president's policy, said both electricity and oil were below the prewar levels. The temporary legislature drafted a constitution unacceptable to the Sunni segment and perhaps to many secularists in the population. The insurgency, a mixed bag of indigenous opponents of U.S. occupation, remnants of Saddam's Baath Party, and outside jihadists, intensified their attacks on Americans and Iraqis who cooperated with them. Even Republican politicians began to question the management of the war and the absence of an exit strategy. The commander in chief rebuffed critics with a litany of catchphrases about staying the course, fighting the terrorists in the Middle East instead of having to battle them at home, and progress toward democracy. He invoked the honor of the dead, arguing that to quit the fight would dishonor their sacrifices. Without disrespect to the fallen, in an economic venue such a practice is known as throwing good money after bad.

In the last throes of the Nixon presidency, the administration had orchestrated a public relations campaign around the motif of "support the troops." Anyone who opposed the war was characterized as a communist sympathizer. Nixon angrily deplored information that damaged the administration, that questioned events in Vietnam, and that investigated the decision-making at home. He tried to persuade the country that "Vietnamization," the development of the indigenous military, would allow Americans to withdraw gracefully. While no one has uttered the barbaric neologism "Iraqization," the Bush reactions bear a painful resemblance to the Nixon administration and its followers. Both presidents placed their faith in a shaky government with thin local support and a homegrown police and troops that in both Vietnam and Iraq seemed inadequate for the task.

The George W. Bush administration, which cloaked itself as "originalist" and preached strict construction when it came to the Constitution, had shown little hesitation in advancing the claims of the commander in chief when it came to war. Forgotten was the warning of Justice Jackson in the 1952 Youngstown Steel case that the hubris of a commander in chief "can vastly enlarge his mastery over internal affairs of the country by his own commitment of the nation's armed forces to some foreign venture." In the twenty-first century, presidential power has expanded to encroach upon civil liberties. The administration protested its innocence, but the evidence indicated that at the very least it had created a climate that skewed intelligence to fit its desires. Similarly, attitudes from the highest echelons led to abuse of prisoners and detainees.

George W. Bush was only the latest in a long line of presidents, starting with Washington and of all political stripes, to have pushed interpretation of the role. However, until the twentieth century, Americans thought of war as a matter of national security or self-defense—the actions against the Barbary pirates, the War of 1812, the Civil War, World Wars I and II. There were exceptions. The conflict with Mexico had more to do with the concept of Manifest Destiny and the expansion of U.S. turf. The Spanish-American War, ginned up by the press, was at best an attempt to fulfill the Monroe Doctrine and flash U.S. power.

Since World War II, the actions of the presidents in the cases of the Cuban Missile Crisis and the September 11, 2001, assault upon U.S. territory would both seem within the bounds of the constitutional demands for a chief executive to defend the nation, having drawn ratification by Congress. In the post–World War II era the idea of national security took on a wider meaning, giving the executive branch much broader considerations. America was now a world power and could not live in isolation. While some questioned Truman's authority to commit the armed forces in Korea, no one seriously disputed that he acted on behalf of national security. Furthermore, his action was supported by the United Nations, and Congress could have shut him down through its control over appropriations. The rubric of national security, however, also explained many of the more dubious ventures, such as meddling in Iran in the 1950s and the interventions in Latin America, overt as in the Dominican Republic and covert in Chile, El Salvador, and Nicaragua. Farther afield came the hidden support for rebels in Afghanistan. Here the legislators were often unaware of exactly what was being done in the name of the United States. The mechanism of a presidential finding plus secret briefings to a few congressional leaders evaded direct confrontation with the mandates of the Constitution. Funding was hidden in the secrecy attendant upon intelligence.

Vietnam was deemed a matter of national security and the flimsy pretext of the Gulf of Tonkin incidents accepted by Congress enabled Johnson and Nixon to carry on massive military operations beyond the fig leaf of a police action. The 1991 Iraqi invasion of Kuwait and the menace to Saudi Arabia qualified as a matter of national security in light of the oil at stake. George H. W. Bush wisely chose to get Capitol Hill to come aboard, and the venture also bore the imprimatur of the UN. Bill Clinton took national security a step further with the use of the armed forces in Mogadishu, Bosnia, and Kosovo. In these instances many believed, as George H. W. Bush did for Yugoslavia, that the United States "had no dog in the hunt." But Clinton's extension of a commander in chief's options, even when American interests were not visibly apparent, established a precedent. Humanitarian causes qualified under his definition. Congress did not foreclose his options, and again backing from NATO and the UN gave the actions a veneer of legitimacy.

Final judgment of the 2003 invasion of Iraq and its aftermath remains for future historians. But at first inspection, while Congress approved in advance, the entire business rested on false intelligence. It is a startling revelation of the possible consequences if a few people in power go unchallenged. The number of deaths, the destruction, the insurgency were not part of the calculus of even those who championed the invasion and continue to support it.

We are a government of laws, but we are governed by men and women. They bring their genes, their personalities honed by their education and experiences. In office they are buffeted by the media and affected by the ideological and partisan climate. As political animals, White House residents are badgered by loud voices in the halls of government, the media (a century ago newspapers drove the country to war on Spain), and public opinion.

Truman, Eisenhower, Kennedy, Johnson, Ford, Carter, Reagan, and their contemporaries thought in terms of a monolithic communist movement bent on conquering the world. The concept held some truth for a few decades after World War II. The invasion of South Korea by its northern brother, the Chinese saber-rattling over Taiwan, and the Cuban Missile Crisis seemed to prove the case. But chief executives tended to react to genuine antiestablishment currents as forerunners of the Red menace rather than as opposition to authoritarian governments and economic

tyranny. Presidents resorted to war, overt and covert, fulfilling the Clausewitz thesis that "war is the extension of policy by other means." Americans helped overthrow governments or suppress indigenous resistance to
oppressive ones in Latin America, meddled in the Middle East, and inter-
jected themselves most egregiously in Vietnam, where Truman, Eisenhower,
Kennedy, Johnson, and Nixon combined to sacrifice tens of thousands of
American lives on the altar of anticommunism. The American presence
there was based upon the domino theory. But when that conflict ended
with a defeat, victory by North Vietnam did not result in an avalanche of
communist movements sweeping into control.

The Vietnam disaster also sprang from partisan politics. Some Republicans—Senator William Knowland, Joe McCarthy, Barry Goldwater—with
allies in the media accused the Democrats of being soft on communism or
of having "lost" China. To preserve themselves, it behooved Democrats to
be resolute against left-wing movements. Both John F. Kennedy and Lyndon Johnson felt obliged to take a hard line. As historian Jeffrey Record
observed, the specter of Munich, appeasement that led to further aggression, haunted White Houses.[1] Bill Clinton was the first president born
after Munich and without a personal memory of that period.

Politics and the press also forced an end to the involvement in Vietnam. As the bodies piled up and a significant portion of the electorate
became unhappy with the war, attitudes in Congress changed. The president could use his bully pulpit to temporarily rally the public, but the legislators read the language in the streets and on the campuses. They zipped
shut the government wallet and forced Nixon to accept an end. But that
is an exception to the rule.

In the twenty-first century, the intensity of partisan politics has skewed
the balance once held by Congress. After World War II, there were those
on both sides of the aisle who offered objective views, regardless of who
held the White House. In contrast to Republicans of the 1940s, like
Arthur Vandenberg, who broke with the isolationist party line to support
an internationalist policy, by the 1990s members of the GOP were unwilling to buck the tide. Clinton said he took action in Bosnia without going
to Congress because he thought Republican leaders like Robert Dole and
Newt Gingrich, "both internationalists," would be relieved not to need to
confront their fellow Republicans. None from his party challenged George
W. Bush on Iraq, and at that Democrats cringed rather than suffer the
accusation of not supporting the troops or being soft on terrorism.

The disaffection with the Vietnam War owed much to the role of
the media. The correspondents' accounts and the television coverage that

belied official statements changed minds and influenced votes. Thirty years later, however, the media failed dismally. It failed to dig hard, scrutinize, or analyze with an intensity that might have challenged the evidence justifying the 2003 invasion of Iraq. The *Washington Post* later published a mea culpa in which executive editor Leonard Downie wrote, "We were so focused on trying to figure out what the administration was doing that we were not giving the same play to people who said it wouldn't be a good idea to go to war and were questioning the administration's rationale."[2] The same press that disseminated information that supported the case for war on Iraq, which had been carefully planted by the administration, took issue with the practice of information leaks after a celebrated case of an alleged outing of CIA official Valerie Plame as payback for her husband Joseph Wilson's publishing material critical of the Bush administration's push for regime change.

The media failure in the case of Iraq underscored the vital role of intelligence. Time and again, the postmortem of wars large and small has revealed deficiencies in the information relied upon by authorities and given the media. MacArthur was badly mistaken in his estimate of the Chinese along the Yalu River. Eisenhower and Kennedy were misled by the predictions of the CIA when they approved the 1961 Bay of Pigs attempt to oust Castro. Kennedy, Johnson, and Nixon all were gulled by brass hats, Defense Department analysts, and Foreign Service specialists with preset opinions, unwilling to admit that sheer firepower could not beat a determined Vietnam guerrilla movement abetted by North Vietnam. In contrast, CIA officials were far less sanguine about progress in Southeast Asia but woefully off the mark on Iraq. The weakness of intelligence was underscored by the astonishing moments of the Ford presidency when photographer David Kennerly casually but correctly provided a more informed view of the situation in Cambodia and with the *Mayaguez* than the regiments of trained professionals from the various intelligence services.

Jimmy Carter was caught by surprise when his embassy staff in Tehran was taken hostage. Reagan stumbled into Iran-Contra because of poor intelligence on the nature of the Iranian government. President George H. W. Bush's intelligence on Iraq indicated that Saddam Hussein was too preoccupied with domestic difficulties to threaten Middle East peace. After the quick but limited victory in the 1991 Gulf War, James Baker, his secretary of state, predicted Saddam would not last six months. George W. Bush went to war in 2003 because he said intelligence warned that a resurgent Saddam possessed weapons of mass destruction and was an imminent danger. As history has reported, the intelligence was spurious but Bush staked his claim upon his administration's interpretation of it. "CIA analysts who provided crucial information about Iraq's alleged weapons of mass destruction had been subjected to a 'hammering' of pressure from the Bush administration that was greater than any previously seen by the agency ombudsman in his thirty-two years of service," Senator Jay Rockefeller would charge, according to the *Boston Globe*. The comment appeared in a 512-page report by the Senate Intelligence Committee on intelligence failures involving Iraq, though the Republican majority chairman of the committee, Pat Roberts, denied evidence of any undue pressure on any analyst. The report also noted that statements by analysts suggesting that no clear link between al-Qaeda and Iraq could be found were discounted by Pentagon undersecretary for policy Douglas Feith, who advised Wolfowitz and Rumsfeld to ignore the CIA's interpretation.[3]

From the start of formal efforts to collect the intelligence that guides a commander in chief (fifteen such agencies currently operate), there have been attempts to improve the performance by purveyors of information, particularly after the vendors have been found at fault. In the latest reform, John Negroponte, the national director of intelligence, has ordered precautions to avoid poorly sourced and inadequately vetted data. Analysts are required to include caveats on the reliability of information as well as to note dissenting conclusions. But all the safeguards installed cannot protect against ideologues or those who bow to the inclinations of their masters. Nor is there a ready means to dispute a chief executive or his minions who choose to cherry-pick intelligence, taking only that which suits their taste.

The Bush administration repeatedly argued that everyone, including congressional Democrats, agreed with its assessment of the WMD threat from Iraq. But that is because they saw intelligence purged of doubts about the reliability of sources like "Curveball." The outsiders were not privy to the reports of the twenty Iraqi exiles who questioned their relatives and friends and heard the WMD programs had not been reconstituted. They were not informed of the inaccuracies and suspicions regarding the existence of mobile germ-warfare laboratories, the fraudulent tales of yellowcake purchases from Niger by Iraq, and that the aluminum tubes supposedly imported by Saddam had nothing to do with nuclear facilities.

The framers of the Constitution hoped to avoid the situation where a single individual, the president, acting on his perception, can send in the troops. Thus they placed the power to authorize war in the legislative branch. But for all the careful language of the Constitution, we do not live in the eighteenth century where oceans provided a shield against enemies, where the range of the largest cannons was measured in yards rather than thousands of miles, where nothing remotely resembled a weapon of mass destruction, where travel and communications moved so slowly that nothing was lost in allowing debate over weeks, even months, before a decision to take action.

The Japanese attack on Pearl Harbor ended any faith in the ability of an ocean to protect the United States. The overnight invasion of South Korea by its northern brother signaled that action delayed by a requirement to talk could mean swift defeat. Development of the long-range ballistic missile emphatically shrank the margins of time. The loss of the American monopoly on the nuclear bomb and its subsequent proliferation along with that of devastating chemical and biological agents added a quantum leap to potential casualties. Instant communication, the ubiquitous eyes first of the camera and then television, destroyed the blissful ignorance of mass savagery through ethnic cleansing or genocide. Unlike 1787, this seems to be a world in which it has become possible to justify wars of preemption and prevention.

Still, except perhaps for the Korean War and the Cuban Missile Crisis, the urgency so far has been largely artificial. There has been time for fuller debate, for more intensive study of intelligence before going to war. The ready resort to the open-ended resolution awarded a commander in chief has been an abdication of the congressional mandate.

A hallmark of American jurisprudence demands that a murder suspect be found guilty "beyond reasonable doubt." It would seem appropriate that before putting the troops in harm's way and embarking on large-scale killing, Congress, as the "jury," should apply a standard that goes beyond reasonable doubt. At the very least, the body that the Constitution vests with the power to declare war ought to engage in critical thinking, and a more rigorous examination of intelligence and the motives of the executive branch. We will be susceptible to future and perhaps deadly adventurism by a president unless the legislative body reasserts its responsibility.

The Constitutional Convention, fearful of the threat to democracy by an indigenous military, gave control of the armed forces to civilian officials. Furthermore, foreign affairs were made the exclusive responsibilities of these same civilians, and deployment of troops, ships, and planes is essentially the ultimate extension of foreign policy. Over time, Americans have been convinced of the truth of the old saw, "War is too important to be left to the generals." To be sure, since war involves political results the stance is understandable. Certainly, when General Douglas MacArthur appeared to challenge the Chinese by his actions in the Korean War, the risk of a free hand to the military commanders was obvious. And during the Cuban Missile Crisis and the Vietnam War, the policies advocated by some of the top brass involved political questions.

However, dangers are attendant upon civilian intrusion into the areas of military expertise. To cite some examples, the meddling with targeting during the Vietnam War by Lyndon Johnson and Robert McNamara added nothing to the prosecution of the war and on occasion jeopardized the lives of those in combat. Ronald Reagan inserted marines into Beirut over the resistance of his secretary of defense and the military. George W. Bush and Secretary of Defense Donald Rumsfeld ignored the counsel of generals who warned against "invasion lite." At the same time, presidents have often allowed what should be a responsibility for the civilian authorities to devolve upon the military, whose training for nation-building has at best been secondary and more often nonexistent. It is apparent that the Kennedy, Johnson, and Nixon administrations all relied on military solutions instead of trying to build a government and infrastructure that would win the hearts and minds of the South Vietnamese. In the Middle East, Asia, and Latin America, from the early 1950s to the present, American policies have focused on shoring up friends in high places by strengthening their armed forces.

The mind-set that gives weaponry and military training top priority shuts out options that might provide widespread support from the people. General Harold K. Johnson, army chief of staff from 1964 to 1968, said, "We did not understand the culture of the Vietnam people."[4] A similar deficit dogs the effort in the Middle East. The countries there have neither a tradition nor an appreciation of freedom of speech, equal rights for men and women, and separation of church and state. The dominant group in Iraq finds the theocracy of Iran far more to its taste than the institutions of the West. Western-style democracy cannot be instilled by an occupying army. President Bush in the ethnocentric hubris of many Americans condemned the opponents: "They hate freedom." What the terrorists and insurgents so fiercely detest is our culture, our presence, our attempts to remake them in our image and our foreign policy.

Yes, it is a different universe than that of 1793. Yet rather than grapple with the issues, those who should be searching for solutions are instead running away from the matter. Time and again since World War II, when the issue of whether to go to war has arisen, Congress has ducked behind open-ended resolutions ceding its rights to presidents or swallowing presidential findings without question. The War Powers Act that followed Vietnam has had little effect.

Former senator George McGovern, the unsuccessful Democratic candidate for president in 1972, whom Republicans like to label as an extreme liberal—that is, a fellow with no regard for the limits on government—said of the conflict between the desires of a commander in chief and the requirement of the legislative branch for its sanction, "A lot of people in Congress don't want that responsibility. They would rather leave it to the executive branch."[5]

NOTES

Introduction: Commander in Chief

1. Schlesinger, *The Imperial Presidency*, 114.
2. Report of the Congressional Committees Investigating the Iran-Contra Affair, 1987, p. 247.
3. Nixon, *New Road for America*, Major Policy Statements, March 1970–October 1971.
4. Schlesinger, *The Imperial Presidency*, 166.
5. Taylor, Oral History.
6. Woodward, *The Commanders*, 39.
7. Fisher, *Presidential War Power*, 6.
8. Scowcroft, interview with author, 2004.
9. Ibid.

1. The Evolution of War Powers and Precedents

1. Fisher, *Presidential War Power*, 10.
2. Ibid., 17.
3. Naval Documents Relating to the U.S. War with Barbary Pirates, 1939, p. 467.
4. Schlesinger, *The Imperial Presidency*, 36.
5. Ibid., 37.
6. Ibid., 41.
7. Thomas, *Abraham Lincoln*, 119.
8. Schlesinger, *The Imperial Presidency*, 42.
9. Ibid., 54.
10. Ibid., 59.

2. World War I, World War II

1. Fisher, *Presidential War Power*, 42.
2. Schlesinger, *The Imperial Presidency*, 89.
3. Ibid., 90.
4. Ibid., 91.
5. Ibid., 113.
6. Ibid., 120.

3. The Truman Years

1. "The Charter of the United Nations," Hearings before the Senate Committee on Foreign Relations, 1st Session, 1945, p. 298.
2. Ibid., 655.
3. Fisher, *Presidential War Power*, 83.
4. Arthur Krock, *New York Times*, April 27, 1951.
5. Pusey, *Charles Evans Hughes*, 795.
6. Nicholas D. Katzenbach, "Foreign Policy, Public Opinion and Secrecy," *Foreign Affairs*, October 1973.
7. *Congressional Record*, February 21, 1949.
8. Hearings before the Committee on Armed Services and Committee on Foreign Affairs, U.S. Senate, June 4, 1951.
9. Haig, interview with author, 2004.
10. Truman, *Memoirs*, 335.
11. *Congressional Record*, July 5, 1950.
12. Chace, *Acheson*, 222.
13. *Congressional Record*, July 5, 1950.
14. Bailey, *A Diplomatic History*, 821.
15. LeMay and Kantor, *Mission with LeMay*, 382.
16. Haig, interview with author.
17. Bailey, *A Diplomatic History*, 821.
18. Haig, interview with author, 2004.
19. Richardson, Oral History.
20. Haig, interview with author, 2004.
21. MacArthur, *Reminiscences*, 442.
22. Morison, *The Oxford History of the American People*, 1070.
23. Ibid., 1072.
24. Ibid.
25. MacArthur, *Reminiscences*, 447.
26. Truman, *Off the Record*, 303–304.
27. Schlesinger, *The Imperial Presidency*, 142.

4. The Reign of Ike

1. Richardson, Oral History.
2. Taylor, Oral History.
3. Haig, interview with author, 2004.
4. *Time*, January 7, 1952.
5. Ibid.

6. Eisenhower, *Mandate for Change*, 159.

7. Saikal, *The Rise and Fall of the Shah*, 215.

8. *Congressional Record*, April 20, 1954.

9. Eisenhower, *Mandate for Change*, 425.

10. Kornbluh, *Bay of Pigs Declassified*, 8.

11. *New York Times*, May 4, 2005.

12. Eisenhower, *Mandate for Change*, 167.

13. Record, *Making War, Thinking History*, 47.

14. *Congressional Record*, February 11, 1954.

15. *New York Times*, February 11, 1954.

16. Eisenhower, *Mandate for Change*, 167.

17. Ibid., 340.

18. Ibid., 347.

19. *Congressional Record*, June 5, 1954.

20. Ibid.

21. Ibid.

22. *Congressional Record*, April 19, 1954.

23. Ibid.

24. Ibid.

25. Anderson, Oral History.

26. Eisenhower, *Public Papers*, 306.

27. Adams, *First Hand Report*, 109.

28. Eisenhower, *Mandate for Change*, 462.

29. Ibid.

30. Ibid.

31. Schlesinger, *The Imperial Presidency*, 160.

32. McGovern, *Grassroots*, 79.

33. *Congressional Record*, July 15, 1958.

34. Ibid.

35. Schlesinger, *A Thousand Days*, 208.

36. Sierra, J. A., "Invasion at Bay of Pigs," www.historyofcuba.com/history/baypigs/pigslong.htm.

5. Camelot's Commander in Chief

1. Sierra, J. A., "Invasion at Bay of Pigs."

2. Schlesinger, *A Thousand Days*, 236.

3. Ibid.

4. Dulles, *The Craft of Intelligence*, 169.

5. Schlesinger, *A Thousand Days*, 270.

6. Kornbluh, *Bay of Pigs Declassified*, 53.

7. Reeves, *President Kennedy*, 103.

8. Mustin, Oral History.

9. Sierra, J. A., "Invasion at Bay of Pigs."

10. Moorer, Oral History.

11. *New York Times*, May 12, 1962.

12. *New York Times*, May 13, 1962.

13. *Congressional Record*, September 21, 1962.

14. Thompson, *The Missiles of October*, 144.

15. Schlesinger, *A Thousand Days*, 731.

16. *New York Times*, September 14, 1962.

17. *Congressional Record*, September 5, 1962.

18. *Congressional Record*, September 6, 1962.

19. *Congressional Record*, September 9, 1962.

20. Ibid.

21. *Congressional Record*, October 10, 1962.

6. The Missile Crisis

1. Schlesinger, *A Thousand Days*, 735.

2. Schlesinger, *Robert Kennedy and His Times*, 507.

3. Reeves, *President Kennedy*, 371.

4. Zumwalt, Oral History.

5. Ibid.

6. Kornbluh, *Bay of Pigs Declassified*, 120.

7. May and Zelikow, *The Kennedy Tapes*, 169.

8. Ibid., 184.

9. Ibid.

10. O'Donnell and Powers, *Johnny, We Hardly Knew You*, 318.

11. Stern, *Averting The Final Failure*, 130.

12. Schlesinger, *A Thousand Days*, 738.

13. Ibid.

14. May and Zelikow, *The Kennedy Tapes*, 204.

15. Ibid., 215.

16. Ibid., 268–283.

17. Zumwalt, Oral History.

7. Resolution and Reverberations

1. Thompson, *The Missiles of October*, 273.

2. Ibid., 281.

3. Stern, *Averting The Final Failure*, 308.

4. Ibid., 361.

5. Stern, *Averting The Final Failure*, 230.

6. May and Zelikow, *The Kennedy Tapes*, 388.

7. Ibid., 390–391.

8. Stern, *Averting The Final Failure*, 233–234.

9. Taylor, Oral History.

10. Stern, *Averting The Final Failure*, 236.

11. May and Zelikow, *The Kennedy Tapes*, 279.

12. Ibid., 608.

13. Ibid.

14. Ibid., 371.

15. Ibid., 171.

16. Stern, *Averting The Final Failure*, 308.

17. Ibid., 388.

18. Haig, *Inner Circles*, 103–104.

19. May and Zelikow, *The Kennedy Tapes*, 18.

20. McNamara, *In Retrospect*, 47.

21. Schlesinger, *A Thousand Days*, 697.

22. Hammond, *The Military and the Media*, 51–52.

23. Schlesinger, *A Thousand Days*, 902.

24. McNamara, *In Retrospect*, 53.

25. Ibid., 54–55.

26. Schlesinger, *A Thousand Days*, 905.

27. Anthony Lake, interview with author, 2004.

28. Schlesinger, *A Thousand Days*, 908.

8. LBJ, Part of the Way

1. Johnson, *The Vantage Point*, 45.

2. McNamara, *In Retrospect*, 97.

3. Record, *Making War, Thinking History*, 58.

4. Beschloss, *Taking Charge*, 248.

5. Johnson, *The Vantage Point*, 64.

6. Ibid., 66.

7. McNamara, *In Retrospect*, 114.

8. Ibid., 118.

9. Telephone conversation, Johnson and Russell, May 27, 1964, LBJ Library, Austin, Tex.

10. Dallek, *Flawed Giant*, 131.

11. Sharp, Oral History.

12. Johnson, *The Vantage Point*, 112.

13. McNamara, Blight, and Schandler, *Argument Without End*, 168.

14. Johnson, *The Vantage Point*, 114.

15. Ibid., 115.

16. Ibid., 117.

17. *New York Times*, August 5, 1964.

18. *Congressional Record*, August 6, 1964.

19. Ibid.

20. *Congressional Record*, August 7, 1964.

21. George McGovern, interview with author, 2004.

22. McNamara, *In Retrospect*, 140.

23. *New York Times*, August 11, 1964.

24. McNamara, *In Retrospect*, 130.

25. Haig, interview with author, January 25, 2005.

26. *Congressional Record*, February 28, 1968.

27. McNamara, *In Retrospect*, 133–134.

28. Sharp, Oral History.

29. Moorer, Oral History.

30. Beschloss, *Reaching for Glory*, 38.

31. Richard Holbrooke, interview with author, 2004.

32. McNamara, Blight, and Schandler, *Argument Without End*, 167.

33. Beschloss, *Reach for Glory*, 137.

34. McNamara, *In Retrospect*, 158.

9. Down the Slope

1. McNamara, *In Retrospect*, 160.

2. Dallek, *Flawed Giant*, 244.

3. Halberstam, *The Best and the Brightest*, 614.

4. McNamara, *In Retrospect*, 171.

5. Ibid., 172–173.

6. Johnson, *The Vantage Point*, 131.

7. Dougherty, Oral History.

8. Moorer, Oral History.

9. Haig, interview with author, January 25, 2005.

10. Haig, *Inner Circles*, 139.

11. Ibid., 127, 152.

12. Beschloss, *Reaching for Glory*, 292.

13. Dallek, *Flawed Giant*, 282.

14. Beschloss, *Reaching for Glory*, 297.

15. Dallek, *Flawed Giant*, 474.

16. McNamara, *In Retrospect*, 183.

17. Beschloss, *Reaching for Glory*, 309.

18. Dallek, *Flawed Giant*, 269.

19. Beschloss, *Reaching for Glory*, 312.

20. McNamara, *In Retrospect*, 350.

21. Ibid., 197.

22. Dallek, *Flawed Giant*, 273.

23. Krulak, Oral History.

24. Dallek, *Flawed Giant*, 286.

25. Weschler, Oral History.

26. Dallek, *Flawed Giant*, 349.

27. Ibid., 283.

10. Toward Peace with Honor

1. Boot, *The Savage Wars*, 293.

2. *Congressional Record*, April 25, 1967.

3. Ibid.

4. Dallek, *Flawed Giant*, 447.

5. Krulak, Oral History.

6. Jones, Oral History.

7. Krulak, Oral History.

8. Jones, Oral History.

9. Train, Oral History.

10. Sharp, Oral History.

11. Dallek, *Flawed Giant*, 491.

12. Ibid., 500.

13. Johnson, *The Vantage Point*, 536.

14. Moorer, Oral History.

15. Johnson, *The Vantage Point*, 384.

16. Alterman, *When Presidents Lie*, 229.

17. McNamara, Blight, and Schandler, *Argument Without End*, 366.

18. Mann, *A Grand Delusion*, 607.

19. Reeves, *President Nixon*, 57.

20. Mann, *A Grand Delusion*, 630.

21. Moorer, Oral History.

22. Abrams, Oral History.

23. Nixon, *RN*, 380.

24. Ibid., 390.

25. Kissinger, *The White House Years*, 252.

26. Haig, *Inner Circles*, 204.

27. Reeves, *President Nixon*, 68.

28. Ibid.

29. Nixon, *RN*, 384.

30. *Congressional Record*, July 2, 1969.

31. Nixon, *RN*, 400.

32. Dallek, *Flawed Giant*, 643.

33. Nixon, *RN*, 394.

34. Kissinger, *The White House Years*, 282.

11. Pieces of Peace

1. Mann, *A Grand Delusion*, 637.

2. Reeves, *President Kennedy*, 143.

3. Stern, *A Murder in Wartime*, 334.

4. Hammond, *The Military and the Media*, 143–144.

5. Hersh, *The Price of Power*, 135.

6. Hammond, *The Military and the Media*, 143–144.

7. Moorer, Oral History.

8. Mann, *A Grand Delusion*, 652.

9. Ibid.

10. Shawcross, *Sideshow*, 134–135.

11. *Congressional Record*, April 2, 1970.

12. Shawcross, *Sideshow*, 138–139.

13. Reeves, *President Kennedy*, 206.

14. Ibid., 206–207.

15. Haig, interview with author, January 25, 2005.

16. Shawcross, *Sideshow*, 150–151.

17. Moorer, Oral History.

18. Reeves, *President Kennedy*, 383.

19. Schlesinger, *The Imperial Presidency*, 191.

20. Ibid., 195, quoting interview of Nixon by Howard K. Smith.

21. Kissinger, *The White House Years*, 515.

22. Mann, *A Grand Delusion*, 668.

23. *Congressional Record*, April 26, 1971.

24. Kissinger, *The White House Years*, 652.

25. Ibid., 659.

26. Isaacson, *Kissinger*, 290.

27. Kissinger, *The White House Years*, 677–678.

28. Coll, *Ghost Wars*, 581.

12. The Bitter End

1. Kissinger, *The White House Years*, 514.

2. Mann, *A Grand Delusion*, 677.

3. Ibid., 684.

4. *Newsweek*, June 28, 1971.

5. Mann, *A Grand Delusion*, 686.

6. Ibid., 696.

7. Haldeman, *The Haldeman Diaries*, 572.

8. Nixon, *RN*, 688.

9. Shawcross, *Sideshow*, 301.

10. Ford, *A Time to Heal*, 250.

11. Ibid., 253.

12. Train, Oral History.

13. Ford, *A Time to Heal*, 256.

14. Isaacson, *Kissinger*, 650.

15. Ford, *A Time to Heal*, 279.

16. Ibid., 279–280.

17. Wetterhahn, *The Last Battle*, 151–152.

18. Train, Oral History.

19. Ford, *A Time to Heal*, 282.

20. Train, Oral History.

21. Wetterhahn, *The Last Battle*, 206, quoting press secretary Ron Nessen.

22. Train, Oral History.

23. Shawcross, *Sideshow*, 476–477.

24. Isaacson, *Kissinger*, 651.

25. Train, Oral History.

13. Iran, Afghanistan, and Lebanon

1. Cannon, *President Reagan*, 342.

2. Brzezinski, *Power and Principle*, 127.

3. Brinkley, *The Unfinished Presidency*, 20.

4. Isaacson, *Kissinger*, 564.

5. Saikal, *The Rise and Fall*, 206.

6. Brzezinski, *Power and Principle*, 394.

7. Morris, *Jimmy Carter*, 176.

8. Train, Oral History.

9. Jones, Oral History.

10. Coll, *Ghost Wars*, 46.

11. Chalmers Johnson, "Abolish the CIA," *London Review of Books*, 2004.

12. Sick, *The October Surprise*, 81–88.

13. *Wall Street Journal*, June 3, 1980.

14. Haig, *Caveat*, 85.

15. Cannon, *President Reagan*, 195.

16. Coll, *Ghost Wars*, 58.

17. Cannon, *President Reagan*, 344.

18. Ibid., 345.

19. Haig, interview with author, January 25, 2005.

20. Cannon, *President Reagan*, 398.

21. Haig, interview with author, 2004.

22. Cannon, *President Reagan*, 414.

23. Martin and Walcott, *Best Laid Plans*, 147.

24. Cannon, *President Reagan*, 439.

14. Beirut, Central America, and Iran

1. Report of the Department of Defense Commission on Beirut International Airport Terrorist Act, October 23, 1983.

2. Cannon, *President Reagan*, 441.

3. Caspar Weinberger, interview with author, May 18, 2004.

4. John Roberts, White House Counsel's Office, 1983.

5. Gary Hart, interview with author, 2004.

6. Reagan, *An American Life*, 451.

7. Cannon, *President Reagan*, 446.

8. Schultz, *Triumph and Turmoil*, 340.

9. Haig, interview with author, January 25, 2005.

10. Weinberger, interview with author, May 18, 2004.

11. *Wall Street Journal*, February 3, 1984.

12. Record, *Making War*, 83.

13. Reagan, *An American Life*, 471, 473.

14. Alterman and Greene, *The Book on Bush*, 250.

15. Ibid., 251.

16. Ibid., 252.

17. Mark Danner, "The Truth of El Mozote," *New Yorker*, December 6, 1993.

18. Ibid.

19. Alterman and Greene, *The Book on Bush*, 257.

20. Danner, "The Truth of El Mozote."

21. Cannon, *President Reagan*, 346.

22. Danner, "The Truth of El Mozote."

23. Alterman and Greene, *The Book on Bush*, 248.

24. Ibid., 259.

25. Weinberger, interview with author, May 18, 2004.

26. Cannon, *President Reagan*, 348.

27. Weinberger, interview with author, May 18, 2004.

28. Shultz, *Triumph and Turmoil*, 311.

29. Cannon, *President Reagan*, 356.

30. Alterman and Greene, *The Book on Bush*, 267.

31. Cannon, *President Reagan*, 388.

15. Iran-Contra

1. Cannon, *President Reagan*, 627.

2. Report of the Congressional Committees Investigating the Iran-Contra Affair, 1987, p. 4.

3. Tower Commission Report, 1987, p. 20.

4. Report of the Congressional Committees, 166.

5. Cannon, *President Reagan*, 625.

6. Tower Commission Report, 32.

7. Report of the Congressional Committees, 198.

8. Ibid., 247.

9. Weinberger, interview with author, May 18, 2004.

10. Report of the Congressional Committees, 255.

11. Ibid., 263.

12. *New York Times*, October 9, 1986.

13. Report of the Congressional Committees, 295–296.

14. Ibid., 298.

15. Ibid., 316.

16. Ibid., 317.

17. Cannon, *President Reagan*, 702.

18. *Time*, December 8, 1986.

19. Report of the Congressional Committees, Oliver North Testimony.

20. Report of the Congressional Committees, John Poindexter Testimony.

21. Ibid.

22. Report of the Congressional Committees, 11.

23. Ibid., 20–21.

24. Tower Commission Report, 65.

25. Ibid., 80.

26. Cannon, *President Reagan*, 711.

27. McGovern, interview with author, 2004.

28. Scowcroft, interview with author, July 29, 2004.

29. Haig, interview with author, January 25, 2005.

16. Bush One

1. Brent Scowcroft, interview with author, July 29, 2004.

2. George H. W. Bush, *Public Papers of the President*, 1989, p. 1393.

3. *Congressional Record*, February 7, 1990.

4. Bush and Scowcroft, *A World Transformed*, 305.

5. Record, *Hollow Victory*, 162.

6. Ibid., 31.

7. Bush and Scowcroft, *A World Transformed*, 311.

8. Sciolino, *The Outlaw State*, 140.

9. Bush and Scowcroft, *A World Transformed*, 317–318.

10. Ibid., 316.

11. Ibid., 324.

12. Ibid., 327.

13. Ibid., 328.

14. Ibid., 333.

15. Woodward, *The Commanders*, 261.

16. Record, *Hollow Victory*, 36.

17. Bush and Scowcroft, *A World Transformed*, 371.

18. Scowcroft, interview with author, July 29, 2004.

19. Freedman and Karsh, *The Gulf Conflict*, 241.

20. Ibid., 291.

21. Ibid., 320.

22. Record, *Hollow Victory*, 65.

23. Freedman and Karsh, *The Gulf Conflict*, 413.

24. Bush and Scowcroft, *A World Transformed*, 464.

25. Scowcroft, interview with author, July 29, 2004.

26. Bush and Scowcroft, *A World Transformed*, 458.

17. Nation-Building and Genocide

1. *Washington Post*, December 5, 1992.

2. *U.S. News and World Report*, December 14, 1992.

3. Clinton, *My Life*, 550.

4. Scowcroft, interview with author, July 29, 2004.

5. Clinton, *My Life*, 550.

6. Ibid., 551.

7. Bowden, *Black Hawk Down*, 379, 409.

8. Clarke, *Against All Enemies*, 86–87.

9. Clinton, *My Life*, 552.

10. Bowden, *Black Hawk Down*, 413–414.

11. Clinton, *My Life*, 553.

12. Holbrooke, *To End a War*, 23–24.

13. Ibid., 27.

14. Fisher, *Presidential War Power*, 158.

15. Ibid., 155–156.

16. Richard Holbrooke, interview with author, 2004.

17. Ibid.

18. Ibid.

19. Holbrooke, *To End a War*, 64.

20. Ibid., 92.

21. Ibid., 132.

22. Ibid., 144–145.

23. Clinton, *My Life*, 674.

24. Ibid., 526.

25. Strasser, *The 911 Investigation*, 63.

26. Clinton, *My Life*, 804.

27. Strasser, *The 911 Investigation*, 120.

18. Prevention and Retaliation

1. Nita Lowey, interview with author, December 14, 2004.

2. Clinton, *My Life*, 859.

3. Clarke, *Against All Enemies*, 243.

4. Dean, *Worse Than Watergate*, 105.

5. Scowcroft, interview with author, July 29, 2004.

6. *New York Times Magazine*, October 17, 2004.

7. Alterman and Greene, *The Book on Bush*, 185.

8. Woodward, *Plan of Attack*, 11–12.

9. Clarke, *Against All Enemies*, 230–232.

10. Ibid., 237.

11. Ibid., 32.

12. Franks, *American Soldier*, 380.

13. *New York Times*, April 8, 2005.

14. Strasser, *The 9/11 Investigation*, 14–15.

15. Ibid.

19. Between Iraq and Hard Places

1. Woodward, *Plan of Attack*, 1, 3.

2. Blix, *Disarming Iraq*, 63.

3. Ibid., 61.

4. *New York Review of Books*, "Text of Downing Street Memo," June 9, 2005.

5. Jules Witcover, *Baltimore Sun*, August 2002.

6. Woodward, *Plan of Attack*, 154–155.

7. *Wall Street Journal*, August 15, 2002.

8. Alterman and Greene, *The Book on Bush*, 256.

9. Ibid., 252.

10. Blix, *Disarming Iraq*, 71.

11. Ibid., 74.

12. Woodward, *Plan of Attack*, 179–191.

13. Ibid., 198–199.

14. *Congressional Record*, October 8, 2002.

15. Lowey, interview with author, December 14, 2004.

16. *Congressional Record*, October 12, 2002.

17. Woodward, *Plan of Attack*, 224.

18. Ibid., 249.

19. *The Nation*, June 11, 2003.

20. Blix, *Disarming Iraq*, 154–155.

21. *Editor and Publisher*, March 26, 2003.

22. *USA Today*, July 22, 2003.

23. *Congressional Record*, October 8, 2002.

24. *New York Times*, October 19, 2004.

25. Ibid.

26. Ibid.

20. Winning the War, Fighting On

1. *New York Times*, October 19, 2004.

2. *Los Angeles Times*, quoted by Paul Krugman, *New York Times*, August 2005.

3. *New York Times*, October 19, 2004.

4. *New York Times*, May 31, 2003.

5. *Washington Post*, October 3, 2003.

6. *New York Times*, April 2, 2004.

7. *Washington Post*, June 5, 2003.

8. *New York Times*, October 15, 2004.

9. *New York Times*, January 17, 2005.

10. *New York Times*, April 8, 2005.

11. *New York Times*, August 1, 2005.

12. Lecture, Princeton University, March 8, 2005.

13. *New York Times*, January 6, 2005.

14. *New York Times*, October 24, 2004.

15. *Time*, January 17, 2005.

16. Ibid.

17. *New York Times*, May 25, 2004.

18. *New York Times*, August 26, 2004.

19. Schlesinger Report, released August 2004.

20. *New York Times*, April 23, 2005.

21. *New York Times*, January 10, 2004.

21. Power and Abdication

1. Record, *Making War, Thinking History*, 4–5.

2. *Washington Post*, August 12, 2005.

3. *Boston Globe*, July 10, 2004.

4. Johnson, Oral History.

5. McGovern, interview with author, 2004.

BIBLIOGRAPHY

Books

Adams, Sherman. *First Hand Report: The Inside Story of the Eisenhower Administration*. New York: Harper, 1962.

Alterman, Eric, and Mark Greene. *The Book on Bush: How George W. (Mis)leads America*. New York: Viking, 2004.

———. *When Presidents Lie: A History of Official Deception and Its Consequences*. New York: Penguin, 2004.

Bailey, Thomas. *A Diplomatic History of the American People*. New York: Appleton-Century-Crofts, 1969.

Baily, Bernard. *The Debate on the Constitution: Federalist and Antifederalist Speeches, Articles and Letters During the Struggle over Ratification*. 2 vols. New York: Library of America, 1993.

Beschloss, Michael. *Reaching for Glory: Lyndon Johnson's Secret White House Tapes, 1964–1965*. New York: Simon & Schuster, 2001.

———. *Taking Charge: The Johnson White House Tapes, 1963–1964*. New York: Simon & Schuster, 1997.

Bissell, Richard. *Memoirs of a Cold War Warrior: From Yalta to the Bay of Pigs*. New Haven, Conn.: Yale University Press, 1996.

Blix, Hans. *Disarming Iraq*. New York: Pantheon, 2004.

Boot, Max. *The Savage Wars of Peace: Small Wars and the Rise of American Power*. New York: Pantheon, 2002.

Bowden, Mark. *Black Hawk Down: A Story of Modern War*. New York: Atlantic Monthly Press, 1999.

Brinkley, Douglas. *The Unfinished Presidency: Jimmy Carter's Journey Beyond the White House*. New York: Penguin, 1999.

Brzezinski, Zbigniew. *Power and Principle: Memoirs of the National Security Adviser, 1977–1981*. New York: Farrar, Straus and Giroux, 1983.

Burns, James MacGregor. *Roosevelt: The Soldier of Freedom*. New York: Harcourt Brace Jovanovich, 1970.

Bush, George H. W., and Brent Scowcroft. *A World Transformed*. New York: Alfred A. Knopf, 1998.

Bush, George H. W. *All the Best: My Life in Letters and Other Writings*. New York: Scribner, 1999.

Cannon, Lou. *President Reagan: The Role of a Lifetime*. New York: Simon & Schuster, 1991.

Chace, James. *Acheson: The Secretary of State Who Created the American World*. New York: Simon & Schuster, 1998.

Clarke, Richard A. *Against All Enemies: Inside America's War on Terror*. New York: Free Press, 2004.

Clinton, Bill. *My Life*. New York: Alfred A. Knopf, 2004.

Coll, Steve. *Ghost Wars: The Secret History of the CIA, Afghanistan, and bin Laden, from the Soviet Invasion to September 10, 2001*. New York: Penguin, 2004.

Corn, David. *The Lies of George Bush: Mastering the Politics of Deception*. New York: Crown, 2003.

Dallek, Robert. *Flawed Giant: Lyndon Johnson and His Times, 1960–1973*. New York: Oxford University Press, 1998.

Dean, John. *Worse Than Watergate: The Secret Presidency of George W. Bush*. New York: Little, Brown, 2004.

Dulles, Allen. *The Craft of Intelligence*. New York: Harper & Row, 1963.

Eisenhower, Dwight D. *Mandate for Change*. Garden City, N.Y.: Doubleday & Company, 1963.

———. *Public Papers of the President 1954*. Abilene, Kans.: Dwight D. Eisenhower Library.

Fisher, Louis. *Presidential War Power*. Lawrence: University Press of Kansas, 1995.

Ford, Gerald. *A Time to Heal*. New York: Harper & Row, 1979.

Franks, Tommy. *American Soldier*. New York: HarperCollins, 2004.

Freedman, Lawrence, and Efraim Karsh. *The Gulf Conflict, 1990–1991*. Princeton, N.J.: Princeton University Press, 1993.

Haig, Alexander M., Jr. *Caveat*. New York: Macmillan, 1984.

———. *Inner Circles: How America Changed the World*. New York: Warner Books, 1992.

Halberstam, David. *The Best and the Brightest*. New York: Random House, 1972.

Haldeman, H. R. *The Haldeman Diaries: Inside the Nixon White House*. New York: G. P. Putnam's Sons, 1994.

Hammond, William. *The Military and the Media, 1962–1968*. Washington, D.C.: Center of Military History, 1990.

Hersh, Seymour. *The Price of Power: Kissinger in the Nixon White House*. New York: Summit, 1983.

Holbrooke, Richard. *To End a War*. New York: Random House, 1998.

Isaacson, Walter. *Kissinger*. New York: Simon & Schuster, 1992.

Johnson, Lyndon B. *The Vantage Point: Perspectives of the Presidency, 1963–1969*. New York: Holt, Rinehart and Winston, 1971.

Kissinger, Henry. *The White House Years*. Boston: Little, Brown & Company, 1979.

Kornbluh, Peter. *Bay of Pigs Declassified: The Secret CIA Report on the Invasion of Cuba*. New York: New Press, 1998.

Lake, Anthony. *Six Nightmares*. Boston: Little, Brown & Company, 2000.

Lake, Anthony, ed. *The Legacy of Vietnam: The War, American Society, and the Future of American Policy*. New York: New York University Press, 1976.

LeMay, Curtis, and McKinlay Kantor. *Mission with LeMay: My Story*. Garden City, N.Y.: Doubleday & Company, 1965.

MacArthur, Douglas. *Reminiscences*. New York: McGraw-Hill, 1964.

Mann, Robert A. *A Grand Delusion: America's Descent into Vietnam*. New York: Basic Books, 2001.

Martin, David C., and John Walcott. *Best Laid Plans: The Inside Story of America's War Against Terrorism*. New York: Harper & Row, 1988.

May, Ernest R., and Philip D. Zelikow, eds. *The Kennedy Tapes: Inside the White House During the Cuban Missile Crisis*. Cambridge, Mass.: Harvard University Press, 1997.

McGovern, George. *Grassroots: The Autobiography of George McGovern*. New York: Random House, 1977.

McNamara, Robert S. *In Retrospect: The Tragedy and Lessons of Vietnam*. New York: Times Books, 1995.

McNamara, Robert, James Blight, and Herbert Schandler. *Argument Without End: In Search of Answers to the Vietnam Tragedy*. New York: Perseus, 1999.

Miller, Merle. *Plain Speaking: An Oral Biography of Harry S. Truman*. New York: G. P. Putnam's Sons, 1973.

Morison, Samuel Eliot. *The Oxford History of the American People*. New York: Oxford University Press, 1965.

Morris, Kenneth. *Jimmy Carter: American Moralist*. Athens: University of Georgia Press, 1996.

Moskin, J. Robert. *Mr. Truman's War: The Final Victories of World War II and the Birth of the Postwar World*. New York: Random House, 1996.

Nixon, Richard M. *RN: The Memoirs of Richard Nixon*. New York: Grosset & Dunlap, 1978.

O'Donnell, Kenneth, and David Powers. *Johnny, We Hardly Knew You*. Boston: Little, Brown, 1970.

Pollack, Kenneth M. *The Threatening Storm: The Case for Invading Iraq*. New York: Random House, 2002.

Pusey, Merle J. *Charles Evans Hughes*. New York: Macmillan, 1951.

Reagan, Ronald. *An American Life: The Autobiography*. New York: Simon & Schuster, 1990.

Record, Jeffrey. *Hollow Victory: A Contrary View of the Gulf War*. McLean, Va.: Brassey's, 1993.

———. *Making War, Thinking History: Munich, Vietnam, and Presidential Uses of Force from Korea to Kosovo*. Annapolis, Md.: U.S. Naval Institute Press, 2002.

Reeves, Richard. *President Kennedy: Profile of Power*. New York: Simon & Schuster, 1963.

———. *President Nixon: Alone in the White House*. New York: Simon & Schuster, 2001.

Rudman, Warren. *Combat: My Twelve Years in the Senate*. New York: Random House, 1996.

Saikal, Amir. *The Rise and Fall of the Shah*. Princeton, N.J.: Princeton University Press, 1980.

Schlesinger, Arthur M., Jr. *The Imperial Presidency*. Boston: Houghton Mifflin, 1973.

———. *Robert Kennedy and His Times*. Boston: Houghton Mifflin, 1978.

———. *A Thousand Days: John F. Kennedy in the White House*. Boston: Houghton Mifflin, 1965.

Sciolino, Elaine. *The Outlaw State: Saddam Hussein's Quest for Power and the War in the Gulf*. New York: John Wiley & Sons, 1991.

Shawcross, William. *Sideshow: Kissinger, Nixon, and the Destruction of Cambodia*. New York: Pocket Books, 1979.

Shultz, George. *Triumph and Turmoil: My Years as Secretary of State*. New York: Charles Scribner, 1993.

Sick, Gary. *The October Surprise: America's Hostages and the Election of Ronald Reagan*. New York: Times Books, 1991.

Sorenson, Theodore C. *Kennedy*. New York: Harper & Row, 1965.

Stein, Jeff. *A Murder in Wartime: The Untold Spy Story That Changed the Course of the Vietnam War*. New York: St. Martin's, 1992.

Stern, Sheldon M. *Averting The Final Failure: John F. Kennedy and the Secret Cuban Missile Crisis Meetings*. Palo Alto, Calif.: Stanford University Press, 2003.

Strasser, Steven, ed. *The 911 Investigation, Public Affairs Reports*. New York: Perseus Group, 2004.

Suskind, Ron. *The Price of Loyalty: George W. Bush, the White House, and the Education of Paul O'Neill*. New York: Simon & Schuster, 2004.

Thomas, Benjamin. *Abraham Lincoln: A Biography*. New York: Alfred A. Knopf, 1952.

Thompson, Robert S. *The Missiles of October: The Declassified Story of John F. Kennedy and the Cuban Missile Crisis*. New York: Simon & Schuster, 1992.

Truman, Harry S. *Memoirs*. Garden City, N.Y.: Doubleday, 1956.

———. *Off the Record*. New York: Harper & Row, 1980.

Wetterhahn, Ralph. *The Last Battle: The Mayaguez Incident and the End of the Vietnam War*. New York: Carroll & Graf, 2001.

Woodward, Bob. *Bush at War*. New York: Simon & Schuster, 2002.

———. *The Commanders*. New York: Simon & Schuster, 1994.

———. *Plan of Attack*. New York: Simon & Schuster, 2004.

Other Written Sources

Congressional Record.
Federalist Papers.

Interviews

Alexander Haig, January 25, 2004.
Gary Hart, 2004.

Richard Holbrooke, November 16, 2004.
Anthony Lake, September 22, 2004.
Nita Lowey, December 14, 2004.
George McGovern, July 19, 2004.
Brent Scowcroft, July 29, 2004.
Caspar Weinberger, May 18, 2004.

Oral Histories by U.S. Naval Institute, U.S. Air Force, U.S. Army Military History Program

Abrams, Creighton, Jr. Oral History. U.S. Air Force. Maxwell Field, Ala.
Anderson, George. Oral History. U.S. Naval Institute. Annapolis, Md.
Dougherty, Russell E. Oral History. U.S. Air Force. Maxwell Field, Ala.
Douglas, James H., Jr. Oral History, U.S. Air Force, Maxwell Field, Ala.
Ellis, Richard H. Oral History. U.S. Air Force. Maxwell Field, Ala.
Fish, Howard M. Oral History. U.S. Air Force. Maxwell Field, Ala.
Johnson, Harold. Oral History. U.S. Army Military History Library. Carlisle, Pa.
Jones, David C. Oral History. U.S. Air Force. Maxwell Field, Ala.
Krulak, Victor H. Oral History. U.S. Marine Corps. Washington, D.C.
Larkin, George R. Oral History. U.S. Air Force. Maxwell Field, Ala.
Moorer, Thomas. Oral History. U.S. Naval Institute. Annapolis, Md.
Mustin, Lloyd. Oral History. U.S. Naval Institute. Annapolis, Md.
Richardson, David. Oral History. U.S. Naval Institute. Annapolis, Md.
Sharp, Adm. Ulysses Grant. Oral History. U.S. Naval Institute. Annapolis, Md.
Taylor, Maxwell. Oral History. U.S. Army Military History Library. Carlisle, Pa.
Train, Adm. Harry D. Oral History. U.S. Naval Institute. Annapolis, Md.
Weschler, Thomas. Oral History. U.S. Air Force Library. Maxwell Field, Ala.
Zumwalt, Adm. Elmo. Oral History. U.S. Naval Institute. Annapolis, Md.

INDEX

ABC News, 98
Abraham Lincoln, 272
Abrams, Creighton, 147, 148, 155, 158–159
Abrams, Elliott, 203–204
Abu Ghraib, 277–280
Acheson, Dean, 39
   Cuban Missile Crisis and, 84, 87
   Korean War and, 35, 36, 39, 41, 44
   Vietnam War and, 131–132
Adams, John, 14
Adams, John Quincy, 17
Adams, Sherman, 55
Adelman, Kenneth, 261
Adenauer, Konrad, 94
Afghanistan, 287–288
   Carter and, 187–189
   Clinton and, 243, 244, 245
   George H. W. Bush and, 222, 223–224
   George W. Bush and, 249, 252–256, 257, 269, 280
   Reagan and, 191, 193, 200–201
Africa, 233–234, 245. *See also individual names of countries*
Aidid, Mohammed Farrah, 234, 236
Allen, Richard, 190
Allende Gossens, Salvador, 164–166
al-Qaeda, 243–245, 249–253
   Iraq and, 250–256, 257–269, 274–276
   prisoners of United States and, 276–280
   September 11 attacks and, 253–256, 269
Al-Shiraa (Lebanon), 214, 216
Alsop, Joseph, 123
aluminum tubes, for nuclear weapons, 265, 267
American Society of Newspaper Editors, 54
Anaconda, 254
Anderson, George, 54, 86, 92–93, 96–97
Anderson, Rudolph, 100
Annan, Kofi, 262
anti-war movement (Vietnam), 128, 140–142, 145, 161–162. *See also* public opinion
Arbenz, Jacobo, 50, 51, 63, 65
Argentina, 182–183
Armas, Castillo, 50
ARVN (South Vietnamese Army), 157
Ashcroft, John, 239–240, 280

Aspin, Les, 235
atomic bombs
   Hiroshima and, 33, 44–45
   Korean War and, 42
   mutual assured destruction (MAD) and, 48
   See also nuclear weapons

Baathist regime, 272. *See also* Iraq
Bacon, Augustus O., 23
Baker, James, 190, 231, 237
   Panama, 223
   Yugoslavia and, 237
Balaguer, Joaquin, 129
Balkans, 237–242, 245
Ball, George, 105
   Cuban Missile Crisis, 78
   Vietnam War, 120–121, 124, 132
Barzani, Mustafa, 184
Batista, Fulgencio, 61–62
Battle of New Orleans, 15
Bay of Pigs, 64–71, 77, 85, 235
Beckwith, Bob, 254
Beecher, William, 149, 159
Begin, Menachem, 193
Beirut. *See* Lebanon
Bennett, Tapley, 129
Berger, Sandy, 234, 244, 249
Berlin Wall, 34, 221
Biden, Joseph, 248–249
Bin Laden, Osama, 227, 243–245, 248–256
"Bin Ladin Determined to Strike in US" (Presidential Daily Brief, August 6, 2001), 252
Bird Air, 173
Bishop, Maurice, 197
Bissell, Richard, 50, 63, 65–66, 70
Black, Hugo, 45–46, 284
Black Hawk helicopter incident, 235–237
Blackstone (legal scholar), 11
Blair, Tony, 258–259, 268
Blix, Hans, 258, 262, 266–270, 274, 276
"blowback," 201
Boland, Edward, 206–207
Boland amendments, 206–208, 209, 217, 219, 220

Bolshakov, Georgi, 95–96
Bolton, John R., 275
Bonner, Raymond, 203–204
Boot, Max, 137
Bosch, Juan, 129
Bosnia and Herzegovina, 237–242, 269
Boston Globe, 291
Boutros-Ghali, Boutros, 234–237, 245
Bowden, Mark, 235
Boxer Rebellion, 23
BP, 49
Bradley, Omar, 43, 44, 131–132
Bremer, L. Paul, 273, 281
Brinkley, David, 141
Brown, Harold, 186
Browne, Malcolm, 103
Brumheller, Tyler, 275
Brzezinski, Zbigniew, 183–189
Buddhists, South Vietnam and, 103–105
Bundy, McGeorge, 77
   Cuban Missile Crisis, 78, 82, 83, 87
   Vietnam War, 111
Bunker, Ellsworth, 155
Burchinal, David, 118
Burke, Arleigh, 68
Burns, John J., 176
Bush, George H. W., 4, 9, 221–222
   Afghanistan, 222, 223–224
   assassination attempt by Hussein, 70–71,
      243, 263
   Iraq, 224–233, 266
   on media, 232
   Panama, 15, 222–223
   public opinion of, 233
   as vice president, 197, 214, 220
   Yugoslavia, 237
Bush, George W., 3, 4, 7–8, 246, 248–249, 293
   on "axis of evil," 258
   Bin Laden and, 249–256
   on due process (Japanese internment
      camps), 28
   electronic "eavesdropping" and, 8, 283–285
   Iraq, 16, 18, 19, 70, 250–256, 257–269,
      274–276
   Iraq, insurgency, 271–274, 277, 279, 282
   Iraq, "Mission Accomplished," 272
   Iraq, war prisoners, 276–281
Bush, Joseph, 157
Bushnell, John, 202
Bybee, Jay S., 277
Byrd, Robert, 169

Calhoun, John C., 16–17
Calley, William L., Jr., 156
Cambodia, 16, 110, 125, 136, 157–163
   Dewey Canyon II, 168
   independence of, 55
   Khmer Rouge, 170, 173

Mayaguez and, 175–181
   U.S. attack on, 146–149
"Camelot," 65
Canada, 234
Cannon, Lou, 189, 191, 194, 195
   on El Salvador, 204
   on Grenada, 198–199
   on Iran-Contra Affair, 219
   on Nicaragua, 207, 208
   views on Poindexter, 211
Carney, William, 57
Carter, Jimmy, 4
   Afghanistan, 187–188
   Central America, 192
   El Salvador, 202
   Iran, 183–189, 206, 290
   Panama Canal, 182
   South America, 182–183
Carter, Marshall, 78, 81
Casablanca Conference, 29
Casey, William, 189, 191, 193
   Iran-Contra Affair and, 209–220
   Nicaragua, 207
Castro, Fidel, 61–63
   Bay of Pigs, 64–71, 77, 85, 235
   Cuban Missile Crisis, 74–77, 95–103
   Operation Mongoose, 70–71, 74, 101
   Reagan administration and, 192
   See also Cuba; Cuban Missile Crisis
CBS
   on Iraq, 278
   on Vietnam War, 106, 133
Chalabi, Ahmad, 275
Charles, Eugenia, 197
Cheney, Dick, 258
   on electronic "eavesdropping," 284–285
   Iraq, 248, 250, 251, 253, 261, 266, 274
   Iraq, and war prisoners, 277
   as Secretary of Defense, 226–229
Chiang Kai-shek, 28, 35, 41, 42, 56, 57–58
Chile, 164–166, 182–183
China, 19
   atomic weapons, 121
   "China Syndrome," 35
   Iraq and, 250
   Kennedy and, 65
   Korean War and, 35–43, 48
   McKinley and, 23
   mujahideen support by, 189
   Nationalist *vs.* Red, 56–58
   Soviet Union relations, during Vietnam
      War, 137–138
   Strait of Formosa, 56
   Tenet on, 250
   Vietnam War and, 51, 54–58, 172–173
   World War II, 27, 28
Chirac, Jacques, 259
Chou En-lai, 56

Christopher, Warren, 235, 239, 240–241, 242
Church, Frank, 137, 173
Churchill, Winston, 28, 29, 53
CIA (Central Intelligence Agency), 6
    Afghanistan, 187–188
    Bay of Pigs, 65, 66, 70, 77
    Bin Laden, 243–245, 250
    Chile, 164–166
    Cuban Missile Crisis, 77–79, 87–88, 90, 91,
        94, 96, 98–99
    established 1947, 33
    Gulf War (1991), 225–226
    Iran, 50
    Iran-Contra Affair, 209–220
    Iraq, 267–268, 274, 276
    Korean War, 41
    Nicaragua, 207, 208
    Operation Mongoose, 101
    PBSUCCESS, 50–51
    "Program of Covert Action Against the
        Castro Regime," 62–63
    Vietnam War, 105, 115–116
    See also individual names of conflicts; individual
        names of presidents
civil disobedience, 145
civil rights movement
    University of Mississippi, 85
    Vietnam War and, 128
Clark, Bill, 199
Clark, Wesley, 247
Clarke, Richard, 235–236, 244
    on al-Qaeda, 249–252
    views on George W. Bush, 248
Clausewitz, Carl von, 1, 289
Clay, Henry, 17
Cleveland, Grover, 21
Clifford, Clark, 141
Clinton, Bill, 4, 9, 246, 249
    Bin Laden and, 243–245, 254
    former Yugoslavia states, 237–242
    Iraq, 243
    Kosovo, 237, 246–248
    1993 World Trade Center bombing, 242
    prisoner interrogation outsourced by,
        279–280
    Rumsfeld's views on, 257
    Somalia, 233–237
Coalition forces (Iraq War), 272, 273–274, 282
Cohen, William, 244, 249, 250
cold war
    containment policy and, 33–34, 36, 65, 188
    mutual assured destruction (MAD), 48
    See also communism
Cole, 247, 249
commander in chief, authority of, 1–9, 27
    personal animosity as motivation of, 70–71
    War Powers Act, 169–172, 177, 180,
        194–195, 260

war powers of, 11–16, 22–23, 29, 237
    (See also war powers; War Powers Act)
    See also U.S. Congress; U.S. Constitution;
        U.S. Senate; individual names of presidents
"Commander-in-Chief Election, The" (Time), 3
communism
    Afghanistan and, 187–189
    Berlin Wall, 34, 221
    containment policy, 33–34, 36, 65, 188
    "evil empire" and, 189
    "falling domino" metaphor, 108, 127
    Iran and, 49–50
    Kennedy on, 72
    Lebanon and, 60–61
    Reagan's speech at Brandenburg Gate, 221
    See also China; Cuba; Korean War; Soviet
        Union; Vietnam War
containment policy, 33–34, 36, 65, 188.
    See also communism
Contras, 206–208
    Iran-Contra Affair, Boland amendment and,
        206–208, 209, 217, 219, 220
    Iran-Contra Affair, events of, 209–216
    Iran-Contra Affair, hearings, 216–220
Conway, James, 273–274
Coolidge, Calvin, 25
Cooper, John Sherman, 114, 173
Cooper-Church amendment, 162–163, 173
Costa Rica, 214
Coudert, Frederick, Jr., 41
Cowles, John, 131–132
Croatia, 237–242
Cronkite, Walter, 106
Crowe, William J., Jr., 2, 4, 213
Cuba
    Bay of Pigs and, 64–71, 77, 85, 235
    Cuban Missile Crisis, 74–77
    Eisenhower, 61–63
    Reagan, 205
    Spanish-American War and, 21–22
    See also Castro, Fidel; Cuban Missile Crisis
Cuban Missile Crisis, 9, 74–79, 82, 292
    Alsop on, 123
    blockade, tactics of, 94–103, 96–97
    blockade vs. airstrikes, 80–89
    Kennedy's speech to nation about, 90–92
    orders for quarantine, 92–93
    strategy, 78–90
"Curveball," 275–276

Daniel Boone teams, 147
Danner, Mark, 204
Darfur, 245
D'Aubuisson, Roberto, 192, 201–205
Da'wa, 213
Dean, Arthur, 131–132
Dearlove, Richard, 259
Deaver, Michael, 190

Declaration of Independence, 14
De Gaulle, Charles, 51
   Cuban Missile Crisis and, 94
   Vietnam War and, 123
DeGette, Diana, 264
Democratic Convention (1968), 145
Desert Storm, 4
DESOTO patrols, 112–113, 116
Dewey Canyon II, 168
Dhahran, 243
Diem, Ngo Dinh, 72–73, 103–108, 133
Dien Bien Phu, 52–55
Dillon, Douglas, 78, 80, 87–88
Dirksen, Everett, 89, 134
Dobrynin, Anatoly, 77, 91, 96, 99–100
Dodd, Thomas, 73
Dole, Robert, 224, 242, 289
Dominica, 197
Dominican Republic, 128–129
Dong, Pham Van, 152
Dougherty, Russell, 125
Douglas, Paul, 38–39
Downie, Leonard, 290
Downing Street Memo, 259
Drain, Richard, 51
Duarte, José Napoleon, 192, 201
Dulles, Allen, 50, 67, 70
Dulles, John Foster, 52, 53, 55, 61

Eagleburger, Lawrence, 229
Eastland, James O., 177
Eden, Anthony, 53
Egypt, 59–61, 225
Eisenhower, Dwight D., 3, 47–48, 64–66
   Bay of Pigs, 68, 70
   Cuban Missile Crisis, 83, 100
   "falling domino" metaphor of, 108, 127
   5412 Committee, 164
   Haig's views on, 220
   Korean War, 43, 48
   Laos, 72
   Latin America, 50–51, 61–63
   Mandate for Change, 50
   Middle East, 49–50, 59–61
   U-2/Soviet Union incident, 75
   Vietnam War, 51–59, 124
"Eisenhower Doctrine," 61
ElBaradei, Mohamed, 266, 267, 270, 274
electronic "eavesdropping," by George W. Bush
      administration, 8, 283–285
El Mozote, 203–204
El Salvador, 192, 201–205
Enders, Thomas, 203, 205
England
   Downing Street Memo, 259
   Falkland Islands and, 199
   Iraq and, 250, 258–259, 266, 267–268
   Operation Vittles, 34
   Suez Canal, 59–60

Vietnam War, 55
War of 1812, 15
war powers of king, 11, 13, 14, 284
World War II, 26, 28
"the Enterprise," 210, 214
Esterline, Jake, 51
"evil empire," 189
Executive Committee (ExCom), National
      Security Council, 77–81, 83, 86–87, 96,
      98. See also Cuban Missile Crisis

Fahd, king of Saudi Arabia, 225, 226–228
Faisal II, king of Iraq, 60
Falkland Islands, 199
"falling domino" metaphor, 108, 127
Fast, Barbara, 280
Fay, George R., 278–279, 279
FBI
   on al-Qaeda, 249, 251
   Nixon and, 167
   on September 11 attacks, 255
Federal Aviation Administration (FAA), 251,
      255
Federalist Papers
   Hamilton, 5, 13, 283–284
   Madison, 12–13
Feingold, Russell, 259–260
Feith, Douglas, 274–275, 291
Felt, Harry, 103
feminism, 128
Fillmore, Millard, 18–19
Fisher, Louis, 13–14, 14
Flanders, Ralph, 54
Fleischer, Ari, 260
Floyd, Henry F., 281
FMLN (Salvadoran rebels), 205
Foley, Tom, 223, 229
Ford, Gerald, 4, 172, 182
   Mayaguez, 175–181
   Vietnam War, 132
   War Powers Act, 177
Ford Motor Company, 71
Foreign Assistance Act of 1974, 166
Foreign Intelligence Surveillance Act (FISA),
      284
Formosa, 35, 37, 40–41
   Resolution, 58
   Strait of Formosa, 56
   See also Taiwan
Forrestal, Mike, 105
Fourteen Points, 25
France
   Iraq and, 250, 258–259, 266
   Somalia and, 234
   Suez Canal and, 59–60
   Vietnam War and, 14, 37, 51–55
   World War II, 26, 27, 28
Franks, Tommy, 254, 271, 273, 281
Freeh, Louis, 255

Freeman, Douglas Southall, 70
Fulbright, J. William, 3, 66
    Cuban Missile Crisis, 89, 90, 96
    Dominican Republic, 129
    on North Vietnam, 158
    on Vietnam War, 114, 132, 134, 137, 154

Gadhafi, Muammar, 220
Garrison, William, 236
Gavin, James M., 156
Gemayel, Bashir, 194
Geneva Convention against Torture,
    276–277
George III, king of England, 11, 13, 14
Germany
    intelligence on bin Laden, 254–255
    Iraq and, 275–276
    reunification, 237
    World War I, 24–25
    World War II, 25–30
Gerry, Elbridge, 5
Giap, Vo Nguyen, 137
Gilpatrick, Roswell, 78, 105
Gingrich, Newt, 242, 289
Glaspie, April, 224–225
Goldberg, Arthur, 141
Goldsmith, Lord, 259
Goldwater, Barry, 144, 164
    on Bay of Pigs, 68
    on *Mayaguez*, 180
    on Nicaragua, 207
    1964 presidential election and, 112
    on Vietnam War, 115
Goldwater-Nichols Act, 269
Gonzales, Alberto, 276–277
Goodell, Charles, 153
Goodwin, Richard, 128
Gorbachev, Mikhail, 221
Government of South Vietnam (GVN), 123.
    See also South Vietnam
Grant, Ulysses S., 3, 48
Gray, Boyden, 228
Graybeal, Sidney, 78, 79
Great Britain. See England
"Great Society," 123–124
Greece, 34
Green, Stanley E., 280
Green Berets, 154–155
Greene, Wallace, 110
Greentree, Todd, 203
Greer, 26–27
Grenada, 196–199
Gromyko, Andrei, 82–85
Grozny, 99, 100
Gruening, Ernest, 114
Guam
    Doctrine, 183
    as U.S. territory, 22
Guantanamo Bay (Gitmo), 62, 276–280

Guatemala, 50, 51, 63, 65
guerrilla wars, 6–7, 8
    counterinsurgency training, 71, 72
    soldier ratio for, 127
    See also individual names of conflicts
Guillermoprieto, Alma, 203–204
Gulf of Tonkin
    event, 27, 112–121, 143, 288
    Resolution, 113–114, 124, 143, 158, 163,
        265–266

habeas corpus, 7–8, 19–20, 46, 276–280
Habib, Philip, 193, 199
Habr Gidr, 235
Hadley, Stephen, 252
Hagel, Chuck, 286
Haig, Alexander M., Jr.
    Cambodia and, 160
    Cuban Missile Crisis and, 102
    Iran-Contra Affair and, 220
    Korean War and, 40–41, 48
    Lebanon and, 199
    McFarlane and, 210
    Nixon administration and, 149
    Reagan administration and, 190–193, 202
    on Vietnam War, 116, 126–127
Haiphong, 132
Hakim, Albert, 210
Halberstam, David, 133
Haldeman, H. R., 146, 155, 159, 170
Hall, Fawn, 215
Halleck, Charles, 89
Halliburton, 261
Hamdi, Yasen Esam, 281
Hamilton, Alexander, 5, 12, 14, 15, 283–284
Hamilton, Lee, 255
Hamlet Evaluation System, 133
Hanna, Mark, 22
Harkins, Paul, 73, 103, 104
Harriman, W. Averell, 44, 104–105, 135
Hart, Gary, 198, 249
Hatfield, Mark, 163
Hatfield-McGovern bill, 168
Hay, John, 22
Hearst, Randolph, 22
Helms, Jesse, 192
Helms, Richard, 105, 128, 155, 165
Hempstone, Smith, 234
Henderson, Loy, 50
Herndon, W. H., 18
Herrick, John, 117–118
Hersh, Seymour, 156
Herter, Christian A., 61
Hezbollah, 211–215
Hickenlooper, Bourke, 76–77, 89
Hilsman, Roger, Jr., 105
Hinton, Deane, 202, 203, 204
Hiroshima, 33, 44–45
Hitler, Adolf, 26, 39, 131

Ho Chi Minh, 51, 151–152
Ho Chi Minh Trail, 125, 146–149, 168
Hoffman, Paul, 131–132
Holbrooke, Richard, 119–120, 237–242
Holland, Henry F., 51
Holland, Spessard, 137–138
Holt, 177, 178
Honduras, 50
Hoover, Herbert, 100
Hoover, J. Edgar, 149
Hosmer, Craig, 76
Houston, 67
Howe, Jonathan, 234
Hughes, Charles Evans, 32
Hughes-Ryan amendment, 166, 187, 212
Hull, Cordell, 2, 29
"humint" (human intelligence), 77
Humphrey, Hubert, 60
   Cuban Missile Crisis, 89
   1968 presidential campaign, 144–145
   Vietnam War, 124, 130
Hussein, king of Jordan, 225
Hussein, Saddam, 257
   assassination attempt against George H. W.
      Bush, 70–71, 243, 263
   George H. W. Bush and, 224–232
   George W. Bush and, 250–256
   Iraqi public opinion and, 283
   Iraq War insurgency and, 272
   Kurds and, 183–184
   September 11 attacks and, 269
   See also Iraq
Hyde, Henry, 263

IAEA, 258, 266
Iceland, 26
Ichiang, 58
Imperial Presidency, The (Schlesinger), 3
Implementation Force (IFOR), 242
Independent Journal (New York), 12
Indochina. *See* Cambodia; Laos; Vietnam
   War
Indonesia, 121
In Retrospect (McNamara), 106
intelligence. *See individual names of agencies;
   individual names of conflicts*
Inter-American Conference, 50
International Atomic Energy Agency (IAEA),
   250
Iran, 59
   Afghanistan and, 188
   Carter, 183–189, 206
   George W. Bush, 253, 258
   Iran-Contra Affair, Boland amendment and,
      206–208, 209, 217, 219, 220
   Iran-Contra Affair, events of, 209–216
   Iran-Contra Affair, hearings, 216–220
   Iraq and, 224
   1985 hostage incident and, 211–215
   Truman and, 49–50

Iraq, 60, 288
   George H. W. Bush, 224–232
   George W. Bush, Iraqi insurgency and,
      271–274, 277, 279, 282
   George W. Bush, on prisoners, 276–281
   George W. Bush on terrorism and, 250–256,
      257–269, 274–276, 290–291
   Kurds and, 183–184
   reconstruction, 269, 272, 282, 286
   U.S. military statistics, 269, 272, 282
   war with Iran, 210, 219
Israel, 187, 193
   Iran and, 211, 212, 215
   Suez Canal and, 59–60
Italy
   Cuban Missile Crisis and, 87, 95–103
   Somalia and, 234
   World War II, 27
Izetbegovic, Alija, 238

Jackson, Andrew, 16
Jackson, Robert H., 7, 46, 284, 287
Jacobsen, David, 213
Japan
   Fillmore and, 18–19
   World War II, 27, 31, 33
Japanese internment camps, in United States,
   28, 277
Javits, Jacob, 169
Jefferson, Thomas, 14–15
Jenco, Lawrence, 213
Jenner, William, 44, 54
Johnson, Alexis U., 78
Johnson, Edwin, 54
Johnson, Harold K., 126, 127, 293
Johnson, Lyndon B., 2, 4, 9, 108–110, 128,
   135, 141, 293
   Asia visit by, 134
   conversations recorded in White House,
      127–128
   Cuban Missile Crisis, 78, 80, 89, 95
   "Great Society," 123–124
   Kennedy's assassination and, 108–109
   National Guard federalized by, 13
   1964 election of, 112, 120
   303 Committee, 164
   Vietnam War, 16, 109–112, 122–124,
      131–135
   Vietnam War, Gulf of Tonkin, 112–121,
      265–266
   Vietnam War, Operation Rolling Thunder,
      124–131, 140
Joint Chiefs of Staff, 6
   Bay of Pigs and, 68–70
   Cuban Missile Crisis and, 101, 102
   Goldwater-Nichols Act and, 269
   Iran-Contra Affair and, 213
   Kennedy and, 85–87
   Korean War and, 42
   Truman and, 47

Vietnam War and, 110
See also individual names of members
Jones, Antony R., 278
Jones, David, 139–140, 185–186
Jordan, 60–61
Journal (New York), 22
Jupiter missiles, 79, 98, 99, 101–103
See also Cuban Missile Crisis

Kamel, Hussein, 262
Karadzic, Radovan, 238, 241, 242
Karpinski, Janis, 279
Katzenbach, Nicholas, 35
Kay, David, 274
Kean, Thomas, 255
Keating, Kenneth, 76
Kennan, George F., 33, 239
Kennedy, Jacqueline, 65
Kennedy, John F., 4, 9
  assassination of, 108
  Bay of Pigs, 64–71, 77, 85, 235
  conversations recorded in White House by,
    78–79
  Cuban Missile Crisis, quarantine orders,
    92–93
  Cuban Missile Crisis, resolution, 94–103
  Cuban Missile Crisis, speech to nation,
    90–92
  Cuban Missile Crisis, strategy, 78–90
  Cuban Missile Crisis and, 74–77
  election of, 64–65
  Vietnam War and, 71–74, 103–107
Kennedy, Robert F.
  assassination of, 143–144
  Bay of Pigs and, 68, 70
  Cuban Missile Crisis, 78, 80–82, 85, 87–89,
    95–96, 99–100
  Johnson and, 138
  on Vietnam War, 105, 137
Kennedy Tapes, The (May, Zelikow), 79
Kennerly, David, 174, 177, 290
Kent State University, 161–162
Kenya, 243–244
Kerry, John, 3, 18, 265
KGB, 98
Khanh, Nguyen, 110, 111
Khmer Rouge, 159
Khomeini, Ayatollah Rhollah, 184–185, 189
Khrushchev, Nikita, 62, 71, 121
  Cuban Missile Crisis, events, 74–75, 77, 79,
    83–84, 89, 91
  Cuban Missile Crisis, resolution, 94–103
Kidd, Ike, 92–93
Kim Il Sung, 41
Kirkpatrick, Jeane, 190
Kirkpatrick, Lyman, 68–69
Kissinger, Henry, 145, 146
  Cambodia and, 158, 160, 163
  Ford and, 172–173, 182
  Haig's views on, 220

Kurds and, 183–184
Mayaguez, 175–181
on 1991 Gulf War, 229
Operation Menu, 147–149
Vietnam War peace talks, 150–154, 164,
  167–175
Knowland, William, 37, 57
Kohler, Foy, 91
Koh Tang, 176–181
Korean War, 8–9, 15, 292
  ceasefire, 47, 48
  Eisenhower visit to Korea, 48
  events leading to, 35–38
  Johnson on, 113
  MacArthur's dismissal, 40–45
  U.S. invasion, 38–41
  Youngstown Co. v. Sawyer, 7, 45–46, 284,
    287
Korry, Edward, 164–165
Kosovo, 237, 246–248, 269
Krauthammer, Charles, 201
Krulak, Victor H., 106, 133, 138–139, 210
Kurds, 183–184, 231–233
Kuwait, 213, 224–232
Ky, Nguyen Cao, 131, 173–174

Laird, Melvin, 154, 155, 161
Lake, Anthony, 106
Lake Resources, 210, 213
Lansdale, Edwin, 73, 104, 133
Laos, 52, 71–72, 110, 136, 147, 170
  "advisers" in, 157
  Dewey Canyon II, 168
  independence of, 55
  Pathet Lao in, 73, 111, 121, 157, 172–173
Latin America, 16
  Eisenhower and, 50–51, 61–63
  Johnson and, 128–129
  See also individual names of countries
Lausche, Frank, 137–138
League of Nations, 25, 37
Lebanon, 60–61, 193–195
  Al-Shiraa, 214, 216
  Reagan and, 196–200
Le Duc Tho, 163
Lee, Robert E., 70
LeMay, Curtis, 40
  Cuban Missile Crisis, 85–86, 100, 102
  Vietnam War, 110, 128
Lemnitzer, Lyman, 68–69, 73
Levin, Carl, 265
Lewis, Anthony, 18
Libby, Lewis, 274–275
Libya, 81, 220
Lincoln, Abraham, 17–19, 87
Lindsey, Lawrence, 269
Lippmann, Walter, 88, 123, 133
Lodge, Henry Cabot, 104–105, 111, 125, 133,
  135, 138
Long, Russell, 137–138

Lon Nol, General, 158, 160, 173
Los Angeles airport, 247
Los Angeles Times, 157
Lovett, Robert, 84, 96, 131–132
Lowey, Nita, 247, 264–265
Lundahl, Arthur, 78

MacArthur, Douglas, 40–45, 293
Macedonia, 237–242
Macmillan, Harold, 94, 96
Madden, Ray J., 50
Maddox, 112–121
Madison, James, 5, 12–13, 15
Mahon, George, 130
Maine, 21–22
Majlis (Iran parliament), 49
Malaysia, 121
Malinovsky, Rodion, 74–75
Mandate for Change (Eisenhower), 50
Manning, David, 268
Mansfield, Mike, 61
    Cuban Missile Crisis, 89
    Vietnam War, 109, 111, 124, 134, 171
Mao Tse-tung, 41
Marshall, George C., 28, 35, 44
Marshall Plan, 34
Martin, Edwin, 78
Martin, Joseph, 43
Martin v. Mott, 16
Matsu, 56–58, 64
May, Ernest, 79, 85
Mayaguez, 4, 175–181
Mayo, Henry Thomas, 24
McCarthy, Eugene, 60, 143–145
McCarthy, Joseph, 35
    John Kennedy and, 65
    Korean War, 44
McCloy, John, 131–132
McCone, John, 77
    Cuban Missile Crisis, 78, 79, 83, 87–89, 96,
        98–99, 101
    Vietnam War, 105, 113, 120
McCormack, John, 89
McFarlane, Robert "Bud," 192, 194
    Grenada, 197
    Iran-Contra Affair, 209–218
    Lebanon, 198, 200
    on Nicaragua, 207, 208
McGovern, George, 60, 294
    Hatfield-McGovern bill, 168
    on Iran-Contra Affair, 219
    on My Lai, 156
    presidential campaign, 168–169
    Vietnam peace talks, 150
    Vietnam War criticism by, 114–115, 137,
        154, 163
McKay, John, 203
McKinley, William, 4, 21–22, 23
McLaughlin, John, 266–267, 276

McMahon, John, 212
McNamara, Robert, 71, 140, 143
    Bay of Pigs and, 66
    Cuban Missile Crisis and, 78–83, 85, 87, 90,
        96–97
    In Retrospect, 106
    Vietnam War and, 73, 105, 106, 109–111,
        115, 121, 122, 129, 131, 141
Meese, Edwin, 190, 214–215, 216
Meiselas, Susan, 203–204
Mendenhall, Joseph, 106
Meredith, James, 85
Metternich, prince of Austria-Hungary, 145
Mexico
    George W. Bush and, 248
    Mexican War, 8, 16–17
    Pancho Villa, 24
    World War I, 25
Middle East. *See individual names of countries*
Middle East Resolution, 60–61
Mikoyan, Anastas, 95
military "advisors." *See* "police actions"
Military Assistance Advisory Group (MAAG),
    52
militias, state, 12–16
Millennium Terrorist Alert, 247
Miller, Geoffrey, 279
Milosevic, Slobodan, 237–242, 246–248
"Mission Accomplished," 272
Mladic, Ratko, 240, 241, 242
Mogadishu, Somalia, 233–237, 245
Monroe Doctrine, 16, 29
Montenegro, 237–242
Moorer, Thomas, 71, 125, 142, 146, 162
    on Gulf of Tonkin, 118–119
    on My Lai, 156
Morison, Samuel Eliot, 44
Morse, Wayne, 114, 115, 116, 117
Mossadegh, Mohammad, 49–50, 65
Motley, Langhorne, 210
Moussaoui, Zacarias, 252
Moyers, Bill, 128
"Mr. Madison's War," 15
Mubarak, Hosni, 225
mujahideen, Afghanistan, 188–189
Muskie, Edmund, 219
Muslims, genocide against, 238–242
Muslims, radical faction
    Afghanistan and, 191
    al-Qaeda and, 243
    Da'wa, 213
    Iran and, 184
    Taliban and, 249
Mustin, Lloyd M., 69–70
mutual assured destruction (MAD), 48
My Lai, 4, 156

Nasser, Gamal, 59–61
Nation, 54

National Guard, 13
National Intelligence Estimate (NIE), 262, 263, 274
national security, as global issue, 30, 46, 47
National Security Act of 1947, 33, 164
National Security Agency (NSA)
    al-Qaeda and, 251
    electronic "eavesdropping" by, 8, 283–285
    Iraq and, 253, 275
    Pueblo, 149–150
    Reagan and, 208
    Vietnam War, 116
National Security Council
    Executive Committee (ExCom), 77–81, 83, 86–87, 96, 98
    Iran-Contra Affair and, 209–220, 217, 219
    Iraq and, 225
    Nixon and, 146
    Vietnam War, 110–111
    See also individual names of members
National Security Presidential Directive (NSPD), 260
"nation-building"
    George W. Bush on, 235, 255
    Kosovo and, 247
    Somalia and, 236–237
NATO (North Atlantic Treaty Organization)
    Cuban Missile Crisis and, 102
    former Yugoslavia and, 238–242, 246–248
    Korean War, 43
    on September 11 attacks, 253
    Suez Canal and, 59–60
    Truman, 34–35
    Vietnam War and, 51
Negroponte, John, 203, 291
New England governors, on state militias, 15–16
New York Evening Post, 22
New York Journal, 12
New York Sun, 22
New York Times
    on Cambodia, 149, 159, 160–161
    on Cuban Missile Crisis, 88
    on El Salvador, 203–204
    on Green Berets incident, 154–155
    on Iraq, 259, 265
    on Laos, 73
    on My Lai, 156
New York World, 22
Nhu, Madame ("Dragon Lady"), 103, 104
Nhu, Ngo Dinh, 103, 105, 108
Nicaragua, 67, 192
    Contras and, 206
    Coolidge and, 25
    George H. W. Bush and, 222
    Haig on, 220
    Nicaraguan Democratic Force (FDN), 214
    Reagan and, 201, 205–208
Nidal, Abu, 217

Niger, 267–268
9/11 Commission, 255–256, 281
Nitze, Paul, 82, 84, 92–93
Nixon, Richard M., 2–4, 145–146, 156, 249
    on Bay of Pigs, 68
    Cambodia, 16, 146–149
    Chile, 164–166
    40 Committee, 164
    Green Berets misconduct and, 154, 155
    Korean War, 42, 44
    Laos and Cambodia invasions, 153–154, 157–161, 157–163
    1968 election of, 143–145
    1964 presidential election and, 112
    "Nixon Doctrine," 150, 158, 183
    Rehnquist and, 162–163, 284
    resignation, 172
    "silent majority" speech, 154
    "support the troops" campaign, 167, 286
    Tet offensive, 155–156
    as vice president, 54, 55, 144
    "Vietnamization" and, 167, 286
    Watergate break-in, 168–169
Nolting, Frederick, 103–104, 104
Noriega, Manuel, 222–223
North, Oliver, 209–218
Northern Alliance, 252, 254
North Korea, 36–38, 47
    George W. Bush, 258
    Pueblo, 141–142, 149
    See also Korean War
North Vietnam, 110
    Gulf of Tonkin, 112–121
    Johnson and, 136, 137
    Kennedy and, 103–107
    Operation Rolling Thunder, 124–131, 140
    Paris peace talks, 150–154, 164, 170–175
    Provisional Revolutionary Government of North Vietnam, 170
    See also Vietnam War
nuclear weapons
    atomic bomb, 33, 44–45
    Cuban Missile Crisis threat and, 102
    Korean War and, 42, 48
    surface-to-air missile sites (SAMs), 79, 100
    Vietnam War and risks of, 121, 122
    See also Cuban Missile Crisis; weapons
Nunn, Sam, 229
nuns, killed in El Salvador, 202

O'Brien, Lawrence, 89
Office of Strategic Services, 6, 33. *See also* CIA (Central Intelligence Agency)
oil, 286
    Iran and, 49–50
    Iraq and, 261
    Oil-for-Food Program, 258
Omar, Mullah, 243, 252, 255
Onassis, Jacqueline Kennedy, 65

O'Neill, Paul, 250
O'Neill, Tip, 195, 198, 200
OPEC (Organization of the Petroleum
    Exporting Countries), 225
Operation Desert Storm, 230–232
Operation Duck Hook, 151, 153
Operation Enduring Freedom, 254–256, 258
Operation Iraqi Freedom, 270, 271
Operation Just Cause, 223
Operation Matterhorn, 28
Operation Menu, 147–149, 159
Operation Mongoose, 70–71, 74, 101
Operation Rolling Thunder, 124–131, 140
Operation Shoemaker, 159–160
Operation Vittles, 34
Organization of American States (OAS), 62
    Cuban Missile Crisis and, 90, 91, 95
    Dominican Republic and, 129
Organization of Eastern Caribbean States,
    196–197
Ormsby-Gore, David, 94

Packard, David, 155
Padilla, Jose, 281
Pahlavi, Reza, shah of Iran, 50, 183–185
Pakistan, 188, 191, 252–253
    Clinton and, 245
    George W. Bush and, 253
Palestine Liberation Organization (PLO), 193
Panama, 15, 222–223
Panama Canal, 182
Pankin, Boris, 223
Pashtuns, 252
Pathet Lao, 73, 111, 121, 157, 172–173
Patriot Act, 280, 283
Paul, Ron, 264
Payne, Donald, 264
PBSUCCESS, 50–51
Pearl Harbor, 27–28, 84, 87, 253, 292
Pell, Claiborne, 223
Pentagon
    Defense Intelligence Agency on Iraq, 266–267
    September 11 attacks, 252–256
Pentagon Papers, 168
Pepper, Claude, 29
Pérez de Cuéllar, Javier, 229
Perle, Richard, 229
Perot, Ross, 118
Perry, Bill, 242
Perry, Matthew C., 18–19
Perry, Merton, 104
Pershing, John J., 24
Pescadore Islands, 57–58
Pfeiffer, Jack, 51
Philippine Islands
    as U.S. territory, 22
    Vietnam War and, 53
Pincus, Walter, 259
Pinochet, Augusto, 183

pirates, 18–19
Plame, Valerie, 290
Plan of Attack (Woodward), 260
Poindexter, John, 209–218
Poland, 50
Polaris missiles, 99, 103
"police actions," 29
    Korean War as, 9, 38–40
    in Laos, 157
    Vietnam as, 72–73, 106, 109
Polk, James, 17–18
Pol Pot, 173
Potsdam Conference, 31
Powell, Colin, 4, 211
    Clinton administration and, 243
    George H. W. Bush administration and,
        226, 229, 234
    George W. Bush administration and, 248,
        250, 252, 261, 272, 275, 284
    UN Security Council address by, 268
Power and Principle (Brzezinski), 188
Powers, Dave, 86
Presidential Daily Brief (August 6, 2001), 252
prisoners
    habeas corpus, 7–8, 19–20, 46, 276–280
    Iraq and 9/11, 276–280
    outsourcing of interrogation, 279–280
    World War II, 28
    World War II Japanese internment camps,
        28, 277
public opinion
    of Cuban Missile Crisis, 95, 101–102
    of George H. W. Bush, 233
    of George W. Bush, 263
    of Iranian hostage situation, 185
    by Iraqis, 283
    of Johnson, 141
    on Korean War, 39, 41
    of Nixon, 154
    of Reagan, 200, 204, 206, 221
    of September 11 attacks, 269
    of Spanish-American War, 22
    of Vietnam War, 109, 128, 132, 137
Publius, 12. See also Madison, James
Pueblo, 141–142, 149
Puerto Rico, 22
Pulitzer, Joseph, 22

Quayle, Dan, 229
Quemoy, 56–58, 64

Radford, Arthur, 53, 55, 57
Radio Moscow, 100
Radio Venceremos (El Salvador), 203
Rangel, Charles, 223
Reagan, Nancy, 190
Reagan, Ronald, 4, 9, 190–191
    Afghanistan, 191, 193, 200–201
    Central America, 192

El Salvador, 201–205
on "evil empire," 189
40 Committee, 220
Gorbachev and, 221
Grenada, 196–199
Iran, 189
Iran-Contra Affair, Boland amendment, 206–208, 209, 217, 219, 220
Iran-Contra Affair, events, 209–216
Iran-Contra Affair, hearings, 216–220
Iraq, 224
Lebanon, 193–200
Libya, 220
mujahideen support by, 188–189
Nicaragua, 201, 205–208
Panama Canal, 182
"Reagan Doctrine," 201
on "shining city on the hill," 232
Weinberger on power of, 2
Record, Jeffrey, 200, 289
Regan, Donald, 190, 215, 216
Rehnquist, William, 162–163, 284
Reminiscences (MacArthur), 43, 44
Resor, Stanley, 155
Reston, James, 88, 133
Rheault, Robert, 154–155
Rhee, Syngman, 36, 56
Rice, Condoleeza, 248–256, 261, 263, 266
Iraq and, reconstruction, 269
Iraq and, "U.S. Goal: Free Iraq" (NSPD), 260
Iraq and, weapons of mass destruction, 265
Richardson, David C., 42, 47
Ridgway, Matthew, 42, 53
Rio Escondido, 67
Roa, Raúl, 67
Robb, Charles, 275
Roberts, Chalmers M., 53, 55
Roberts, John G., 197–198
Roberts, Pat, 291
Rockefeller, Jay, 291
Rockefeller, Nelson, 68, 145
Rogers, William, 147–149, 154
Rohrabacher, Dana, 264
Role of a Lifetime, The (Cannon), 189
Romero, Oscar Arnulfo, 201
Roosevelt, Franklin Delano, 2, 4, 31
Japanese internment camps, 28, 277
recorded conversations by, 78
World War II, 14, 25–30, 253
Roosevelt, Theodore, 23
Root, Elihu, 23
Ros-Lehtinen, Ileana, 264
Rothblatt, Henry, 155
Rudman, Warren, 249
Rumsfeld, Donald, 257–258
Ford administration, 179
George W. Bush administration, 248, 250, 253, 267, 269, 272, 273, 278, 279
Nixon administration, 159

Rusk, Dean
Bay of Pigs and, 66
Cuban Missile Crisis and, 78, 79, 90, 91, 95, 99
Vietnam War and, 104, 110–111, 115
Russell, Richard, 160
Cuban Missile Crisis, 89–90
Vietnam War, 111, 120, 134
Russia, Iraq and, 250. See also Soviet Union
Rwanda, 245

Safer, Morley, 133
Saltonstall, Leveret, 89
Sanchez, Ricardo, 279, 280
Sandinistas, 192, 205–208, 214, 218, 222
Sandino (Nicaraguan rebel), 25
Santayana, George, 181
Sarajevo, 238, 239
Saudi Arabia, 49, 191
George H. W. Bush and, 225, 226–228, 230–231, 243
George W. Bush and, 253
Scali, John, 98
Schlesinger, Arthur, Jr.
on Bay of Pigs, 64, 66, 67, 70
on commander in chief title, 2, 27
on Cuba, 62, 75–76, 79, 87
on Formosa Resolution, 58
The Imperial Presidency, 3
on Vietnam War, 103, 108
views on Rehnquist, 162
on war powers, 16
on World War II, 27
Schlesinger, James, 174–175, 176, 279
Schneider, René, 165
Schwarzkopf, Norman, 226, 230
Sciaroni, Bretton G., 209
Sciolino, Elaine, 225
Scowcroft, Brent, 222
on commander in chief title, 9
on definition of war, 5
on Iran-Contra Affair, 219–220
on Iraq, 224, 260–261
Mayaguez, 179
on 1991 Gulf War, 226, 228–229, 231
on power of president, 8
Somalia and, 234
on Tower Commission, 219
Vietnam War and, 174
views on George W. Bush, 248
Yugoslavia and, 237
Secord, Richard, 210
September 11, 2001 attacks, 252–256, 269
Serbia, 237–242, 246–248
Shackley, Theodore, 155
Shapiro, Alan, 20
Sharon, Ariel, 194
Sharp, Ulysses Grant, Jr., 92–93, 112, 113, 116, 129, 139

Shawcross, William, 160–161, 173
Shelton, Hugh, 244
Shiites, 231–233, 282
Shultz, George, 193, 194
    Grenada and, 197, 199
    Iran-Contra Affair and, 211, 212, 214–216
    Lebanon and, 200
    Nicaragua and, 206
Sick, Gary, 189
Sidey, Hugh, 216
Sihanouk, Norodom, prince of Cambodia, 148,
    157–158, 172–173
Silberman, Lawrence, 275
"silent majority," 154
Simpson, Alan, 224
60 Minutes (CBS), 278
Slovenia, 237–242
Smathers, George, 76, 89
Smith, Nick, 263
Solana, Javier, 247
Somalia, 233–237, 245
Somoza, Anastasio, 192, 201, 205–208
Sorenson, Ted, 68, 78, 86–87
Southeast Asia Resolution, 113–115
Southeast Asia Treaty Organization (SEATO),
    55–56
South Korea, 36–38, 56, 71, 292. See also
    Korean War
South Vietnam, 71–72
    ARVN (South Vietnamese Army), 157
    Dewey Canyon II, 168
    Johnson support of, 128–129
    Kennedy and, 103–107
    Vietnam War, end, 171
Soviet Union
    Afghanistan and, 187–189, 222, 223–224
    Castro and, 74
    Cuba and, 62
    Cuban Missile Crisis and, 90–92, 94–103
    Iran and, 49
    Korean War and, 35–43
    U.S. missiles aimed at, 79
    Vietnam War, China and, 137–138
    Vietnam War, North supplied by, 125–131
    Vietnam War, peace talks, 142
    World War II, 29
    See also communism; Cuban Missile Crisis
Spain, 21–22
Spanish-American War, 8, 21–23
Srebrenica, 238, 240
Stalin, Joseph, 41, 43
Stanton, Frank, 133
Stars and Stripes, 156
states, militias of, 12–16
steelworkers strike (1952), 7, 45–46, 284, 287
Stennis, John, 52, 162, 169
Stevenson, Adlai E.
    Cuban Missile Crisis, 67, 78, 84, 88, 93, 95,
    98
    presidential campaign of, 48

Stilwell, Joseph, 28
Stockdale, James B., 118
Strait of Formosa, 56, 57
Straw, Jack, 259
Sudan, 243–245
Suez Canal, 59–60
Sullivan, 247
Sullivan, William, 184
Sulzberger, C. L., 180
Sunnis, of Iraq, 272, 282
"support the troops" campaign, 167, 286
surface-to-air missile sites (SAMs), 79, 100.
    See also Cuban Missile Crisis
Sweeney, Walter C., 88
Syngman Rhee, 36, 56

Tabor, John, 89
Tachen Islands, 58
Taft, Robert A., 26, 39, 47
Taft, William Howard, 23
Taft-Hartley Act, 45
Taguba, Anthony, 278
Taiwan, 57–58
    Korean War, 35, 37, 40–41
    Korean War, Formosa Resolution, 58
    Vietnam War, 56
Taliban, 224, 243–245, 249, 252–256,
    254–256
Talmadge, Herman, 169–170
Tambs, Lewis, 214
Taney, Roger B., 19
Tanzania, 243–244
TASS (Soviet News Agency), 83
Taylor, Maxwell, 48, 73–74
    Cuban Missile Crisis and, 78–82, 84, 97,
    102
    on Eisenhower's military decisions, 3
    The Uncertain Trumpet, 71
    Vietnam War and, 106, 110, 111, 123, 125,
    126, 129
Taylor, Zachary, 4, 17–18
Tenet, George, 240, 250–251, 255, 263, 266,
    276, 281
terrorism, 7–8
    Iraq and, 250–256
    Marines killed in Lebanon, 196–197
    Millennium Terrorist Alert, 247
    1993 World Trade Center bombing, 242
    September 11 attacks, 252–256, 269
    Yemen, 247, 249
Tet offensive, 142–143, 155–156
Texas
    George W. Bush and, 248
    Mexican War and, 16–17
Thailand, 71–72
Thant, U, 96, 98, 101
"theater of war," 45–46
Thieu, Nguyen Van, 131, 151, 169, 170,
    173–174
Thompson, Lewellyn, 78

Ticonderoga, 112, 118
Time
    on Mossadegh, 49
    "The Commander-in-Chief Election," 3
    on Vietnam War, 104
TIPOFF, 251
Tito, 237, 246
Tora Bora, 254
Tower, John, 212, 219
Tower Commission Report, 212
Train, Harry D., 140, 174–175, 177–179, 180
Trujillo, Rafael, 128–129
Truman, Harry S., 4, 8–9, 287
    on Bay of Pigs, 68
    Cuban Missile Crisis, 100
    Holbrooke's views on, 240
    Johnson's views on, 113
    Korean War, 19, 35–46, 45–46, 47, 48,
        230
    Middle East and, 49–50
    "Truman Doctrine," 33–35
    Vietnam War and, 51–52
    World War II, 31–33
Tudeh (Iran communist party), 49
Turkey
    Cuban Missile Crisis and, 79, 83, 87, 95–103
    1991 Gulf War and, 231–232
    Truman Doctrine, 34
Turner Joy, 113–121
Twining, Nathan, 57
Tyler, John, 16–17

U-2 incident, Cuban Missile Crisis, 100–101
UN (United Nations)
    creation of, 29
    Cuban Missile Crisis and, 96, 98–101
    former Yugoslavia and, 238–242
    Iraq and, 225, 250, 258, 261, 262
    Iraq embassy of, 273
    Korean War and, 36–41, 48
    Oil-for-Food Program, 258
    Somalia, peacekeepers in, 234–237, 245
    Suez Canal, 59–60
    UN Participation Act, 31–32
    Vietnam War and, 51–52, 127–128
Uncertain Trumpet, The (Taylor), 71
United Arab Republic, 60, 61
United Fruit Company, 50
University of Mississippi, 85
uranium, Iraq and, 267–268
Urgent Fury, 197–199
U.S. Congress, 6, 8–9, 13, 14, 21–23, 293–294
    Cuban Missile Crisis and, 76–77, 83, 89, 91,
        101–102
    Eisenhower and, 51, 54–55, 58–63
    George H. W. Bush and, 229–230
    George W. Bush and, 259–260, 263–265,
        267
    George W. Bush and, Foreign Intelligence
        Surveillance Act, 284

George W. Bush and, Patriot Act, 283
Johnson and, 113, 119, 121, 125, 130–131
Kennedy and, 73–74
Mexican War, 16
National Security Act, 33
Reagan and, 199, 206, 207, 209–220,
    211–220
Supreme Court on "theater of war,"
    45–46
Truman and, 113–114
UN Participation Act, 31–32
War of 1812, 15
War Powers Act, 169–172, 177, 180
World War I declaration, 25
U.S. Constitution, 291–293
    Articles of Confederation, 11
    on commander in chief designation, 1–9
    George W. Bush on, 283–284
    Mexican War and, 18
    Morse on Gulf of Tonkin and, 114
    Smathers on, 76
    on title of "president," 2
"U.S. Goal: Free Iraq" (National Security
    Presidential Directive), 260
U.S. Senate
    Cuban Missile Crisis, 89
    Iraq, 2002 resolution, 265–266
    Korean War, 41–42
    See also U.S. Congress
U.S. Supreme Court
    on habeas corpus, 20
    on Japanese internment camps, 28
    Martin v. Mott, 16
    on "theater of war," 45–46
    Youngstown Co. v. Sawyer, 7, 45, 284, 287

Vandenberg, Arthur, 29, 32, 35, 289
Vessey, John W., 193, 195, 196, 205–206
Vichy France, 27
Vietcong, 110
    Kennedy and, 103–107
    Operation Rolling Thunder, 124–131, 140
    as Provisional Revolutionary Government
        of North Vietnam, 170
    See also North Vietnam; Vietnam War
Viet Minh, 51
Vietnam War, 4, 13, 14, 16, 37, 122–124,
    131–135, 289
    casualties of, 171
    Green Berets incident, 154–155
    Gulf of Tonkin, 27, 112–121, 124, 143,
        288
    Gulf of Tonkin Resolution, 265–266
    Johnson, 136–145
    Kennedy, John F. and, 71–74, 103–107
    Mayaguez, 175–181
    media coverage of, 289–290
    Nixon, 145–152
    Operation Rolling Thunder, 124–131,
        140

Vietnam War (continued)
  pacification, 133–135
  Paris peace agreement, 150–154, 164,
    170–175
  Tet offensive, 155–156
  "Vietnamization," 167, 286
  See also North Vietnam; South Vietnam
Villa, Francisco "Pancho," 24
Vinson, Carl, 89, 160
Vogt, John, 186–187

Waite, Terry, 213
Walker, Walton, 42
Wall Street Journal
  on El Salvador, 204
  on Iraq, 260–261, 261
War of 1812, 8, 15
war powers
  of commander in chief vs. Congress, 16–20
  state militias and, 12–16
  U.S. Constitution on, 11–12
  war as defense, 12–14, 22–23, 29, 237
  See also War Powers Act; individual names of
    events; individual names of presidents
War Powers Act, 177
  George W. Bush and, 260
  Nixon and, 169–172, 180
  Reagan and, 194–195
Warren, Mac, 280
Washington, George, 3, 7
Washington Post
  on El Salvador, 203–204
  on Iraq, 259, 290
Washington Post and Times-Herald, 53
Watergate, 168–169
Watkins, James, 195
Watson, Albert, 155
weapons
  Afghanistan and, 191
  El Salvador and, 205
  Honduras and, 50–51
  Iran-Contra Affair and, 209–220
  UN embargo of Bosnia, Serbia, 238
  weapons of mass destruction (WMD), Iraq
    and, 250, 258–269, 274, 275
  See also nuclear weapons
Weinberger, Caspar, 190
  Cuba and, 205
  Grenada, 197
  Iran-Contra Affair, 211, 212, 214–215
  Lebanon, 193–195, 199–200

  on Nicaragua, 207
  on Reagan's power, 2
  "Weinberger Doctrine," 205
Weschler, Thomas, 134
Westermann, Christian P., 275
Westmoreland, William, 136–139, 143, 147
  Green Berets incident, 155
  Operation Rolling Thunder and, 125–126,
    129, 132
Weyand, Frederick C., 174
Wheeler, Earle "Bus," 135, 138, 155
  Cambodia and, 148
  Cuban Missile Crisis, 86
  Vietnam War, 136
Whiskey Rebellion, 14
White, Robert, 202
White, Thomas E., 273
Wilson, 178, 179
Wilson, Charles, 3
Wilson, Joseph, 267–268, 290
Wilson, Woodrow, 24–25
wiretaps, by George W. Bush administration, 8,
    283–285
Woerner, Fred E., 202
Wojdakowski, Walter, 280
Wolfowitz, Paul, 251, 253, 259, 266, 269,
    274–275
Woodward, Bob, 260
World Trade Center
  1993 bombing, 242
  September 11 attacks, 252–256, 269
World War I, 8, 24–25
World War II, 8
  atomic bomb, 44–45
  Hiroshima, 44–45
  Pearl Harbor, 253, 292
  Truman, 31–33
Wright, Jim, 216

Xuan Thuy, 150, 152

Yeh, George K. C., 57
yellowcake, Iraq and, 268
Yemen, 247, 249, 253
Yoo, John, 260
Youngstown Co. v. Sawyer, 7, 45, 284, 287
Yugoslavia (former), 233, 237–242, 269

Zelikow, Philip, 79, 85
Zorin, Valerian, 98
Zumwalt, Elmo R. "Bud," Jr., 82, 84, 92–93

CPSIA information can be obtained
at www.ICGtesting.com
Printed in the USA
BVHW030914171219
566915BV00003B/119/P